KU-296-570

WITHDRAWN
THE LIBRARY OF
TRINITY COLLEGE DUBLIN

AUTHORISED: MK

DATE: 9/5/24

50633728
506337 28

Case Law
of the European Court
# of Human Rights

VOLUME III: 1991–1993

Case Law
of the European Court
# of Human Rights

VOLUME III: 1991–1993

Vincent Berger

Head of Division at the Registry of
the European Court of Human Rights,
Professor at the College of Europe at Bruges and Warsaw

WITH A FOREWORD BY

The Honourable Mr Justice Brian Walsh

Former Judge of the Supreme Court of Ireland
Judge of the European Court of Human Rights

THE ROUND HALL PRESS
DUBLIN

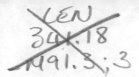

The typesetting of this book was input by
Carrigboy Typesetting Services, Bantry, Co. Cork
and output by Koinonia Ltd, Bury, Lanchashire for
THE ROUND HALL PRESS
Kill Lane, Blackrock, Co. Dublin.

**This serial is available in North America from
The Round Hall Press
c/o ISBS, 5804 N.E. Hassalo Street, Portland, OR 97213
and from
UNIFO Publishers
PO Box 42556, Washington, DC 20015.**

© Vincent Berger 1995

ISBN 1-85800-038-6
ISSN 0791-1866

Earlier volumes in the series
Volume 1: 1960-1987
ISBN: 0-947686-37-1

Volume 2: 1988-1990
ISBN: 0-947686-66-5

A catalogue record for this book is available
from the British Library.

All rights reserved.
No part of this publication may be reproduced,
stored in or introduced into a retrieval system, or transmitted,
in any form or by any means (electronic, mechanical, photocopying
recording or otherwise), without the prior written permission of both
the copyright owner and publisher of this book.

Printed in Great Britain by
Cambridge University Press, Cambridge.

For Lydie Baton-Vermeersch, my wife,
and Marie-Caroline, our daughter

Contents

Contents

Contents

Contents

Foreword

The unique institution which is the European Court of Human Rights continues to flourish and to grow. In this the third volume of Dr Berger's work on the case law of the Court, which brings us to the end of 1993, that progress is fully evidenced. The period covered in this volume, from 1991 to 1993 inclusive, records the more than two hundred cases decided by the Court in those three years. When one compares that case load with the ninety-three decisions of the previous three years, recorded in volume II, and the one hundred and seventeen decisions for the first twenty seven years of the Court's existence, recorded in volume III, it is clear that the Court has earned the respect and the confidence of the free peoples of Europe.

Each member state of the Council of Europe is entitled to nominate a judge to the Court. The member states now number thirty-four. When one recalls that no state is admitted to membership of the Council unless it is one in which there exists a genuine pluralistic democracy, the rule of law and the enjoyment of human rights and fundamental freedoms by all persons within the jurisdiction of the state, one can appreciate what great strides Europe itself has made in the field of human rights. The desire to have the opportunity to participate in the decision-making process of the Court and to have the national benefit of the protection of the European Convention of Human Rights, whose final interpretation rests exclusively with the Court, has undoubtedly spurred many states into ensuring that their internal order satisfies the criteria of the Council of Europe and ensures the protection afforded by the right of ultimate recourse to the Court. As the Court itself is subsidiary to the national courts in that domestic remedies must first be exhausted before resort is had to Strasbourg the national legal and political systems are at all times reminded of the existence of the Court's supervisory function.

Protocol No. 11, which now awaits ratification by all the member states, proposes to abolish the European Commission of Human Rights and to make the Court a full-time Court whose judges will serve on that basis and will reside in or near Strasbourg. If adopted, that will mean that all cases will in the first instance be received by the Court which will in special procedures decide all questions of admissibility as a prelude to a hearing. In other words the Court would become the first and final instance and the competence of the Committee of Ministers to deal with applications under the present Article 32 of the Convention would be abolished. That should greatly reduce the delays at present experienced before a case reaches the Court. Furthermore the proposed new structure would enable the Court to sit as several chambers at the same time and also to have an effective procedure to enable friendly settlements to be achieved.

These radical changes, coupled with the fact that there are at present many applications for membership of the Council of Europe from new states, should ensure that Dr Berger, who is still a young man, will be kept busy chronicling the case law in his usual expert way and which, hopefully, the Round Hall Press will continue to bring to the world. They are both to be warmly congratulated on the present publication.

BRIAN WALSH
February 1995

Abbreviations

A.A.	Ars Aequi
A.C.D.P.	Annuaire canadien des droits de la personne
A.D.	Annales de droit (Leuven)
A.E.H.R.Y.B.	All-European Human Rights Yearbook
A.F.D.I.	Annuaire français de droit international
A.J.C.L.	American Journal of Comparative Law
A.J.D.A.	L'actualité juridique. Droit administratif
A.J.I.L.	American Journal of International Law
A.J.P./P.J.A.	Aktuelle Juristische Praxis/Pratique juridique actuelle
A.S.D.I.	Annuaire suisse de droit international
B.D.H.	Bulletin des droits de l'homme (Luxembourg)
B.Y.B.I.L.	British Year Book of International Law
C.D.E.	Cahiers de droit européen
C.H.R.Y.	Canadian Human Rights Yearbook
C.L.J.	The Cambridge Law Journal
D.	Recueil Dalloz Sirey
D.D.	Delikt en Delinkwent
E.J.C.	European Journal of Crime, Criminal Law and Criminal Justice
E.J.I.L.	European Journal of International Law
E.L.R.	The European Law Review
EuGRZ	Europaïsche Grundrechte-Zeitschrift
Foro it.	Il Foro italiano
G. P.	Gazette du Palais
G.Y.I.L.	German Yearbook of International Law
Harv. I.L.J.	Harvard International Law Journal
H.R.L.J.	Human Rights Law Journal
H.R.Q.	The Human Rights Quarterly
H.R.R.	The Human Rights Review
I.C.L.Q.	International and Comparative Law Quarterly
J.Bl.	Juristische Blätter
J.C.P.	Juris-classeur périodique (Semaine juridique)
J.D.I.	Journal du droit international
J.E.D.I.	Journal européen de droit international
J.L.M.B.	Revue de jurisprudence de Liège, Mons et Bruxelles
J.Ö.R.	Jahrbuch des öffentlichen Rechts der Gegenwart
J.R.	Juristische Rundschau

J.T.	Journal des tribunaux
J.Z.	Juristen Zeitung
L.P.	Legipresse
L.P.A.	Les petites affiches
L.Q.R.	Law Quarterly Review
M.L.R.	Modern Law Review
N.I.L.R.	Netherlands International Law Review
N.J.	Nederlandse Jurisprudentie
N.J.B.	Nederlands Juristenblad
N.J.C.M.	Nederlands Juristen Comité voor de Mensenrechten
N.J.W.	Neue Juristische Wochenschrift
N.Q.H.R.	Netherlands Quarterly of Human Rights
Ö.J.Z.	Österreichische Juristenzeitung
Ö.Z.Ö.R.	Österreichische Zeitschrift für öffentliches Recht und Völkerrecht
R.B.D.I.	Revue belge de droit international
R.C.A.D.I.	Recueil des cours de l'Académie de droit international
R.C.J.B.	Revue critique de jurisprudence belge
R.D.H.	Revue des droits de l'homme
R.D.I.D.C.	Revue de droit international et de droit comparé
R.D.P.	Revue du droit public et de la science politique en France et à l'étranger
R.D.P.C.	Revue de droit pénal et de criminologie
R.F.D.A.	Revue française de droit administratif
R.G.D.I.P.	Revue générale de droit international public
R.H.D.I.	Revue hellénique de droit international
R.I.D.P.	Revue internationale de droit pénal
R.I.E.	Revista de instituciones europeas
Riv.D.E.	Rivista di diritto europeo
Riv.D.I.	Rivista di diritto internazionale
Riv.I.D.P.P.	Rivista italiana di diritto e procedura penale
Riv.I.D.U.	Rivista internazionale dei diritti dell'uomo
Riv.T.D.P.	Rivista trimestrale di diritto pubblico
R.P.D.P.	Revue pénitentiaire et de droit pénal
R.S.C.D.P.C.	Revue de science criminelle et de droit pénal comparé
R.T.D.B.	Revue trimestrielle de droit belge
R.T.D.H.	Revue trimestrielle des droits de l'homme
R.U.D.H.	Revue universelle des droits de l'homme
R.W.	Rechstkundig Weekblad
S.J.	Semaine judiciaire (Geneva)
Y.E.L.	Yearbook of European Law
Z.A.Ö.R.V.	Zeitschrift für ausländisches Recht und Völkerrecht

Introduction

1. What is the European Court of Human Rights? The litigant will complain that it is the promised land reached only seldom after a procedural marathon. For the jurist it is the only genuinely judicial institution set up by the Convention for the Protection of Human Rights and Fundamental Freedoms.[1] For the historian it is the first international court of fundamental rights. For the politician it is the ultimate mainstay of democracy in Europe. These formulas are not wrong, nor do they contain the whole truth, and they certainly do provide a definition of the Court of Human Rights; yet, when all is said and done the Court remains a discreet institution about which the man in the street knows very little. Even in Strasbourg itself, where the Court has its seat and where its presence is announced on street signs in three languages, for years it used to stand almost unnoticed between the imposing Palais de l'Europe and the ancient Marne Rhine canal until the completion in 1995 of a fitting building, designed by Sir Richard Rogers. Yet the rôle conferred upon the Court by the democratic States of Europe (the Thirty-four)[2] affects all those who come under the jurisdiction of those States, be they nationals, foreigners or stateless persons. Beyond that, it concerns all who are anxious to see certain universal values take concrete shape.

2. The number of judges of the Court is equal to that of the member States of the Council of Europe. No two judges may be nationals of the same State. For the most part, they are judges of the highest national courts and professors of law. They may be still in office or retired. The judges are elected by the Parliamentary Assembly of the Council of Europe from a list of three persons nominated by the member States. Their term of office is nine years and they may be re-elected. The judges sit on the Court in their individual capacity and enjoy full independence in the discharge of their duties. Over the years their duties

---

1 More commonly referred to as the European Convention on Human Rights (and in this book as 'the Convention'), it is set out in Annex A.
2 Andorra, Austria, Belgium, Bulgaria, Cyprus, Czech Republic, Denmark, Estonia, Finland, France, Federal Republic of Germany, Greece, Hungary, Iceland, Ireland, Italy, Latvia, Liechtenstein, Lithuania, Luxembourg, Malta, the Netherlands, Norway, Poland, Portugal, Romania, San Marino, Slovakia, Slovenia, Spain, Sweden, Switzerland, Turkey and the United Kingdom (at 10 February 1995).

1

have become increasingly onerous: in addition to the public hearings, there are the numerous deliberative meetings of judges held in closed session, not to mention the time spent studying the documents and written submissions. At present, the Court meets, in Strasbourg (but the judges do not live there), on average one week each month for ten months of the year.

The Court elects its President and Vice-President (for terms of three years) and its Registrar and Deputy Registrar (for terms of seven years). The function of the latter, aided by a staff of about forty, is to assist the Court. The Court's expenses are borne by the Council of Europe.

3. Apart from the power to give advisory opinions on legal questions concerning the interpretation of the Convention and the Protocols thereto—a power conferred upon the Court in 1970[1] but which has not yet been exercised—the Court has jurisdiction in contentious matters. It consists of deciding cases referred to it concerning alleged breaches of the Convention. This jurisdiction can, however, be exercised only with regard to States which have declared that they recognize the Court's decision as binding *ipso facto* or which have given their consent to a particular case being referred to the Court. To date thirty member States have accepted the Court's compulsory jurisdiction, generally for a specific period. Andorra, Estonia, Latvia and Lithuania have still to accept it. (Annex B)

4. Under the Convention, any case submitted to the Court necessarily originates in an application lodged with another body, the European Commission of Human Rights, by a State or by a person, non-governmental organization or group of individuals. The Commission first considers the admissibility of the application: in particular it checks whether all domestic remedies have been exhausted and whether the time limit of six months as from a final decision by the courts or authorization of the State in question has not been exceeded. If it accepts the application, it ascertains the facts and tries to bring about a friendly settlement. Should this attempt fail, the Commission draws up a report containing an opinion as to whether or not the facts found disclose a breach by the respondent State of its obligations under the Convention. The report is transmitted to the Committee of Ministers of the Council of Europe, whereupon the case may be brought before the Court, within three months, by the Commission or any Contracting State concerned, but only by them. If this does not occur, the Committee of Ministers decides whether or not there has been a violation of the Convention.[2]

1 Protocol No. 2, see Annex A.
2 See the Scheme of the procedure introduced by the Convention, in Annex C.

5. For the consideration of each case brought before it, the Court sits in a chamber of nine judges including, as *ex officio* members, the President or the Vice-President and the judge who is a national of any State Party concerned. If the 'national' judge is unable to sit or withdraws, or if there is none, the State in question is entitled to appoint a member of the Court (an elected judge of a different nationality: this has not yet occurred) or a person from outside the Court (an *ad hoc* judge). To date, an *ad hoc* judge has been appointed in sixteen cases. The names of the other judges are chosen by lot by the President. In certain circumstances, the chamber thus constituted may, or must, relinquish jurisdiction in favour of a Grand Chamber of nineteen judges; and the Grand Chamber itself may in turn, in exceptional cases, relinquish jurisdiction in favour of the plenary Court.[1]

6. The first stage of the procedure is generally written: memorials and other documents are filed with the Court's registry in the order and within the time limit laid down by the President. Once the case is ready for hearing, the oral proceedings take place. These hearings are normally held in public. Not only the State or States concerned take part in the proceedings (through an agent); the Commission also takes part and appoints one or more of its members as Delegates for this purpose, but it does not appear as a party. The Commission's main function at this stage is to assist the Court as defender of the public interest in order to enlighten the Court. As for the individual applicants, the Convention does not empower them to refer a case to the Court or to appear before it as parties. By virtue of the case law and practice of the Court, however, the Commission was entitled to put forward any observations made by the applicants. The former Rules of Court also permitted the Delegates of the Commission to have the assistance of a person of their choice; this could, for example, be and often was the lawyer or former lawyer of the individual applicant, or the applicant himself. The new Rules of Court, which came into force on 1 January 1983, include a similar provision but allow the applicant to take part in the proceedings. However, since the coming into force of Protocol No. 9 on 1 October 1994 individual applicants are entitled to bring their cases before the Court, provided that the respondent State has ratified that instrument and that the Commission has adopted its report.

---

1 Prior to October 1993—when the system of Grand Chambers was first instituted—eighty-seven cases had come before the plenary Court; since then, one case has been referred to a Grand Chamber.

7. Between 20 April 1959, when it started sitting, and 31 December 1993, the Court has had referred to it 447 cases (cases brought mainly by the Commission) (Annex D). They originated in 526 applications lodged with the Commission, only one of which was lodged by a State. Fifty-three cases are pending before the Court (not counting those cases in which the only outstanding question of that of the award is 'just satisfaction') (Annex E).

The Court has delivered 448 judgments, of which 49 are concerned with the application of Article 50 ('just satisfaction') and 50 solely with questions of jurisdiction or admissibility, procedure, friendly settlements or the interpretation of a judgment.

8. These rapidly rising figures do not by themselves reflect the scale of the Court's work, much less the importance of the problems considered and of the solutions adopted. However, summaries of the judgments to be found in this book do give an accurate picture of the Court's work, identifying as they do all the stages in the Court's reasoning. For the sake of clarity, the judgments have been grouped under the names of the case(s) where they arise, since a single case may be the subject of two or even three judgments which, albeit of differing interest, necessarily complement each other. Before the legal arguments are set out, there is a brief account of the facts and complaints of the applicant(s). Each case is rounded off by a specific bibliography.

177. Case of Fox, Campbell and Hartley v. the United Kingdom[1]

Judgment of 27 March 1991 *(Chamber)—Application of Article 50 (Series A No. 190–B)*

9. Since the applicants had received 32,257.19 French francs in respect of their travel and subsistence expenses from the Council of Europe, the Court did not find it necessary to make any further award under that head.

As regards lawyers' fees, it awarded the applicants jointly £11,000, plus any value added tax that might be chargeable (unanimously). The Court took account of the fact that it had found a violation in respect of only one of the applicants' claims.

10. As for non-pecuniary damage, the Court considered that the finding in the principal judgment itself constituted sufficient just satisfaction (six votes to one).[2]

---

1 See *Fox, Campbell and Hartley*, Series A No. 182 and Vol. II of this work, 444–454.
2 Section 6 of the Northern Ireland (Emergency Provisions) Act 1987, which entered into force on 15 June 1987 after the material events, replaced section 11(1) of the Northern Ireland (Emergency Provisions) Act 1978.

182. Case of Windisch v. Austria[1]

Judgment of 28 June 1993 *(Chamber)—Application of Article 50* *(Series A No. 255–D)*

11. At the Government's request, the President of the Court agreed on two occasions to stay the proceedings on the ground that, on the Attorney General's entering a plea of nullity in the interest of the law, the Supreme Court had quashed the Innsbruck Regional Court's judgment of 20 November 1985 finding the applicant guilty, and referred the case back to that court for retrial and decision. By judgment of 25 June 1991, the Regional Court convicted the applicant of burglary and attempted intimidation and sentenced him to three years' imprisonment. On 20 February and 25 March 1992, respectively, the Supreme Court rejected the applicant's plea of nullity and the Court of Appeal rejected his appeal against sentence. The Court then resumed the Article 50 proceedings.

12. The Court noted that the proceedings subsequently brought in Austria had redressed the violation found by the Court in its principal judgment. Following the annulment of the judgment finding Mr Windisch guilty, the Innsbruck Regional Court had retried the applicant and imposed a sentence identical to that originally passed, but on that occasion the trial had been attended by all the guarantees laid down by the Convention; in particular, the two anonymous witnesses who had not been heard in public during the first trial had given evidence at the retrial. The end-result of the fresh set of proceedings had brought about a situation as close to *restitutio in integrum* as was possible in the nature of things.

As for the compensation sought in respect of the length of the national proceedings, it was not recoverable because the violation found in the principal judgment did not concern this point.

The Court rejected the remainder of the claims for just satisfaction (unanimously).

13. *Summary bibliography*

SUDRE (F.) and others.—'Chronique de la jurisprudence de la Cour européenne des droits de l'homme. Deuxième partie : juin–décembre 1993', *R.U.D.H.* 1993, pp. 377 *et seq.*

---

1 See *Windisch*, Series A No. 186 and Vol. II of this work, 480–485.

185. Case of Moreira de Azevedo v. Portugal[1]

Judgment of 28 August 1991 *(Chamber)—Application of Article 50 (Series A No. 208–C)*

14. The Court considered that the excessive length of the criminal proceedings must have caused the applicant pecuniary and non-pecuniary damage. Taking its decision on an equitable basis, the Court awarded him 4,000,000 escudos on this count (unanimously).

15. The Court did not regard the amounts claimed by way of costs and expenses relating to the European proceedings as excessive (946,800 escudos), but deducted the 20,153.90 French francs paid as legal aid (held unanimously).

16. *Summary bibliography*

MERRILLS (J.G.).—'Decisions on the European Convention on Human Rights during 1991', *B.Y.B.I.L.* 1991, p. 524.
RENUCCI (J.-F.).—'Droit européen des droits de l'homme', *D.* 1992, sommaires commentés, pp. 335 and 336.

---

1 See *Moreira de Azevedo*, Series A No. 189 and Vol. II of this work, 497–503.

190. Case of Djeroud v. France

Deportation order made against an Algerian, who had arrived in France at a very young age, and causing him to be separated from his family

17. *Mohamed Djeroud, an Algerian national who was born in Algeria in 1958, arrived in France the following year with his family, who set up home in Mulhouse. His mother and his six brothers and sisters, four of whom had French nationality, lived in France.*

He was convicted on several occasions in 1977 and 1978, inter alia, *on theft charges, the first two sentences being suspended. In February 1979 the Minister of the Interior ordered his deportation on the ground that he represented a danger to public order (section 23 of the Order of 2 November 1945 on the conditions for the entry and residence of foreign nationals). The applicant went to Algeria of his own accord in 1980, but in 1982 returned to France, where he lived until 1985 under a provisional residence permit and committed further offences. He was deported in February 1985 and again in April 1987 in pursuance of the 1979 order, but each time he returned to France. In December 1987 he refused to board an aeroplane for Algeria, as a result of which he served a prison sentence in France.*

Since 1988 he had been the subject of a compulsory residence order confining him to the municipality of Villeneuve-Saint-Georges, near Paris, until such time as he complied with the deportation order. Various attempts to secure the revocation of that order failed, as did an application for political asylum lodged in 1987.

18. *In his application made to the Commission on 25 September 1987, Mr Djeroud alleged that his deportation from France infringed the right to respect for his private and family life, guaranteed by Article 8 of the Convention, and constituted inhuman and degrading treatment contrary to Article 3.*[1]

Judgment of 23 January 1991 *(Chamber) (Series A No. 191–B)*

19. The Court took formal note of the settlement reached by the Government and Mr Djeroud under which the deportation order was

---

1 In its report of 15 March 1990, the Commission expressed the opinion that there had been a violation of Article 8 (family life) (thirteen votes to one) but not of Article 3 (unanimously).

revoked and Mr Djeroud was issued a residence permit valid for ten years and paid compensation of 150,000 French francs. The Court discerned no reason of *ordre public* militating against striking the case out of the list (Rule 49 §§ 2 and 4 of the Rules of Court) (held unanimously).

20. *Summary bibliography*

COUSSIRAT-COUSTÈRE (V.).—'Jurisprudence de la Cour européenne des droits de l'homme de 1989 à 1991', *A.F.D.I.* 1991, p. 586.

DECAUX (E.) and TAVERNIER (P.).—'Chronique de jurisprudence de la Cour européenne des droits de l'homme', *J.D.I.* 1992, pp. 774 and 775.

MERRILLS (J.G.).—'Decisions on the European Convention on Human Rights during 1991', *B.Y.B.I.L.* 1991, pp. 486 and 487.

RENUCCI (J.-F.).—'Droit européen des droits de l'homme', *D.* 1992, sommaires commentés, p. 327.

SUDRE (F.).—'Chronique de la jurisprudence de la Cour européenne des droits de l'homme—1991', *R.U.D.H.* 1992, Nos 1 and 2, pp. 1 *et seq.*

191. Case of Fredin v. Sweden (no. 1)

Revocation of a permit to exploit gravel and absence of judicial review of the relevant decision

21. *In 1963, the County Administrative Board of Stockholm County granted Anders Fredin's parents a permit, subject to certain conditions, to extract gravel from an old pit located on a parcel of land in the municipality of Botkyrka. The permit provided that exploitation had to be carried out in three stages, each of which should not exceed ten years. However, commercial operations never started.*

In 1973, an amendment to the Nature Conservation Act 1964 empowered the County Administrative Board to revoke permits of the type in question after 1 July 1983. In 1977, the applicant and his wife Maria became sole proprietors of the property. They began to exploit the pit in 1980 and invested some 2,250,000 kronor to that end. The permit was transferred to them in April 1983. At the same time, they were officially informed that it was intended to re-examine the permit question in 1983 with a view to a possible termination of the activities.

In December 1984, the County Administrative Board decided that the permit should remain in force until the end of 1987, by which time the exploitation of gravel should cease and the area should be restored. The Fredins were also ordered to increase the security intended to cover possible restoration costs. In 1985, the Government dismissed an appeal brought by the couple, but extended the validity of the permit until 1 June 1988. It subsequently put the deadline back to 1 December 1988, at which date the extraction of the gravel ceased.

At the time, the Government's decisions were not open to judicial review.

22. *In their application to the Commission of 5 March 1986, Mr and Mrs Fredin relied on Article 1 of Protocol No. 1 and Articles 6 and 14 of the Convention.*[1]

---

1 In its report adopted on 6 November 1989, the Commission expressed the unanimous opinion that there had been a violation of Article 6 § 1 of the Convention, but not of Article 1 of Protocol No. 1 taken either alone or in conjunction with Article 14.

Judgment of 18 February 1991 *(Chamber) (Series A No. 192)*

23. There had been no formal expropriation and the consequences of the revocation of the permit had not been so serious as to amount to a *de facto* deprivation: the revocation had not taken away all meaningful use of the properties in question; the applicants were still the owners of the gravel resources; and the 1973 amendments to the 1964 Act had already made the applicants' possibilities of continuing their gravel exploitation business uncertain. Consequently, the measure had to be considered as a control of the use of property falling within the scope of the second paragraph of Article 1 of Protocol No. 1.

The legislation in issue incontestably had a legitimate aim, namely the protection of nature, which in today's society was an increasingly important consideration. The Court's power to review compliance with domestic law was limited and the evidence available did not show that the revocation decision had been contrary to Swedish law. The 1964 Act had indicated the scope and manner of exercise of the discretion conferred on the authorities with sufficient precision. Lastly, the absence of judicial review did not amount, in itself, to a violation of Article 1 of Protocol No. 1.

The effects of the revocation of the permit had to be assessed, not only in the light of the substantial losses incurred by the applicants, having regard to the potential of the gravel pit if it had been exploited in accordance with the 1963 permit, but also of the restrictions lawfully imposed on the use of the pit. When the applicants had initiated their investment and operations in 1980, they could not have nurtured the justified hope of continuing their operations for a long time: as a result of the 1973 amendment, they risked losing their permit after 1983.

Having regard to those considerations and the closing-down period (almost four years), the Court found that it could not be said that the revocation decision complained of by the applicants had been disproportionate to the legitimate aim pursued. Therefore, no violation of Article 1 of Protocol No. 1 had been established (held unanimously).

24. The applicants had not tried to refute the Commission's assessment that there was nothing to show that the applicants were in a similar situation to those gravel companies whose permits had not been revoked. Since the Court perceived no reason why it should assess the evidence otherwise than the Commission, it held that there had been no violation of Article 1 of Protocol No. 1 in conjunction with Article 14 of the Convention (unanimously).

25. Mr and Mrs Fredin's right to develop their property in accordance with the applicable laws and regulations was a 'civil' one. The 'genuine and serious' dispute between them and the authorities regarding the lawfulness of the impugned decisions which had manifestly arisen could have been determined only by the Government as the final instance. The applicants had therefore not had the benefit of their right to access to a court guaranteed by Article 6 § 1 of the Convention (held unanimously).

26. There remained the question of the application of Article 50 of the Convention. In the absence of a causal link between the violation of Article 6 and the alleged prejudice, the Court awarded nothing under this head. Deciding on an equitable basis, it awarded the applicants 10,000 kronor for non-pecuniary damage and 75,000 kronor for costs and expenses (unanimously).[1]

27. *Summary bibliography*

COUSSIRAT-COUSTÈRE (V.).—'Jurisprudence de la Cour européenne des droits de l'homme de 1989 à 1991', *A.F.D.I.* 1991, pp. 587 *et seq.*

DECAUX (E.) and TAVERNIER (P.).—'Chronique de jurisprudence de la Cour européenne des droits de l'homme', *J.D.I.* 1992, pp. 775 and 776.

MERRILLS (J.G.).—'Decisions on the European Convention on Human Rights during 1991', *B.Y.B.I.L.* 1991, pp. 487–489.

SUDRE (F.).—'Chronique de la jurisprudence de la Cour européenne des droits de l'homme—1991', *R.U.D.H.* 1992, Nos 1 and 2, pp. 1 *et seq.*

WARBRICK (C.).—'The European Convention on Human Rights', *Y.E.L.* 1991, p. 589.

---

1 Under a law enacted on 21 April 1988, the Supreme Administrative Court may now review the legality of numerous administrative decisions, such as a decision to revoke a permit to extract gravel.

192. Case of Moustaquim v. Belgium

Deportation of a Moroccan who arrived in the country at a very early age, separating him from his close relatives

28. *Abderrahman Moustaquim, who was born in Morocco in 1963, arrived in Belgium with his mother in July 1965 at the latest. His parents and seven brothers and sisters also lived in Belgium.*

On 9 November 1982, the Liège Court of Appeal found him guilty of twenty-two offences committed between February and December 1980 while he was still a minor for the purposes of the criminal law, and sentenced him to a total of twenty-six months' imprisonment. This represented a fraction of the charges brought against him which had previously come up before the juvenile courts and later the Liège Criminal Court.

A royal order of 28 February 1984 required him to be deported from Belgium on the ground that he constituted a real danger to society and had seriously prejudiced public order. On 22 June 1984 and 16 October 1985, respectively, the Conseil d'Etat *rejected his applications (a) to have execution of the deportation order stayed and (b) to have the order itself quashed. He was released in April 1984 after spending eighteen months in detention and deported in late June 1984; he took refuge first in Spain, until he was asked to leave, and subsequently in Greece and Sweden. However, a royal order of 14 December 1989 authorized him to return to Belgium for a two-year trial period; he came back to Belgium on 20 January 1990.*

29. *In his application of 13 May 1986 to the Commission, Mr Moustaquim alleged that his deportation from Belgium infringed several provisions of the Convention: Article 8, on account of interference with his family and private life; Article 14 taken together with Article 8, on account of discrimination based on nationality; Article 3, on account of inhuman and degrading treatment; Article 6, because the* Conseil d'Etat *was not in this case an impartial tribunal; and Article 7, because the deportation was a punishment imposed in respect of acts which did not all amount to criminal offences at the time they were committed.*[1]

---

1 On 10 April 1989, the Commission declared the application admissible as to the consequences of the deportation but rejected the complaint based on Article 6. In its report of 12 October 1989, it expressed the opinion that there had been a breach of Article 8 (ten votes to three) but not of Article 14 taken together with Article 8 or of Articles 3 and 7 (unanimously).

13

Judgment of 18 February 1991 *(Chamber) (Series A No. 193)*

30. Contrary to the view taken by the Belgian Government, the Court considered that the application had not become devoid of purpose. The order of 14 December 1989 had only suspended the deportation order and had not made reparation for its consequences, which Mr Moustaquim had suffered for more than five years.

31. Mr Moustaquim lived in Belgium, where his parents and his seven brothers and sisters also resided. He had never broken off relations with them. His deportation had resulted in his being separated from them for more than five years, although he had tried to remain in touch by correspondence. There had accordingly been interference with the right to respect for family life guaranteed in paragraph 1 of Article 8.

32. The Court then considered whether the interference satisfied the requirements of Article 8 § 2.

It was common ground that its legal basis was to be found in provisions of the Act of 15 December 1980 on the entry, residence, settlement and expulsion of aliens.

The interference in question pursued an aim which was fully compatible with the Convention, that of the prevention of disorder.

Was the interference necessary in a democratic society? The Court did not in any way underestimate the Contracting States' concern to maintain public order, in particular in exercising their right, as a matter of well-established international law and subject to their treaty obligations, to control the entry, residence and expulsion of aliens.

Mr Moustaquim's alleged offences in Belgium had a number of special features. They all went back to his adolescence. Furthermore, proceedings had been brought in the criminal courts in respect of only twenty-six of them, which had been spread over a fairly short period—about eleven months—, and on appeal the Liège Court of Appeal had acquitted him on four charges and convicted him on twenty-two. There had been a relatively long interval between the last of those offences and the deportation order. Moreover, at the time the deportation order had been made, all the applicant's close relatives had been living in the host country; one of the older children had acquired Belgian nationality and the three youngest had been born in Belgium. Mr Moustaquim himself had been very young when he arrived in Belgium. He had spent about twenty years there with his family or not far away from them, had returned to Morocco only twice, for holidays, and had received all his schooling in French. His family life had thus been seriously disrupted by the deportation measure, which the Advisory Board

14

on Aliens had judged to be 'inappropriate'. Consequently, the means employed had been disproportionate to the legitimate aim pursued and, accordingly, there had been a violation of Article 8 (seven votes to two).

33. This conclusion made it unnecessary for the Court to consider whether the deportation had also been in breach of the applicant's right to respect for his private life.

34. The applicant could not be compared to juvenile delinquents who were nationals of Belgium or another member State of the European Community. Belgian nationals had a right of abode in their own country and there was objective and reasonable justification for the preferential treatment given to nationals of the other member States of the Community, as Belgium belonged, together with those States, to a special legal order. There had accordingly been no breach of Article 14 taken together with Article 8 (held unanimously).

35. As the complaints based on Articles 3 and 7 had not been raised again before the Court, it did not consider itself bound to deal with them of its own motion (held unanimously).

36. The Court dismissed the applicant's claim for compensation for pecuniary damage (unanimously) since it perceived no causal link between the breach of Article 8 and the alleged loss of earnings. In contrast, it awarded him 100,000 Belgian francs compensation for non-pecuniary damage (seven votes to two).

Belgium had to pay the costs and lawyer's fees incurred by the applicant before the Advisory Board on Aliens and the *Conseil d'Etat*, amounting to 90,000 Belgium francs (seven votes to two). As far as the costs and expenses incurred before the Convention institutions were concerned, the Court took account of the inadequacy of the particulars and vouchers supplied by Mr Moustaquim and awarded him only 250,000 Belgian francs, less 10,730 French francs paid by the Council of Europe by way of legal aid (seven votes to two).

37. *Summary bibliography*

COUSSIRAT-COUSTÈRE (V.).—'Jurisprudence de la Cour européenne des droits de l'homme de 1989 à 1991', *A.F.D.I.* 1991, pp. 586 *et seq.*

DECAUX (E.) and TAVERNIER (P.).—'Chronique de jurisprudence de la Cour européenne des droits de l'homme', *J.D.I.* 1992, pp. 777 and 778.

DUFFAR (J.).—'La protection du droit au respect de la vie familiale des étrangers', *L.P.A.*, 24 May 1991, No. 62, pp. 32–34.

MERRILLS (J.G.).—'Decisions on the European Convention on Human Rights during 1991', *B.Y.B.I.L.* 1991, pp. 489–491.

RENUCCI (J.-F.).—'Droit européen des droits de l'homme', *D.* 1992, sommaires commentés, pp. 326 and 327.

STEENBERGEN (J.D.M.).—'Noot', *NJCM-Bulletin* 1991, pp. 252–254.

SUDRE (F.).—'Chronique de la jurisprudence de la Cour européenne des droits de l'homme—1991', *R.U.D.H.* 1992, Nos 1–2, pp. 1 *et seq.*

WARBRICK (C.).—'The European Convention on Human Rights', *Y.E.L.* 1991, pp. 553–556.

193. Case of Isgrò v. Italy

Criminal conviction based in part on the statements made by a witness before an investigating judge and read out at the trial, the witness in question being 'untraceable'

38. *In November 1978, criminal proceedings were brought against Salvatore Isgrò for the kidnapping and death of a young man. In March 1980, he was found guilty by the Monza District Court, which sentenced him to thirty years' imprisonment. The Milan Court of Appeal upheld the verdict in December 1981 but reduced the sentence by ten years. The Court of Cassation dismissed Mr Isgrò's appeal on a point of law in March 1984.*

The guilty verdict was based essentially on statements made by a witness (Mr D.) during the investigation in the absence of Mr Isgrò and his lawyer and on a confrontation between Mr D. and the accused when Mr Isgrò was not assisted by his lawyer. Neither the Monza District Court nor the Milan Court of Appeal heard the witness, who remained impossible to trace, even though he was summoned to appear.

39. *In his application to the Commission of 12 September 1984, Mr Isgrò complained that he had been convicted on the basis of statements by a witness who could not be traced during the trial and whom his lawyer had never had the opportunity to examine. He relied on paragraphs 1, 2 and 3(d) of Article 6 of the Convention.*[1]

Judgment of 19 February 1991 *(Chamber) (Series A No. 194–A)*

40. The Government argued that, since Mr Isgrò had not objected to Mr D.'s statements being read out at the trial, he had not exhausted domestic remedies and could not claim to be a 'victim'.

The Court held that an objection of that kind would not have constituted a sufficient and effective remedy, and hence declared the first submission to be unfounded (unanimously). It further considered that the Government was estopped from relying on the second preliminary objection on the ground that it had not first raised it before the Commission (held unanimously).

---

1 In its report of 14 December 1989, the Commission expressed the opinion that there had been a violation of Article 6 §§ 1 and 3(d) (ten votes to three).

41. As for the merits, the Court proceeded on the basis that it had not been possible to secure Mr D.'s presence in Court. Mr D. was not an anonymous witness: in particular, the investigating judge had questioned him several times and two confrontations had been organized in order to compare the earlier statements of Mr D. with those respectively of Mr Isgrò and a co-accused. Thus the applicant had been in a position to put questions directly to the witness and to discuss his statements. Furthermore, the District Court and the Court of Appeal had not based their decisions solely on Mr D.'s statements to the examining judge. They had also had regard to other testimony and to the observations submitted by the applicant during the investigation and at the trial. Lastly, the applicant's lawyer had been able to challenge at the trial the accuracy of Mr D.'s allegations and his credibility.

The rights of the defence had therefore not been subject to restrictions of such a kind as to deprive the applicant of a fair trial. Consequently, the Court held that there had been no violation of paragraph 3(d) of Article 6, in conjunction with paragraph 1 (unanimously).

42. *Summary bibliography*

COUSSIRAT-COUSTÈRE (V.).—'Jurisprudence de la Cour européenne des droits de l'homme de 1989 à 1991', *A.F.D.I.* 1991, pp. 585 *et seq.*

MERRILLS (J.G.).—'Decisions on the European Convention on Human Rights during 1991', *B.Y.B.I.L.* 1991, pp. 491 and 492.

MYJER (E.).—'De onmiddellijke getuige en artikel 6 EVRM—deel 2', *NJCM–Bulletin* 1991, pp. 358–360.

SUDRE (F.).—'Chronique de la jurisprudence de la Cour européenne des droits de l'homme—1991', *R.U.D.H.* 1992, Nos 1–2, pp. 1 *et seq.*

194. Case of Brigandi v. Italy
195. Case of Zanghi v. Italy
196. Case of Santilli v. Italy

Length of civil proceedings

43. *Natale Brigandi, Claudio Zanghi and Franco Santilli were Italian nationals. Mr Brigandi sued Mr B. in the Reggio Calabria District Court. He sought an injunction requiring a new building to be demolished and the rebuilding of the warehouse which had formerly stood on the site. He also sought compensation. Mr Zanghi brought proceedings in the Catania District Court for a declaration that there was a right of view for the benefit of his secondary residence, an injunction requiring his neighbour to restore the situation as it had been before—his neighbour had built a dividing wall—and damages. Mr Santilli sued his bank in the Pescara District Court so as to obtain leave to invest a sum borrowed from another credit institution and compensation for the damage suffered.*

44. *In their applications to the Commission made on 22 February, 16 April and 4 March 1985, the applicants complained principally or solely of the length of the civil proceedings which they had brought and of the disregard of their right to respect for their possessions. They relied on Article 6 § 1 of the Convention and Article 1 of Protocol No. 1.[1]*

Judgments of 19 February 1991 *(Chamber) (Series A No. 194–B to D)*

45. The Court started by determining in each case the period to be taken into consideration for assessing whether the length of the proceedings had been reasonable:

Brigandi: more than seventeen years (from the date on which Italy's declaration recognizing the right of individual petition had taken effect to the date when the Messina Court of Appeal's judgment had been filed);

1 In its reports of 6 December, 11 December and 6 November 1989, the Commission expressed the opinion that there had been a violation of Article 6 § 1 (unanimously) but not of Article 1 of Protocol No. 1 (Brigandi: twelve votes to seven; Zanghi and Santilli: unanimously).

Zanghi: almost nine years (from the date when the proceedings had been instituted to the date of the judgment of the European Court of Human Rights, since the proceedings were still pending before the Catania Court of Appeal);

Santilli: approximately six years and nine months (from the date when the summons had been served on the applicant to the date when the judgment of the Aquila Court of Appeal had been filed).

The Court found that the cases of Brigandi and Zanghi were not complex, even though the former had been considered by courts at various levels. Matters were different as regards the Santili case—where, in addition, the parties had been responsible for one of the adjournments—, but the trial court had allowed excessively long periods to elapse between hearings and had been totally inactive for nearly two years. Hence there had been a breach of Article 6 § 1 (held unanimously).

46. The Court considered it unnecessary also to determine the complaint based on Article 1 of Protocol No. 1 (unanimously).

47. The Court reached the following conclusions with regard to the claims based on Article 50:

Brigandi: 15,000,000 lire awarded for damage (unanimously);

Zanghi: as matters stood, the claim for compensation for the pecuniary damage resulting from the alleged breach of Article 1 of Protocol No. 1 was dismissed on the ground that it was still possible that the national courts might make reparation for the financial consequences of failing to try the case within a reasonable time (held unanimously);

Santilli: 10,000,000 lire awarded for non-pecuniary damage and 4,000,000 lire for costs and expenses before the Court (unanimously).

Judgment of 10 February 1993 *(Zanghi case) (Chamber)—Application of Article 50 (Series A No. 257–A)*

48. The Court considered that the judgment delivered on 31 May 1980 by the Catania Court of Appeal, which had become final on 26 September 1991, was not of such a nature as to call for a reconsideration of the Strasbourg decision (eight votes to one).

49. Summary bibliography

COUSSIRAT-COUSTÈRE (V.).—'Jurisprudence de la Cour européenne des droits de l'homme de 1989 à 1991', *A.F.D.I.* 1991, pp. 599 *et seq.*

MERRILLS (J.G.).—'Decisions on the European Convention on Human Rights during 1991', *B.Y.B.I.L.* 1991, pp. 492 and 493.

RENUCCI (J.-F.).—'Droit européen des droits de l'homme', *D.* 1992, sommaires commentés, pp. 333 and 334.

SUDRE (F.).—'Chronique de la jurisprudence de la Cour européenne des droits de l'homme—1991', *R.U.D.H.* 1992, Nos 1–2, pp. 1 *et seq.*

SUDRE (F.) and others.—'Chronique de la jurisprudence de la Cour européenne des droits de l'homme. Première partie : janvier-mai 1993', *R.U.D.H.* 1993, pp. 217 *et seq.*

197. Case of Motta v. Italy

Length of civil and criminal proceedings

50. *Luciano Motta, an Italian national, practised as a doctor at Carlentini (Syracuse). He brought civil proceedings against the national health insurance institute for the payment of medical services. Shortly afterwards, criminal proceedings were brought against him for forgery and fraud.*

51. *In his application to the Commission of 22 April 1985, the applicant alleged several violations of Article 6 of the Convention and Article 1 of Protocol No. 1.*[1]

Judgment of 19 February 1991 *(Chamber) (Series A No. 195–A)*

52. The Court started by establishing the period to be taken into consideration for assessing whether the duration of the proceedings had been reasonable: in the civil proceedings, more than seven and a half years had elapsed between 20 October 1979, when the investigating judge had advised Mr Motta of the opening of an investigation, and the decision of the Court of Cassation on an appeal brought by the applicant against a judgment of the Catania Court of Appeal that the proceedings should be discontinued because of an amnesty. The civil proceedings had been stayed pending the outcome of the criminal proceedings and had not been resumed since.

As regards the criminal proceedings, the Court noted that the criminal case was not a complex one. Moreover, the applicant had caused hardly any delay. As for the civil case, the proceedings had been prevented from pursuing their course by the slowness of the criminal proceedings. There had therefore been, in both cases, a violation of Article 6 § 1 (held unanimously).

53. Under Article 50, the evidence did not show that the applicant had suffered pecuniary damage, but the Court awarded him 10,000,000

---

1 On 14 December 1988, the Commission declared the application admissible solely as regards the length of two sets of proceedings. In its report of 6 November 1989, it expressed the opinion that there had been a violation of Article 6 § 1 (unanimously for the criminal proceedings and fourteen votes to three for the civil proceedings).

lire for non-pecuniary damage and 2,000,000 lire for such of his costs and expenses as were not covered by legal aid (unanimously).

54. *Summary bibliography*

198. Case of Manzoni v. Italy
199. Case of Pugliese v. Italy (no. 1)
200. Case of Alimena v. Italy
201. Case of Frau v. Italy
202. Case of Ficara v. Italy
203. Case of Viezzer v. Italy
204. Case of Angelucci v. Italy
205. Case of Maj v. Italy
206. Case of Girolami v. Italy
207. Case of Ferraro v. Italy
208. Case of Triggiani v. Italy
209. Case of Mori v. Italy
210. Case of Colacioppo v. Italy
211. Case of Adiletta and Others v. Italy

Length of criminal proceedings

55.   *The following list sets out the name and, where it is mentioned in the judgment, the occupation of each applicant at the material time, followed by (a) the charge and (b) the outcome or the present state of the proceedings:*

*Giovanni **Manzoni**: (a) principally, drug trafficking; (b) judgment of the Naples Court of Appeal sentencing him* inter alia *to six years' imprisonment upheld by the Court of Cassation;*

*Vincenzo **Pugliese** (journalist): (a) trespass; (b) amnesty pronounced by the Rieti District Court on appeal;*

*Bernardino **Alimena** (lawyer): (a) contempt of court; (b) judgment of the Salerno Court of Appeal acquitting him on the ground of insufficient evidence upheld by the Court of Cassation;*

*Aventino **Frau** (Member of Parliament): (a) obtaining money with menaces; (b) acquittal by the Milan Court of Appeal;*

Antonino **Ficara**: *(a) malicious accusations; (b) acquittal by the Reggio di Calabria Court of Appeal;*

Antonio **Viezzer** *(colonel in the* Carabinieri*): (a) political espionage (obtaining secret documents for the purpose of espionage and disclosure of confidential information); (b) investigation by an investigating judge in Rome still pending;*

Roberto **Angelucci** *(businessman): (a) criminal association and drug trafficking; (b) discharge by the investigating judge of the Rome District Court;*

Giuseppe **Maj** *(engineer): (a) carrying weapons unlawfully, infringing exchange control regulations and treasonable conspiracy; discharge by the investigating judge at Bergamo;*

Dino **Girolami** *(butcher's assistant): (a) aggravated fraud; (b) acquittal by the Livorno District Court because of insufficient evidence;*

Enrico **Ferraro** *(inspector with the Ministry of Transport): (a) forgery and corruption; (b) acquittal by the Rome District Court;*

Emanuele **Triggiani** *(bank employee): (a) fraud, forgery and use of forged documents, and criminal association; (b) acquittal by the Rome Court of Appeal;*

Bruna **Mori** *(teacher): (a) defamation of a judge of an administrative court; (b) proceedings held to be time-barred by the Court of Cassation following acquittal by the Genoa District Court on appeal;*

Antonio **Colacioppo** *(civil servant employed by the National Pensions Institute): (a) extortion; (b) discharge by the Perugia investigating judge applying an Amnesty Act;*

Anna **Adiletta**, Maria **Adiletta** *and Aniello* **Agovino** *(post-office employees): (a) forging signatures on receipts for pensions; (b) acquittal by the Salerno District Court.*

56. *In their applications to the Commission made between December 1982 and March 1988, the applicants complained of the length of the criminal proceedings brought against them and relied on Article 6 § 1 of the Convention. Mr Alimena further criticized the procedure* *followed by the Court of Cassation on the ground that it was contrary to Article 6 § 3(c).*[1]

Judgments of 19 February 1991 *(Chamber) (Series A Nos 195–B to E, 196–A to E and 197–A to E)*

57. The Court started by determining in each case the period to be taken into consideration for assessing whether the length of the proceedings had been reasonable:

Manzoni:	more than seven years and one month;
Pugliese (no. 1):	more than five years and two months;
Alimena:	more than seven years and four months;
Frau:	more than six years and eight months;
Ficara:	nine years and seven months;
Viezzer:	more than nine and a half years;
Angelucci:	at least eight years and two months;
Maj:	more than five years and eight months;
Girolami:	about eight years;
Ferraro:	almost eight years and five months;
Triggiani:	more than twelve years and two months;
Mori:	almost six years;
Colacioppo:	more than ten years and two months;
Adiletta and others:	thirteen years and five months.

The Court held that Article 6 § 1 had been violated (unanimously) after commenting on various aspects of the proceedings in question (notably the lack of complexity of the cases and the absence of delays caused by the applicants).

58. In the Alimena case, it also held that there had been a violation of Article 6 § 3(c) (unanimously) on the ground that the Court of Cassation had held its hearing without notifying Mr Alimena's lawyer.

59. Under Article 50, the Court awarded the following sums (unanimously):

Manzoni: 1,000,000 lire for non-pecuniary damage and 2,000,000 lire for costs and expenses;

---

1 In its reports of 5 and 13 December 1989, the Commission expressed the opinion that there had been, in each case, a violation of Article 6 § 1 (unanimously) and, in the Alimena case, of Article 6 § 3(c) (unanimously).

Pugliese (no. 1): nothing, since the judgment constituted sufficient just satisfaction;

Alimena: 10,000,000 lire for non-pecuniary damage and 3,000,000 lire for costs and expenses;

Frau: 20,000,000 lire for non-pecuniary damage;

Ficara: 10,000,000 lire for non-pecuniary damage and 20,000,000 lire for costs and expenses;

Viezzer: 25,000,000 lire for non-pecuniary damage and 4,800,400 lire for costs and expenses;

Angelucci: 30,000,000 lire for non-pecuniary damage and costs and expenses;

Maj: 5,000,000 lire for non-pecuniary damage and for costs and expenses;

Girolami: nothing for non-pecuniary damage, since the judgment constituted sufficient just satisfaction; 1,210,000 lire for costs and expenses;

Ferraro: 60,000,000 lire for damage; 6,008,600 lire and 743 French francs for costs and expenses;

Triggiani: 150,000,000 lire for non-pecuniary and pecuniary damage and 5,200,000 lire for costs and expenses;

Mori: 2,000,000 lire for non-pecuniary damage and 5,000,000 lire for costs and expenses;

Colacioppo: 20,000,000 lire for non-pecuniary damage;

Adiletta and others: for each applicant, 15,000,000 lire for non-pecuniary damage; 4,000,000 lire for costs and expenses.

60. *Summary bibliography*

COUSSIRAT-COUSTÈRE (V.).—'Jurisprudence de la Cour européenne des droits de l'homme de 1989 à 1991', *A.F.D.I.* 1991, pp. 597 *et seq.*

MERRILLS (J.G.).—'Decisions on the European Convention on Human Rights during 1991', *B.Y.B.I.L.* 1991, pp. 493–495.

RENUCCI (J.-F.).—'Droit européen des droits de l'homme', *D.* 1992, sommaires commentés, pp. 330 and 331.

SUDRE (F.).—'Chronique de la jurisprudence de la Cour européenne des droits de l'homme—1991', *R.U.D.H.* 1992, Nos 1–2, pp. 1 *et seq.*

212. Case of Vernillo v. France

Length of civil proceedings

61.   *In October 1967, Generoso Vernillo and his wife Maria,* née *Siciliano, Italian nationals, bought a three-room flat in Nice from Ange Torzuoli and his wife (their aunt) for a down payment of 10,000 French francs followed by monthly payments of 100 French francs to the vendors during their lifetimes. In July 1977, the applicants were served with formal notice to pay arrears and co-ownership service charges, but they did not act on it.*

   In December 1977, Mr and Mrs Torzuoli summoned Mr and Mrs Vernillo before the Nice tribunal de grande instance. *They asked the court to declare that the sale was automatically rescinded. In June 1981, the court refused to make such a declaration. In June 1985, the Court of Cassation dismissed an appeal brought against the decision of the Aix-en-Provence Court of Appeal of June 1983 declaring that the sale was rescinded through the fault of the applicants.*

62.   *In their application to the Commission of 22 November 1985, Mr and Mrs Vernillo complained that the length of the civil proceedings brought against them in the Nice* tribunal de grande instance *was incompatible with Article 6 § 1 of the Convention.*[1]

Judgment of 20 February 1991 *(Chamber) (Series A No. 198)*

63.   The Government maintained that the applicants had not exhausted domestic remedies, since they had not brought an action for compensation against the State under Article L 781–1 of the Code of Judicial Organization.

   The Court rejected that objection (unanimously). The article in question laid down very strict conditions for eligibility. Moreover, the applicants did not claim to be the victims of a denial of justice or even of gross negligence, and it did not appear from the decisions drawn to the Court's attention by the Government that the French courts had interpreted the concept of gross negligence sufficiently broadly to include, for example, every delay exceeding the 'reasonable time' laid down in Article 6 § 1 of the Convention.

1   In its report of 6 February 1990, the Commission expressed the (unanimous) opinion that there had been a violation of Article 6 § 1.

64.   The period to be considered had begun when the applicants had been summoned before the Nice *tribunal de grande instance*, and had ended when the Court of Cassation had delivered its judgment. It had therefore amounted to about seven and a half years.

The case was not very complex and the parties' conduct had contributed decisively to the slowing down of the proceedings. The periods which might seem abnormal and due to the conduct of the judicial authorities had not been so long as to warrant the conclusion that the overall duration of the proceedings had been excessive. The Court therefore considered that Article 6 § 1 had not been violated (held unanimously).

65.   *Summary bibliography*

COUSSIRAT-COUSTÈRE (V.).—'Jurisprudence de la Cour européenne des droits de l'homme de 1989 à 1991', *A.F.D.I.* 1991, pp. 585 *et seq.*

DECAUX (E.) and TAVERNIER (P.).—'Chronique de jurisprudence de la Cour européenne des droits de l'homme', *J.D.I.* 1992, pp. 779 and 780.

JUNOSZA-ZDROJEWSKI (G.).—'Arrêt Vernillo c. France du 20 février 1991 de la Cour européenne', *G.P.* 6–7 March 1992, doctrine, p. 196.

MERRILLS (J.G.).—'Decisions on the European Convention on Human Rights during 1991', *B.Y.B.I.L.* 1991, pp. 495 and 496.

RENUCCI (J.-F.).—'Droit européen des droits de l'homme', *D.* 1992, sommaires commentés, p. 333.

SUDRE (F.).—'Chronique de la jurisprudence de la Cour européenne des droits de l'homme—1991', *R.U.D.H.* 1992, Nos 1–2, pp. 1 *et seq.*

213. Case of Stocké v. Germany

Arrest and detention of a person who claimed to have been the victim of collusion between the authorities and a police informer for the purpose of bringing him back to Germany against his will

66. *Walter Stocké was a German citizen. In 1975, following the bankruptcy of his building firm, he was investigated in Germany, where he was suspected of fraud and tax offences. He fled abroad. When he was living in Strasbourg, he was, he alleged, lured into a trap with the connivance of the German authorities by a police informer, Mr Köster, who, on 7 November 1978, got him to board an aeroplane, which was supposed to land in Luxembourg, but actually landed in Saarbrücken, where he was arrested by the German police. Mr Stocké was put in custody before being sentenced in 1982 to six years' imprisonment by the Kaiserslautern Regional Court for fraud and tax evasion. He unsuccessfully appealed to the Federal Court of Justice and the Federal Constitutional Court.*

67. *In his application to the Commission of 20 September 1985, Mr Stocké relied on Article 5 § 1 and Article 6 § 1 of the Convention.*[1]

Judgment of 19 March 1993 *(Chamber) (Series A No. 199)*

68. The German Government denied the allegations of collusion between the German authorities and Mr Köster. Not only had the authorities not been warned of Mr Köster's intentions, but they had done their best to clarify the situation. As for Mr Köster, the authorities had neither shielded him nor dealt leniently with him. He had been arrested in February 1988 and sentenced to nine years' imprisonment for other offences.

69. Whilst the proceedings were pending before the Court, Mr Stocké asked for five witnesses to be called, four of whom had not been heard by the Commission. The Court recalled that under the Convention system, the establishment and verification of the facts was primarily a matter for the Commission. It was only in exceptional circumstances that the Court would use its powers in this area. Having regard to the

---

1 In its report of 12 October 1989, the Commission expressed the opinion that there had been no breach of Article 5 § 1 and Article 6 § 1 (unanimously).

conclusions reached by the French and German authorities after thorough investigations, to the evidence of numerous witnesses already heard by the Commission and to the fact that the Commission had considered it unnecessary to hear other witnesses, the Court saw no reason to accede to that request.

The Court considered that it had not been established that the cooperation between the German authorities and Mr Köster had extended to unlawful activities abroad. Accordingly, it did not deem it necessary to examine whether, if it had been otherwise, the applicant's arrest in the Federal Republic of Germany would have violated the Convention.

In conclusion, the Court found that there had been no violation of Article 5 or Article 6 (unanimously).

70. *Summary bibliography*

DECAUX (E.) and TAVERNIER (P.).—'Chronique de jurisprudence de la Cour européenne des droits de l'homme', *J.D.I.* 1992, pp. 780 and 781.

MERRILLS (J.G.).—'Decisions on the European Convention on Human Rights during 1991', *B.Y.B.I.L.* 1991, pp. 496–498.

SUDRE (F.).—'Chronique de la jurisprudence de la Cour européenne des droits de l'homme—1991', *R.U.D.H.* 1992, Nos 1–2, pp. 1 *et seq.*

WARBRICK (C.).—'The European Convention on Human Rights', *Y.E.L.* 1991, pp. 556–559.

214. Case of Cardot v. France

Criminal conviction based partly on statements by former co-defendants, who were examined by the investigating judge and each confronted with the accused before him, but not by the trial courts

71. *Jean-Claude Cardot, a French national, worked as a road haulier. In 1979, he and fourteen others were charged with offences and attempted offences under drugs legislation. The proceedings brought against the other fourteen persons at first instance and on appeal culminated in February 1982 with the majority of them being convicted. In contrast, the proceedings brought against Mr Cardot were adjourned and his trial deferred on the ground that he was in detention in Italy.*

In September 1982, the Valence Criminal Court sentenced Mr Cardot —who had since been extradited from Italy to France—to a term of six years' imprisonment. The Grenoble Court of Appeal upheld that judgment in March 1983, but increased the sentence to seven years' imprisonment. Mr Cardot's conviction was based to some extent on evidence gathered during the course of the proceedings brought against his co-accused and, in particular, of statements made by them. They had been confronted by him before the investigating judge, but had not been heard by the Valence Criminal Court or the Grenoble Court of Appeal; no application to that effect had been made by either Mr Cardot or the public prosecutor. An appeal brought by Mr Cardot on points of law in the Court of Cassation was dismissed in February 1984.

72. *In his application to the Commission of 12 December 1983, Mr Cardot complained that he had been convicted on the strength of evidence gathered in connection with proceedings to which he had not been a party and that he had not had an opportunity, either at his trial or on appeal, to challenge or have challenged those who had testified against him. He also impugned his conviction for aiding and abetting an offence for which the principal offender, who had been amnestied in Iran, could no longer be prosecuted in France. He alleged, lastly, that the Court of Cassation had not been able to satisfy itself that the principle* non bis in idem *had been complied with.*[1]

---

1 On 7 September 1989, the Commission declared the application admissible as regards the conduct of the judicial investigation and the court proceedings. In its report of 13 April 1990, the Commission expressed the (unanimous) opinion that there had been a breach of Article 6 §§ 1 and 3(d).

Judgment of 19 March 1991 *(Chamber) (Series A No. 200)*

73. The Government argued in the first place that domestic remedies had not been exhausted as Mr Cardot had failed to raise in the French courts, even in substance, the complaint based on a violation of Article 6 § 3(d) of the Convention.

The Delegate of the Commission submitted, on the contrary, that Mr Cardot had satisfied the requirements of Article 26 of the Convention by appealing on points of law.

74. The Court pointed out that Article 26 must be applied with some degree of flexibility and without excessive formalism, but it did not require merely that applications should be made to the appropriate domestic courts and that use should be made of remedies designed to challenge decisions already given. It normally required also that the complaints intended to be made subsequently at Strasbourg should have been made to those same courts, at least in substance and in compliance with the formal requirements and time-limits laid down in domestic law. Further, any procedural means which might prevent a breach of the Convention should have been used. Practice in international arbitration would appear to reflect a similar approach; an example was to be found in the award of 6 March 1956 in the *Ambatielos* case.

75. In the Valence Criminal Court, Mr Cardot had not expressed any wish that evidence should be heard from his former co-defendants, although they had said that he had played a major part in organizing the smuggling of drugs and three of them, when confronted with him before the investigating judge, had confirmed their earlier statements. Nor had he made any application to the Grenoble Court of Appeal for such evidence to be heard. The case-file disclosed no special reason which could have excused him from calling those witnesses or applying to have them called.

As to his appeal on points of law, only one of the three grounds put forward had related to the proceedings in respect of the former co-defendants who had been heard in that capacity at the time. Above all, it had not relied on paragraph 3(d) of Article 6 or even on the general principle in paragraph 1 and had not referred to the statements that the persons in question had made to the investigating judge; accordingly, it had been too vague to draw the Court of Cassation's attention to the issue subsequently submitted to the Convention institutions, namely the failure to hear prosecution witnesses at any stage of the court proceedings against Mr Cardot.

In sum, Mr Cardot had not provided the French courts with the opportunity which was in principle intended to be afforded to Contracting States by Article 26, namely the opportunity of preventing or putting right the violations alleged against them. The Court held that the objection that domestic remedies had not been exhausted was therefore well founded (six votes to three).

76. *Summary bibliography*

COUSSIRAT-COUSTÈRE (V.).—'Jurisprudence de la Cour européenne des droits de l'homme de 1989 à 1991', *A.F.D.I.* 1991, p. 585.

DECAUX (E.) and TAVERNIER (P.).—'Chronique de jurisprudence de la Cour européenne des droits de l'homme', *J.D.I.* 1992, pp. 781 and 782.

FLAUSS (J.-F.).—'La condition de l'épuisement des griefs au sens de l'article 26 CEDH : les enseignements de l'arrêt Cardot', *R.U.D.H.* 1991, pp. 529–536.

FLAUSS (J.-F.).—'Note', *D.* 1992, jurisprudence, pp. 178–181.

MERRILLS (J.G.).—'Decisions on the European Convention on Human Rights during 1991', *B.Y.B.I.L.* 1991, pp. 498–500.

MYJER (E.).—'De onmiddelligke getuige en artikel 6 EVRM—deel 2', *NJCM–Bulletin* 1991, pp. 358–360.

RENUCCI (J.-F.).—'Droit européen des droits de l'homme', *D.* 1992, sommaires commentés, p. 332.

SUDRE (F.).—'Chronique de la jurisprudence de la Cour européenne des droits de l'homme—1991', *R.U.D.H.* 1992, Nos 1–2, pp. 1 *et seq.*

215. Case of Cruz Varas and Others v. Sweden

Decision to deport a husband, wife and son of Chilean nationality to Chile, implemented as regards the husband despite an indication given by the European of Human Rights

77. *Hector Cruz Varas, his wife, Magaly Maritza Bustamento Lazo, and their son Richard Cruz were Chilean citizens. The first applicant came to Sweden on 28 January 1987 and applied the following day for political asylum. He was joined there by the second and third applicants on 5 June 1987.*

On 21 April 1988, the National Immigration Board decided to expel the applicants and rejected their requests for declarations of refugee status. The applicants appealed to the Government, which dismissed their appeal on 29 September 1988. Mr Cruz Varas told the Varberg police that he had worked in Sweden for a radical organization which had tried to kill Colonel Pinochet, and that he was at risk of political persecution if he returned to Chile. He also claimed that he had been tortured on several occasions in his home country. The police forwarded the file to the National Immigration Board, which referred the case to the Government (Ministry of Labour), expressing the view that there was no impediment to the enforcement of the expulsion order. Mr Cruz Varas submitted to the Government two medical reports relating to the allegations that he had been tortured. On 5 October 1989, the Government found that there was no impediment under sections 77 and 80 of the Aliens Act 1980 to the enforcement of the expulsion order. On the same day, the Cruz Varas family lodged a petition with the European Commission in Strasbourg.

On 6 October, the National Immigration Board decided not to stop the expulsion. However, at 9.10 a.m. on 6 October, the Government's agent was informed of a decision taken by the European Commission of Human Rights under Rule 36 of its Rules of Procedure: it was desirable in the interests of the parties and the proper conduct of the proceedings before the Commission not to deport the applicants to Chile until the Commission had had an opportunity to examine the application further. Nevertheless, Mr Cruz Varas was deported to Chile at 4.40 p.m. on the same day; he stayed there for three weeks, before leaving for Argentina. His wife and three children went into hiding in Sweden.

78. *The applicants complained to the Commission that the first applicant's expulsion amounted to a breach of Article 3 because of the risk*

that he would be tortured by the Chilean authorities. They also claimed
that the expulsion of Richard would be in breach of Article 3. In addition, they complained that the separation of the family constituted a
breach of Article 8 of the Convention. They further invoked Articles 6
and 13.[1]

Judgment of 20 March 1991 *(Plenary Court) (Series A No. 201)*

79. Referring to its judgment in *Soering v. the United Kingdom*,[2] the
Court reaffirmed the principle that Article 3 applied to extradition; the
article also applied to deportation and *a fortiori* to cases of actual
expulsion.

The Court then ruled on the application of Article 3 in the circumstances of the case, distinguishing between the four questions in issue.

The first question: the determination of the facts. Under the
Convention system, the establishment and verification of the facts was
primarily a matter for the Commission. It was only in exceptional circumstances that the Court would use its powers in this area. The Court
was not, however, bound by the Commission's findings of fact, and
remained free to make its own appreciation in the light of all the material before it. In assessing whether the risk of maltreatment existed, it
had to refer primarily to those facts which had been known or ought to
have been known to the Contracting State at the time of the expulsion.
However, information which had come to light subsequently to the
expulsion might be of value in confirming or refuting the appreciation
that had been made by the Contracting Party of the well-foundedness
of an applicant's fears.

The second question: had Mr Cruz Varas's expulsion exposed him
to a real risk of inhuman treatment? Whilst the medical evidence supported the view that the applicant had, at some stage in the past, been
subjected to inhuman or degrading treatment, Mr Cruz Varas' complete
silence as to his alleged clandestine activities and torture by the

1   The application was declared admissible on 7 December 1989 as regards
    the applicants' complaints under Articles 3 and 8 and inadmissible as regards
    the complaints under Articles 6 and 13. The Commission also retained for
    further examination the issues arising from the Government's failure to
    comply with the Rule 36 indications. In its report adopted on 7 June 1990,
    the Commission expressed the opinion that there had been no violation of
    Article 3 (eight votes to five) or Article 8 (unanimously) but that there had
    been a failure on the part of Sweden to comply with Article 25 § 1 *in fine*
    (twelve votes to one).
2   Series A No. 161; see Vol. II of this work, 248–262.

Chilean authorities until more than eighteen months after his first interrogation by the Chilean police cast doubt on his credibility. His credibility was further called into question by the continuous changes in his story following each police interrogation and by the fact that no material had been presented to the Court which substantiated his claims of clandestine political activity. In addition, several factors had to be taken into account: the improvement in the political situation in Chile; the voluntary return of refugees; the particular knowledge and experience of the Swedish authorities in evaluating claims of this nature; and the fact that the final decision to expel Mr Cruz Varas had been taken after thorough examinations of his case. In the light of those considerations, the Court found that substantial grounds had not been shown for believing that Mr Cruz Varas' expulsion exposed him to a real risk of being subjected to inhuman or degrading treatment on his return to Chile.

The third question: had Mr Cruz Varas' expulsion involved such trauma that it amounted to a breach of Article 3? No substantial basis had been shown for his fears. Hence the Court did not consider that his expulsion had exceeded the threshold set by Article 3.

The fourth question: could the possible expulsion of Mr Cruz Vara amount to a breach of Article 3? The applicants did not appear to have maintained that complaint before the Court. In any event, the facts did not reveal a breach in this respect.

80.   In sum, there had been no breach of Article 3 (eighteen votes to one).

81.   With regard to Article 8, the Court recalled that Mr Cruz Varas' wife and son had gone into hiding in order to evade enforcement of the expulsion order. Having regard to the evidence adduced and the Court's finding with regard to Article 3, it held that there had been no obstacles to their establishing family life in their home country. In those circumstances, responsibility for the separation of the family could not be imputed to Sweden. Accordingly, there had been no breach of Article 8 (held unanimously).

82.   There remained the question of Article 25 § 1. Unlike other international instruments, the Convention did not contain a specific provision with regard to interim measures. The *travaux préparatoires* of the Convention were silent as to any discussion which might have taken place on this question. When the Consultative Assembly of the Council of Europe had called on the Committee of Ministers to draft an additional Protocol (Recommendation 623 (1971)), the Committee of Ministers had taken the view that such a protocol would not be expedient.

The Assembly and the Committee had later recommended in 1977 and 1980 respectively that the member States should suspend extradition or expulsion to a non-Contracting State where the Commission or the Court had been called on to take a decision on allegations under Article 3.

Could the Commission nevertheless derive a power to order interim measures from Article 25 § 1 or other sources?

In the absence of a provision in the Convention for interim measures, an indication given under Rule 36 of the Commission's Rules of Procedure could not be considered to give rise to a binding obligation. Indeed, this was borne out by the wording of Rule 36 itself and of the indications which had been made under it in this case.

Article 25 § 1 prohibited interferences with an individual's right effectively to present and pursue his complaint with the Commission. Although that right was procedural and distinguishable from the substantive rights set out under Section I of the Convention, it must be open to individuals to complain that it had been infringed. Nevertheless, it would strain the language of Article 25 to infer from it an obligation to comply with a given Commission indication under Rule 36. That conclusion was not altered by considering Article 25 § 1 in conjunction with Rule 36 or in conjunction with Articles 1 and 19 of the Convention.

In practice, the Contracting Parties had a record of almost total compliance with Rule 36 indications. That practice could be taken as establishing the agreement of Contracting States regarding the interpretation of a Convention provision but not as creating rights and obligations which had not been included in the Convention at the outset. In any event, it reflected a desire to co-operate in good faith with the Commission, as the various recommendations of the Council of Europe bodies referred to above confirmed.

Lastly, general principles of international law afforded no assistance in this regard, since there was no uniform legal rule.

Accordingly, the Court considered that the power to order interim measures could not be inferred from either Article 25 § 1 or from other sources. It was for the Contracting Parties to assess whether it was expedient to remedy this situation. However, if a member State were to decide not to comply with an indication given under Rule 36, it would knowingly assume the risk of being found by the Convention institutions to be in breach of Article 3 and this would be aggravated by the failure to comply with the indication in question.

Had the expulsion actually hindered the effective exercise of the right of petition? Although compliance with the Rule 36 indication would no doubt have facilitated the presentation of the applicants' case before the Commission, there was no evidence that they had been hindered in the exercise of the right of petition to any significant degree: Mr Cruz Varas had remained at liberty following his return to Chile and counsel for the applicants had in fact been able to represent them fully before the Commission. Nor had it been established that his inability to confer with his lawyer had hampered the gathering of evidence additional to that already adduced during the lengthy immigration proceedings in Sweden. In sum, there had been no breach of Article 25 § 1 *in fine* (ten votes to nine).

83. *Summary bibliography*

COUSSIRAT-COUSTÈRE (V.).—'Jurisprudence de la Cour européenne des droits de l'homme de 1989 à 1991', *A.F.D.I.* 1991, pp. 582 *et seq.*

DECAUX (E.) and TAVERNIER (P.).—'Chronique de jurisprudence de la Cour européenne des droits de l'homme', *J.D.I.* 1992, pp. 783–785.

GARCIA DE ENTERRIA (E.).—'De la légitimité des mesures provisoires prises par la Commission et la Cour européennes des droits de l'homme. L'affaire Cruz Varas', *R.T.D.H.* 1992, pp. 251–280.

MACDONALD (R.St.J.).—'Interim measures in international law, with special reference to the European system for the protection of human rights', *Z.A.O.R.V.* 1992, pp. 703–740.

MERRILLS (J.G.).—'Decisions on the European Convention on Human Rights during 1991', *B.Y.B.I.L.* 1991, pp. 500–503.

OELLERS-FRAHM (K.).—'Zur Verbindlichkeit einstweiliger Anordnungen der Europäischen Kommission für Menschenrechte. Anmerkung zum Urteil des EGMR im Fall Cruz Varas gegen Schweden', *EUGRZ* 1991, pp. 197–199.

RENUCCI (J.-F.).—'Droit européen des droits de l'homme', *D.* 1992, sommaires commentés, pp. 327 and 328.

STEENBERGEN (H.).—'Noot 1', *NJCM–Bulletin* 1991, pp. 345–347.

SUDRE (F.).—'Chronique de la jurisprudence de la Cour européenne des droits de l'homme—1991', *R.U.D.H.* 1992, Nos 1–2, pp. 1 *et seq.*

VANDE LANOTTE (J.) and VAN DE PUTTE (M.).—'De verantwoordelijkheid van de vitwijzende Staat: de zaak Cruz Varas', *Tijdschrift voor bestuursweten-schappen en publiekrecht* 1992, pp. 3–8.

WARBRICK (C.).—'The European Convention on Human Rights', *Y.E.L.* 1991, pp. 544–553.

ZWART (T.).—'Noot 2', *NJCM–Bulletin* 1991, pp. 347–349.

216. Case of Ezelin v. France

Disciplinary sanction imposed on an avocat because he had not dissociated himself from a public and unrestrained demonstration in which protests were made against judicial decisions, and had refused to give evidence to an investigating judge

84. *Roland Ezelin lived at Basse-Terre (Guadeloupe), where he practised as a lawyer* (avocat). *In February 1983, he took part in a public demonstration in his capacity as a lawyer to protest against court decisions whereby prison sentences and fines were imposed on three members of independence movements for criminal damage to public buildings. During the demonstration, slogans hostile to the police were chanted and graffiti referring in particular to the judiciary were daubed on public buildings. On a complaint from the principal public prosecutor, disciplinary proceedings were initiated against the applicant: the Bar Council of Guadeloupe considered that there was no occasion to impose any disciplinary sanction on him, but, on 12 December 1983, on an appeal by the principal public prosecutor the Basse Terre Court of Appeal imposed on the applicant the disciplinary penalty of a warning. The Court of Cassation dismissed Mr Ezelin's appeal on 19 June 1985.*

85. *In his application to the Commission of 16 October 1985, Mr Ezelin relied on Articles 10 and 11 of the Convention: he submitted that the disciplinary sanction imposed on him seriously interfered with his freedom of expression and of peaceful assembly.*[1]

Judgment of 26 April 1991 *(Chamber) (Series A No. 202)*

86. The applicant had been punished for having neither shown his disapproval of the 'demonstrators' offensive and insulting acts' nor left the procession in order to dissociate himself from them, and also for having refused to give evidence. Nevertheless, he had been summoned before the investigating judge as a result of his having taken part in the demonstration. That being so, the question of the refusal to give evidence—an issue which in itself did not come within the ambit of Articles 10 and 11—was a secondary one.

---

1 In its report of 14 December 1989, the Commission expressed the opinion that there had been a violation of Article 11 (fifteen votes to six) and that no separate issue arose under Article 10 (unanimously).

87. In the circumstances of the case, Article 10 was to be regarded as a *lex generalis* in relation to Article 11, a *lex specialis*, so that it was unnecessary to take it into consideration separately (held unanimously).

88. The main question in issue concerned Article 11. The term 'restrictions' in paragraph 2 of that article could not be interpreted as not including measures taken after a meeting. In joining the demonstration—of which prior notice had been given and which was not prohibited—the applicant had availed himself of his freedom of peaceful assembly; he himself had not made threats or daubed graffiti. The Court accordingly found that there had been in this instance an interference with the exercise of the applicant's freedom of peaceful assembly.

Was such an interference justified? In this case, the legal basis of the sanction complained of was to be found solely in the special rules governing the profession of *avocat*; hence it had been 'prescribed by law'. It pursued a legitimate aim, the 'prevention of disorder'.

It remained to be considered whether the interference had been necessary. The proportionality principle demanded that a balance be struck between the requirements of the purposes listed in Article 11 § 2 and those of the free expression of opinions by word, gesture or even silence by persons assembled on the streets or in other public places. The pursuit of a just balance must not result in *avocats* being discouraged, for fear of disciplinary sanctions, from making clear their beliefs on such occasions.

According to the Court, the penalty imposed on Mr Ezelin was at the lower end of the scale of disciplinary penalties and had mainly moral force. However, the freedom to take part in a peaceful assembly—in this instance a demonstration that had not been prohibited—was of such importance that it could not be restricted in any way, even for an avocat, so long as the person concerned did not himself commit an reprehensible act on such an occasion. In short, the sanction complained of, however minimal, did not appear to have been necessary in a democratic society. It accordingly had contravened Article 11 (six votes to three).

89. The Court held that this finding afforded Mr Ezelin sufficient just satisfaction (unanimously).

The Court, making an assessment on an equitable basis, allowed the applicant's claim for 40,000 French francs for costs and expenses in full (unanimously).

90. Summary bibliography

Bossi (P.).—'"Liberté de réunion pacifique", "liberté d'expression" e deontologia professionale: a proposito della sentenza Ezelin', *Riv. I.D.U.* 1991, pp. 728–740.

Coussirat-Coustère (V.).—'Jurisprudence de la Cour européenne des droits de l'homme de 1989 à 1991', A.F.D.I. 1991, pp. 604 *et seq.*

Decaux (E.) and Tavernier (P.).—'Chronique de jurisprudence de la Cour européenne des droits de l'homme', *J.D.I.* 1992, pp. 785–787.

Merrills (J.G.).—'Decisions on the European Convention on Human Rights during 1991', *B.Y.B.I.L.* 1991, pp. 504–506.

Renucci (J.-F.).—'Droit européen des droits de l'homme', *D.* 1992, sommaires commentés, p. 335.

Sudre (F.).—'Chronique de la jurisprudence de la Cour européenne des droits de l'homme—1991', *R.U.D.H.* 1992, Nos 1–2, pp. 1 *et seq.*

Warbrick (C.).—'The European Convention on Human Rights', *Y.E.L.* 1991, pp. 586 and 587.

217. Case of Asch v. Austria

Criminal conviction based in part on statements made by a witness before a police officer and read out at the trial, the witness in question having refused to testify before the court

91. *In the night of 5 to 6 July 1985 a dispute broke out at their home between Johann Asch, an Austrian national, and his cohabitee, Mrs J.L. She subsequently reported the incident to the police, alleging that the applicant had beaten and threatened to kill her. Some time later, she returned to the police station, saying that she and the applicant had been reconciled and that she wished to withdraw her complaint. Proceedings were then brought against Mr Asch for intimidation and actual bodily harm. Availing herself of her right to that effect under Austrian law, she refused to testify against him at the hearing at the St Pölten Regional Court held in November 1985. The statement which she had made to the police was then read out. The court heard the officer who had taken down her statement and had in its possession medical certificates dated 9 and 11 July 1985 saying that she had bruises on her head and body. Although he maintained he was innocent, Mr Asch was sentenced to fines payable on a daily basis over a fixed period. His appeal to the Vienna Court of Appeal was dismissed in March 1986.*

92. *In his application to the Commission of 22 August 1986, Mr Asch complained that he had been convicted solely on the basis of the statements of Mrs J.L., who had not given evidence before the Regional Court; he relied on Article 6 §§ 1 and 3(d) of the Convention.*[1]

Judgment of 26 April 1991 *(Chamber) (Series A No. 203)*

93. Following a reference to its case law, the Court made a number of observations. Before the trial court only the police officer had recounted the facts of the case, as Mrs J.L. had described them to him on the very day of the incident. Subject to the rights of the defence being respected, it had been open to the national court to have regard to this statement, in particular in view of the fact that it could consider it to be corroborated by other evidence before it. Furthermore, Mr Asch had had the opportunity to discuss Mrs J.L.'s version of events and to put

---

1   In its report of 3 April 1990, the Commission expressed the opinion that there had been a violation of Article 6 §§ 1 and 3(d) (twelve votes to five).

his own. Moreover, the applicant had chosen not to question the police officer or to call other witnesses. As for his application for expert medical opinion, it had been made at too late a stage and was insufficiently reasoned. Above all, it was clear from the file that Mrs J.L.'s statements did not constitute the only item of evidence on which the first-instance court had based its decision.

In sum, the fact that it had been impossible to question Mrs J.L. at the hearing had not violated the rights of the defence or deprived the accused of a fair trial. Consequently, the Court held that there had been no breach of paragraphs 1 and 3(d) of Article 6, taken together (seven votes to two).

94. *Summary bibliography*

COUSSIRAT-COUSTÈRE (V.).—'Jurisprudence de la Cour européenne des droits de l'homme de 1989 à 1991', *A.F.D.I.* 1991, p. 602.

MERRILLS (J.G.).—'Decisions on the European Convention on Human Rights during 1991', *B.Y.B.I.L.* 1991, pp. 506–508.

MYJER (E.).—'De onmiddellijke getuige en artikel 6 EVRM—deel 3', *NJCM–Bulletin* 1991, pp. 459–462.

SUDRE (F.).—'Chronique de la jurisprudence de la Cour européenne des droits de l'homme—1991', *R.U.D.H.* 1992, Nos 1–2, pp. 1 *et seq.*

WARBRICK (C.).—'The European Convention on Human Rights', *Y.E.L.* 1991, p. 570.

218. Case of Oberschlick v. Austria

Journalist's conviction for defamation of a politician; same bench sitting at first instance and on the appeal court

95. *On 20 April 1983, Gerhard Oberschlick and several other people laid a criminal information against an Austrian politician, Mr Grabher-Meyer, who had made certain statements concerning the family allowances, which he maintained should be paid (a) to Austrian women and (b) to immigrant women. On the same day, Mr Oberschlick published in the periodical* Forum, *for which he worked as a journalist, the complete text of the complaint, in which he alleged, among other things, that Mr Grabher-Meyer was guilty of the offences of incitement to hatred and of activities contrary to the Act prohibiting the National Socialist Party.*

The politician brought a private prosecution for defamation. The Review Chamber of the Vienna Regional Criminal Court decided on the same day to order the discontinuance of the proceedings, but the Vienna Court of Appeal quashed that decision on 31 May 1983 and remitted the case back to the Regional Court. On 11 May 1984, that court imposed a fine on Mr Oberschlick; it also ordered the relevant issue of Forum *to be seized and the publication of its judgment in the periodical. On 17 December 1984, the Vienna Appeal Court, consisting of the same bench which had delivered the judgment of 31 May 1983, dismissed an appeal brought by the applicant. It considered that the applicant had insinuated, without a sufficient basis in the facts, that Mr Grabher-Meyer held National Socialist attitudes.*

96. *In his application to the Commission of 16 June 1985, Mr Oberschlick alleged violations of Articles 6 § 1 and 10 of the Convention as a result of the defamation proceedings instituted against him, and his subsequent conviction.*[1]

Judgment of 23 May 1991 *(Plenary Court) (Series A No. 204)*

97. The Court dismissed the Government's preliminary objection to the effect that Mr Oberschlick had not lodged his application within the six-month period: (a) as regards his main complaints under Articles

---

1 In its report of 14 December 1989, the Commission expressed the opinion that there had been a violation of Article 10 (nineteen votes to two) and also of Article 6 § 1 in relation to the proceedings before the Court of Appeal (twenty votes to one), but not in relation to the proceedings before the Regional Court (unanimously).

6 § 1 and 10, he had posted the application within the six-month period and (b) as regards the complaint concerning the refusal to rectify the trial record, the six-month period had begun to run only as from the same date as that which was relevant with regard to the final decision on the merits.

98. With regard to the merits, the Court considered the case in the light of Article 6 § 1, starting with the proceedings before the Vienna Regional Court. Before the Court, the applicant had not gone further into the question of the Regional Court's refusal to rectify the trial record. In those circumstances, the Court saw no reason to examine this matter.

The fact that the Regional Court had considered itself bound by the Court of Appeal's decision of 31 May 1983, albeit contrary to domestic law, did not constitute of itself a violation of Article 6 § 1, because the court had considered the evidence before it and reached the fully-reasoned conclusion that the applicant was guilty; its decision had subsequently been upheld on appeal.

As for the proceedings before the Vienna Court of Appeal, Mr Oberschlick alleged that, when hearing his appeal on 17 December 1984, that Court had not been 'impartial' or 'established by law', because, contrary to Austrian legislation, it had consisted of the same bench that had sat on 31 May 1983. The Court noted that the applicant's two complaints coincided in substance. The relevant provision of domcstic law manifested the national legislature's concern to remove all reasonable doubts about judicial impartiality. Accordingly, the failure to abide by that rule meant that the applicant's appeal had been heard by a tribunal whose impartiality was recognized by national law to be open to doubt. It had not been established that the applicant had waived his right to have his case determined by an impartial tribunal: neither the applicant nor his counsel had been aware at the time that the three members of the Court of Appeal had participated in both decisions. There had accordingly been a violation of Article 6 § 1 in this respect (held unanimously).

99. As regards Article 10, it was not disputed that the applicant's conviction had constituted an 'interference' with his right to freedom of expression, which was 'prescribed by law' (Criminal Code, Article 111) and had the legitimate aim of protecting the 'reputation or rights of others'.

The Court concentrated above all on the necessity for the interference in a democratic society. After recalling the principles emerging from its case law, the Court observed that the applicant had been convicted for having reproduced in a periodical the text of a criminal information which he and other persons had laid against a politician.

The applicant had expressed the opinion that the politician's proposal corresponded to the philosophy and the aims of National Socialism. The publication had contributed to a public debate on a political question of general importance, namely the issue of different treatment of nationals and foreigners in the social field. Mr Oberschlick's criticisms had sought to draw the public's attention in a provocative manner to a proposal made by a politician which had been likely to shock many people. He had been found guilty because he had been unable to prove the truthfulness of his allegations. According to the Court, the publication had consisted of a factually correct version of the facts (the politician's proposal), followed by an analysis of that proposal made by the authors of the information. The latter part of the information constituted a value-judgment which could not be proved to be true and was itself an infringement of freedom of opinion. In addition, in view of the importance of the issue at stake, Mr Oberschlick could not be said to have exceeded the limits of freedom of expression by choosing that particular form of publication. There had, accordingly, been a violation of Article 10 (sixteen votes to three).

100. Under Article 50, the Court awarded Mr Oberschlick 18,123.84 schillings for pecuniary damage and 85,285 schillings for costs and expenses incurred in Austria and before the Convention institutions (unanimously).[1]

101. *Summary bibliography*

COUSSIRAT-COUSTÈRE (V.).—'Jurisprudence de la Cour européenne des droits de l'homme de 1989 à 1991', *A.F.D.I.* 1991, pp. 585 *et seq.*

DECAUX (E.) and TAVERNIER (P.).—'Chronique de jurisprudence de la Cour européenne des droits de l'homme', *J.D.I.* 1992, pp. 787 and 788.

CREMONA (J.J.).—'The thick hide of politicians and Article 10 of the European Convention on Human Rights', in *Présence du droit public et des droits de l'homme. Mélanges offerts à Jacques Velu*, Brussels, Bruylant, 1992, Vol. III, pp. 1799–1811.

LAMBERT (P.).—'La liberté de la presse et la réputation de l'homme politique', *R.T.D.H.* 1992, pp. 383–388.

MERRILLS (J.G.).—'Decisions on the European Convention on Human Rights during 1991', *B.Y.B.I.L.* 1991, pp. 508–510.

SUDRE (F.).—'Chronique de la jurisprudence de la Cour européenne des droits de l'homme—1991', *R.U.D.H.* 1992, Nos 1–2, pp. 1 *et seq.*

WARBRICK (C.).—'The European Convention on Human Rights', *Y.E.L.* 1991, p. 586.

1 By judgment of 18 May 1993, the Supreme Court adapted Austrian case law on the interpretation of Article 111 of the Criminal Code to suit the requirements of the Convention.

219. Case of Quaranta v. Switzerland

Refusal of the president of a criminal court in Vaud to afford free legal assistance to an accused during the investigation and at the trial

102. *Claudio Quaranta, an Italian national born in 1962 and resident in Switzerland, was an assistant plumber. In 1985, the investigating judge of the Vevey-Lavaux district opened an investigation with regard to him on suspicion of an offence under the Federal Misuse of Drugs Act. Mr Quaranta requested free legal assistance on several occasions for the investigation and subsequently for the trial, but this was refused by the President of the Vevey Criminal Court. The court sentenced the accused to six months' imprisonment and ordered the activation of a previous suspended sentence handed down in 1982. Mr Quaranta unsuccessfully appealed to the Criminal Court of Cassation of the Vaud Cantonal Court and to the Federal Court.*

103. *In his application of 18 December 1986 to the Commission, Mr Quaranta claimed to be the victim of a violation of Article 6 § 3(c) of the Convention. He maintained that he had not had the means to pay a lawyer of his choice and that, in view of the nature of the case, a lawyer should have been appointed to represent him.*[1]

Judgment of 24 May 1991 *(Chamber) (Series A No. 205)*

104. The Court pointed out that the right of an accused to be given, in certain circumstances, free legal assistance constituted one aspect of the notion of a fair trial in criminal proceedings. Article 6 § 3(c) attached two conditions to this right. The first, lack of 'sufficient means to pay for legal assistance', was not in dispute in the present case. The Court therefore confined itself to examining whether the 'interests of justice' required that Mr Quaranta should have been granted such assistance. In so doing, the Court had regard to various criteria, which, to a large extent, corresponded to those used by the cantonal and federal authorities in rejecting Mr Quaranta's application. However, the way in which the Swiss authorities appeared to have applied them might differ—and in the present case had differed—from the Court's approach.

The seriousness of the offence and the severity of the possible sentence: Mr Quaranta was accused of use of and traffic in narcotics, which

1 In its report of 12 February 1990, the Commission expressed the unanimous opinion that there had been a violation of Article 6 § 3(c).

might attract a penalty of up to three years' imprisonment. Free legal assistance should have been afforded because so much had been at stake.

The complexity of the case: although the case had not raised special difficulties as regards the establishment of the facts, the outcome of the trial had been of considerable importance for the applicant, since the alleged offences had occurred during his probationary period and a wide range of measures had been available to the court. The participation of a lawyer at the trial would have created the best conditions for the accused's defence.

The applicant's personal situation: he was a young adult of foreign origin from an underprivileged background without any real vocational training, who had a long criminal record and had been taking drugs since 1975, almost daily since 1983.

Consequently, his appearance in person before the investigating judge, and then before the Criminal Court, without the assistance of a lawyer, had not enabled him to present his case in an adequate manner.

That defect had not been cured either in the Criminal Court of Cassation of the Canton of Vaud or in the Federal Court, because of the limits on the scope of the review which might be carried out by those two courts. Consequently, Article 6 § 3(c) had been violated (held unanimously).

105. With regard to the application of Article 50, the Court did not perceive any causal connection between the breach of Article 6 and the alleged pecuniary damage. On the other hand, the violation found must have caused the applicant non-pecuniary damage justifying the award, assessed on an equitable basis, of 3,000 Swiss francs.

The Court awarded Mr Quaranta a total of 7,000 Swiss francs in respect of costs incurred before the Criminal Court of Cassation and the Strasbourg institutions.

106. *Summary bibliography*

COUSSIRAT-COUSTÈRE (V.).—'Jurisprudence de la Cour européenne des droits de l'homme de 1989 à 1991', *A.F.D.I.* 1991, p. 603.

MERRILLS (J.G.).—'Decisions on the European Convention on Human Rights during 1991', *B.Y.B.I.L.* 1991, pp. 510–512.

SCHÜRMANN (F.).—'Der Anspruch auf amtliche Verteidigung. Bemerkungen zum Urteil des Europäischen Gerichthofs für Menschenrechte i. S. Q. gegen die Schweiz', *A.J.P./P.J.A.* 1992, pp. 661–665.

SUDRE (F.).—'Chronique de la jurisprudence de la Cour européenne des droits de l'homme—1991', *R.H.D.H.* 1992, Nos 1–2, pp. 1 *et seq.*

WARBRICK (C.).—'The European Convention on Human Rights', *Y.E.L.* 1991, pp. 571–573.

220. Case of Pugliese v. Italy (no. 2)
221. Case of Caleffi v. Italy
222. Case of Vocaturo v. Italy

Length of civil proceedings

107. *Vincenzo Pugliese, Massimo Caleffi and Nicola Vocaturo were Italian nationals. Mr Pugliese obtained from the President of the Rome District Court an order for payment against a company as reimbursement of the expenses incurred by him as a director of that company. Mr Caleffi brought an action against his employer before the Rome magistrate's court, seeking backdated promotion and backpay. Mr Vocaturo, who was the property manager of a company, was sued by an employee in the Rome District Court together with the company.*

108. *In their applications to the Commission of 29 June and 20 September 1985, the applicants complained of the length of the civil proceedings brought by or against them and relied on Article 6 § 1 of the Convention.[1]*

Judgments of 24 May 1991 *(Chamber) (Series A No. 206 A–C)*

109. The Court started by determining in each case the period to be taken into consideration for assessing whether the length of the proceedings had been reasonable:

Pugliese (no. 2): just over four years and five months (from the date of the order to pay to the date when the judgment of the Rome District Court had become final);

Caleffi: just over seven years and seven months (from the date of the summons to the date on which a friendly settlement had been reached);

Vocaturo: almost twelve years and four months (from the date on which the Italian declaration recognizing the right of individual petition had taken effect and the date on which the Court of Cassation's judgment had been deposited).

---

1 In its reports of 6 March 1990, the Commission expressed the opinion that there had been a violation of Article 6 § 1 (unanimously).

The Court went on to hold as follows:

in **Pugliese (no. 2)**, the intervention of a third party had not given rise to any special complexity and the period of almost two years between the termination of the investigation and the hearing before the trial court did not seem reasonable;

in the **Caleffi** and **Vocaturo** cases, the reduced time-limits for employment disputes had not been complied with, in the Court of Cassation in the both cases and also at first instance in the case of Mr Vocaturo.

Accordingly, Article 6 § 1 had been violated (held unanimously).

110.   With regard to the application of Article 50, the Court dismissed Mr Pugliese's claims (unanimously) on the ground that there was no causal link between the violation found and either the alleged damage or any costs relating to the domestic proceedings.

In contrast, it granted Mr Caleffi 10,000,000 Italian lire as compensation for non-pecuniary damage and Mr Vocaturo 10,500,000 Italian lire in respect of pecuniary and non-pecuniary damage (unanimously). It also awarded Mr Caleffi and Mr Vocaturo the 3,000,000 lire each which they had claimed for costs and expenses incurred before the Convention organs (unanimously).

Lastly, the Court held that it had no jurisdiction to order the Italian State to publish its judgment (unanimously).

111.   *Summary bibliography*

Coussirat-Coustère (V.).—'Jurisprudence de la Cour européenne des droits de l'homme de 1989 à 1991', *A.F.D.I.* 1991, pp. 600 *et seq.*

Merrills (J.G.).—'Decisions on the European Convention on Human Rights during 1991', *B.Y.B.I.L.* 1991, pp. 512 and 513.

Sudre (F.).—'Chronique de la jurisprudence de la Cour européenne des droits de l'homme—1991', *R.U.D.H.* 1992, Nos 1–2, pp. 1 *et seq.*

223. Case of Letellier v. France

Length of detention on remand

112. *Suspected of being an accessory to the murder of her husband, Mrs Monique Merdy, née Letellier, was arrested on 8 July 1985. On 24 December, the Créteil investigating judge ordered her release subject to court supervision, but the indictments division of the Paris Court of Appeal set aside the order on 22 January 1986. In February, it rejected a further application for release, which the applicant had made on 24 January 1986. The Court of Cassation set its judgment aside in May and remitted the case back to it, whereupon in September it rejected the application again. The Court of Cassation set the judgment aside again in December and remitted the case to the indictments division of the Amiens Court of Appeal, which rejected the application. The Court of Cassation upheld that judgment on 15 June 1987. The Paris indictments division rejected six further applications for release in 1986 and 1987. Subsequently, the applicant remained in custody on remand until 10 May 1988, when the Val-de-Marne Assize Court sentenced her to three years' imprisonment for being an accessory to murder.*

113. *In her application to the Commission of 21 August 1986, the applicant complained that her detention on remand had exceeded a 'reasonable time' (Article 5 § 3 of the Convention) and that the various courts which had in turn examined her application for release of 24 January 1986 had not ruled 'speedily' (Article 5 § 4).*[1]

Judgment of 26 June 1991 *(Chamber) (Series A No. 207)*

114. For the purposes of Article 5 § 3, the period to be taken into consideration had lasted two years and nine months: it had begun on 8 July 1985, the date on which the applicant had been remanded in custody, and had ended on 10 May 1988, with the judgment of the Assize Court, less the period during which she had been released subject to court supervision.

The French courts had put forward in particular four reasons for refusing to release the applicant.

---

1 In its report of 15 March 1990, the Commission expressed the opinion that there had been a violation of paragraph 3 (unanimously) and paragraph 4 (seventeen votes to one) of Article 5.

First, there was the risk of pressure being brought to bear on the witnesses. The Court accepted that a genuine risk of pressure being brought to bear on the witnesses might have existed initially, but took the view that it had diminished and indeed disappeared with the passing of time. In fact, after 23 December 1986—after which the courts had no longer referred to such a risk—the continuing detention of the applicant had no longer been justified under this head.

Secondly, there was the risk of the applicant's absconding. The Court pointed out that such a danger could not be gauged solely on the basis of the severity of the sentence risked: it had to be assessed with reference to a number of other relevant factors which might either confirm the existence of such a danger or make it appear so slight that it could not justify detention pending trial. In this case, the decisions of the indictments divisions did not give the reasons why, notwithstanding the arguments put forward by the applicant in support of her applications for release, they had considered the risk of her absconding to be decisive.

Thirdly, there was the question of the inadequacy of court supervision. When the only remaining reason for continued detention was the fear that the accused would abscond and thereby subsequently avoid appearing for trial, he had to be released if he was in a position to provide adequate guarantees to ensure that he would so appear. The Court noted that the indictments divisions had not established that this had not been the case in this instance.

Fourthly, there was the question of the preservation of public order. The Court accepted that, by reason of their particular gravity and public reaction to them, certain offences might give rise to a social disturbance capable of justifying pre-trial detention, at least for a time. In exceptional circumstances, this factor might therefore be taken into account for the purposes of the Convention, in any event in so far as domestic law recognized—as in Article 144 of the Code of Criminal Procedure—the notion of disturbance to public order caused by an offence. However, this ground could be regarded as relevant and sufficient only provided that it was based on facts capable of showing that the accused's release would actually disturb public order. In addition, detention would continue to be legitimate only if public order remained actually threatened; its continuation could not be used to anticipate a custodial sentence. In this case, those conditions had not been satisfied. The courts had assessed the need to continue the deprivation of liberty from a purely abstract point of view, taking into consideration only the gravity of the offence.

At least from 23 December 1986, the contested detention had ceased to be based on relevant and sufficient grounds. There had consequently been a violation of Article 5 § 3 (held unanimously).

115. The Court had certain doubts about the overall length of the examination of the second application for release, but the applicant had retained the right to submit a further application at any time. Indeed, she had lodged other applications, which had all been dealt with in periods ranging from eight to twenty days. There had therefore been no violation of Article 5 § 4 (held unanimously).

116. Under Article 50, the Court rejected the claim for compensation for pecuniary damage, since the pre-trial detention had been deducted in its entirety from the sentence (unanimously). As to non-pecuniary damage, the Court considered that the judgment constituted sufficient reparation.

In respect of the costs and expenses referable to the proceedings before the Convention institutions, the applicant claimed 21,433 French francs. The Court considered it equitable to allow the applicant's claims under this head in their entirety (unanimously).

117. *Summary bibliography*

COUSSIRAT-COUSTÈRE (V.).—'Jurisprudence de la Cour européenne des droits de l'homme de 1989 à 1991', *A.F.D.I.* 1991, pp. 592 *et seq.*

DECAUX (E.) and TAVERNIER (P.).—'Chronique de jurisprudence de la Cour européenne des droits de l'homme', *J.D.I.* 1992, pp. 788–790.

MERRILLS (J.G.).—'Decisions on the European Convention on Human Rights during 1991', *B.Y.B.I.L.* 1991, pp. 513–515.

PETTITI (L.-E.).—'Droits de l'homme', *R.S.C.D.P.C.* 1991, pp. 805–814.

RENUCCI (J.-F.).—'Droit européen des droits de l'homme', *D.* 1991, sommaires commentés, pp. 328 and 329.

SUDRE (F.).—'Chronique de la jurisprudence de la Cour européenne des droits de l'homme—1991', *R.U.D.H.* 1992, Nos 1–2, pp. 1 *et seq.*

WARBRICK (C.).—'The European Convention on Human Rights', *Y.E.L.* 1991, pp. 559 and 560.

224. Case of Owners' Services Ltd v. Italy

Length of civil proceedings

118. *A limited company incorporated under English law, Owners' Services Ltd, took proceedings against the I. company by summons served on 13 March 1982 to recover 29,850,000 Italian lire which it had paid in error.*

On 2 December 1986 the court allowed the applicant's claim. The text of the decision was lodged with the registry on 6 March 1987. On 2 June 1987, Owners' Services Ltd agreed to a friendly settlement of the case.

119. *In its application of 13 March 1986 to the Commission, the applicant company complained of the length of the civil proceedings brought by it. It relied on Article 6 § 1 of the Convention.[1]*

Judgment of 28 June 1991 *(Chamber) (Series A No. 208–A)*

120. The Court considered that although the applicant's decision did not strictly speaking constitute a withdrawal, since it had not been taken by a party to the case, it was in any event a 'fact of a kind to provide a solution of the matter' (Rules of Court, Rule 49 § 2). In addition, the Court discerned no reason of *ordre public* (public policy) for continuing the proceedings (Rule 49 § 4). It therefore decided to strike the case out of the list (unanimously).

121. *Summary bibliography*

SUDRE (F.).—'Chronique de la jurisprudence de la Cour européenne des droits de l'homme—1991', *R.U.D.H.* 1992, Nos 1–2, pp. 1 *et seq.*

---

1 In its report of 15 January 1991, the Commission expressed the unanimous view that there had been a violation of Article 6 § 1.

225. Case of Philis v. Greece

Access to civil courts for recovery of fees owed by public corporations

122. *Nicolaos Philis was a consultant engineer in Athens. Between 1971 and 1978 he designed a number of central-heating and electro-mechanical installations for the Autonomous Organization for Labour Housing (A.O.E.K.), the Penteli children's hospital (P.N.P.) and a public works contractor (A.S.).*

As he was not paid for this work, he brought a number of actions in the Athens first-instance court either indirectly through the Technical Chamber of Greece (T.E.E.), acting on his behalf, or, in the case of the hospital project, directly. His action in respect of the hospital project was dismissed as inadmissible on the ground that under Royal Decree No. 30/1956 laying down the rules for the remuneration of engineers only T.E.E. had the capacity to bring proceedings to recover payment of fees.

123. *In his applications lodged with the Commission on 5 January 1987, 6 April 1988 and 24 June 1988, Mr Philis relied on Articles 6, 13 and 14 of the Convention and Article 1 of Protocol No 1.*[1]

Judgment of 27 August 1991 *(Chamber) (Series A No. 209)*

124. The Court began by considering the question of access to a court.

Although it recognized the advantages afforded by the system of subrogation, it pointed to the ambivalent wording of paragraphs 4 and 5 of Article 2 of Royal Decree No. 30/1956. Read literally, they conferred on T.E.E. the exclusive capacity to bring proceedings on behalf of engineers. Existing practice was consistent with this interpretation. In accordance with such practice, Mr Philis had requested T.E.E., in connection with his disputes with A.O.E.K. and A.S., to bring proceedings in the courts. When he himself had sued P.N.P. in the Athens

---

1 The Commission ruled on the admissibility of the three applications on 7 December 1988 and 11 October 1989. It found admissible the complaints concerning the right of access to a court and the duration of the proceedings as well as that concerning Article 13, and declared the other complaints inadmissible. In its report of 8 March 1990, it expressed the opinion that (a) there had been a violation of the applicant's right of access to a court (unanimously), (b) the case had not been heard within a reasonable time (eleven votes to two), and (c) no separate question arose under Article 13 (unanimously).

Court of Appeal, that court had dismissed his action on the ground that he lacked the capacity to bring proceedings. That practice was confirmed by the prevailing case law. A judgment of the Larissa Administrative Court of Appeal holding that T.E.E.'s capacity to sue was 'parallel' to that of the true beneficiary seemed to be clearly out of line with the rest of the case law.

The Government contended that, notwithstanding the effect of the subrogation system, the applicant could have asserted his rights in person through the numerous means available to him in Greek civil procedure. That reasoning did not persuade the Court. Intervention and third-party objection were possible only once the proceedings had been instituted by T.E.E., whereas an action for damages made it possible for the engineer to claim compensation, not his fees as such. As to a subrogation action, the prevailing case law of the Greek courts indicated that the general provision of Article 72 of the Code of Civil Procedure did not override the specific provision of Article 2 § 4 of Royal Decree No. 30/1956. Since the applicant had not been able to institute proceedings, directly and independently, to seek payment from his clients—even from T.E.E. in the first instance—of fees which were owed to him, the very essence of his 'right to a court' had been impaired, and it had not been possible for this to have been redressed by any remedy available under Greek law. The Court held that there had therefore been a violation of Article 6 § 1 in this regard (eight votes to one).

125.   In the light of this finding, the Court held that it was unnecessary to examine the complaint based on the length of the proceedings (unanimously) or that based on Article 13 (unanimously).

126.   There remained the alleged violation of Article 14 in conjunction with Article 6. In its decision on the admissibility of the application, the Commission had rejected the first complaint relating to discrimination because it concerned a period prior to 20 November 1985, when the Greek declaration accepting the right of individual petition had taken effect. Accordingly, the Court was not entitled to entertain it.

As to the second complaint to the effect that the profession of engineer was the only one whose members did not enjoy direct access to the courts in order to assert their civil rights, the Court held (unanimously) that no useful purpose was to be served in considering it, since it had already found that the restriction on Mr Philis's right of access to a court had infringed Article 6.

127. As regards Article 50, the Court could not speculate as to the conclusions which the national courts would have reached had Mr Philis been able to bring legal proceedings himself. As no causal connection had been established, it dismissed the claims concerning the amounts sought from A.O.E.K., P.N.P. and A.S. and the alleged loss of earnings (unanimously).

In contrast, the feeling of frustration generated by the impossibility of assuming control of the defence of his own interests, as well as the prolonged anxiety as to the outcome of his disputes with his debtors, must have caused the applicant some non-pecuniary damage, which the Court assessed at 1,000,000 drachmas (unanimously).

Greece had to reimburse the applicant 6,000,000 drachmas in respect of the proceedings brought in the Greek courts and at Strasbourg (held unanimously).

Lastly, the Court refused the applicant's request that the Court should specify in its judgment that the sums awarded under Article 50 should be exempt from attachment (unanimously).

128. *Summary bibliography*

COUSSIRAT-COUSTÈRE (V.).—'Jurisprudence de la Cour européenne des droits de l'homme de 1989 à 1991', *A.F.D.I.* 1991, pp. 584 *et seq.*

MERRILLS (J.G.).—'Decisions on the European Convention on Human Rights during 1991', *B.Y.B.I.L.* 1991, pp. 516 and 517.

SUDRE (F.).—'Chronique de la jurisprudence de la Cour européenne des droits de l'homme—1991', *R.U.D.H.* 1992, Nos 1–2, pp. 1 *et seq.*

VANDERNOOT (P.).—'L'accès au juge, la prééminence du droit et quelques autres considérations . . . ', *R.T.D.H.* 1992, pp. 489–511.

WARBRICK (C.).—'The European Convention on Human Rights', *Y.E.L.* 1991, pp. 562 and 563.

226. Case of Demicoli v. Malta

Sanction imposed on a journalist by the House of Representatives for breach of parliamentary privilege

129. *Carmel Demicoli, a Maltese national, was the editor of the political satirical periodical* MHUX fl-Interesstal-Poplu *(NOT in the people's interest). On 13 January 1986, two Members of Parliament brought an article recently published in the periodical commenting on a parliamentary session that had been transmitted live on television to the attention of the House of Representatives as an alleged breach of privilege. In their view, it contained insulting references to themselves. On 10 February, the House passed a resolution which stated that it considered the article in question to be a breach of its privileges within the meaning of section 11(1)(k) of the House of Representatives (Privileges and Powers) Ordinance (1942–1983) on the publication of a libel concerning a Member of the House. A motion was adopted on 4 March repeating the earlier resolution and ordering the applicant to appear before the House in order to answer a charge of defamation. After appearing at a session which lasted three days and at which the two Members of Parliament concerned made declarations, Mr Demicoli was found guilty by resolution of 19 March; the House deferred the question of the sanction to be imposed.*

In the interim, Mr Demicoli brought an application before the Civil Court of Malta challenging the proceedings instituted against him by the House of Representatives on the ground that those proceedings, which were penal in nature, violated his right under section 40 of the Constitution to a fair trial before an independent, impartial court. On 16 May 1986, the Civil Court delivered judgment in favour of the applicant, although it found that the proceedings were not criminal in nature. On 13 October 1986, the Constitutional Court, on appeals by both parties, disagreed with the conclusions of the Civil Court: the lower court had not been entitled to look further into the matter or to afford the remedies indicated in its judgment.

On 9 December 1986, the House of Representatives summoned the applicant before it in order to decide the penalty to be imposed upon him. He was fined 250 Maltese liri and ordered to publish the resolution of 19 March 1986 in his periodical. The applicant had not as yet paid the fine and no steps had been taken to enforce its recovery.

130. *In his application of 22 May 1987 to the Commission, Mr Demicoli submitted that he had not received a fair and public hearing by an*

independent and impartial tribunal (Article 6 § 1 of the Convention).
He also alleged a failure to observe the presumption of innocence
(Article 6 § 2).[1]

Judgment of 27 August 1991 *(Chamber) (Series A No. 210)*

131.   According to the Government, Mr Demicoli had failed to lodge
his application within the time-limit laid down in Article 26 of the
Convention, namely within a period of six months from the date on
which the final decision had been taken nationally. The Court dismissed the preliminary objection (unanimously). It held that the proceedings against the applicant had culminated in the decision of 9
December 1986 as to the penalty, which had finally determined his
position; that was the date to be taken into consideration.

132.   The first question to be resolved was that of the applicability of
Article 6 § 1. In the Government's view, the breach of privilege proceedings taken against the applicant for breach of parliamentary privilege
owing to libel had not been 'criminal' but disciplinary in character.

In ruling on this question, the Court used the three criteria which it
had laid down for the first time in the judgment of 8 June 1976 in
Engel and Others v. the Netherlands[2] and which had been consistently
applied in the Court's subsequent case law.

The first criterion was the definition of the offence in issue according to the legal system of the respondent State: breach of Parliamentary
privilege was not classified as a crime in Maltese law; however, the
indication afforded by national law was not decisive for the purpose of
Article 6. The second criterion was the actual nature of the offence in
question: the proceedings taken against Mr Demicoli, who was not a
Member of the House, for an act carried out outside the House could
not be taken to be disciplinary since they did not relate to the internal
regulation and orderly functioning of the House; as the relevant legislation potentially affected the whole population, the offence thereby
defined to which the imposition of a penal sanction was attached was
akin to a criminal offence under the Press Act 1974. The third criterion
was the degree of severity of the potential penalty: what was at stake (a
maximum of sixty days' imprisonment or a fine of 500 Maltese liri or
both) was sufficiently important to warrant classifying the offence with

1   In its report of 15 March 1990, the Commission expressed the opinion that
    there had been a breach of Article 6 § 1 and that no separate issue arose
    under Article 6 § 2 (unanimously).
2   Series A No. 22; see Vol. I of this work, 131–141.

which the applicant had been charged as a criminal one. Consequently, Article 6 was applicable (held unanimously).

133. The House of Representatives had undoubtedly exercised a judicial function in determining the applicant's guilt. The fact that the two Members of the House whose behaviour in Parliament had been criticized in the impugned article had participated throughout the proceedings sufficed to cast doubt on the impartiality of the adjudicating body and the applicant's fears were justified. Accordingly, there had been a breach of Article 6 § 1 on the point considered and it was not necessary to go into other aspects of that provision (held unanimously).

134. The applicant submitted that the resolution of 10 February 1986 and the motion of 4 March 1986 had placed the burden of proving innocence on him and accordingly had violated Article 6 § 2. In view of the finding of a violation of Article 6 § 1, the Court did not consider it necessary to examine this issue (held unanimously).

135. It awarded Mr Demicoli 5,000 Maltese liri for his costs and expenses incurred in Malta and before the Convention institutions, and dismissed his claims for compensation for pecuniary and non-pecuniary damage (unanimously).

136. *Summary bibliography*

COUSSIRAT-COUSTÈRE (V.).—'Jurisprudence de la Cour européenne des droits de l'homme de 1989 à 1991', *A.F.D.I.* 1991, pp. 585 *et seq.*
DECAUX (E.) and TAVERNIER (P.).—'Chronique de jurisprudence de la Cour européenne des droits de l'homme', *J.D.I.* 1992, p. 792.
MERRILLS (J.G.).—'Decisions on the European Convention on Human Rights during 1991', *B.Y.B.I.L.* 1991, pp. 518 and 519.
SUDRE (F.).—'Chronique de la jurisprudence de la Cour européenne des droits de l'homme—1991', *R.U.D.H.* 1992, Nos 1–2, pp. 1 *et seq.*
WARBRICK (C.).—'The European Convention on Human Rights', *Y.E.L.* 1991, pp. 563–565.

227. Case of Brandstetter v. Austria

Appointment of court experts and hearing of witnesses in two sets of criminal proceedings; defamation proceedings instituted against an applicant on account of statements made in his defence in the first set of proceedings

137. *Karl Brandstetter, an Austrian wine merchant residing at Hadres (Lower Austria), had three consecutive sets of criminal proceedings brought against him.*

At the end of the first set of criminal proceedings, the Haugsdorf District Court convicted Mr Brandstetter of adulterating wine contrary to the 1961 Wine Act and fined him 5,600 schillings. It also ordered the forfeiture of a total of 27,000 litres of wine and the publication of its judgment. The court had appointed as official expert a member of the staff of the Federal Agricultural Chemical Research Institute, which had drawn up the report which had led to the institution of the criminal proceedings, and refused to appoint other experts.

In the second proceedings, the Korneuburg Regional Court found the applicant guilty of tampering with evidence in the wine case and sentenced him to three months' imprisonment. It had appointed as expert a member of the staff of the Federal Agricultural Chemical Research Institute which had been at the origin of the first suspicions against Mr Brandstetter, whereas it had heard Mr Brandstetter's expert only as a witness.

In the third proceedings, the Regional Court found Mr Brandstetter guilty of defamation in so far as he had wrongly accused an Inspector of Cellars in the wine case of improper conduct, and sentenced him to a suspended term of three months' imprisonment. On appeal, the Vienna Senior Public Prosecutor filed observations (croquis) which had not been served on the applicant's lawyer and of which the applicant himself had had no knowledge.

138. *In his applications to the Commission of 6 September 1984, 13 March 1987 and 21 October 1987, the applicant made several complaints based on Article 6 §§ 1, 2 and 3(c) and (d) of the Convention.*[1]

---

1 On 14 July 1987 the Commission declared the first application admissible in part. On 10 July 1989, it declared the two other applications admissible and ordered their joinder with the remaining claims of the first application. In its report of 8 May 1990, the Commission expressed the opinion that:
 (a) in the case concerning the quality of the wine, there had been a violation of Article 6 § 1, taken in conjunction with Article 6 § 3(d), inasmuch as

Judgment of 28 August 1991 *(Chamber) (Series A No. 211)*

139. With regard to Article 6, the Court examined the proceedings relating to the quality of the wine.

Turning to the principle of equality of arms with regard to the expert evidence, the Court observed that the person appointed as expert by the District Court had not participated in drawing up the initial report. The fact that the expert had been employed by the same institute as the expert on whose opinion the indictment had been based did not in itself justify fears that he would be unable to act with proper neutrality. In addition, the defence had not raised any objection to his appointment until after he had filed a report unfavourable to Mr Brandstetter. Nor did the file disclose other grounds for regarding him as a witness for the prosecution. Accordingly, the District Court's refusal to appoint other experts and to call a witness had not violated Article 6 § 1 in conjunction with Article 6 § 3(d) (held unanimously).

As regards the right to a fair trial and the right to obtain the attendance and examination of witnesses, the Court noted that the applicant had never sought the attendance and examination of the members of the Agricultural Institute's panel, but had merely requested the examination of the minutes of their wine-tasting session. The results of that session had formed only part of the written expert opinions and did not constitute conclusive evidence but merely an indication. There had thus been no violation of Article 6 § 1, taken in conjunction with Article 6 § 3(d), under this head either (held unanimously).

Lastly, the Court rejected Mr Brandstetter's allegation that there had been an interference with the rights of the defence contrary to Article 6 § 3(c) (unanimously). Article 6 § 3(c) did not provide for an unlimited right to use any defence arguments. It would be overstraining the concept

      the expert evidence for the prosecution and that for the defence had not been treated on an equal footing (unanimously);

(b) the same was true in the proceedings concerning the charge of tampering with evidence (unanimously);

(c) the applicant's conviction for defamation had infringed Article 6 § 3(c) (nine votes to three);

(d) no separate issue arose concerning the question whether, in the proceedings concerning the charge of tampering with evidence, there had been in other respects an infringement of the applicant's right to a fair trial (Article 6 § 1) or a breach of the principle of the presumption of innocence (Article 6 § 2) (unanimously); and

(e) in the defamation proceedings, there had not been, on appeal, a breach of the principle of equality of arms guaranteed in Article 6 § 1 (eleven votes to one).

of the rights of defence of those charged with a criminal offence if it were to be assumed that they could not be prosecuted when, in exercising those rights, they intentionally aroused false suspicions of punishable behaviour concerning a witness or any other person involved in the criminal proceedings. It was not for the Court to determine whether Mr Brandstetter had rightly been found guilty of having done so. Although the Regional Court had taken the relevant statements into account as an aggravating circumstance when determining sentence on the charge of adulterating wine, it did not appear from the file that Mr Brandstetter had been stopped from making them or in any way restrained from airing the views which he had expressed.

140. Turning to the proceedings concerning the charge of tampering with evidence, the Court rejected the Government's objection that Mr Brandstetter had failed to exhaust domestic remedies (unanimously): the applicant's complaint did not relate to the appointment of the official expert; what he was complaining about was the refusal to appoint his privately commissioned expert as the second court expert.

Had there been a violation of the principle of equality of arms? The Court took into consideration the position occupied by the court-appointed expert throughout the proceedings and the manner in which he had performed his functions. The charge of tampering with the evidence was based on a report which he had drawn up. The applicant's apprehensions with regard to the expert's neutrality and objectivity could therefore be held justified. Under the principle of equality of arms, persons who had been or could have been called, in whatever capacity, by the defence should have been examined under the same conditions as the court-appointed expert. However, the latter had not played a dominant role. Although Mr Brandstetter's expert had not been heard under the same conditions, in view of the line taken by the defence and the evidence before the courts the refusal to appoint him as the second official expert had not failed to satisfy the requirements of a fair trial. There had therefore been no violation of Article 6 § 1, taken in conjunction with Article 6 § 3(d) (held unanimously).

141. There remained the defamation proceedings. Although the defence could have enquired of the registry whether the Senior State Prosecutor had filed a *croquis* and then requested leave to inspect the file under section 82 of the Code of Criminal Procedure, that section did not seem to grant an unconditional right. The Court considered that that practice did not sufficiently ensure that appellants were aware that such a *croquis* had been filed. An indirect and purely hypothetical possibility for an accused to comment on prosecution arguments included in the text of a judgment could scarcely be regarded as a proper substitute for the right to examine, and reply directly to, submissions made by the prosecution. There had therefore been a violation of Article 6 § 1 of the Convention in this regard (six votes to three).

142. Under Article 50, the Court rejected Mr Brandstetter's claims for compensation and costs and expenses in relation to the proceedings concerning the quality of the wine, the charge of tampering with the evidence and the charge of defamation (unanimously).

In contrast, it awarded him 60,000 schillings, including interest, for his costs and expenses incurred before the Commission and the Court (unanimously).

143. *Summary bibliography*

COUSSIRAT-COUSTÈRE (V.).—'Jurisprudence de la Cour européenne des droits de l'homme de 1989 à 1991', *A.F.D.I.* 1991, pp. 581 *et seq.*

MERRILLS (J.G.).—'Decisions on the European Convention on Human Rights during 1991', *B.Y.B.I.L.* 1991, pp. 519–522.

SUDRE (F.).—'Chronique de la jurisprudence de la Cour européenne des droits de l'homme—1991', *R.U.D.H.* 1992, Nos 1–2, pp. 1 *et seq.*

WARBRICK (C.).—'The European Convention on Human Rights', *Y.E.L.* 1991, pp. 568–570.

228. Case of F.C.B. v. Italy

Accused tried in his absence on appeal while in custody in another country

144. *Mr F.C.B. was sentenced in 1977 by the Bergamo Assize Court to twenty-four years' imprisonment for armed robbery, murder and attempted murder, committed with others. On 26 March 1980 the Brescia Assize Court of Appeal acquitted him for lack of evidence and ordered his release. On that occasion he was required to give an address for service for subsequent notifications. On 13 April 1983, the Court of Cassation quashed the judgment of 26 March 1980 and remitted the case to the Milan Assize Court of Appeal. The applicant, who had in the meantime left Italy without informing the authorities of his change of address and had been placed in detention in the Netherlands, failed to appear. Although various statements were made explaining that he was prevented from appearing, he was tried* in absentia *and sentenced once again to twenty-four years' imprisonment. On 13 November 1985, the Court of Cassation dismissed an appeal brought by Mr F.C.B. on the ground that it had been for the trial court to assess the alleged inability to attend and that its decision, which was duly reasoned, was not susceptible to review; in addition, the written evidence of his inability to attend had been offered in evidence only after judgment had been given and therefore had no probative value.*

Mr F.C.B., who was in custody in Belgium, would have to return to the Netherlands to serve one year's imprisonment there, and if the Italian authorities succeeded in obtaining his extradition, he would then serve in Italy six years and six months of the prison sentence imposed by the Milan Assize Court of Appeal.

145. *In his application to the Commission of 9 May 1986, Mr F.C.B. complained of a violation of the rights of the defence; he relied on Article 6 §§ 1 and 3(c) of the Convention.[1]*

Judgment of 28 August 1991 *(Chamber) (Series A No. 208–B)*

146. Since the case related to the opportunity for a person charged with a criminal offence to attend his trial alongside his counsel and the requirements of Article 6 § 3 were to be seen as particular aspects of the right to

---

1 In its report of 17 May 1990, the Commission expressed the unanimous opinion that there had been a violation of Article 6 §§ 1 and 3(c).

a fair trial guaranteed by paragraph 1, the Court examined the complaint from the point of view of those two provisions in conjunction.

It observed in the first place that Mr F.C.B., who had not been present at the hearing before the Milan Assize Court of Appeal, had not expressed the wish to waive attendance. Moreover, that court had learnt from concurring sources that he appeared to be in custody in the Netherlands. Yet it had not adjourned the trial, but merely stated that it had not been provided with proof that he was unable to attend.

Although the Dutch authorities had requested the co-operation of the Italian authorities, the latter had not drawn the necessary inferences as regards the proceedings pending against Mr F.C.B. in Milan. That behaviour had scarcely been compatible with the diligence which the Contracting States had to exercise in order to ensure that the rights guaranteed by Article 6 were enjoyed in an effective manner.

Even supposing that indirect knowledge of the trial date sufficed to allow the applicant to participate in the trial and satisfied the requirements of Article 6, it did not appear from the case-file that Mr F.C.B., whether expressly or at least in an unequivocal manner, had intended to waive his right to appear at the trial and defend himself. There had therefore been a violation of paragraph 1 in conjunction with paragraph 3(c) of Article 6 (held unanimously).

147. As far as Article 50 was concerned, the finding that there had been a violation in itself afforded sufficient just satisfaction.

The Court awarded Mr F.C.B. 5,000,000 lire for costs and expenses incurred before the Strasbourg institutions (unanimously).[1]

148. *Summary bibliography*

COUSSIRAT-COUSTÈRE (V.).—'Jurisprudence de la Cour européenne des droits de l'homme de 1989 à 1991', *A.F.D.I.* 1991, p. 603.

DECAUX (E.) and TAVERNIER (P.).—'Chronique de jurisprudence de la Cour européenne des droits de l'homme', *J.D.I.* 1992, p. 791.

MERRILLS (J.G.).—'Decisions on the European Convention on Human Rights during 1991', *B.Y.B.I.L.* 1991, pp. 522–524.

SUDRE (F.).—'Chronique de la jurisprudence de la Cour européenne des droits de l'homme—1991', *R.U.D.H.* 1992, Nos 1–2, pp. 1 *et seq.*

WARBRICK (C.).—'The European Convention on Human Rights', *Y.E.L.* 1991, pp. 570 and 571.

---

1 The new code of criminal procedure, which entered into force on 24 October 1989, provides that the court should stay the proceedings or adjourn the trial, if necessary of its own motion, where it seems probable that the accused's absence is due to the fact that it is absolutely impossible for him to appear.

229. Case of Muyldermans v. Belgium

Proceedings conducted in the Audit Court without a public hearing and in the absence of the applicant

149. *In the night of 5 to 6 September 1979, a sum of around 5,000,000 Belgian francs disappeared from the post office in Courcelles (Hainaut). Marie-Louise Muyldermans, a Post Office employee, had worked there as an accountant since 3 September 1979. An investigation opened by the police terminated with an order closing the case. In the course of an administrative investigation carried out by the Post Office, Mrs Muyldermans had the opportunity to be informed of the views of her superiors and the report drawn up by a chief inspector and to submit her observations.*

On 5 May 1982, the Audit Court ruled on the question in private on the basis solely of the administrative file: it held Mrs Muyldermans and two other employees responsible for the shortfall, found that the former had failed to perform her duties and ordered her to repay the Post Office the sum of 2,000,000 Belgian francs, the balance being payable by the two other employees.

The Court of Cassation dismissed the applicant's appeal in June 1983.

150. *In her application lodged with the Commission on 22 December 1983, Mrs Muyldermans relied on Article 6 § 1 of the Convention inasmuch as she had not received a fair public hearing and on Article 1 of Protocol No. 1 in that she had been deprived of all or part of her assets.[1]*

Judgment of 23 October 1991 *(Chamber) (Series A No. 214–B)*

151. The Agent of the Government, and subsequently the applicant's lawyer, communicated to the Court Registry the text of an agreement whereby the Government agreed not to enforce the judgment of the Audit Court and further undertook to amend the Act of 29 October 1846 on the Organization of the Audit Court and the Act of 28 June 1963 on public accounts and to pay Mrs Muyldermans compensation amounting to 70,000 Belgian francs.

---

1 On 17 January 1989, the Commission declared the second complaint inadmissible, but the first one admissible. In its report of 2 October 1990, it expressed the opinion that there had been a breach of Article 6 § 1 of the Convention (nine votes to two).

152. The Court took formal note of the agreement. It observed that the agreement would give satisfaction to the applicant and that the amendment of the above-mentioned legislation would remove any reason of public policy *(ordre public)* such as would necessitate a decision by the European Court on the merits of the case (Rules of Court, Rule 49 § 4). Consequently, it decided to strike the case out of its list (unanimously).

153. *Summary bibliography*

COUSSIRAT-COUSTÈRE (V.).—'Jurisprudence de la Cour européenne des droits de l'homme de 1989 à 1991', *A.F.D.I.* 1991, pp. 586 *et seq.*

MERRILLS (J.G.).—'Decisions on the European Convention on Human Rights during 1991', *B.Y.B.I.L.* 1992, pp. 533 and 534.

SUDRE (F.).—'Chronique de la jurisprudence de la Cour européenne des droits de l'homme—1991', *R.U.D.H.* 1992, Nos 1–2, pp. 1 *et seq.*

230. Case of Helmers v. Sweden

Judgment in a private prosecution for defamation, joined with a civil action for damages, upheld on appeal without a public hearing

231. Case of Jan-Åke Andersson v. Sweden
232. Case of Fejde v. Sweden

First-instance conviction upheld by the Court of Appeal without a public hearing

154. *Reinhard Helmers, a German citizen, applied for appointment in 1979 to an academic post at the University of Lund. His application was unsuccessful and he appealed to the National Board of Universities and Colleges. In the course of that procedure, a university committee submitted a report containing information which the applicant considered to be defamatory. When the public prosecutor refused to bring criminal proceedings, Mr Helmers availed himself of his entitlement under the Code of Judicial Procedure to bring a private prosecution for defamation, which he joined with an action for damages. Following a public hearing, the Lund District Court dismissed Mr Helmer's claims on 19 November 1981.*

Mr Helmers contested the judgment in the Court of Appeal of Skåbe and Blekinge, but his appeal was rejected on 9 December 1981 without the public hearing which he had requested being held. Subsequently, the Supreme Court refused him leave to appeal.

155. *On 26 February 1983, Jan-Åke Andersson, an engineer, was stopped by the police while driving a tractor on a highway on the ground that that type of vehicle was not permitted to be driven on a highway. He refused to pay a fine, maintaining that he had not seen any road sign indicating the category of the road or the prohibition in question. On 21 September 1983, the District Court of Ronneby, after a public hearing, found the applicant guilty of an offence under the Traffic Ordinance and sentenced him to a fine of 400 Swedish kronor. Mr Andersson appealed to the Court of Appeal of Skåne and Blekinge to hold fresh discussions. His appeal was dismissed on 10 February 1984 on the basis of the case-file, including his written observations and those of the prosecution. Mr Andersson applied for leave to appeal to the Supreme Court but his application was refused.*

156. *In connection with the bankruptcy of Hans Fejde's removal firm in 1984, a rifle was found among the goods stored on its business premises and this was notified to the police. On 27 August 1984, following a public hearing at which the applicant was heard, the City Court of Göteborg found him guilty of the offence of unlawful possession of a firearm contrary to the Weapons Act 1973 and fined him 300 Swedish kronor.*

During the subsequent appeal proceedings, the Court of Appeal for Western Sweden dismissed, by a specific decision pursuant to certain amendments of July 1984 to the Code of Judicial Procedure, the applicant's request for a new hearing, on the ground that a public hearing was 'manifestly unnecessary'. It dismissed the appeal on 2 October 1985 on the basis of the file, including Mr Fejde's written observations. Mr Fejde also unsuccessfully sought to contest his conviction in the Supreme Court.

157. *Mr Helmers applied to the Commission on 6 February 1985, Mr Andersson on 16 October 1984 and Mr Fejde on 28 July 1986: the first relied on Articles 6, 9, 10, 13, 14, 17 and 25 of the Convention, the second on Article 6 § 1 and the third on Article 3, Article 6 §§ 1, 2 and 3(c) and (d) and Article 13.*[1]

Judgments of 29 October 1991 *(Plenary Court) (Series A No. 212–A, B and C)*

158. With regard to the preliminary questions raised in the case of Helmers, the Court pointed out that it had no jurisdiction to reopen an earlier application to the Commission as Mr Helmers had requested; a decision by the Commission that an application was inadmissible was final and not open to appeal (held unanimously).

It also considered that Article 6 § 1 was applicable to the proceedings brought by Mr Helmers in the Swedish courts: although Article 6 did not guarantee a right for an individual to institute a criminal prosecution himself, such a right was conferred on Mr Helmers by the Swedish legal system in order to allow him to protect his reputation; moreover, both the private prosecution and the claim for damages were decisive as regards his right to his good reputation, which was a 'civil right' for the purposes of Article 6 § 1.

1 On 5 May, 10 July and 4 October 1989, the Commission declared the complaints admissible in part. In its reports of 6 February, 15 March and 8 May 1990, it expressed the opinion that Article 6 § 1 had been violated (unanimously in the *Helmers* case, by seventeen votes to two in the two other cases).

159. With regard to the merits, the Court held in the first place that, provided a public hearing had been held at first instance, the absence of such a hearing at second or third instance might be justified by the special features of the proceedings at issue. Secondly, it observed that, under Swedish law, in each of these cases the Court of Appeal had been called upon to examine both questions of fact and questions of law. In the Helmers case, it also had had to make a full assessment of the guilt or innocence of defendant members of the university committee. However, the Court made a distinction: whereas Mr Helmers' appeal had gone to the merits of the case and raised serious questions relating to the facts and the application of the law, the appeals brought by Mr Andersson and Mr Fejde had not raised any questions of fact or of law which could not be adequately resolved on the basis of the case-file. In the light of those considerations and having regard also to the seriousness of what had been at stake in each case, the Court concluded in the case of Helmers that there had been no special features to justify the decision not to hold a public hearing. In the other two cases, it held that such special features had been present.

In sum, the Court held that Article 6 § 1 had been violated in the Helmers case (eleven votes to nine) but not in the cases of Jan-Åke Andersson and Fejde (thirteen votes to seven).

160. Under Article 50, Mr Helmers claimed compensation for pecuniary and non-pecuniary damage. The Court dismissed the claim in respect of pecuniary damage on the ground that it could not speculate on whether the Court of Appeal would have ruled in the applicant's favour had a public hearing been held at the appeal stage. Making an assessment on an equitable basis, the Court awarded Mr Helmers 25,000 kronor for non-pecuniary damage.

161. *Summary bibliography*

CLOSSET-MARCHAL (G.).—'Le droit à la comparution personnelle et son applicabilité en cas de pluralité de degrés de juridiction', *R.T.D.H.* 1992, pp. 394–402.

COUSSIRAT-COUSTÈRE (V.).—'Jurisprudence de la Cour européenne des droits de l'homme de 1989 à 1991', *A.F.D.I.* 1991, pp. 583 *et seq.*

DECAUX (E.) and TAVERNIER (P.).—'Chronique de jurisprudence de la Cour européenne des droits de l'homme', *J.D.I.* 1992, pp. 793–795.

MERRILLS (J.G.).—'Decisions on the European Convention on Human Rights during 1992', *B.Y.B.I.L.* 1992, pp. 534–536.

SUDRE (F.).—'Chronique de la jurisprudence de la Cour européenne des droits de l'homme—1991', *R.U.D.H.* 1992, Nos 1–2, pp. 1 *et seq.*

WARBRICK (C.).—'The European Convention on Human Rights', *Y.E.L.* 1991, pp. 574–578.

233. Case of Wiesinger v. Austria

Length of land-consolidation proceedings and its bearing on property rights

162. *On 22 July 1975, land-consolidation proceedings were commenced pursuant to the Upper Austria Agricultural Land Planning Act in respect of the area in which Mr and Mrs Wiesinger's property was located.*

On 13 October 1978 the District Agricultural Authority ordered them provisionally to transfer 25,206 square metres of land to third parties. In return, they were granted rights over other plots. On 16 November 1979, the municipal council amended the area zoning plan and classified as building land plots which had previously belonged to the applicants. As from 10 August 1982, Mr and Mrs Wiesinger initiated a series of proceedings with a view, inter alia, *to recovering their land or obtaining damages on the ground that their former land was now worth more.*

On 16 July 1986, the District Authority published the land-consolidation plan; it gave the Wiesingers back part of their former land and granted them additional plots. However, they contested the plan before the higher agricultural authorities and their situation improved further.

The applicants' appeal to the Constitutional Court was still pending.

163. *In their application to the Commission of 12 August 1985, the applicants relied on Article 6 § 1 of the Convention and Article 1 of Protocol No. 1 in conjunction with Article 14 of the Convention.*[1]

Judgment of 30 October 1991 *(Chamber) (Series A No. 213)*

164. The Court considered the case first from the point of view of Article 6 of the Convention.

The consolidation had started on 22 July 1975, yet no dispute had arisen until 10 August 1982. The consolidation proceedings had had to be considered as a whole and no decision had been taken on the

---

1 The Commission declared the application admissible on 10 July 1989, except as regards the complaint concerning the independence and impartiality of the agricultural authorities. In its report of 6 June 1990, it expressed the unanimous opinion that there had been a violation of Article 6 § 1 of the Convention and Article 1 of Protocol No. 1, and that it was not necessary to consider whether there had been a breach of Article 14 of the Convention.

dispute, since the applicants' appeal to the Constitutional Court was still pending. The proceedings had therefore lasted more than nine years thus far.

Land consolidation was a complex process. The proceedings appeared, however, to have developed relatively smoothly until the municipal authorities redesignated the applicants' former plots as building land. The resultant complication of the case could not be held against the applicants.

The remedies which the applicants had pursued in the interim proceedings had not delayed the determination of the main issue, namely the question of the compensation to which they were entitled under the consolidation scheme: they had been brought to a close before the scheme was published (on 16 July 1986). The further remedies pursued by the applicants had not been useless since they had secured an improvement in their situation.

There remained the question of the conduct of the Austrian authorities. The failure to abide by the time-limit prescribed by Austrian law for completing the consolidation scheme did not in itself contravene Article 6 § 1. However, since the competent agricultural authorities had initiated the consolidation process of their own motion, they had been under a special duty to act with diligence. The main feature of the present case was the amendment of the area zoning plan by the municipal council; it had upset the balance which had been struck between the different landowners at the time of the provisional transfer, since the enhancement in value of the applicants' former plots had, under Austrian law, to be taken into account in determining which compensatory parcels should be allotted to them. The difficulties in this case had thus stemmed from a lack of co-ordination between the municipal and the agricultural authorities in finalizing, respectively, the plan and the scheme. Furthermore, the duration of the negotiations with a view to reaching a friendly settlement after the publication of the scheme had exceeded what was reasonable.

There had thus been a violation of Article 6 § 1 (held unanimously).

165. As regards Article 1 of Protocol No. 1, the Court confined itself to considering the applicants' complaint that they had suffered an unjustified interference with their property rights pending the adoption of the final consolidation scheme.

It noted that the applicants had expressly agreed to the draft scheme, had not objected to the provisional transfer and had accepted the plots which had been allocated to them in exchange. However, the redesignation of their former plots as building land had upset the initial balance and created a situation comparable to that in the cases of *Erkner and Hofauer*[1] and *Poiss*[2] since the applicants had still not received the compensation in kind stipulated by the legislation. There had therefore been an interference with the applicants' right of property.

The Court considered the complaint from the point of view of the general rule set out in Article 1, which guaranteed respect for possessions, and inquired whether a proper balance had been struck between the demands of the community's general interest and the requirements of protecting the fundamental rights of the individual. In that respect, a temporary disadvantage might in principle be justified if it was not disproportionate to the aim sought to be achieved.

In the event, only a small fraction (two and a half hectares out of 172) of the area covered by the consolidation scheme had been the object of any dispute. The authorities had considered that the plots should remain within the scheme, despite their reclassification, until it became final; the agricultural authorities, having been in direct contact with the local situation, had enjoyed a margin of appreciation.

Although the interference complained of by the applicants had continued over a long period, the Court's ruling on the alleged breach of Article 6 § 1 of the Convention in this case was not conclusive as to the issue under the Protocol. Other elements were also relevant: Mr and Mrs Wiesinger had agreed to the provisional transfer, and had accepted and exploited the compensatory parcels; the area zoning plan had been amended in 1980, but the applicants had not manifested their disagreement until 10 August 1982; as from 16 July 1986, the consolidation scheme had reallocated to the Wiesingers some of their former land and their appeals had further improved their position.

Since the interference with the applicants' right of property could not be held to be disproportionate to the demands of the general interest involved in the consolidation proceedings, no violation of Article 1 of Protocol No. 1 had been established (eight votes to one).

166. The applicants had also alleged before the Commission that they had been treated less favourably than the provisional owners of their former land (Article 14 of the Convention, taken in conjunction with Article 1 of Protocol No. 1). However, they had not pursued the matter as a separate issue before the Court, which saw no reason to examine it (held unanimously).

167. Under Article 50 of the Convention, the Court rejected the applicants' claim for a total of 8,704,700.66 schillings in respect of

1 Series A No. 117; see Vol. I of this work, 754–762.
2 Series A No. 117; see Vol. I of this work, 754–762.

pecuniary damage: there was no causal link between one item (relating to a loan) and the violation of Article 6 § 1; the other item (relating to compensation for the increase in value of the applicants' former land) was outside the scope of the case (held unanimously).

The Court awarded Mr Wiesinger 200,000 schillings for non-pecuniary damage (unanimously).

Lastly, it awarded the applicants 300,000 schillings for costs and expenses in Austria and 200,000 schillings for those before the Commission and the Court (unanimously).

168. *Summary bibliography*

COUSSIRAT-COUSTÈRE (V.).—'Jurisprudence de la Cour européenne des droits de l'homme de 1989 à 1991', *A.F.D.I.* 1991, pp. 583 *et seq.*

DECAUX (E.) and TAVERNIER (P.).—'Chronique de jurisprudence de la Cour européenne des droits de l'homme', *J.D.I.* 1992, pp. 795–797.

MERRILLS (J.G.).—'Decisions on the European Convention on Human Rights during 1991', *B.Y.B.I.L.* 1992, pp. 536–538.

SUDRE (F.).—'Chronique de la jurisprudence de la Cour européenne des droits de l'homme—1991', *R.U.D.H.* 1991, Nos 1–2, pp. 1 *et seq.*

WARBRICK (C.).—'The European Convention on Human Rights', *Y.E.L.* 1991, pp. 589 and 590.

234. Case of Borgers v. Belgium

Accused precluded from replying to submissions made at the hearing before the Court of Cassation by an official of the *procureur général's* department at that court who had participated in the deliberations

169. *André Borgers, a Belgian lawyer, was sentenced on 19 May 1982 by the Antwerp Court of Appeal on charges of forgery and using forged documents to a suspended sentence of six months' imprisonment and a fine of 40,000 Belgian francs. On 20 March 1984, the Court of Cassation quashed the contested decision and remitted the case to the Ghent Court of Appeal; in accordance with Belgian practice, the* avocat général *had also attended the deliberations. On 14 November 1984, that court found him guilty and imposed on him identical sanctions. The Court of Cassation dismissed a further appeal on 18 June 1985; on that occasion also the* avocat général *had attended the deliberations.*

170. *In his application lodged with the Commission on 5 December 1985, Mr Borgers relied* inter alia *on Article 6 § 1 of the Convention. He complained that an* avocat général *at the Court of Cassation had attended the deliberations of that court. He subsequently criticized, in addition, the fact that he had not been able to reply to that official's submissions or address the court last at the hearing on 18 June 1985.*[1]

Judgment of 30 November 1991 *(Plenary Court) (Series A No. 214–B)*

171. The Court noted in the first place that the findings in the *Delcourt* judgment[2] on the question of the independence and impartiality of the Court of Cassation and its *procureur général's* department remained entirely valid. The Court did not perceive any breach of the Convention requirements on this issue.

---

1 On 12 April 1989, the Commission declared these complaints admissible, while finding the remainder of the application inadmissible. In its report of 17 May 1990, it expressed the opinion that there had been a violation of Article 6 § 1 (fourteen votes to one).

2 Series A no. 11; see Vol. I of this work, 70–77.

172. It went on to consider whether the proceedings at issue had also respected the rights of the defence and the principle of equality of arms, features of the wider concept of a fair trial. That principle had undergone a considerable evolution in the Court's case law, notably in respect of the importance attached to appearances and the increased sensitivity of the public to the fair administration of justice.

In that regard, the Court observed that, even though there was no question as the objectivity with which the *procureur général's* department at the Court of Cassation had discharged its functions, its opinion could not be regarded as neutral from the point of view of the parties to the cassation proceedings. By recommending that an accused's appeal be allowed or dismissed, the official of the *procureur général's* department became objectively speaking his ally or his opponent. In the latter event, Article 6 § 1 required that the rights of the defence and the principle of equality of arms should be respected.

At no time had Mr Borgers been able to reply to the *avocat général's* submissions made at the conclusion of the hearing on 18 June 1985: before hearing them, he had been unaware of their contents because they had not been communicated to him in advance; thereafter he had been prevented from doing so by statute. The Court could not see the justification for such restrictions on the rights of the defence. Once the *avocat général* had made submissions unfavourable to the applicant, the latter had a clear interest in being able to submit his observations on them before argument was closed. The fact that the Court of Cassation's jurisdiction was confined to questions of law made no difference in this respect. Further and above all, the inequality had been increased even more by the *avocat général's* participation, in an advisory capacity, in the court's deliberations. Even if such assistance had been limited to stylistic questions, it could reasonably have been thought that the deliberations had afforded the *avocat général* an additional opportunity to promote, without fear of contradiction by the applicant, his submissions to the effect that the appeal should be dismissed. There had therefore been a violation of Article 6 § 1 (eighteen votes to four).

173. Mr Borgers claimed compensation for non-pecuniary damage. The Court considered that the finding of a violation of Article 6 § 1 constituted in itself sufficient just satisfaction (unanimously).

As for the claim in respect of lawyer's fees and expenses, the Court awarded him the whole of the amount claimed (113,250 Belgian francs) (twenty-two votes to two).

174. Summary bibliography

CALLEWAERT (J.).—'Au-delà des apparences . . . d'un revirement', *R.T.D.H.* 1992, pp. 204–209.

COUSSIRAT-COUSTÈRE (V.).—'Jurisprudence de la Cour européenne des droits de l'homme de 1989 à 1991', *A.F.D.I.* 1991, pp. 587 *et seq.*

DECAUX (E.) and TAVERNIER (P.).—'Chronique de jurisprudence de la Cour européenne des droits de l'homme', *J.D.I.* 1992, pp. 797–799.

KIRKPATRICK (J.).—'La procédure en cassation en matière repressive après l'arrêt de la Cour européenne des droits de l'homme du 30 octobre 1991', *J.T.* 1992, pp. 161–166.

LAMBERT (P.).—'De la participation du ministère public au délibéré de la Cour de cassation . . . à "l'erreur de menuiserie"', *J.T.*, 1992, pp. 167–169.

MARCUS-HELMONS (S.).—'La présence du ministère public aux délibérations de la Cour de cassation ou l'affaire Borgers', in *Présence du droit public et des droits de l'homme. Mélanges offerts à Jacques Velu*, Brussels, Bruylant, 1992, Vol. III, pp. 1379–1390.

MERRILLS (J.G.).—'Decisions on the European Convention on Human Rights during 1992', *B.Y.B.I.L.* 1992, pp. 538–540.

PIRET (J.-M.).—'Le parquet de cassation', *J.T.* 1994, pp. 621–631.

SUDRE (F.).—'Chronique de la jurisprudence de la Cour européenne des droits de l'homme—1991', *R.U.D.H.* 1992, Nos 1–2, pp. 1 *et seq.*

WAUTERS (A.).—'Het arrest Borgers van het Europees Hof voor de rechten van de mens', *R.W.* 1991–1992, pp. 1105–1107.

WAUTERS (A.).—'L'arrêt Borgers de la Cour européenne des droits de l'homme', *R.D.I.D.C.* 1992, pp. 125–131.

WARBRICK (C.).—'The European Convention on Human Rights', *Y.E.L.* 1991, pp. 565–568.

235. Case of Vilvarajah and Others v. the United Kingdom

Decision to remove five Sri Lankan asylum seekers to Sri Lanka

175. *Nadarajah Vilvarajah, Vaithialingam Skandarajah, Saravamuthu Sivakumaran, Vathanan Navratnasingam and Vinnasithamby Rasalingam, who were all Sri Lankan Tamils, arrived in the United Kingdom at different dates in 1987 and requested asylum under the 1951 United Nations Convention relating to the Status of Refugees (as amended): they feared persecution if they were returned to their country, where their families and themselves had been victims of the excesses of the army carried out against the Tamil community. The Home Secretary considered and refused their requests. They then sought judicial review of his decisions, but the House of Lords dismissed their applications at last instance on 16 December 1987.*

They were returned to Sri Lanka on 10 and 12 February 1988. The first, second and third of them claimed that they had been arrested, detained and (in the case of the second and third applicants) mistreated by the Indian Peace Keeping Forces ('the IPKF'); the fourth maintained that he had been arrested and beaten by the police. On 13 March 1989, the Adjudicator upheld their appeals against the refusal of asylum. They were then allowed to return to the United Kingdom in the second half of 1989, where they were granted exceptional leave to remain initially for twelve months and thereafter until 22 March 1992.

176. *Mr Vilvarajah, Mr Skandarajah and Mr Sivakumaran lodged their applications with the Commission on 26 August 1987, Mr Navratnasingam and Mr Rasalingam on 15 December 1987. In their applications they alleged that, as young male Tamils, they had reasonable grounds to fear that they would be subjected to persecution, torture, arbitrary execution or inhuman or degrading treatment contrary to Article 3 of the Convention. They further alleged that they had no effective remedy under United Kingdom law in respect of their complaint under Article 3.[1]*

---

1 In its report adopted on 8 May 1990, the Commission expressed the opinion that there had been no breach of Article 3 (seven votes to seven, with a casting vote by the President) but that there had been a breach of Article 13 (thirteen votes to one).

Judgment of 30 October 1991 *(Chamber) (Series A No. 215)*

177. The right to political asylum was contained in neither the Convention or its Protocols. However, the expulsion by a Contracting State of an asylum seeker might give rise to an issue under Article 3 where substantial grounds had been shown for believing that the person concerned faced a real risk of being subjected to torture or to inhuman or degrading treatment or punishment in the country to which he was returned.

In determining whether such grounds had been shown, the Court would assess the issue in the light of all the material placed before it or, if necessary, material obtained *proprio motu*. It had to do this primarily by reference to those facts which were known or ought to have been known to the Contracting State at the time of the expulsion, even if information obtained subsequently might be of value in confirming or refuting the Contracting State's appreciation. It had to apply rigorous criteria in view of the absolute character of Article 3 and of the fact that that article enshrined one of the fundamental values of the democratic societies making up the Council of Europe.

The Court found that substantial grounds had not been established for believing that the applicants would be exposed to a real risk of being subjected to inhuman or degrading treatment within the meaning of Article 3 on their return to Sri Lanka in February 1988. At the time, there had been an improvement in the situation in the north and east of Sri Lanka. Although occasional fighting had still been taking place, the IPKF had, in accordance with the Accord of July 1987, taken over from the Sinhalese dominated security forces in these areas and the major fighting at Jaffna had stopped. Moreover, the voluntary programme of the United Nations High Commission for Refugees had enabled numerous refugees to be repatriated to Sri Lanka.

The evidence before the Court concerning the background of the applicants, as well as the general situation in Sri Lanka, did not establish that the applicants' personal position had been any worse than that of the generality of other members of the Tamil community or other young male Tamils who had been returning to their country. A mere possibility of ill-treatment, however, in such circumstances, was not in itself sufficient to give rise to a breach of Article 3. As regards the second, third and fourth applicants, who had in fact been subjected to ill-treatment following their return, there had existed no special distinguishing features in their cases that could or ought to have enabled the Secretary of State to foresee that they would have been treated in this way. The removal to Sri Lanka of the fourth and fifth applicants without identity cards was open to criticism but had not exposed them to a real risk of treatment going beyond the threshold set by Article 3. The Court also attached importance to the knowledge and experience that the United Kingdom authorities had had in dealing with large numbers of asylum seekers from Sri Lanka and to the fact that the personal circumstances of each applicant had been carefully considered by the Secretary of State. There had therefore not been a violation of Article 3 (eight votes to one).

178. As regards Article 13, the Court could see no material difference between the *Soering* case[1] and the present one. The English courts were able in asylum cases to review the Secretary of State's refusal to grant asylum with reference to the same principles of judicial review and to quash a decision in similar circumstances and they had done so on several occasions. Indeed they had stressed their special responsibility to subject administrative decisions in this area to the most anxious scrutiny. Moreover, the practice was that an asylum seeker would not be removed from the United Kingdom until proceedings were complete once he had obtained leave to apply for judicial review. The applicants thus had had available to them an effective remedy, with the result that there had been no violation of Article 13 (seven votes to two).

179. *Summary bibliography*

Bossuyt (M.) and Lammerant (I.).—'La conformité à la Convention européenne des droits de l'homme des mesures d'éloignement du territoire de demandeurs d'asiles déboutés', *R.T.D.H.* 1993, pp. 417–430.

Coussirat-Coustère (V.).—'Jurisprudence de la Cour européenne des droits de l'homme de 1989 à 1991', *A.F.D.I.* 1991, pp. 589 *et seq.*

Decaux (E.) and Tavernier (P.).—'Chronique de jurisprudence de la Cour européenne des droits de l'homme', *J.D.I.* 1992, pp. 801–803.

Merrills (J.G.).—'Decisions on the European Convention on Human Rights during 1992', *B.Y.B.I.L.* 1992, pp. 540–542.

Pedrazzi (F.).—'Corte europea dei diritti dell'uomo, richiedenti asilo e procedure di riconoscimento dello status di rifugiato. Considerazioni critiche sulla sentenza Vilvarajah', *Riv. I.D.U.* 1992, pp. 187–202.

Sudre (F.).—'Chronique de la jurisprudence de la Cour européenne des droits de l'homme—1991', *R.U.D.H.* 1992, Nos 1–2, pp. 1 *et seq.*

Warbrick (C.).—'The European Convention on Human Rights', *Y.E.L.* 1991, pp. 544–553.

---

1 *Soering v. the United Kingdom*, Series A No. 16; see Vol. II of this work, 248–262.

236. Case of the *Observer* and the *Guardian* v. the United Kingdom
237. Case of the *Sunday Times* v. the United Kingdom (no. 2)

Interlocutory injunctions restraining newspapers from publishing details of the content of a book

180. *The two cases were concerned with interlocutory injunctions— the precise terms of which had varied in the course of the proceedings—granted by courts in the United Kingdom with regard to* Spycatcher, *the memoirs of Peter Wright, a retired member of the British security services who lived in Australia. The book included an account of alleged illegal activities by the Security Service. Part of the material in* Spycatcher *had already been published in the United Kingdom in other books and television interviews. In September 1985, the Attorney General of England and Wales instituted, on behalf of the United Kingdom Government, proceedings in Australia to restrain publication of* Spycatcher. *The memoirs were finally published after the New South Wales Court of Appeal found in favour of the author and his publishers.*

181. *In June 1986, short articles appeared in the* Observer *and the* Guardian *giving details of some of the contents of* Spycatcher. *The Attorney General instituted proceedings for breach of confidence, seeking permanent injunctions restraining them from making any publication of* Spycatcher *material. On 27 June 1986* ex parte *interim injunctions—modified on 11 July 1986—were granted to the Attorney General essentially restraining the* Observer *and the* Guardian, *pending the substantive trial, from any further publication concerning the allegedly illegal activities of the Security Service described in* Spycatcher *or further information deriving from Mr Wright and obtained by him in his capacity as a member of the Security Service. In April 1987, following the publication of summaries of certain of Mr Wright's allegations in three other British newspapers, the* Observer *and the* Guardian *applied for the discharge of the injunctions. In mid-July, the book was published in the United States, where it became a best-seller. A substantial number of copies were bought by United Kingdom residents. The Government took no steps to prevent such imports of the book.*

Shortly before Spycatcher *was published in the United States, the first instalment of extracts from the book appeared in the* Sunday Times, *which had purchased the British newspaper serialization rights. This prompted the Attorney General to commence proceedings for contempt of court, and subsequently for breach of confidence, against the* Sunday Times. *On 30 July 1987, the House of Lords decided by a majority that the injunctions should continue against the* Observer *and the* Guardian. *As a result of the law relating to contempt of court, they bound the whole of the United Kingdom media and had the effect, for instance, of preventing the* Sunday Times *from publishing further extracts from* Spycatcher. *In the meantime and subsequently, publication and dissemination of* Spycatcher *continued worldwide. Interlocutory injunctions remained in force until 13 October 1988 when, after substantive consideration of the actions for breach of confidence brought by the Attorney General, the House of Lords held,* inter alia, *that it would not be appropriate to grant permanent injunctions against the* Observer, *the* Guardian *and the* Sunday Times.

182. (a) *The* Observer, *that is to say, The Observer Ltd, the owners and publishers of that newspaper, Donald Trelford, its editor, and David Leigh and Paul Lashmar, two of its reporters, and (b) the* Guardian, *that is to say, Guardian Newspapers Limited, the owners and publishers of the* Guardian, *Peter Preston, its editor, and Richard Norton-Taylor, one of its reporters, applied to the Commission on 27 January 1988.*

The Sunday Times, *that is to say, Times Newspapers Ltd, the publishers of that newspaper, and Andrew Neill, its editor, did likewise on 31 July 1987.*

They complained that the injunctions imposed by the English courts restraining them from publishing infringed Articles 10, 13 and 14 of the Convention.[1]

---

1 In its reports of 12 July 1990, the Commission expressed the opinion that:
   (a) in the cases of the *Observer* and the *Guardian* there had been a violation of Article 10 in respect of temporary injunctions imposed on them for the period from 11 July 1986 to 30 July 1987 (six votes to five); there had been a violation of Article 10 in respect of temporary injunctions imposed on them for the period from 30 July 1987 to 13 October 1988 (unanimously); there had been no violation of Article 13 or Article 14 (unanimously);
   (b) in the case of the *Sunday Times* there had been a violation of Article 10, but not of Articles 13 and 14 (unanimously).

Judgments of 26 November 1991 *(Plenary Court) (Series A Nos 216 and 217)*

183. The restrictions complained of clearly constituted, as was not disputed, an interference with the applicants' exercise of their freedom of expression.

184. The Court started by conceding—and thus rejecting an argument raised by the *Observer* and the *Guardian*, but not by the *Sunday Times*—that the interference had been 'prescribed by law': the guidelines for the grant of interlocutory injunctions had been enunciated by the House of Lords several years previously and had been formulated with a sufficient degree of precision.

185. The Court went on to hold that the interference had the legitimate aim of 'maintaining the authority of the judiciary' in so far as it had preserved the rights of the Attorney General *qua* litigant and protected national security until the substantive proceedings, since the application for permanent injunctions had been based on evidence of the damage that publication of the content of *Spycatcher* might do to the Security Service.

186. The Court then considered whether the interference had been 'necessary in a democratic society'.

It was observed in each of the two judgments that, whilst Article 10 did not in terms prohibit the imposition of prior restraints on publication, such measures called for the most careful scrutiny on the part of the Court, especially so as far as the press was concerned.

As far as the period from 11 July 1986 to 30 July 1987 (not covered by the complaints made by the *Sunday Times*) was concerned, the Court noted that, when the restrictions had been imposed for the first time, the *Observer* and the *Guardian* had wished to publish further information deriving from Mr Wright and disclosing alleged unlawful activity on the part of the Security Service. In addition, Mr Wright's memoirs (which in July 1986 had existed only in manuscript form) had been liable to comprise material the disclosure of which might be detrimental to the interests of national security and it was unlikely that all the contents of the book would have raised questions of public concern outweighing the interests of national security. In issuing interlocutory injunctions, the English courts had based themselves on relevant criteria (the publication of the information in question before the substantive trial would have made nugatory the actions brought by the Attorney General and hence his aim of protecting national security) and had carefully weighed the conflicting interests. In view of the nature and possible contents of *Spycatcher*, the interests of national security involved and the potential prejudice to the Attorney General's breach of confidence actions, the English courts had been entitled, having regard to their margin of appreciation, to consider the grant of injunctive relief to be necessary and their reasons for so concluding had been sufficient. Lastly, the Court held that the restrictions actually imposed were proportional to the aims pursued, since their scope had been mitigated in several respects and their duration was justified.

Consequently, there had been no violation of Article 10 during the first period (fourteen votes to ten).

As for the period from 30 July 1987 to 13 October 1988 (covered by the complaints of the *Sunday Times*, in addition of those of the *Observer* and the *Guardian*), the fact that the further publication of *Spycatcher* material could have been prejudicial to the trial of the Attorney General's claims for permanent injunctions did not constitute a sufficient reason for extending the interlocutory injunctions: if the Attorney General had succeeded in obtaining permanent injunctions, they would have borne on material the confidentiality of which had been destroyed in any event as a result of the publication of *Spycatcher* in the United States. No more were the interests of national security a sufficient reason: as the material concerned was no longer secret, the purpose of the injunctions had thus become confined to the promotion of the efficiency and reputation of the Security Service and the refusal to discharge them had prevented newspapers from purveying information, already available, on a matter of legitimate public concern. The Court therefore held that after 10 July 1987 there had been a violation of Article 10 (unanimously).

187. The Court then considered whether the *Observer* and the *Guardian* and the *Sunday Times* had been victims of discrimination in so far as foreign newspapers or publishers had not been subject to the contested restrictions. The Court held that they had not been victims of such discrimination. If there had been a difference in treatment, this was because those newspapers and publishers were not subject to the jurisdiction of the English courts and hence had not been in a situation similar to that of applicants. Hence, there had been no violation of Article 14 in conjunction with Article 10 (held unanimously).

188. The Court dismissed claims by the *Observer*, the *Guardian* and the *Sunday Times* that, contrary to Article 13, they had not had an effective remedy before a national authority in respect of their complaints based on the Convention (unanimously). They had raised the relevant issues in substance before the domestic courts and the effectiveness of a remedy did not depend on the certainty of a favourable outcome.

189. Under Article 50, the Court upheld, but only in part, the claims in respect of costs and expenses incurred in the domestic proceedings and at Strasbourg made by the *Sunday Times* (£224,340.67) and the *Observer* and the *Guardian* (£212,430.28): it awarded each group of applicants £100,000 (unanimously).

190. *Summary bibliography*

COHEN-JONATHAN (G.).—'Cour européenne des droits de l'homme. Arrêts du 26 novembre 1991. Sunday Times c. Royaume-Uni (n° 2) et Observer et Guardian c. Royaume-Uni', *L.P.* No. 88, January-February 1992, chroniques et opinions, pp. 1–16.

COUSSIRAT-COUSTÈRE (V.).—'Jurisprudence de la Cour européenne des droits de l'homme de 1989 à 1991', *A.F.D.I.* 1991, pp. 605 *et seq.*

DECAUX (E.) and TAVERNIER (P.).—'Chronique de jurisprudence de la Cour européenne des droits de l'homme', *J.D.I.* 1992, pp. 803–807.

MERRILLS (J.G.).—'Decisions on the European Convention on Human Rights during 1992', *B.Y.B.I.L.* 1992, pp. 542–546.

SUDRE (F.).—'Chronique de la jurisprudence de la Cour européenne des droits de l'homme—1991', *R.U.D.H.* 1992, Nos 1–2, pp. 1 *et seq.*

WARBRICK (C.).—'The European Convention on Human Rights', *Y.E.L.* 1991, pp. 579–586.

238. Case of Kemmache v. France (nos 1 and 2)

Length of detention on remand and of criminal proceedings

191. *Michel Kemmache, a French national, was charged on 16 February 1983 with importing counterfeit money into French territory and with the use and unlawful circulation of counterfeit banknotes, and remanded in custody. On 29 March 1983 he was released subject to court supervision and the payment of a security of 500,000 French francs. On 22 March 1984 he was remanded in custody again.*

The investigation closed on 29 June 1984 and, following a judgment of the Court of Cassation in October 1985, Mr Kemmache was committed for trial in the Alpes-Maritimes Assize Court. He subsequently brought four appeals on points of law. Eventually the case was set down for trial in the first quarter of 1986, but the Assize Court President adjourned the trial to a subsequent session on account of the link between the main charges brought against Mr Kemmache and a charge of suborning a witness, which was brought in February 1986.

After being released on 19 December 1986, subject to court supervision and to the payment of a security amounting to 300,000 French francs, Mr Kemmache was acquitted on the charge of suborning a witness on 20 October 1987. Since the case relating to the main charges was ready for judgment, he was summoned to appear before the Alpes-Maritimes Assize Court. On 11 June 1990 he reported to be taken into custody. However, on 12 June the Assize Court severed the proceedings brought against one of the co-accused and, on the application of the latter and Mr Kemmache, adjourned the proceedings to a subsequent session. On 4 July 1990 Mr Kemmache was released subject to court supervision and the payment of a security of 800,000 French francs. In December, Mr Kemmache failed to surrender to custody on the eve of the trial. Re-arrested on 14 March 1991, he was sentenced on 25 April 1991 by the Alpes-Maritimes Assize Court to eleven years' imprisonment and a fine of 2,600,000 French francs. On the following day, he lodged an appeal with the Court of Cassation, which was still pending.

192. *In his applications of 1 August 1986 and 28 April 1989 to the Commission, Mr Kemmache alleged that there had been violations, on the one hand, of Article 5 § 2 and 3 and Article 6 of the Convention and, on the other, of Article 6 § 1 as regards the length of the criminal proceedings.*[1]

---

1 On 10 March 1989, the Commission declared the complaints based on Article 5 § 2 and Article 6 § 2 inadmissible and the complaint under

Judgment of 27 November 1991 *(Chamber) (Series A No. 218)*

193. The applicant had undergone four periods of detention on remand. Only the first two periods (16 February to 29 March 1983 and 22 March 1984 to 19 December 1986), which had lasted a total of two years, ten months and ten days, were to be taken into consideration in this instance: the others were subsequent to the Commission's report on the alleged violation of Article 5 § 3 and were the subject of new, pending applications.

194. In the Court's view, the nature of the offences to be investigated and the requirements of the investigation were capable of justifying the first period of detention.

195. In dismissing Mr Kemmache's applications for release during the second period of detention, the relevant courts cited four main grounds.

The first was the seriousness of the offences and the severity of the sentence risked. The existence and persistence of serious indications of the guilt of the person concerned undoubtedly constituted relevant factors, but the Court considered that they alone could not justify such a long period of pre-trial detention.

The second ground was requirements of public order. In this case, the conditions laid down in the Court's case law had not been satisfied. Some of the indictments divisions had assessed the need to continue the deprivation of liberty from a purely abstract point of view, taking into consideration only the gravity of the offences. Others had confined themselves to noting the effects of the alleged offences.

The third ground was the risk of pressure being brought to bear on the witnesses and the co-accused. The Court found that that risk had ceased to exist after the investigation into the main offence had been concluded by the investigating judge, and could no longer serve as a justification for detention.

The final ground was the risk of the applicant's absconding. It appeared from the documents produced that the courts in question had been entitled to believe that there was a risk that Mr Kemmache would evade trial. However, they had no longer relied on such a risk after 18 April 1986 so that, at least subsequent to that date, detention had no longer been justified on that account.

Article 5 § 3 admissible. On 7 June 1990, it found the second application (Article 6 § 1) admissible in its entirety. In its reports of 8 June and 3 July 1990, it expressed the opinion that there had been a violation of Article 5 § 3 (thirteen votes to three) and of Article 6 § 1 (unanimously).

In sum, the contested detention had infringed Article 5 § 3 in so far as it had lasted until 19 December 1986 (held unanimously).

196. For the purposes of Article 6 § 1, the period to be taken into consideration had begun on 16 February 1983, the date on which Mr Kemmache had been charged; it had not yet ended, as the Court of Cassation had still to rule on the latter's appeal against the Assize Court's decision of 25 April 1991. It had therefore already lasted more than eight and a half years.

The duration of the investigation (16 February 1983 to 29 June 1984, or sixteen and a half months) could not be regarded as excessive. In any event, the applicant had not accused the judge in question of any lack of diligence.

In contrast, a 'reasonable time' had been exceeded and hence Article 6 § 1 had been violated (held unanimously) during the trial phase, that is to say, after 29 June 1984. The Court used its usual criteria in order to reach that conclusion.

The complexity of the case: before the Commission, the Government had cited the complexity of the case, but they had not reverted to this point once the case had been brought before the Court.

The applicant's conduct: the judicial authorities could not be held responsible for two prolongations of the proceedings. Mr Kemmache had consented to one of them and had caused the other by not reporting to the prison on the day before his trial in December 1990, despite the fact that according to a medical report his state of health had not prevented him from appearing at the Assize Court.

The conduct of the judicial authorities: the Court considered that although the subornation proceedings had had some effect on the course of the main proceedings, that did not justify the length of the latter proceedings. As for the severance of Mr Kemmache's case from that of a co-accused who had been provisionally handed over to the Swiss authorities, examination of the case-file did not disclose any insurmountable obstacle which would have prevented the trial from being held during one of the sessions in the first half of 1988.

197. The Court held that the question of the application of Article 50 was not ready for decision as the main criminal proceedings had not yet been concluded. Accordingly, it reserved that question (unanimously).

Judgment of 2 November 1993 *(Chamber)—Application of Article 50*
(Series A No. 270–B)

198. The criminal proceedings conducted subsequently to the principal judgment included the following decisions:

(a) on 18 December 1991, the judgment of the Alpes-Maritimes Assize Court of 25 April 1991 sentencing Mr Kemmache to eleven years' imprisonment and fining him 2,600,000 French francs was quashed;

(b) on 21 March 1992, the Var Assize Court, to which the case had been remitted, adopted a judgment sentencing the accused to nine years' imprisonment and fining him 2,600,000 francs for aiding and abetting the importation and use on French territory of counterfeit foreign banknotes and the unlawful circulation of such notes within the customs area;

(c) on 3 February 1993, the applicant's appeal on points of law was dismissed by the Court of Cassation.

199. The Court noted that the entire period which Mr Kemmache had spent in detention on remand had been reckoned as part of his sentence. This being so, it did not find sufficient causal connection between the violations found in the principal judgment and the deterioration of the applicant's financial and professional circumstances. It accordingly dismissed the claim for compensation in respect of pecuniary damage (unanimously). In contrast, the Court took the view that the applicant must have suffered non-pecuniary damage, for which it awarded him 75,000 French francs (unanimously).

The security had been paid several years after the end of the pre-trial detention at issue. Consequently, it could not be taken into consideration (held unanimously).

200. Although the applicant had not provided any itemized accounts or supporting documents, the Court considered it reasonable to accept, making an assessment on an equitable basis, the claims for the costs incurred in Strasbourg and part of those referable to the applicant's attempts to secure release from detention on remand. It therefore awarded him a total of 150,000 French francs (unanimously).

201. *Summary bibliography*

COUSSIRAT-COUSTÈRE (V.).—'Jurisprudence de la Cour européenne des droits de l'homme de 1989 à 1991', *A.F.D.I.* 1991, pp. 592 *et seq.*

DECAUX (E.) and TAVERNIER (P.).—'Chronique de jurisprudence de la Cour européenne des droits de l'homme', *J.D.I.* 1992, pp. 807–810.

MÉRAL (C.).—'L'arrêt Kemmache de la Cour européenne des droits de l'homme en date du 27 novembre 1991', *G.P.* 18–19 March 1992, doctrine, pp. 35–37.

MERRILLS (J.G.).—'Decisions on the European Convention on Human Rights during 1992', *B.Y.B.I.L.* 1992, pp. 546–548.

PETTITI (L.-E.).—'Droits de l'homme', *R.S.C.D.P.C.* 1992, pp. 143–153.

PETTITI (L.-E.).—'Note', *G.P.* 1992, jurisprudence, pp. 105 and 106.

RENUCCI (J.-F.).—'Droit européen des droits de l'homme', *D.* 1992, sommaires commentés, pp. 329 and 330.

RENUCCI (J.-F.).—'Note', *D.* 1993, jurisprudence, pp. 515 and 516.

SUDRE (F.).—'Chronique de la jurisprudence de la Cour européenne des droits de l'homme—1991', *R.U.D.H.* 1992, Nos 1–2, p. 1 *et seq.*

SUDRE (F.) and others.—'Chronique de la jurisprudence de la Cour européenne des droits de l'homme. Deuxième partie : juin-décembre 1993', *R.U.D.H.* 1993, pp. 377 *et seq.*

WARBRICK (C.).—'The European Convention on Human Rights', *Y.E.L.* 1991, pp. 560 and 561.

239. Case of Oerlemans v. the Netherlands

Access of a farmer to a court to challenge the designation of part of his land as a protected natural site

202. *Johannes Oerlemans, a citizen of the Netherlands, raised cattle on a farm of approximately 110 hectares. By an order of 20 September 1982, made pursuant to the Nature Protection Act 1967, the Minister of Culture, Recreation and Publics Works designated a large part of the area known as the Markiezaatsmeer, which included a parcel of land of which the applicant was a co-owner, as a 'protected natural site'. The order provided that farming of the land located within the area could continue as usual but that certain actions should be subject to authorization. In October 1982, Mr Oerlemans, whose objections to the proposed designation had previously been considered by the competent authorities, appealed against the designation order to the Crown on the ground,* inter alia, *of its effects on the use which he might make of his land. The Crown—that is to say, the Queen and the competent minister—dismissed the appeal on 14 March 1986 by royal decree on the ground that it saw no reason to take issue with the contested measure in view of the unquestionable importance of the public interest pursued. In accordance with the law in force at the time, the Crown had previously sought the opinion of the Administrative Disputes Division of the Council of State, which considered the matter on 8 November 1985.*

203. *In his application to the Commission of 24 November 1986, Mr Oerlemans invoked Article 6 § 1 of the Convention on the ground that he had been unable to challenge the legality of the designation before a court; he also claimed that his property rights had been infringed contrary to Article 1 of Protocol No. 1.*[1]

Judgment of 27 November 1991 *(Chamber) (Series A No. 219)*

204. The Court first had to assure itself that Article 6 § 1 was applicable. A dispute concerning the lawfulness of the designation order existed. Moreover, the legal consequences of the designation order were that the applicant was no longer free to cultivate his land as he saw fit and was required to seek an authorization from the Minister for various

---

1 On 10 July 1989, the Commission declared the complaint based on Article 6 § 1 admissible. In its report of 3 April 1990, it expressed the opinion that there had been a violation of Article 6 § 1 (fifteen votes to two).

purposes, for example if he sought to alter or intensify existing use or carry out certain farming activities. The extent to which he was restricted in his use of the land could be seen from the subsequent disputes that he had had with the Minister. There had thus existed a serious dispute concerning the resultant restrictions on the applicant's use of his property.

Regard being had to the Court's case law, the property right in question was a 'civil' one within the meaning of Article 6 § 1. Consequently, that provision was applicable in this case.

205.   In considering whether Article 6 § 1 had been complied with, the Court noted that under Netherlands law it was clearly established, in extensive case law which predated this dispute, that where an administrative appeal to a higher authority was not considered to offer sufficient guarantees as to a fair procedure it was possible to have recourse to the civil courts for a full review of the lawfulness of the administrative decision. The fact that the dispute was of a public law nature was irrelevant in this context. Following the judgment in *Benthem*[1] it was the view of many authorities on Netherlands law that the civil courts would thus be able to examine the lawfulness of any administrative decision coming within the scope of Article 6 against which an appeal lay to the Crown. Indeed that opinion had already been expressed by several commentators. The Supreme Court had upheld this view concerning the competence of the civil courts in a decision of 12 December 1986 and confirmed the principle in several subsequent judgments. The Court concluded that, under well-established principles of Netherlands law which existed at the time of the Royal Decree in the present case, the applicant could have submitted his dispute to the civil courts for examination. The Court held that, accordingly, there had been no violation of Article 6 § 1 (unanimously).

206.   *Summary bibliography*

DECAUX (E.) and TAVERNIER (P.).—'Chronique de jurisprudence de la Cour européenne des droits de l'homme', *J.D.I.* 1992, pp. 810 and 811.

ERGEC (R.).—'L'accès à un tribunal lors du classement de terres agricoles en site protégé', *R.T.D.H.* 1993, pp. 531–535.

MERRILLS (J.G.).—'Decisions on the European Convention on Human Rights during 1991', *B.Y.B.I.L.* 1992, pp. 548 and 549.

SUDRE (F.).—'Chronique de la jurisprudence de la Cour européenne des droits de l'homme—1991', *R.U.D.H.* 1992, Nos 1–2, pp. 1 *et seq.*

---

1   Judgment of 23 October 1975, Series A No. 97; see Vol. I of this work, 618–623.

240. Case of S. v. Switzerland

Surveillance of meetings between an accused remanded in custody in the Canton of Zürich and his lawyer

207. *S., a mason from Zürich, who was charged on 28 May 1985 with having caused an explosion and arson, was remanded in custody on the grounds of the risk of flight and of collusion with his co-accused. He was subsequently further charged with arson and criminal damage. Whilst he was in custody, S.'s communications with his lawyer were placed under surveillance between 31 May 1985 and 10 January 1986: police officers listened to their conversations and took notes; S. and his lawyer were also required to show the police officers the documents which they were using. On 15 October and 4 December 1985, the Federal Court dismissed arguments based on the fact that S. had been unable freely to consult with his lawyer on the grounds, inter alia, that the offences constituted attacks on public order and that S. was dangerous. Consequently, surveillance of the lawyer's contacts with his client was in accordance with the Swiss Constitution and the European Convention. On 9 February 1990, the Zürich Court of Appeal sentenced him to seven years' imprisonment.*

208. *In his applications to the Commission of 18 November 1986 and 28 May 1988, S. invoked Article 6 § 3(b) and (c), Article 5 § 4 and Article 13 of the Convention.[1]*

Judgment of 28 November 1991 *(Chamber) (Series A No. 220)*

209. As far as Article 6 § 3(c) was concerned, S. criticized the Swiss authorities for having exercised surveillance of his meetings with his lawyer and for having authorized his lawyer to consult only a minute fraction of the case-file, with the alleged effect that it had been difficult for him to challenge the decisions by which his detention on remand had been extended.

---

1 On 9 November 1989, the Commission declared the complaints based on Articles 5 and 6 admissible. In its report of 12 July 1990, it concluded that:
  (a) there had been a violation of Article 6 § 3(c) in that the applicant had from 31 May 1985 to 10 January 1986 been unable to converse freely with his lawyer (fourteen votes to one);
  (b) no separate issue was raised with reference to Article 6 § 3(b) (fourteen votes to one) and Article 5 § 4 (unanimously).

The Government argued that the 'particularly drastic' restriction that had been imposed was justified by the exceptional circumstances of the case, in particular the 'extraordinarily dangerous' character of the accused and the risk of collusion between his lawyer and the co-accused.

The Court noted that, unlike some national laws and international instruments, the European Convention did not expressly guarantee the right of a person charged with a criminal offence to communicate with defence counsel out of hearing of a third person. The Court considered that such a right on the part of the accused was one of the basic requirements of a fair trial in a democratic society and followed from Article 6 § 3(c) of the Convention. If a lawyer were unable to confer with his client and receive confidential instructions from him without such surveillance, his assistance would lose much of its usefulness.

The risk of 'collusion' relied on by the Government and based, according to the Swiss courts, on 'indications pointing to' such a risk 'in the person of defence counsel' could not justify the restriction in issue in the absence of other sufficiently cogent reasons. There had therefore been a violation of Article 6 § 3(c) (held unanimously).

210. Since S. had no longer relied on Article 6 § 3(b) before the Court, there was no need for it to consider the question of its own motion (held unanimously).

211. Having regard to the conclusion which it had reached with regard to Article 6 § 3(c), the Court saw no need to consider the matter from the point of view of Article 5 § 4 (held unanimously).

212. Making an assessment on a equitable basis, the Court awarded S. 2,500 Swiss francs in respect of non-pecuniary damage (unanimously).

The Court awarded S. 12,500 Swiss francs in respect of the costs and expenses which he had incurred in Switzerland and in connection with the proceedings before the Strasbourg institutions (unanimously).

213. *Summary bibliography*

COUSSIRAT-COUSTÈRE (V.).—'Jurisprudence de la Cour européenne des droits de l'homme de 1989 à 1991', *A.F.D.I.* 1991, pp. 594 *et seq.*

DECAUX (E.) and TAVERNIER (P.).—'Chronique de jurisprudence de la Cour européenne des droits de l'homme', *J.D.I.* 1992, pp. 812 and 813.

HOTTELIER (M.).—'Vers une procédure pénale "euro-compatible". Remarques à propos de l'arrêt S. contre Suisse', *A.J.P./P.J.A.* 1992, pp. 363–368.

LOMBARDINI (C.) and CAMBI (A.).—'Le droit du détenu de communiquer librement avec son conseil', *R.T.D.H.* 1993, pp. 297–308.

MERRILLS (J.G.).—'Decisions on the European Convention on Human Rights during 1991', *B.Y.B.I.L.* 1992, pp. 549 and 550.

SUDRE (F.).—'Chronique de la jurisprudence de la Cour européenne des droits de l'homme—1991', *R.U.D.H.* 1992, Nos 1–2, pp. 1 *et seq.*

WARBRICK (C.).—'The European Convention on Human Rights', *Y.E.L.* 1991, pp. 573 and 574.

241. Case of Koster v. the Netherlands

Appearance before the Military Court of a conscript placed in detention on remand during military manoeuvres

214. *On Wednesday 11 March 1987, Jacobus Koster, a Netherlands national, repeatedly refused to obey an order that he should take receipt of a weapon and a uniform while completing his compulsory military service. He was arrested forthwith and placed in custody, the measure being confirmed on the same day by the officer commanding his unit. He appeared before the investigating officer on 13 March and before the Arnhem Military Court on Monday 16 March. That court confirmed the earlier detention and extended it by thirty days. When Mr Koster's lawyer invoked Article 5 § 3 of the Convention, the court stated that it had sat as soon as possible, regard being had to the circumstances: a Sunday had fallen in the interval and the applicant had been arrested during major military manoeuvres in which its military members had been participating.*

215. *In his application to the Commission of 31 March 1987, Mr Koster complained that he had not been brought promptly before the Military Court, as was required under Article 5 § 3 of the Convention.*[1]

Judgment of 28 November 1991 *(Chamber) (Series A No. 221)*

216. Following a reference to its case law, the Court held that the manoeuvres did not justify any delay in the proceedings: as they took place at periodic intervals and therefore had been foreseeable, they had in no way prevented the military authorities from ensuring that the Military Court had been able to sit so as to enable it to comply with the requirements of the Convention, if necessary on Saturday or Sunday.

Accordingly, and even taking into account the demands of military life and justice, the applicant's appearance before the judicial authorities had not complied with the requirement of promptness laid down in Article 5 § 3, which had therefore been violated (held unanimously).

217. Applying Article 50, the Court held that that finding afforded sufficient just satisfaction for the alleged damage (unanimously).

1 In its report of 3 September 1990, the Commission expressed the opinion that there had been a violation of Article 5 § 3 (unanimously).

It awarded the whole of the amount claimed for costs and expenses incurred before the Strasbourg institutions (11,626 guilders), less the sum of 9,382.50 French francs which had been received by way of legal aid (unanimously).

218. *Summary bibliography*

COUSSIRAT-COUSTÈRE (V.).—'Jurisprudence de la Cour européenne des droits de l'homme de 1989 à 1991', *A.F.D.I.* 1991, p. 583 *et seq.*

MERRILLS (J.G.).—'Decisions on the European Convention on Human Rights during 1991', *B.Y.B.I.L.* 1992, pp. 550 and 551.

SUDRE (F.).—'Chronique de la jurisprudence de la Cour européenne des droits de l'homme—1991', *R.U.D.H.* 1992, Nos 1–2, pp. 1 *et seq.*

WARBRICK (C.).—'The European Convention on Human Rights', *Y.E.L.* 1991, p. 561 and 562.

242. Case of Pine Valley Developments Ltd and Others v. Ireland

Outline planning permission on the strength of which the applicants had purchased land declared by the Supreme Court to be a nullity and absence of compensation

219.   *Pine Valley Developments Ltd and Healy Holdings Ltd, its parent company, were incorporated in Ireland and used to have as their principal business the purchase and development of land. Daniel Healy, an Irish national, was the managing director of Healy Holdings Ltd and its sole beneficial shareholder. Pine Valley Developments Ltd was dissolved in 1990, a receiver was appointed to Healy Holdings Ltd in 1985 and Mr Healy was adjudged bankrupt in England in 1990.*

In 1978 Pine Valley Developments Ltd had agreed to purchase land at Clondalkin (County Dublin) for IR£550,000 in reliance on outline planning permission which had been granted to the previous owner for industrial warehouse and office development by the Minister for Local Government. In July 1981 Pine Valley Developments Ltd sold the land to Healy Holdings Ltd for the same price. Subsequently, by judgment of 5 February 1982, the Supreme Court declared the grant of planning permission a nullity. The land depreciated sharply. It was later sold in the open market for IR£50,000.

Subsequently, the Government obtained the passage of the Local Government (Planning and Development) Act 1982 with a view to validating planning permissions and approvals the validity of which had come into question as a result of the decision of the Supreme Court. Once that law had entered into force, Pine Valley Developments Ltd applied to Dublin County Council for planning permission, but was turned down. Pine Valley Developments Ltd considered itself to be precluded from benefiting by that law and brought an action against the Minister for the Environment (as the successor to the Minister for Local Government) seeking damages for breach of statutory duty, negligent misrepresentation, negligence and breach of their constitutional rights of property. On 30 July 1986, the Supreme Court, upholding a judgment of the High Court, held that no cause of action lay.

220.   *The applicants applied to the Commission on 6 January 1987. They submitted that Ireland's alleged failure to validate retrospectively the outline planning permission or to provide compensation or other remedy for the reduction in value of their property constituted a violation of Article 1 of Protocol No. 1. They also complained of discrimination* *in the enjoyment of their property rights, contrary to Article 14 of the Convention taken in conjunction with the said Article 1. Finally, they claimed that they had not had an effective remedy under Irish law in respect of the foregoing complaints as required by Article 13 of the Convention.*[1]

Judgment of 29 November 1991 *(Chamber) (Series A No. 222)*

221. The Government raised several preliminary objections.

The Court started by dismissing the submission that the applicants could not claim to be 'victims' of a violation of the Convention (unanimously). It would be artificial to draw distinctions between the three applicants. The financial status of Healy Holdings Ltd and Mr Healy was of no relevance in this respect.

The Government submitted that the applicants had not exhausted domestic remedies because they had failed to take advantage of certain avenues available to them when Dublin County Council had refused them planning permission. The Court held that the Government were estopped because they had not duly put this to the Commission (unanimously).

According to the Government, the applicants had failed to seek a judgment declaring that they were entitled to the benefit of the Local Government (Planning and Development) Act 1982 or ruling on its constitutionality. The Court held that the Government was not entitled to raise this point regard being had to the attitude which they had adopted in the domestic proceedings (unanimously); furthermore, the remedy would have taken too much time to be effective.

Lastly, the Court rejected the Government's argument that the applicants had been under a duty to institute certain actions against the former owner of the land (unanimously).

222. Until the Supreme Court's decision invalidating the planning permission had been rendered, the applicants had had at least a legiti-

---

1 In its report of 6 June 1990, the Commission expressed the opinion that:
  (a) there had been no violation of the rights under Article 1 of Protocol No. 1 of Pine Valley Developments Ltd (unanimously), of Healy Holdings Ltd (nine votes to four) or of Mr Healy (ten votes to three);
  (b) there had been a violation of the rights under Article 14 of the Convention in conjunction with the said Article 1 of Healy Holdings Ltd and of Mr Healy (twelve votes to one), but not of those of Pine Valley Developments Ltd (unanimously);
  (c) there had been no violation of Article 13 of the Convention (unanimously).

mate expectation of being able to carry out their proposed development and this had to be regarded as a component part of the property in question. Having regard to the views expressed by some members of the Supreme Court and to the stance taken by the Government in the domestic proceedings, it could not now be claimed that the outline planning permission had been retrospectively validated by the 1982 Act. The annulment of planning permission had therefore been an interference with the right of Healy Holdings Ltd and Mr Healy to the peaceful enjoyment of their property (but not of Pine Valley Development Ltd's right, since it had previously sold the land). It constituted a control of the use of property failing within the scope of Article 1 of Protocol No. 1.

The decision of the Supreme Court, the result of which had been to prevent building in an area zoned for the further development of agriculture so as to preserve a green belt, must be regarded as a proper way—if not the only way—of ensuring that the relevant planning legislation was correctly applied. The applicants had been engaged on a commercial venture and had been aware of the zoning plan, and so the Court did not consider that the annulment of the permission without any remedial action being taken in their favour could be regarded as disproportionate. There had therefore been no violation of Article 1 of Protocol No. 1 in respect of Pine Valley Developments Ltd (held unanimously) or in respect of Healy Holdings Ltd and Mr Healy (six votes to three).

223. Article 14 was not applicable as far as Pine Valley Developments Ltd was concerned because it had sold the land in 1981. As regards Healy Holdings Ltd and Mr Healy, the Government had not advanced any other justification for the difference of treatment between the applicants and the other holders of permissions in the same category as theirs which had been validated retroactively by the 1982 Act. The Court therefore held that Article 14 of the Convention, taken together with Article 1 of Protocol No. 1, had not been violated as far as the first applicant was concerned, but that it had as regards the other two applicants (unanimously).

224. There had been no violation of Article 13 of the Convention (held unanimously): the applicants not only could raise, but also had raised, the substance of their Convention complaints before the Irish courts.

225. Healy Holdings Ltd and Mr Healy claimed compensation for pecuniary and non-pecuniary damage, together with reimbursement of certain costs and expenses they had incurred in Ireland. The Court considered that this question was not ready for decision and reserved it (unanimously).

Judgment of 9 February 1993 *(Chamber)—Application of Article 50*
(Series A No. 246–B)

226. The applicants argued that the loss to be made good consisted of the difference between the values, on 28 July 1982 (the date of the entry into force of the Local Government (Planning and Development) Act 1982), of the site with and without the outline planning permission. The Government did not contest the fact that compensation should be granted. The main point at issue was the value which the site would have had at that date with planning permission.

Making an assessment on an equitable basis, the Court held that the applicants should be awarded a global sum, including interest, of IR£1,200,000 for pecuniary damage (unanimously).

227. The violation of the Convention had caused Mr Healy non-pecuniary damage and the finding in the principal judgment did not of itself constitute sufficient just satisfaction for this. Making an assessment on an equitable basis, the Court awarded him IR£50,000 under this head.

228. The Court held that the amount sought in respect of costs and expenses incurred in the domestic proceedings should be reimbursed in full (IR£42,655.11). On the other hand, the Court found that the claim in respect of the Strasbourg proceedings (IR£406,760) was excessive and it awarded for this item IR£70,000, together with any value-added tax that might be due (unanimously).

229. As for the claim for interest on the sum awarded, the Court did not consider it appropriate to accede to it (held unanimously).

230. *Summary bibliography*

CLEMENT (J.-N.).—'Note', *G.P.* 15–19 July 1994, p. 47.
COUSSIRAT-COUSTÈRE (V.).—'Jurisprudence de la Cour européenne des droits de l'homme de 1989 à 1991', *A.F.D.I.* 1991, pp. 581 *et seq.*
DECAUX (E.) and TAVERNIER (P.).—'Chronique de jurisprudence de la Cour européenne des droits de l'homme', *J.D.I.* 1992, pp. 813–815.
FLAUSS (J.-F.).—'L'octroi d'intérêts moratoires par la Cour européenne des droits de l'homme', *R.T.D.H.* 1993, pp. 580–586.
MERRILLS (J.G.).—'Decisions on the European Convention on Human Rights during 1992', *B.Y.B.I.L.* 1992, pp. 551–554.
SUDRE (F.).—'Chronique de la jurisprudence de la Cour européenne des droits de l'homme—1991', *R.U.D.H.* 1992, Nos 1–2, p. 1 *et seq.*
WARBRICK (C.).—'The European Convention on Human Rights', *Y.E.L.* 1991, pp. 587–589.

243. Case of Vermeire v. Belgium

Granddaughter excluded from the estates of her deceased grandparents because of the 'illegitimate' nature of the kinship

231. *Astrid Vermeire, a Belgian national, was the recognized illegitimate daughter of Jérôme Vermeire, one of the three children of the marriage of Camiel Vermeire and Irma Vermeire, née Van den Berghe. The latter, who had brought Astrid Vermeire up after her father's death in 1939, died intestate on 22 July 1980 and 16 January 1975, respectively. Their estates were wound up after Carmel Vermeire's death and distributed to the 'legitimate' heirs, namely the two children of their son Robert. Astrid Vermeire was excluded under the old Article 756 of the Civil Code (since repealed), which provided that recognized 'illegitimate' issue had no claim on the estate of their father and mother.*

In June 1981, she brought an action before the Brussels Court of First Instance against the 'legitimate' grandchildren for a share in the estates. In a judgment of 3 June 1983 based on the judgment given by the European Court in the Marckx *case on 13 June 1979,[1] the Brussels first-instance court allowed her the same rights as a legitimate descendant in her grandparents' estates on the ground that no distinction could be drawn between 'legitimate' and 'illegitimate' children. On an appeal brought by the 'legitimate' grandchildren, the Brussels Court of Appeal set aside the judgment in May 1985 on the ground that the judgment in* Marckx *was not binding on courts and tribunals. In February 1987, the Court of Cassation dismissed an appeal brought by Astrid Vermeire.*

232. *In her application lodged with the Commission on 1 April 1987, Mrs Vermeire complained that the Belgian courts had denied her the status of an heir of her grandparents. She claimed that she had thereby suffered a discriminatory interference with the exercise of her right to respect for her private and family life, which was not compatible with Article 8 in conjunction with Article 14 of the Convention.[2]*

---

1 Series A No. 31; see Vol. I of this work, 212–223.
2 In its report of 5 April 1990, the Commission expressed the opinion that the decisions in question had not violated the said articles as regards her grandmother's estate (seven votes to six), but that they had violated them with respect to her grandfather's (unanimously).

Judgment of 29 November 1991 *(Chamber) (Series A No. 214–C)*

233. Mrs Vermeire maintained that the domestic courts should have applied Articles 8 and 14, as interpreted by the Court of Human Rights in the judgment of 13 June 1979 in *Marckx*, directly to the estates in which she was interested; at the very least, the Belgian legislature should have given the Law of 21 March 1987, amending the legislation complained of in that case, retrospective effect as from the date of that judgment.

As the principle of legal certainty dispensed the Belgian State from reopening legal acts or situations that antedated the delivery of the judgment in *Marckx*, the Court considered separately the successions of the grandmother and of the grandfather, which had become effective respectively before and after the date of the judgment in *Marckx*.

The succession to the grandmother's estate had taken place on her death and the estate had devolved on her 'legitimate' heirs as of that date. What had been in issue in that case, therefore, was a legal situation antedating the delivery of the *Marckx* judgment and there was no occasion to reopen it (eight votes to one).

As regards the grandfather's estate, the Court pointed out that the *Marckx* judgment had held that the total lack of inheritance rights on intestacy, based only on the 'illegitimate' nature of the affiliation, was discriminatory. That finding had related to facts which were so close to those of the instant case that it applied equally to the succession in issue, which had taken place after its delivery. It could not be seen what could have prevented the Brussels Court of Appeal and the Court of Cassation from complying with the findings of the *Marckx* judgment, as the Court of First Instance had done. There was nothing imprecise or incomplete about the rule which prohibited discrimination against Astrid Vermeire compared with her cousins Francine and Michel, on the grounds of the 'illegitimate' nature of the kinship between her and the deceased. An overall revision of the legislation, with the aim of carrying out a thoroughgoing and consistent amendment of the whole of the law on affiliation and inheritance on intestacy, had not been necessary as an essential preliminary to compliance with the Convention as interpreted by the Court in the *Marckx* case. The freedom of choice allowed to a State as to the means of fulfilling its obligation under Article 53 could not allow it to suspend the application of the Convention while waiting for such a reform to be completed, to the extent of compelling the Court to reject in 1991, with respect to a succession which had taken effect on 22 July 1980, complaints identical to those which it had upheld on 13 June 1979. Consequently the applicant's exclusion from the estate of her grandfather had violated Article 14 in conjunction with Article 8 of the Convention (held unanimously).

234. The Court considered that the question of the application of Article 50 was not ready for decision and therefore reserved it (unanimously).

Judgment of 4 October 1993 *(Chamber)—Application of Article 50 (Series A No. 270–A)*

235. In its judgment of 29 November 1991, the Court had held that Mrs Vermeire had suffered pecuniary damage, the amount of which was equivalent to the share of her grandfather's estate which she would have obtained had she been his 'legitimate'granddaughter; it had added that inheritance taxes and interest would have to be taken into account in calculating the compensation. Making its assessment on an equitable basis, the Court awarded Mrs Vermeire 22,192,511 Belgian francs plus interest from 1 October 1993 (unanimously).

Again making its assessment on an equitable basis, it awarded Mrs Vermeire 2,000,000 Belgian francs in respect of costs and expenses (unanimously).

236. *Summary bibliography*

COUSSIRAT-COUSTÈRE (V.).—'Jurisprudence de la Cour européenne des droits de l'homme de 1989 à 1991', *A.F.D.I.* 1991, pp. 588 *et seq.*

DECAUX (E.) and TAVERNIER (P.).—'Chronique de jurisprudence de la Cour européenne des droits de l'homme', *J.D.I.* 1992, pp. 799–801.

LAMBERT (P.).—'Observations', *R.T.D.H.* 1994, pp. 241 and 242.

MERRILLS (J.G.).—'Decisions on the European Convention on Human Rights during 1992', *B.Y.B.I.L.* 1992, pp. 554 and 555.

POLAKIEWICZ (J.).—'Die innerstaatliche Durchsetzung der Urteile des Europäischen Gerichtshofs für Menschenrechte. Gleichzeitig eine Anmerkung zum Vermeire-Urteil des Europäischen Gerichtshofs für Menschenrechte vom 29. November 1991', *Z.A.Ö.R.V.* 1992, pp. 149–185 (English summary, pp. 185–190).

RIGAUX (F.).—'Le droit successoral des enfants naturels devant le juge international et le juge constitutionnel', *R.T.D.H.* 1992, pp. 215–225.

SUDRE (F.).—'Chronique de la jurisprudence de la Cour européenne des droits de l'homme—1991', *R.U.D.H.* 1992, Nos 1–2, pp. 1 *et seq.*

SUDRE (F.) and others.—'Chronique de la jurisprudence de la Cour européenne des droits de l'homme. Deuxième partie : juin-septembre 1993', *R.U.D.H.* 1993, pp. 377 *et seq.*

WARBRICK (C.).—'The European Convention on Human Rights', *Y.E.L.* 1991, pp. 590 and 591.

244. Case of Macaluso v. Italy
245. Case of Manunza v. Italy

Length of civil proceedings

237. *Maria Macaluso and Grazia Manunza were Italian citizens, both of whom were unemployed. They brought actions against the* Istituto Nazionale della Previdenza Sociale *(national social security institution) before the Rome magistrate's court in order to establish their rights to disability pensions.*

238. *In their applications to the Commission made on 14 May and 20 June 1987, the applicants complained of the length of the civil proceedings which they had brought and relied on Article 6 § 1 of the Convention.*[1]

Judgments of 3 December 1991 *(Chamber) (Series A No. 223–A and B)*

239. The Court held that the applicants' death, together with the silence of their heirs, who had shown no interest in the proceedings before the Court, constituted a 'fact of a kind to provide a solution of the matter' (Rules of Court, Rule 49 § 2). In addition, the Court discerned no reason of *ordre public* (public policy) for continuing the proceedings (Rule 49 § 4). Accordingly, it struck the cases out of the list (unanimously).

240. *Summary bibliography*

MERRILLS (J.G.).—'Decisions on the European Convention on Human Rights during 1992', *B.Y.B.I.L.* 1992, p. 556.

---

1 In its reports of 15 January 1991, the Commission expressed the opinion that there had been a violation of Article 6 § 1 (unanimously).

246. Case of Gilberti v. Italy
247. Case of Nonnis v. Italy
248. Case of Trotto v. Italy
249. Case of Cattivera v. Italy
250. Case of Seri v. Italy
251. Case of Gori v. Italy
252. Case of Casadio v. Italy
253. Case of Testa v. Italy
254. Case of Covitti v. Italy
255. Case of Zonetti v. Italy
256. Case of Simonetti v. Italy
257. Case of Dal Sasso v. Italy

Length of civil proceedings

241. *Silvia Gilberti, Anna Maria Nonnis, Maria Trotto, Loreto Cattivera, Maria Seri, Maria Gori, Alvaro Casadio, Giancarlo Testa, Bianca Maria Covitti, Remo Zonetti, Spartaco Simonetti and Ernestina Dal Sasso were Italian nationals. They all took proceedings in the Rome magistrate's court against the* Istituto Nazionale della Previdenza Sociale *(national social security institution), with the exception of Mr Cattivera, who sued the* Istituto Nazionale per l'Assicurazione contro gli Infortuni sul Lavoro *(national institution for industrial accidents), in order to obtain—or reinstate—a right to a disability pension.*

242. *In their applications to the Commission made between 21 January and 15 October 1987, the applicants complained of the length of the civil proceedings which they had brought and relied on Article 6 § 1 of the Convention.*[1]

---

1 In its reports of 15 January (Gilberti–Gori) and 5 March 1991 (Casadio–Dal Sasso), the Commission expressed the opinion that there had been a violation of Article 6 § 1 (unanimously except in the cases of Zonetti and Simonetti, where the voting was ten votes to one).

Judgments of 3 December 1991 *(Chamber) (Series A No. 223–C to N)*

243.   The Court regarded the lack of interest shown by the applicants in the proceedings before it as an implied withdrawal which constituted a 'fact of a kind to provide a solution of the matter' (Rules of Court, Rule 49 § 2). In addition, the Court discerned no reason of *ordre public* (public policy) for continuing the proceedings (Rule 49 § 4). Accordingly, it struck the cases out of the list, but reserved the right to restore the cases to the list if a new situation arose which was capable of justifying such a course (unanimously).

244.   *Summary bibliography*

MERRILLS (J.G.).—'Decisions on the European Convention on Human Rights during 1992', *B.Y.B.I.L.* 1992, p. 556.

258. Case of Toth v. Austria

Length of detention on remand and appeal procedures for reviewing detention

245. *Stefan Toth, an Austrian national, was arrested on 11 January 1985 on suspicion of aggravated fraud involving an amount in excess of 2,000,000 schillings. In detention on remand until February 1987, he made several applications to be released which were ultimately rejected by the Review Chamber of the Regional Court of Salzburg and, on appeal, by the Linz Court of Appeal. The latter court also decided on several occasions to extend his detention on remand. Neither the applicant nor his lawyer attended the Court of Appeal hearings on his detention.*

246. *In his application to the Commission of 12 October 1985, Mr Toth formulated a number of complaints concerning his arrest and his detention on remand and the length of the criminal proceedings as well as the conduct of the Austrian authorities and courts. He relied on Article 5 §§ 3 and 4 of the Convention.*[1]

Judgment of 12 December 1991 *(Chamber) (Series A No. 224)*

247. With regard to Article 5 § 3, the period to be taken into consideration had begun on 11 January 1985, the date of the arrest, and had ended on 18 February 1987, with the applicant's release following the decision of the Linz Court of Appeal allowing his appeal, less the brief period during which the applicant had served a prison sentence. It had therefore lasted two years, one month and two days.

Could that period be regarded as reasonable? The Court started by examining the reasonableness of the detention. The national courts had had reasonable cause to fear that the accused would commit new offences in view of the nature of offences previously committed by him and the number of sentences imposed as a result. They had based their decisions on grounds which provided a sufficient explanation as

---

1 On 8 May 1989, the Commission declared the application admissible as regards the length of the detention on remand and in relation to the proceedings before the Linz Court of Appeal. In its report of 3 July 1990, it expressed the opinion that there had been a violation of Article 5 §§ 3 and 4 (unanimously).

to why they considered the danger of his absconding to be decisive. In sum, the reasons put forward for dismissing Mr Toth's applications were both relevant and sufficient.

As for the conduct of the proceedings, the evidence disclosed that the Austrian courts had not in this instance acted with all necessary dispatch. The length of the proceedings seemed essentially not to have been attributable either to the complexity of the case or to the applicant's conduct: the offences of which Mr Toth had been accused were relatively commonplace and repetitive; as far as his appeals were concerned, some of which had been bound to fail from the outset, they had scarcely slowed down the examination of the case. In contrast, the speed of the investigation had suffered considerably from the transmission of the whole file to the relevant court, not only on the occasion of each application for release and each appeal by Mr Toth, but also on that of each request from the investigating judge or public prosecutor for the extension of the detention. Preferred to the use of copies, which was the practice in other Member States of the Council of Europe, such toing and froing of the file could hardly be reconciled with the importance attached to the right to liberty secured under Article 5 § 1 of the Convention. In conclusion, there had been a violation of Article 5 § 3 (held unanimously).

248. In Mr Toth's contention, the proceedings before the Linz Court of Appeal had not been adversarial either when it had ruled on his applications for release or when it had authorized the extension of his pre-trial detention, which constituted a breach of Article 5 § 4.

As far as the first point was concerned, the Government had raised a preliminary objection based on the claim that Mr Toth had not formulated before the Commission, within the six-month period provided for in Article 26 of the Convention, any complaint concerning his absence and that of his lawyer during the examination of his appeals against the dismissal of his applications for release by the Salzburg Regional Court. In the light of its case law and of all the evidence, the Court dismissed the objection (unanimously).

It therefore considered the merits of the complaint. The Linz Court of Appeal had ruled on Mr Toth's appeals without having summoned or heard him or his lawyer, whereas an official of the principal public prosecutor's office had attended the hearing and been able to reply to the court's questions. For his part, Mr Toth had not had the opportunity to contest properly the reasons invoked to justify the continuation of his detention. Any questions by the Court of Appeal would have enabled the representative of the prosecuting authority to put forward his views; they could have prompted, on the part of the accused, reactions warranting consideration by the members of the court before they reached their decision. As the proceedings had not ensured equal treatment, they had not been truly adversarial. There had therefore been a violation of Article 5 § 4 on this point (eight votes to one).

The applicant had made a similar complaint concerning the proceedings instituted in the Linz Court of Appeal by the investigating judge for the extension of the pre-trial detention. The Court held that Article 5 § 4 did not apply to the proceedings in question (eight votes to one), since their purpose was to fix a maximum period of detention and they were separate from the 'proceedings' which Mr Toth had been entitled to take under that provision.

249. As regards the application of Article 50, the Court dismissed the applicant's claim in respect of pecuniary damage on the ground that the entire period of pre-trial detention had been deducted from his sentence. As for non-pecuniary damage, it considered that the judgment constituted sufficient satisfaction (held unanimously).

Mr Toth had received legal aid before the Convention institutions and claimed nothing in respect of the proceedings conducted before them. The Court awarded him 7,853.40 schillings in respect of the costs and expenses relating to only one of his counsel before the Austrian courts (unanimously).[1]

250. *Summary bibliography*

COUSSIRAT-COUSTÈRE (V.).—'Jurisprudence de la Cour européenne des droits de l'homme de 1989 à 1991', *A.F.D.I.* 1991, pp. 581 *et seq.*

MARCUS-HELMONS (S.).—'La durée de la détention provisoire et la nécessité d'une procédure contradictoire lors des demandes d'élargissement', *R.T.D.H.* 1993, pp. 544–548.

MERRILLS (J.G.).—'Decisions on the European Convention on Human Rights during 1992', *B.Y.B.I.L.* 1992, pp. 556–558.

SUDRE (F.).—'Chronique de la jurisprudence de la Cour européenne des droits de l'homme—1991', *R.U.D.H.* 1992, Nos 1–2, p. 1 *et seq.*

WARBRICK (C.).—'The European Convention on Human Rights', *Y.E.L.* 1991, p. 561.

---

1 A circular of the Minister of Justice dated 5 October 1992 called on members of the public prosecutor's office no longer to exercise their right to participate in deliberations before appeal courts under Article 35 § 2 of the Code of Criminal Procedure, pending the adoption of an amendment submitted to Parliament in January 1993. It also made provision for the production of photocopies of the case file in order to avoid delays due to the transmission of the case file to another court in the event of an appeal.

259. Case of Clooth v. Belgium

Length of detention on remand

251. *Serge Clooth, a Belgian national, was arrested and remanded in custody on 13 September 1984 on suspicion of murder and arson. He was detained on remand until 17 November 1987, when the indictments division of the Brussels Court of Appeal upheld the order of the review chamber that he should be released on the ground that a 'reasonable time' within the meaning of Article 5 § 3 of the Convention had been exceeded. However, the applicant remained in custody on other charges.*

During the period in question, Mr Clooth's detention was extended by orders of the review chamber of the Brussels Court of First Instance made at intervals of approximately a month, which were upheld, when Mr Clooth appealed against them, by the indictments chamber. Mr Clooth also appealed unsuccessfully on points of law to the Court of Cassation on three occasions. On 6 November 1990, the review chamber held that there was no case to answer.

252. *In his application of 12 February 1987 to the Commission, Mr Clooth complained of the length of his detention on remand and relied on Article 5 § 3 of the Convention.*[1]

Judgment of 12 December 1991 *(Chamber) (Series A No. 225)*

253. The detention in question had lasted three years, two months and four days from the applicant's arrest on 13 September 1984 until 17 November 1987, the date of the judgment of the indictments chamber.

In extending Mr Clooth's detention, the national courts relied essentially on three grounds, in addition to the serious indications of his guilt:

First ground: the danger of repetition. The offences which had given rise to the applicant's previous convictions were not comparable, either in nature or in the degree of seriousness, to the charges preferred against him in the contested proceedings. In addition, an expert report of 21 June 1985 had described Mr Clooth as dangerous and mentioned

---

1 In its report of 10 July 1990, the Commission expressed the unanimous opinion that there had been a violation of Article 5 § 3.

the need for him to be taken into psychiatric care. The Court considered that such conclusions, submitted more than nine months after the beginning of the detention, ought to have persuaded the competent courts not to extend it without an accompanying therapeutic measure. The ground based on the risk of repetition did not therefore in itself justify the continuation of the detention after 21 June 1985.

Second ground: the needs of the inquiry and the risks of collusion. The Court acknowledged that this had been a very complicated case necessitating difficult inquiries. By his conduct, Mr Clooth had considerably impeded and indeed delayed them. The authorities' belief that he should consequently be kept in detention in order to prevent him from disrupting the inquiry even more was easy to understand, at least at the outset. In the long term, however, the requirements of the investigation did not suffice to justify the detention of a suspect: in the normal course of events the risks alleged diminished with the passing of time as the inquiries were effected, statements taken and verifications carried out. In this case, orders or decisions which specified the cause or the purpose of the inquiries under way precluding the release of the applicant had been rare. The majority of them merely mentioned, without more ado, the requirements of the investigation, when they were not simply confined to referring, by means of a stereotyped formula, to an earlier decision, adopted more than eleven months previously in one case. Where the needs of the investigation were invoked in such a general and abstract fashion they did not suffice to justify the continuation of detention. In addition, there had been delays in the investigation.

Third ground: the danger of absconding. It was on 16 April 1987 that the indictments division had first mentioned the danger of the applicant's absconding. The Court considered that such fears had become immaterial by the time at which they were expressed, not less than thirty-one months after the applicant's arrest. In addition, the decisions referring thereto did not put forward any argument capable of showing that those fears were well-founded.

In conclusion, the Court found that the length of Mr Clooth's detention on remand had exceeded the reasonable time referred to in Article 5 § 3 (unanimously).

254. As the Court considered that the question of the application of Article 50 was not ready for decision, it reserved its decision (unanimously).

255. *Summary bibliography*

Coussirat-Coustère (V.).—'Jurisprudence de la Cour européenne des droits de l'homme de 1989 à 1991', *A.F.D.I.* 1991, pp. 593 *et seq.*

MERRILLS (J.G.).—'Decisions on the European Convention on Human Rights during 1991', *B.Y.B.I.L.* 1992, pp. 558 and 559.

SCOUFLAIRE (I.).—'Le délai raisonnable de la détention provisoire', *R.T.D.H.* 1992, pp. 517–524.

SUDRE (F.).—'Chronique de la jurisprudence de la Cour européenne des droits de l'homme—1991', *R.U.D.H.* 1992, No. 1–2, p. 1 *et seq.*

WARBRICK (C.).—'The European Convention on Human Rights', *Y.E.L.* 1991, p. 560.

260. Case of Margareta and Roger Andersson v. Sweden

Restrictions on access between a mother and her son taken into public care

256. *Margareta Andersson and Roger Andersson, both Swedish citizens, were mother and son. Roger was born in 1974. On 17 July 1985, acting on the application of the Social Council of Växjö, the County Administrative Court of that town ordered Roger to be taken into care—he had already been taken into public care on a provisional basis the month before—under the 1980 Act containing Special Provisions on the Care of Young Persons, essentially on the ground that his mother was not capable of providing him with the support and assistance which he needed. Following periods spent in a clinic and at his mother's home, Roger was placed in a foster home in August 1986.*

On 6 August 1986, the social welfare authorities at Växjö decided, pursuant to section 16 § 1 of the 1980 Act, to prohibit access between the applicants until further notice. In a report of 15 August, the social welfare officer responsible for the case set out the reasons for the prohibition and recommended that it be continued as part of a care-plan for Roger. On 21 August, the Social Committee endorsed the proposed care-plan, including the prohibition of access. With the authorization of the social welfare authorities, the mother and son met on 5 October 1986 at a support foster home. Further meetings took place fairly irregularly, often at long intervals, under close supervision. As from June 1987, supervision was relaxed and in November 1987 Roger was allowed to visit his mother at her home. As from February 1988, it was decided to organize regular meetings. When Roger was hospitalized between 26 February and 3 May 1988, his mother visited him in hospital, where she stayed overnight. They spent approximately two weeks there altogether.

Between 6 August 1986 and 5 February 1988, contact by telephone or letter was prohibited. As from 5 February 1988, that prohibition was revoked on condition that communication by telephone was initiated by Roger. Mrs Andersson brought a number of appeals, most of them unsuccessful, before the administrative courts against the various restrictions on access.

257. In their application of 13 February 1987 to the Commission, Margareta and Roger Andersson relied on Articles 8 and 13 of the Convention; Roger also invoked Articles 2, 3, 4, 9, 10 and 25.[1]

Judgment of 25 February 1992 *(Chamber) (Series A No. 266–A)*

258. Were the interferences with the Andersson's right to respect for their family life and their correspondence 'in accordance with the law'? The Court answered this question in the affirmative. Since the total prohibition of access was only in force for a time—from 6 August 1986 until 5 October 1986—it had a basis in Swedish law, which afforded certain guarantees. Moreover, as interpreted by the administrative appeal courts, the relevant legislation empowered the social services to extend a ban on contacts to cover telephone calls and letters. Although only some of the relevant judgments pre-dated the judgments in the instant case, those which followed were in principle capable of illustrating the previous understanding of the law. Moreover, it was clear that the contested restrictions all concerned restrictions on access by telephone and by letter.

Since the restrictions had been aimed at protecting Roger's 'health or morals' and 'rights and freedoms', they had pursued legitimate aims with regard to Article 8.

The Court then considered whether the restrictions had been 'necessary in a democratic society'. Besides the fact that the applicants' right to visits had been severely restricted, they had also been prohibited from having any contact by mail or telephone during the period from 6 August 1986 to 5 February 1988. The measures relating to this period had been particularly far-reaching. They had to be supported by strong reasons and to be consistent with the ultimate aim of reuniting the Andersson family in order to be justified under Article 8 § 2. The reasons adduced by the Government were of a general nature. Although they were relevant, they did not sufficiently show that it had been necessary to deprive the applicants of almost every means of maintaining contact with each other for a period of approximately one and a half years. Indeed, it was questionable whether the measures were compatible with the aim of reuniting the applicants. The aggregate of the

---

1 On 10 October 1989, the Commission declared admissible the complaints relating to the prohibition of access and the absence of an effective remedy. In its report of 3 October 1990, the Commission expressed the opinion that there had been a violation of Article 8 (unanimously), but no violation of Article 13 with regard to Margareta Andersson (unanimously) or with regard to Roger Andersson (ten votes to two).

restrictions imposed had been disproportionate to the legitimate aims pursued and there had therefore been a breach of Article 8 (eight votes to one).

259. The Court considered that it was not necessary to consider whether Mrs Andersson had had an effective remedy before a national authority with regard to the restrictions on contacts, since that issue had not been pursued before it (held unanimously). It held that Article 13 had not been breached in the case of Roger (five votes to four).

260. Under Article 50, the Court awarded the applicants 50,000 Swedish kronor each for non-pecuniary damage and 125,000 Swedish kronor for costs and expenses (unanimously).

261. *Summary bibliography*

COUSSIRAT-COUSTÈRE (V.).—'La jurisprudence de la Cour européenne des droits de l'homme en 1992', *A.F.D.I.* 1992, pp. 629 *et seq.*

DECAUX (E.) and TAVERNIER (P.).—'Chronique de jurisprudence de la Cour européenne des droits de l'homme (année 1992)', *J.D.I.* 1993, pp. 715–718.

MERRILLS (J.G.).—'Decisions on the European Convention on Human Rights during 1992', *B.Y.B.I.L.* 1992, pp. 559–562.

SUDRE (F.), LEVINET (M.), PEYROT (B.) and ECOCHARD (B.).—'Chronique de la jurisprudence de la Cour européenne des droits de l'homme—1992', *R.U.D.H.* 1993, Nos 1–2, pp. 1 *et seq.*

TULKENS (F.).—'Le placement des mineurs et le droit au respect de la vie familiale', *R.T.D.H.* 1993, pp. 557–573.

WARBRICK (C.).—'The European Convention on Human Rights', *Y.E.L.* 1992, pp. 706–713.

261. Case of Pfeifer and Plankl v. Austria

Two Regional Court judges exercising investigative and judicial functions in turn in the same criminal proceedings; deletion of passages in a letter sent from one person in detention on remand to another

262. *In October 1983, following trial before the Klagenfurt Regional Court composed of two professional judges and two lay assessors, Heinrich Pfeifer was convicted of receiving stolen goods and unlawful possession of firearms and sentenced to three years' imprisonment. Before the trial, the President of the court informed him that the two judges were disqualified from sitting in the trial under the Code of Criminal Procedure on the ground that they had acted as investigating judges. Mr Pfeifer stated, without consulting his lawyer, that he would waive his right to lodge a plea of nullity on that ground. The defence did not raise that question at the trial. In February 1984, a plea of nullity lodged by Mr Pfeifer and an appeal against sentence were dismissed by the Supreme Court.*

263. *In summer 1983, a letter from Margrit Plankl to Mr Pfeifer (who were both in detention on remand) was censored by the investigating judge on the ground that passages in it were 'jokes of an insulting nature against prison officers' and therefore defamed officials in the exercise of their duty. During the subsequent proceedings, the court held that the method used (rendering the offending passages illegible) was unlawful, but considered the censorship to be justified as Mrs Plankl could justifiedly be suspected of the offence of insulting officials in the course of their duties.*

264. *In their application to the Commission of 23 September 1983, Mr Pfeifer and Mrs Plankl alleged various violations of Articles 3, 5, 6, 7, 8 and 13 of the Convention.*[1]

---

1 The Commission, by decisions of 13 May 1987, 15 December 1988 and 8 May 1989, declared the application inadmissible, apart from two complaints which it found admissible. In its report of 11 October 1990, it expressed the opinion that there had been violations of Article 6 § 1 (unanimously) and of Article 8 (ten votes to one).

Judgment of 25 February 1992 *(Chamber) (Series A No. 227)*

265. On the basis of well-established case law, the Court reaffirmed that it had jurisdiction to consider the Government's objections which had been rejected by the Commission (eight votes to one). It decided that the Government's objection to the effect that domestic remedies had not been exhausted should be joined to the merits on the ground that the question was inextricably linked with that of the validity of Mr Pfeifer's waiver of his right to lodge a plea of nullity (held unanimously).

266. In the Court's view, the applicant's two complaints under Article 6 § 1 coincided in substance. The provision under which a judge was disqualified from hearing a case if he had already had to deal with it as investigating judge, manifested the legislature's concern to remove all reasonable doubt as to the impartiality of trial courts. Its non-observance meant that Mr Pfeifer had been tried by a court whose impartiality was recognized by national law itself to be open to doubt.

Mr Pfeifer's waiver of his rights, which had been expressed forthwith and in the absence of his lawyer, was not valid under the Convention, even supposing that the rights in question could be waived by a defendant. In conclusion, the Court rejected the Government's preliminary objection and considered that there had been a violation of Article 6 § 1 (held unanimously).

267. With regard to Article 8, the Government raised a preliminary objection. The Court held that since the deletion of passages in a letter had affected both applicants at the same time, it appeared pointless to inquire whether one of them had exhausted domestic remedies with reference thereto, given that the other had undeniably done so without success (unanimously).

In the Court's view, there had been an interference with the exercise of the applicants' right to respect for their correspondence. It was based on Article 187(2) of the Code of Criminal Procedure and was aimed at ensuring the protection of the rights of others and the prevention of crime. The Court went on to consider whether it was necessary in a democratic society. Although some of the expressions used were doubtless rather strong ones, they were part of a private letter which should have been read by Mr Pfeifer and the investigating judge only. Although the deletion of passages was a less serious interference than the interception of correspondence, it was disproportionate and there had therefore been a violation of Article 8 (held unanimously).

268. Under Article 50, the Court rejected the applicants' claim for compensation for non-pecuniary damage because there was no causal link between the violations found in the present judgment and the duration and conditions of the applicants' detention (held unanimously).

The Court awarded Mr Pfeifer and Mrs Plankl 20,000 schillings and 1,500 schillings, respectively, for costs and expenses incurred in Austria and awarded them 60,000 schillings jointly for lawyer's fees in connection with the Strasbourg proceedings (unanimously).

269. *Summary bibliography*

COUSSIRAT-COUSTÈRE (V.).—'La jurisprudence de la Cour européenne des droits de l'homme en 1992', *A.F.D.I.* 1992, pp. 629 *et seq.*

DECAUX (E.) and TAVERNIER (P.).—'Chronique de jurisprudence de la Cour européenne des droits de l'homme (année 1992)', *J.D.I.* 1993, pp. 718 and 719.

MERRILLS (J.G.).—'Decisions on the European Convention on Human Rights during 1992', *B.Y.B.I.L.* 1992, pp. 562–564.

RENUCCI (J.-F.).—'Droit européen des droits de l'homme', *D.* 1992, sommaires commentés, pp. 331 and 332.

SUDRE (F.), LEVINET (M.), PEYROT (B.) and ECOCHARD (B.).—'Chronique de la jurisprudence de la Cour européenne des droits de l'homme—1992', *R.U.D.H.* 1993, Nos 1–2, pp. 1 *et seq.*

SWART (B.).—'The case law of the European Court of Human Rights in 1992', *E.J.C.* 1993, pp. 167 *et seq.*

WARBRICK (C.).—'The European Convention on Human Rights', *Y.E.L.* 1992, p. 732.

262. Case of Nibbio v. Italy
263. Case of Borgese v. Italy
264. Case of Biondi v. Italy
265. Case of Monaco v. Italy
266. Case of Lestini v. Italy

Length of civil proceedings

270. *Silvana Nibbio, Michelangelo Borgese, Ida Biondi, Angelina Monaco and Fernanda Lestini, who were all Italian nationals, were unemployed, with the exception of Ida Biondi, who was a housewife. Each of them sued the* Istituto Nazionale della Previdenza Sociale *(National Social Security Institution) in the Rome magistrate's court to obtain a declaration of his or her right to a disability pension.*

271. *In their applications to the Commission of 3 April, 15 April, 17 April, 14 May and 10 April 1987, the applicants complained of the length of the civil proceedings brought by them and relied on Article 6 § 1 of the Convention.*[1]

Judgments of 26 February 1992 *(Chamber) (Series A No. 228–A to E)*

272. The Court started by determining in each case the period to be taken into consideration for assessing whether the length of the proceedings had been reasonable:

Nibbio: just over nine years and three months (from the date on which proceedings had been brought in the magistrate's court; proceedings were still pending before the Court of Cassation);

Borgese: just over four years and ten months (from the date on which proceedings had been brought in the magistrate's court until the date when the Rome District Court's judgment on the appeal had become final);

Biondi: over five years and ten months (from the date on which proceedings had been brought in the magistrate's court to the date of the judgment of the Court of Human Rights as proceedings were still pending before the Rome District Court);

---

1 In its reports of 15 January 1991 (Nibbio, Borgese, Biondi and Monaco) and 5 March 1991 (Lestini), the Commission expressed the opinion that there had been a violation of Article 6 § 1 (unanimously).

Monaco: almost five years and nine months (from the date on which proceedings had been brought in the magistrate's court until the date when the Rome District Court's judgment on the appeal had become final);

Lestini: more than six years and nine months (from the date on which proceedings had been brought in the magistrate's court until the date when the Rome District Court's judgment on the appeal had become final).

The Court stressed that special diligence was necessary in employment disputes, which included pension disputes. It found that in Nibbio's case the magistrate's court had taken more than three years to give judgment—it did not appear to have displayed the diligence necessary to ensure that the expert appointed by it had carried out his task within the period prescribed—and that in each of the five cases the appeal proceedings had remained dormant for somewhat more or less than two years without any investigative measures having been taken. Consequently, there had been a violation of Article 6 § 1 (Nibbio: unanimously; Borgese: five votes to four; Biondi: unanimously; Monaco: unanimously; Lestini: six votes to three).

273. With regard to the application of Article 50, the Court held that there was no evidence that the violation had caused the applicants to sustain the alleged pecuniary damage (unanimously).

In respect of non-pecuniary damage, it awarded Mrs Nibbio 6,000,000 lire, Mr Borgese 3,000,000 lire, Mrs Biondi 5,000,000 lire, Mrs Monaco 5,000,000 lire and Mrs Lestini 3,000,000 (unanimously).

The Court awarded part payment of the costs and expenses incurred before the Convention institutions (2,000,000 lire to each applicant) (unanimously).

Lastly, the Court did not consider it appropriate to require the defendant State to pay default interest on the sums awarded (held unanimously).

274. *Summary bibliography*

COUSSIRAT-COUSTÈRE (V.).—'La jurisprudence de la Cour européenne des droits de l'homme en 1992', *A.F.D.I.* 1992, pp. 629 *et seq.*

MERRILLS (J.G.).—'Decisions on the European Convention on Human Rights during 1992', *B.Y.B.I.L.* 1992, pp. 564 and 565.

SUDRE (F.), LEVINET (M.), PEYROT (B.) and ECOCHARD (B.).—'Chronique de la jurisprudence de la Cour européenne des droits de l'homme—1992', *R.U.D.H.* 1993, Nos 1–2, pp. 1 *et seq.*

267. Case of G. v. Italy
268. Case of Andreucci v. Italy
269. Case of Arena v. Italy
270. Case of Cormio v. Italy

Length of civil proceedings

275. *G., Aldo Andreucci, Carlo Arena and Armando Cormio were Italian nationals. G. sued his former employer in the Rome magistrate's court for arrears of salary. Mr Andreucci brought an action for assault in the Rome District Court for injuries sustained in a dispute. Mr Arena brought an action for damages in the Rome magistrate's court for damage resulting from a traffic accident. Mr Cormio brought an action in the Rome District Court for the termination of an agreement for the sale of a building.*

276. *In their applications to the Commission of 6 March, 23 May, 10 September and 17 July 1987, the applicants complained of the length of the civil proceedings brought by them and relied on Article 6 § 1 of the Convention.*[1]

Judgments of 27 February 1992 *(Chamber) (Series A No. 228–F to I)*

277. The Court started by determining in each case the period to be taken into consideration for assessing whether the length of the proceedings had been reasonable. It took as the starting point the date of the action in the court and as the end of period the date on which the judgment became final (Arena) or could become final (G.) or the date on which the judgment was executed (Andreucci) or the date on which the case was struck out of the list (Cormio). It arrived at the following periods:

G.: just over four years;
Andreucci: more than four years and seven months;
Arena: more than five years; and
Cormio: more than five years and nine months.

---

1 In its reports of 5 December 1990 (G.), 15 January 1991 (Andreucci and Arena) and 5 March 1991 (Cormio), the Commission expressed the opinion that there had been a violation of Article 6 § 1 (unanimously).

The Court found that there had been delays, but they had not been so substantial as to constitute an infringement of Article 6 § 1 (held unanimously).

278. *Summary bibliography*

271. Case of Diana v. Italy
272. Case of Ridi v. Italy
273. Case of Casciaroli v. Italy
274. Case of Manieri v. Italy
275. Case of Mastrantonio v. Italy
276. Case of Idrocalce S.r.l. v. Italy
277. Case of Cardarelli v. Italy
278. Case of Golino v. Italy
279. Case of Taiuti v. Italy
280. Case of Maciariello v. Italy
281. Case of Manifattura FL v. Italy
282. Case of Steffano v. Italy
283. Case of Ruotolo v. Italy
284. Case of Vorrasi v. Italy
285. Case of Cappello v. Italy
286. Case of Caffè Roversi S.p.a. v. Italy
287. Case of Gana v. Italy
288. Case of Barbagallo v. Italy
289. Case of Cifola v. Italy
290. Case of Pandolfelli and Palumbo v. Italy
291. Case of Pierazzini v. Italy
292. Case of Tusa v. Italy
293. Case of Cooperativa Parco Cuma v. Italy
294. Case of Serrentino v. Italy
295. Case of Lorenzi, Bernardini and Gritti v. Italy
296. Case of Tumminelli v. Italy

Length of civil proceedings

279.   For each case, (a) the subject-matter of the action and (b) the outcome or the stage reached in the case is listed below against the applicant's name.

Giovanni **Diana**: (a) scope and conditions for the use of a right of way; (b) confirmation by the Genoa Court of Appeal of a judgment of the Savona District Court in the applicant's favour;

Antonio **Ridi**: (a) compensation for damage arising from the unlawful widening of a cart track crossing land and reinstatement of the track; (b) award of damages by the Venice Court of Appeal;

Rosina **Casciaroli**: (a) damages in respect of her husband's death in a road accident; (b) pending before the Venice Court of Appeal;

Anna Aurora **Manieri**: (a) recovery from a managing agent of real property inherited by the applicant; (b) pending before the Teramo District Court;

Alberto **Mastrantonio**: (a) compensation for damage resulting from a road traffic accident; (b) pending before the Teramo District Court;

Idrocalce S.r.l.: (a) recovery of a debt; (b) confirmation by the Lecce Court of Appeal of a judgment of the Taranto District Court dismissing the claim;

Achille **Cardarelli**: (a) compensation for damage caused to a flat by seepage of water; (b) pending before the Florence District Court;

Luigi **Golino**: (a) compensation for injury sustained in a road traffic accident; (b) award of damages by the District Court of Santa Maria Capua Vetere;

Renzo **Taiuti**: (a) spouses' rights and obligations as a result of divorce; (b) judgment of the Florence District Court;

Vittorio **Maciariello**: (a) spouses' rights and obligations as a result of divorce; (b) judgment of the District Court of Santa Maria Capua Vetere;

Manifattura FL (a limited company): (a) existence of a contract of sale; (b) pending before the Bologna Court of Appeal;

Silvia **Steffano**: (a) remuneration for serving on an examination board; (b) pending before the Consiglio di Stato (supreme administrative court);

Luigi **Ruotolo**: *(a) reinstatement in his job and compensation for dismissal; (b) pending before the Court of Cassation;*

Maria **Vorrasi**: *(a) proceedings for the division of the estate of the applicant's father; (b) pending before the Melfi District Court;*

Catarina **Cappello**: *(a) compensation for injury sustained in a road traffic accident; (b) dismissal by the Cagliari Court of Appeal of the defendants' appeal and increase in the damages awarded by the Tempio Pausania District Court;*

Caffè Roversi S.p.a.: *(a) recovery of a debt; (a) claim upheld by the Modena District Court;*

Serena **Gana**: *(a) spouses' rights and obligations resulting from separation; (b) confirmation by the Court of Cassation of the judgment of the Rome Court of Appeal dismissing the appeal of applicant's husband;*

Emilia **Barbagallo**: *(a) validity of an attachment of moveable property effected at the applicant's request in debt-recovery proceedings; (b) finding by the Messina District Court that the attachment was invalid in respect of one item of property but otherwise valid;*

Attilio **Cifola**: *(a) claim made against co-owners of a building for recognition of proprietary rights in part of that building; (b) claim upheld by the Rome District Court, subject to a right of way for the defendants;*

Gennaro **Pandolfelli** and Domenica **Palumbo**: *(a) right of way; (b) pending before the Court of Cassation;*

Paola **Pierazzini**: *(a) application for a settlement in respect of the applicant's holdings in companies which she claimed to have inherited from her father; (b) pending before the Tempio Pausania District Court;*

Antonio **Tusa**: *(a) claim for compensation for damage caused by a road traffic accident; (b) dismissal by the Palermo Court of Appeal of an appeal brought by one of the defendants and finding in favour of the applicant's cross-appeal;*

Cooperativa Parco Cuma: *(a) recovery of a debt; (b) pending before the Naples District Court;*

*Ignazio **Serrentino**: (a) compensation for injuries sustained in a road traffic accident; (b) pending before the Court of Cassation;*

*Giovanni **Lorenzi**, Ivano **Bernardini** and Alessio **Gritti**: (a) compensation for damage caused by flooding; (b) judgment of the Brescia Court of Appeal finding for the applicants quashed;*

*Salvatore **Tumminelli**: (a) claim for fees for professional services; (b) pending before the Caltanissetta District Court.*

280. *The applicants lodged their applications with the Commission at various dates between October 1985 and October 1987. They all complained of the length of the various civil proceedings and invoked Article 6 § 1 of the Convention.*[1]

Judgments of 27 February 1992 *(Chamber) (Series A Nos 229–A to I, 230–A to I and 231–A to H)*

281. The Court started by determining in each case the period to be taken into consideration for assessing whether the length of the proceedings had been reasonable:

Diana: eleven years and ten months;
Ridi: almost thirteen years;
Casciaroli: approximately fifteen years and eleven months;
Manieri: more than eight years and ten months;
Mastrantonio: more than thirteen years and ten months;
Idrocalce S.r.l.: nine years and eight and a half months;
Cardarelli: just over fourteen years and one month;
Golino: more than seven years and eight months;
Taiuti: eight and a half years;
Maciariello: four years and nine and a half months;
Manifattura FL: more than nine years and three months;
Steffano: just over nine years and two months;
Ruotolo: more than ten years and seven months;
Vorrasi: just over thirteen years and ten months;
Cappello: just over eleven years and four months;
Caffè Roversi S.p.a.: just over seven and a half years;

---

1 In its reports of 5 December 1990, 15 January 1991 and 5 and 6 March 1991, the Commission expressed the opinion that there had been violations of Article 6 § 1 (unanimously, except in the case of Serrentino, where the voting was nine votes to three).

Gana: twelve years;
Barbagallo: just over eight years and ten months;
Cifola: just over five years;
Pandolfelli and Palumbo: seventeen years and ten months;
Pierazzini: more than eight years;
Tusa: approximately eighteen years and two months;
Cooperativa Parco Cuma: more than eleven years and two months;
Serrentino: more than seven years and four months;
Lorenzi, Bernardini and Gritti: more than sixteen years and one month;
Tumminelli: more than twelve years and seven months.

The Court held that Article 6 § 1 had been violated (unanimously, except in the case of Ruotolo, where the voting was eight votes to one) after commenting on various aspects of the proceedings in question.

282.   Under Article 50, the Court awarded the following sums (unanimously):

Diana: 2,000,000 lire for non-pecuniary damage and 2,000,000 lire for costs and expenses;
Ridi: nothing, since the judgment constituted sufficient just satisfaction;
Casciaroli: 60,000,000 lire for non-pecuniary damage and 8,000,000 lire for costs and expenses;
Manieri: 20,000,000 lire for non-pecuniary damage and 2,609,500 lire plus 845 French francs for costs and expenses;
Mastrantonio: 10,000,000 lire for non-pecuniary damage and 2,606,000 lire plus 772 French francs for costs and expenses;
Idrocalce S.r.l.: 8,040,000 lire for costs and expenses; the Court held that it had no jurisdiction to order Italy to implement certain legislative measures;
Cardarelli: the Court held that it was unnecessary to apply Article 50;
Golino: 2,000,000 lire for non-pecuniary damage;
Taiuti: 2,000,000 lire for non-pecuniary damage and 327,500 lire for costs and expenses;
Maciariello: 2,000,000 lire for non-pecuniary damage;
Manifattura FL: 8,000,000 lire for costs and expenses;
Steffano: nothing, since the judgment constituted sufficient just satisfaction;
Ruotolo: 5,000,000 lire for non-pecuniary damage;
Vorrasi: 4,000,000 lire for costs and expenses;

Cappello: 10,000,000 lire for non-pecuniary damage and 3,000,000 lire for costs and expenses;

Caffè Roversi S.p.a.: 8,000,000 lire for costs and expenses;

Gana: 4,000,000 lire for non-pecuniary damage and 4,000,000 lire for costs and expenses;

Barbagallo: 1,734,430 lire for costs and expenses;

Cifola: the Court held that the finding of a violation constituted sufficient just satisfaction;

Pandolfelli and Palumbo: 5,000,000 lire for non-pecuniary damage and 3,850,000 lire for costs and expenses;

Pierazzini: 15,000,000 lire for non-pecuniary damage and 8,000,000 for costs and expenses;

Tusa: 10,000,000 lire for non-pecuniary damage and 2,000,000 for costs and expenses;

Cooperativa Parco Cuma: 3,090,334 lire for costs and expenses;

Serrentino: 10,000,000 lire for non-pecuniary damage and 4,710,000 lire for costs and expenses;

Lorenzi, Bernardini and Gritti: 2,000,000 lire for costs and expenses;

Tumminelli: 1,996,500 lire for costs and expenses.

283. *Summary bibliography*

COUSSIRAT-COUSTÈRE (V.).—'La jurisprudence de la Cour européenne des droits de l'homme en 1992', *A.F.D.I.* 1992, pp. 629 *et seq.*

MAURO (J.).—'Sur la voie de la compréhension et de l'indulgence en matière de lenteur de la justice?', *G.P.* 8–10 November 1992, chronique, p. 28.

MERRILLS (J.G.).—'Decisions on the European Convention on Human Rights during 1992', *B.Y.B.I.L.* 1992, pp. 565 and 566.

SUDRE (F.), LEVINET (M.), PEYROT (B.) and ECOCHARD (B.).—'Chronique de la jurisprudence de la Cour européenne des droits de l'homme—1992', *R.U.D.H.* 1993, Nos 1–2, pp. 1 *et seq.*

297. Case of Société Stenuit v. France

Fine imposed by the Minister of Economic and Financial Affairs after consulting the Competition Commission

284. *Stenuit, a company limited by shares incorporated under French law, undertook landscape-gardening projects. On 16 October 1981, the Minister of Economic and Financial Affairs imposed a fine of 50,000 French francs on it pursuant to the Order of 30 June 1945 on prices and the punishment of infringements of economic legislation. He accused it of having acted in concert with competitors with a view to sharing out various public contracts. He had previously consulted the Competition Commission, which had recommended a fine of twice the amount finally imposed.*

The applicant company appealed to the Minister to reconsider his decision, requesting application in its favour of the Amnesty Law of 4 August 1981, but the Minister dismissed this appeal on 1 February 1982 on the ground that the Amnesty Law did not cover administrative penalties. On 2 April 1982 the applicant company appealed against this decision to the Conseil d'Etat. The appeal was dismissed on 22 June 1984.

285. *In its application to the Commission of 20 December 1984, Stenuit complained on the basis of Article 6 § 1 of the Convention that its case had not been heard by an independent tribunal responsible for examining the justification of the criminal charge brought against it.*[1]

Judgment of 27 February 1992 *(Chamber) (Series A No. 232–A)*

286. By letter dated 12 December 1991, the applicant company informed the Court of its wish to 'withdraw'. The Government were consulted and expressed the view that the case should be struck out of the list, especially since, in their opinion, the President of the Republic's Order No. 86–1243 of 1 December 1986 on free prices and competition, which provided in particular for the creation of a Competition Council, had to a large extent remedied the problems of principle raised by the Commission in its report.

---

1 In its report of 30 May 1991, the Commission expressed the unanimous opinion that there had been a violation of Article 6 § 1.

287. The applicant's decision constituted a 'fact of a kind to provide a solution of the matter'. In view of the fact that the Court could discern no reason of *ordre public* (public policy) for continuing the proceedings, the case should be struck out of the list (Rules of Court, Rule 49 §§ 2 and 4) (held unanimously).

288. *Summary bibliography*

Coussirat-Coustère (V.).—'La jurisprudence de la Cour européenne des droits de l'homme en 1992', *A.F.D.I.* 1992, pp. 629 *et seq.*

Decaux (E.) and Tavernier (P.).—'Chronique de jurisprudence de la Cour européenne des droits de l'homme', *J.D.I.* 1993, pp. 719 and 720.

Goy (R.).—'L'affaire Stenuit c. France', *Cahier du CREDHO* No. 1, 1994, pp. 51–59.

Mello (X.A. de).—'Droit de la concurrence et droits de l'homme', *R.T.D.E.* 1993, pp. 601–633.

Merrills (J.G.).—'Decisions on the European Convention on Human Rights during 1992', *B.Y.B.I.L.* 1992, p. 566.

Renucci (J.-F.).—'Droit européen des droits de l'homme', *D.* 1993, sommaires commentés, pp. 385 and 386.

Sudre (F.).—'L'arrêt de la Cour européenne des droits de l'homme du 27 février 1992, Société Stenuit c. France : à propos des droits . . . de l'entreprise', *Cahiers de droit de l'entreprise* 1992, No. 4, p. 26.

Sudre (F.), Levinet (M.), Peyrot (B.) and Ecochard (B.).—'Chronique de la jurisprudence de la Cour européenne des droits de l'homme—1992', *R.U.D.H.* 1993, Nos 1–2, pp. 1 *et seq.*

Swart (B.).—'The case-law of the European Court of Human Rights in 1992', *E.J.C.* 1993, pp. 167 *et seq.*

298. Case of Birou v. France

Length of detention on remand

289. *Roland Birou, a French national suspected of having taken part in two armed robberies, was charged and remanded in custody by an investigating judge at Aix-en-Provence on 23 July 1983.*

He submitted a series of unsuccessful applications for release to the indictments division of the Aix-en-Provence Court of Appeal (judgments of 12 December 1984 and 27 August 1985) and to the Bouches-du-Rhône Assize Court (judgments of 16 April, 19 June and 28 October 1986, 28 January and 1 October 1987 and 7 January 1988). On 30 June 1987, the applicant's appeal to the Court of Cassation against the judgment of 28 January 1987 on grounds of formal defects was dismissed. On 3 October 1988, the Court of Cassation quashed for want of jurisdiction the indictments division's decision of 23 June 1988 dismissing a further application for release by Mr Birou. The case was remitted to the Assize Court, which granted the application on 19 October 1988. Two days later, the court convicted the applicant and sentenced him to eight years' imprisonment; the period spent in detention on remand fell, by operation of law, to be deducted from the term of imprisonment.

290. *In his application to the Commission of 16 September 1987, Mr Birou alleged that the length of his detention on remand had exceeded the 'reasonable time' required under Article 5 § 3 of the Convention.[1]*

Judgment of 27 February 1992 *(Chamber) (Series A No. 232–B)*

291. The French Government sent the Registrar a document setting out a friendly settlement, which the applicant's lawyer confirmed that his client accepted, under which the Government stated that it was prepared to pay Mr Birou compensation of 30,000 French francs.

292. The Court took formal note of the friendly settlement. It decided to strike the case out of the list (unanimously), since it discerned no reason of *ordre public* why it should not be struck out (Rules of Court, Rule 49 §§ 2 and 4).

---

1 In its report of 17 April 1991, the Commission expressed the opinion that there had been a violation of Article 5 § 3 (unanimously).

293. *Summary bibliography*

COUSSIRAT-COUSTÈRE (V.).—'La jurisprudence de la Cour européenne des droits de l'homme en 1992', *A.F.D.I.* 1992, pp. 629 *et seq.*

KOERING-JOULIN (R.).—'Les affaires Birou et Tomasi et la détention avant jugement', in *Le droit français et la Convention européenne des droits de l'homme. 1974–1992*, Kehl, Engel, 1994, pp. 185–195.

MERRILLS (J.G.).—'Decisions on the European Convention on Human Rights during 1992', *B.Y.B.I.L.* 1992, pp. 566 and 567.

SUDRE (F.), LEVINET (M.), PEYROT (B.) and ECOCHARD (B.).—'Chronique de la jurisprudence de la Cour européenne des droits de l'homme—1992', *R.U.D.H.* 1993, Nos 1–2, pp. 1 *et seq.*

SWART (B.).—'The case-law of the European Court of Human Rights in 1992', *E.J.C.* 1993, pp. 167 *et seq.*

299. Case of B. v. France

Non-recognition in law of the new sexual identity of a post-operative transsexual

294. *The applicant, who was born in 1935 in Algeria, was registered as being of male sex, with the forenames Norbert Antoine. She adopted female behaviour from a very early age, since she looked female and was considered as a girl by her family. After completing her military service, she moved to Paris, where she was still living at the time of the proceedings and working in the entertainment industry. She was treated for depression between 1963 and 1967. She then underwent hormone therapy which feminized her appearance. She underwent a sex-change operation in Morocco in 1972, after which she lived with a man, whom she hoped to marry.*

In 1978, she brought proceedings for a declaration that she was of the female sex and for the rectification of her birth certificate so as to indicate her change of sex and her new forenames, Lyne Antoinette. The Libourne tribunal de grande instance dismissed her action in November 1979. Appeals to the Bordeaux Court of Appeal and to the Court of Cassation were dismissed in May 1985 and March 1987 respectively. Her official papers, including her passport, identity card and driving licence, were made out in the names of 'Norbert B.' and her social security card bore the code number used for males.

295. *In her application of 28 September 1987 to the Commission, Ms B. complained of the refusal of the French authorities to recognize her true sexual identity, in particular their refusal to allow her the change of civil status sought. She relied on Articles 3, 8 and 12 of the Convention.*[1]

Judgment of 25 March 1992 *(Plenary Court) (Series A No. 232–C)*

296. The Commission asked the Court to declare inadmissible the two objections entered by the Government. To examine them would render more burdensome the proceedings of the Convention institutions,

---

1 The Commission declared the application admissible on 13 February 1990, with the exception of the complaint based on Article 12. In its report of 6 September 1990, it expressed the opinion that there had been a violation of Article 8 (seventeen votes to one) but not of Article 3 (fifteen votes to three).

and create a further lack of equality between governments and applicants, as the latter were not able to appeal against findings of inadmissibility by the Commission.

The Court saw no reason, as matters stood, for abandoning a line of case law which had been followed constantly for over twenty years and had found expression in a large number of judgments. It therefore considered that it had jurisdiction to examine the Government's preliminary objections (sixteen votes to five).

297.   The Court found that the applicant had complained in substance of a violation of her right to respect for her private life before the Libourne *tribunal de grande instance* and the Bordeaux Court of Appeal. The Court of Cassation had not declared the ground of appeal inadmissible on the grounds of novelty. The Court therefore dismissed the objection of non-exhaustion of domestic remedies (unanimously).

The applicant had put to the Court of Cassation a point of law relating to Article 8. There was moreover no consistent case law in existence at the time to show in advance that the applicant's appeal was pointless. An appeal to the Court of Cassation was after all in principle one of the remedies which should be exhausted in order to comply with Article 26 and had the effect at the very least of postponing the starting-point of the six-month period. Accordingly, the Court dismissed the objection that the application was out of time (unanimously).

298.   According to the applicant, the refusal to recognize her true sexual identity infringed her right to respect for her private life guaranteed by Article 8. By failing to allow the indication of her sex to be corrected in the civil status register and on her official identity documents, the French authorities had forced her to disclose intimate personal information to third parties and caused her great difficulties in her professional life.

The Court noted first of all that the notion of 'respect' was not clear-cut. In determining whether or not a positive obligation existed, regard must be had to the fair balance that had to be struck between the general interest and the interests of the individual.

The Court considered that it was undeniable that attitudes towards transsexualism had changed, science had progressed and increasing importance was attached to the problem. It noted, however, in the light of the relevant studies carried out and work done by experts in this field, that there still remained some uncertainty as to the essential nature of transsexualism and that the legitimacy of surgical intervention in such cases was sometimes questioned. The legal situations which resulted were moreover extremely complex and there was as yet no sufficiently broad consensus between the member States of the Council of Europe to persuade the Court to reach opposite conclusions to those in its *Rees*[1] and *Cossey*[2] judgments concerning the United Kingdom.

The Court found that there were noticeable differences between France and England with reference to their law and practice on civil status, change of forenames, the use of identity documents, etc.

Nothing would have prevented the insertion, once judgment had been given, in Miss B.'s birth certificate of an annotation so as to reflect the applicant's present position. Numerous French first instance and appeal courts had already ordered similar insertions in the case of other transsexuals. The Court of Cassation had adopted a contrary position in its case law, but this could change. It was true that the applicant had undergone the surgical operation abroad, without the benefit of all the medical and psychological safeguards which were required in France. The operation had nevertheless involved the irreversible abandonment of the external marks of Miss B.'s original sex. The Court considered that the applicant's manifest determination was a factor which was sufficiently significant to be taken into account, together with other factors, with reference to Article 8.

The judgments supplied to the Court by the Government did indeed show that non-recognition of the change of sex did not necessarily prevent the person in question from obtaining a new forename which would better reflect his or her physical appearance. However, this case law was not settled at the time when the Libourne and Bordeaux courts had given their rulings. Indeed, it did not appear to be settled even at the time of this judgment, as the Court of Cassation had apparently never had an occasion to confirm it. The refusal to allow the applicant the change of forename requested by her was also a relevant factor from the point of view of Article 8.

The Court considered that the inconveniences complained of by the applicant in connection with the discrepancy between her legal sex as stated in various official papers and her appearance reached a sufficient degree of seriousness to be taken into account for the purposes of Article 8.

299. The Court thus reached the conclusion, on the basis of the above-mentioned factors which distinguished the present case from the

1 *Rees v. the United Kingdom*, Series A No. 106; see Vol. I of this work, 672–677.
2 *Cossey v. the United Kingdom*, Series A No. 184; see Vol. II of this work, 466–471.

Rees and *Cossey* cases and without its being necessary to consider the applicant's other arguments, that she found herself daily in a situation which, taken as a whole, was not compatible with the respect due to her private life. Consequently, even having regard to the State's margin of appreciation, the fair balance which had to be struck between the general interest and the interests of the individual had not been attained, and there had thus been a violation of Article 8 (fifteen votes to six). The respondent State had several means to choose from for remedying this state of affairs. It was not the Court's function to indicate which was the most appropriate.

300. Before the Commission, Miss B. had also claimed that she had been treated by the law in a manner which was both inhuman and degrading within the meaning of Article 3. She had not repeated this complaint since, and the Court did not consider it necessary to examine the question of its own motion (held unanimously).

301. The Court considered that Miss B. had suffered non-pecuniary damage as a result of the situation found in the present judgment to be contrary to the Convention, and awarded her 100,000 French francs under that head (fifteen votes to six). In contrast, it dismissed her claims in respect of pecuniary damage: her difficulty in finding work because of having to disclose her circumstances, although real, was not insurmountable (held unanimously).

The Court held that the respondent State had to reimburse the applicant the entire amount claimed for costs and expenses (35,000 French francs) (fifteen votes to six).

302. *Summary bibliography*

COUSSIRAT-COUSTÈRE (V.).—'La jurisprudence de la Cour européenne des droits de l'homme en 1992', *A.F.D.I.* 1992, pp. 629 *et seq.*

DECAUX (E.) and TAVERNIER (P.).—'Chronique de jurisprudence de la Cour européenne des droits de l'homme', *J.D.I.* 1993, pp. 720–723.

DURY-GHERRAK (F.).—'L'affaire B. c. France (transsexuels)', *Cahiers du CREDHO* No. 1, 1994, pp. 61–78.

GARÉ (T.).—'Note', *J.C.P.* 1992, édition générale, II, No. 21955, pp. 417–419.

HAUSER (J.).—'Jurisprudence française en matière de droit civil', *R.T.D.C.* 1992, pp. 540 and 541.

LOMBOIS (C.).—'La position française sur le transsexualisme devant la Cour européenne des droits de l'homme', *D.* 1992, chronique, pp. 323–326.

MARGUÉNAUD (P.-J.).—'Note', *D.* 1993, jurisprudence, pp. 103–108.

MERRILLS (J.G.).—'Decisions on the European Convention on Human Rights during 1992', *B.Y.B.I.L.* 1992, pp. 567–569.

RENUCCI (J.-F.).—'Droit européen des droits de l'homme', *D.* 1992, sommaires commentés, pp. 325 and 326.

RUBELLIN-DEVICHI (J.).—'L'état de la personne', in *Le droit français et la Convention européenne des droits de l'homme. 1974–1992*, Kehl, Engel, 1994, pp. 165–184.

SUDRE (F.), LEVINET (M.), PEYROT (B.) and ECOCHARD (B.).—'Chronique de la jurisprudence de la Cour européenne des droits de l'homme—1992', *R.U.D.H.* 1993, Nos 1–2, pp. 1 *et seq.*

WARBRICK (C.).—'The European Convention on Human Rights', *Y.E.L.* 1992, pp. 703–706.

ZWAAK (L.).—'Noot', *NJCM–Bulletin* 1993, pp. 81–83.

300. Case of Campbell v. the United Kingdom

Control by prison authorities in Scotland of a prisoner's correspondence to and from his solicitor and with the European Commission of Human Rights

303. *Thomas Campbell, a British national, was serving a sentence of life imprisonment for murder after being found guilty on 10 October 1984 by the Glasgow High Court; the judge recommended that he should serve not less than twenty years' imprisonment.*

Mr Campbell was initially classified as a Category B prisoner, but following an incident at Peterhead Prison he was charged with a number of offences and re-classified as a Category A prisoner, the classification pertaining to the group of inmates requiring the highest degree of security. Despite the abandonment of those charges by the Crown, he remained a Category A prisoner from 4 November 1985 until 9 March 1988. Since then he had been a Category B prisoner again. He had been detained in, inter alia, Perth and Peterhead Prisons, which were situated at a considerable distance from the offices of his solicitor in Glasgow. At the time of the proceedings, he was serving his sentence in the Special Unit in Barlinnie Prison, Glasgow.

Since his imprisonment the applicant had been advised by his solicitor in respect of legal proceedings which were contemplated or pending and other matters. He had also corresponded with the Commission. Since 1985, his correspondence with his solicitor and the Commission was regularly opened and scrutinized by the prison authorities. The applicant made several complaints to the Home Secretary and to the Scottish Home and Health Department, but was informed that all correspondence would be opened under standing instructions, with the exception of complaints to the Commission.

304. *Mr Campbell lodged his application with the Commission on 14 January 1986. He complained of interference by the prison authorities with his correspondence with his solicitor, the Commission and a Member of Parliament, contrary to Articles 8 and 10 of the Convention. He also complained of a violation of Article 6 § 1 of the Convention in that he had been refused legal aid to challenge in the civil courts the actions of the prison authorities in respect of his correspondence.[1]*

1 On 8 November 1989, the Commission found admissible the complaint that correspondence with his solicitor and the Commission had been opened by the prison authorities in violation of his right to respect for

Judgment of 25 March 1992 *(Chamber) (Series A No. 233)*

305. The Court found that there had been an interference with Mr Campbell's right to respect for his correspondence to and from his solicitor. That interference was based on the Prison Rules and orders providing for the opening and reading of such letters which were designed to maintain order and prevent the commission of criminal offences.

As far as the necessity for such measures was concerned, the Court saw no reason to distinguish between the different categories of correspondence with lawyers: such letters, whatever their purpose, concerned matters of a private and confidential character and, in principle, were privileged under Article 8. Accordingly, the prison authorities might open a letter from a lawyer to a prisoner when they had reasonable cause to believe that it contained an illicit enclosure which the normal means of detection had failed to disclose, but the letter should only be opened and should not be read. Suitable guarantees preventing the reading of the letter should be provided—for instance, opening the letter in the presence of the prisoner. As for the reading of a prisoner's mail to and from a lawyer, it should be permitted only in exceptional circumstances when the authorities had reasonable cause to believe that the privilege was being abused in that the contents of the letter endangered prison security or the safety of others or were otherwise of a criminal nature.

The European Agreement relating to persons participating in proceedings of the European Commission and Court of Human Rights of 6 May 1969, referred to by the Government, was not to be interpreted as limiting the obligations assumed under the Convention. Further,

correspondence under Article 8. It declared the other complaints inadmissible but decided to examine further whether the opening of the applicant's correspondence with the Commission was compatible with Article 25 § 1 of the Convention.

In its report of 12 July 1990, the Commission expressed the opinion that:
(a) there had been a violation of Article 8 in respect of the opening of the applicant's correspondence with his solicitor concerning contemplated and pending proceedings (eleven votes to one);
(b) there had been a violation of Article 8 in respect of the opening of the applicant's general correspondence with his solicitor (eight votes to four);
(c) there had been a violation of Article 8 as a result of the opening of the applicant's correspondence with the Commission (eleven votes to one); and
(d) the applicant had not been hindered in the effective exercise of the right of individual petition under Article 25 § 1 (ten votes to two).

correspondence was a different medium of communication which was afforded separate protection under Article 8. The right to respect for correspondence was of special importance in a prison context where it might be more difficult for a legal adviser to visit his client in person because, as in the present case, of the distant location of the prison. Finally, the objective of confidential communication with a lawyer could not be achieved if this means of communication were the subject of automatic control.

The Government argued that the professional competence and integrity of solicitors could not always be relied on. If it were known that all correspondence with solicitors would pass unopened, there existed a risk that they would become the target of pressure from those wishing to smuggle forbidden material into or out of prisons. The Court was not persuaded by these submissions. The possibility of examining correspondence for reasonable cause provided a sufficient safeguard against the possibility of abuse. Solicitors were subject to disciplinary sanctions for professional misconduct and it had not been suggested that there had been any reason to suspect the applicant's solicitor. In sum, the mere possibility of abuse was outweighed by the need to respect the confidentiality attached to the lawyer-client relationship. As there had been no pressing social need for the opening and reading of the applicant's correspondence with his solicitor, there had been a breach of Article 8 in this respect (eight votes to one).

306. There remained the question of the correspondence with the Commission. Mr Campbell had not shown that his letters to the Commission had been opened, since the prison authorities habitually subjected such letters to no scrutiny.

In contrast, there had been an interference with the applicant's correspondence from the Commission: that interference was based, *inter alia*, on Standing Orders, which were published and available and pursued the legitimate aim of 'the prevention of disorder or crime'. The Court considered that it was of importance to respect the confidentiality of mail, not only to, but from the Commission, since it might concern allegations against the prison authorities or prison officials. Moreover, there had been no compelling reason why such letters from the Commission should have been opened. The risk, adverted to by the Government, of Commission stationery being forged in order to smuggle prohibited material or messages into prison, was so negligible that it must be discounted. Accordingly, the Court found that the opening of letters from the Commission had not been 'necessary in a democratic society' within the meaning of Article 8 § 2 and there had therefore been a breach of Article 8 (eight votes to one).

307. The question of compliance with Article 25 § 1 had been raised by the Commission of its own motion but had not been pursued before the Court. There was therefore no reason to examine this matter (held unanimously).

308. The Court awarded the applicant all the sum claimed in respect of costs and expenses incurred in Scotland and before the Convention institutions, and dismissed his claim for compensation for damage (unanimously).[1]

309. *Summary bibliography*

Coussirat-Coustère (V.).—'La jurisprudence de la Cour européenne des droits de l'homme en 1992', *A.F.D.I.* 1992, pp. 629 *et seq.*

Merrills (J.G.).—'Decisions on the European Convention on Human Rights during 1992', *B.Y.B.I.L.* 1992, pp. 569–572.

Sudre (F.), Levinet (M.), Peyrot (B.) and Ecochard (B.).—'Chronique de jurisprudence de la Cour européenne des droits de l'homme—1992', *R.U.D.H.* 1993, Nos 1–2, pp. 1 *et seq.*

Swart (B.).—'The case-law of the European Court of Human Rights in 1992', *E.J.C.* 1993, pp. 167 *et seq.*

Warbrick (C.).—'The European Convention on Human Rights', *Y.E.L.* 1992, pp. 737–739.

---

1 An administrative circular which entered into force on 12 October 1992 describes in detail the steps to be taken in scrutinizing a prisoner's correspondence with his lawyer or the Convention institutions. Henceforward, except in exceptional cases, such correspondence will be dispatched and received without being read.

301. Case of Beldjoudi v. France

Deportation order against an Algerian, born in France of parents who were then French, and married to a Frenchwoman

310. *Mohand Beldjoudi was born in France in 1950 of parents of Algerian origin, who, like him, lost their French nationality in 1963 following the independence of Algeria. He was brought up in France, where he had always lived, either with his parents or with Martine Teychene, a French citizen, whom he married in 1970. His parents and his five brothers and sisters were all resident in France.*

In 1969, 1974, 1977 and 1978 he was convicted of various offences, including aggravated theft, for which he was sentenced to eight years' imprisonment.

In November 1979, the Minister of the Interior issued a deportation order against Mr Beldjoudi, on the ground that his presence on French territory was a threat to public order (ordre public). *In April 1988, the Versailles Administrative Court dismissed Mr Beldjoudi's application for the order to be set aside. In the meantime, he had been convicted of several other offences in 1986. In 1983 and 1984, he unsuccessfully applied for a certificate of French nationality. On 18 January 1991, the* Conseil d'Etat *dismissed Mr Beldjoudi's application contesting the Administrative Court's judgment and the deportation order. The deportation order had not yet been carried out and Mr Beldjoudi was subject to an order to reside in Hauts-de-Seine. He was also placed under judicial supervision following a charge of aggravated receiving of stolen property.*

311. *In their application of 28 March 1986 to the Commission, Mr and Mrs Beldjoudi alleged that the deportation order against Mr Beldjoudi had violated several provisions of the Convention: Article 8, by infringing their right to respect for their private and family life; Article 3, as the probable refusal of the Algerian authorities to issue Mr Beldjoudi with a passport allowing him to leave Algeria would constitute inhuman and degrading treatment; Article 14 in conjunction with Article 8, by discriminating on the grounds of Mr Beldjoudi's religious beliefs or ethnic origin; Article 9, by interfering with their freedom of thought, conscience and religion; and Article 12, by infringing their right to marry and to found a family.*[1]

1 In its report of 6 September 1990, the Commission expressed the opinion that the deportation of Mr Beldjoudi would violate his and his spouse's

Judgment of 26 March 1992 *(Chamber) (Series A No. 234–A)*

312. In the Court's view, enforcement of the deportation order would constitute an interference by a public authority with the exercise of the applicants' right to respect for their family life, as guaranteed by paragraph 1 of Article 8.

313. It therefore had to be determined whether the expulsion in issue would comply with the conditions of paragraph 2.

The legal basis for the interference was clearly section 23 of the Order of 2 November 1945 relating to the conditions of entry and residence of aliens in France.

The interference in issue was directed at aims which were entirely in accordance with the Convention: the prevention of disorder and the prevention of crime.

As regards the question as whether the interference had been necessary in a democratic society, Mr Beldjoudi's criminal record appeared much worse than that of Mr Moustaquim[1] and the Court therefore held that it should be examined whether the other circumstances of the case—relating to both applicants or to one of them only—were enough to compensate for this important fact.

Having regard to the applicants' age and the fact that they had no children, the interference in question primarily affected their family life as spouses. They had been married in France over twenty years ago and had always had their matrimonial home there. The periods when Mr Beldjoudi had been in prison had not terminated their family life, which remained under the protection of Article 8.

Mr Beldjoudi, the person immediately affected by the deportation, had been born in France of parents who were then French, and had had French nationality until 1 January 1963. A year after his first conviction but nine years before the adoption of the deportation order, he had manifested the wish to recover French nationality. Secondly, he had married a Frenchwoman and his close relatives had all had French nationality for a time, and had resided in France for several decades. Finally, he had spent his whole life—over forty years—in France, had been educated in French and appeared not to know Arabic. He did not seem to have any links with Algeria apart from that of nationality.

right to respect for their family life within the meaning of Article 8 (twelve votes to five), but would not violate Article 3 (unanimously), and that there had not been a failure to comply with the requirements of Article 14 in conjunction with Article 8 (unanimously) or with those of Articles 9 and 12 (unanimously).

1 *Moustaquim v. Belgium*, Series A No. 193; see Chapter 192, above.

As for Mrs Beldjoudi, she had been born in France of French parents, had always lived there and had French nationality. Were she to follow her husband after his deportation, she would have to settle abroad, presumably in Algeria, a State whose language she probably did not know. To be uprooted like this could cause her great difficulty in adapting, and there might be real practical or even legal obstacles.

Consequently, the decision to deport Mr Beldjoudi, if put into effect, would not be proportionate to the legitimate aim pursued and would therefore violate Article 8 (seven votes to two).

314. Having reached this conclusion, the Court did not have to examine whether the deportation would also infringe the applicants' right to respect for their private life.

315. In view of the finding that Article 8 had been violated, the Court did not consider it necessary also to examine the complaint that there had been discrimination contrary to Article 14 in the enjoyment of the applicants' right to respect for their family life (eight votes to one).

316. Since the complaints based on Articles 3, 9 and 12 had not been mentioned before the Court, it did not consider it necessary to examine them of its own motion (eight votes to one).

317. Mr and Mrs Beldjoudi alleged that they had suffered damage and claimed 10,000,000 French francs. The Court held that the applicants must have suffered non-pecuniary damage, but that the present judgment provided them with sufficient compensation in this respect (unanimously).

The Court considered it reasonable to award 60,000 French francs in respect of costs and expenses incurred before the Strasbourg institutions (held unanimously).

318. *Summary bibliography*

CARLIER (J.-Y.).—'Vers l'interdiction d'expulsion des étrangers intégrés?', *R.T.D.H.* 1993, pp. 449–466.

COUSSIRAT-COUSTÈRE (V.).—'La jurisprudence de la Cour européenne des droits de l'homme en 1992', *A.F.D.I.* 1992, pp. 629 *et seq.*

DECAUX (E.) and TAVERNIER (P.).—'Chronique de jurisprudence de la Cour européenne des droits de l'homme (année 1992)', *J.D.I.* 1993, pp. 723–727.

LESCÈNE (P.).—'Affaires Beldjoudi c. France et Vijayanathan et Pusparajah c. France', *Cahiers du CREDHO*, no. 1, 1994, pp. 81–84.

MERRILLS (J.G.).—'Decisions on the European Convention on Human Rights during 1992', *B.Y.B.I.L.* 1992, pp. 572–574.

PETTITI (L.-E.).—'Droits de l'homme', *R.S.C.D.P.C.* 1992, pp. 635–644.

SUDRE (F.), LEVINET (M.), PEYROT (B.) and ECOCHARD (B.).—'Chronique de la jurisprudence de la Cour européenne des droits de l'homme—1992', *R.U.D.H.* 1993, Nos 1–2, pp. 1 et seq.

SWART (B.).—'The case-law of the European Court of Human Rights in 1992', *E.J.C.* 1993, pp. 167 *et seq.*

WARBRICK (C.).—'The European Convention on Human Rights', *Y.E.L.* 1992, pp. 698–702.

302. Case of Editions Périscope v. France

Length of proceedings for damages before administrative courts

319. *In October 1960, Editions Périscope, a limited company incorporated under French law, applied to the Joint Committee on Press Publications and Press Agencies for a certificate of registration for its review* 'Périscope de l'usine et du bureau' *in order to secure the tax concessions and preferential postal charges accorded to the press. The Joint Committee rejected the application and three others made in 1961, 1964 and 1966 on the ground that the main purpose of the review was not to provide technical information but to act as a link between suppliers of goods and potential purchasers through a 'readers' service'. In 1974 the company stopped trading.*

In March 1976, the company appealed to the competent ministers for compensation from the State for the damage caused by the refusal to register its review. As its appeal was impliedly rejected, it brought an action in the Tribunal administratif *of Paris on 12 November 1976 for compensation for the loss of 200 million French francs which it had allegedly incurred on account of the discriminatory treatment afforded to it by comparison with its competitors in the matter of tax concessions and preferential postal charges. The* Tribunal administratif *dismissed its action on 27 April 1981. The company's appeal of 15 July 1981 to the Conseil d'Etat was dismissed on 22 March 1985.*

320. *In its application of 20 September 1985 to the Commission, Editions Périscope alleged two violations of Article 6 § 1 of the Convention: the administrative courts had not heard its case within a reasonable time; the* Conseil d'Etat *had not constituted an impartial tribunal.*[1]

Judgment of 26 March 1992 *(Chamber) (Series A No. 234–B)*

321. The Court first ruled on the applicability of Article 6 § 1, which was denied by the Government. The Court found that there had been a dispute relating to a right: the trial had concerned compensation for the

---

1 On 12 April 1989, the Commission declared the application admissible as regards the length of the proceedings, but inadmissible as regards the other complaint. In its report of 11 October 1990, it expressed the opinion that there had been a violation of Article 6 § 1 (seventeen votes to two).

damage which the State had allegedly caused Editions Périscope by refusing to accord to it the reductions granted to competing undertakings; the arguments relating to faults committed by the public authorities were sufficiently tenable, since the two courts before which the case had come had found the application admissible and ruled on the merits of the case. In addition, the Court observed that the subject-matter of the applicant company's action was 'pecuniary' in nature and that the action was founded on an alleged infringement of rights which were likewise pecuniary rights. The right in question was, therefore, a 'civil right', notwithstanding the origin of the dispute and the fact that the administrative courts had jurisdiction. Accordingly Article 6 § 1 applied in this case (held unanimously).

322. The period to be taken into consideration had begun on 12 November 1976, when the proceedings had been instituted in the Paris Administrative Court. It had ended on 22 March 1985 when the *Conseil d'Etat* had delivered its judgment. It had therefore covered more than eight years.

Examination of the two decisions of the administrative courts showed that the case was not a particularly complex one. In addition, the applicant company had done nothing to delay the conclusion of the proceedings; on the contrary, it had made repeated attempts to compel the ministries concerned to submit their memorials more rapidly. Accordingly, a 'reasonable time' had been exceeded and there had been a violation of Article 6 § 1 (held unanimously).

323. Under Article 50, the Court rejected the claim for compensation for pecuniary damage (unanimously) on the ground that it could discern no causal connection between the violation of Article 6 § 1 and the dismissal of the company's action by the national courts.

Making an assessment on an equitable basis, the Court awarded the applicant company 50,000 French francs for the costs and expenses which it had incurred in the proceedings in the French courts and at the Strasbourg institutions.

324. *Summary bibliography*

Coussirat-Coustère (V.).—'La jurisprudence de la Cour européenne des droits de l'homme en 1992', *A.F.D.I.* 1992, pp. 629 *et seq.*

Decaux (E.) and Tavernier (P.).—'Chronique de jurisprudence de la Cour européenne des droits de l'homme', *J.D.I.* 1993, pp. 727 and 728.

Merrills (J.G.).—'Decisions on the European Convention on Human Rights during 1992', *B.Y.B.I.L.* 1992, pp. 574 and 575.

RENUCCI (J.-F.).—'Droit européen des droits de l'homme', *D*. 1993, sommaires commentés, pp. 385 and 386.

SUDRE (F.), LEVINET (M.), PEYROT (B.) and ECOCHARD (B.).—'Chronique de la jurisprudence de la Cour européenne des droits de l'homme—1992', *R.U.D.H.* 1993, Nos 1–2, pp. 1 *et seq.*

TAMION (E.).—'Affaire Editions Périscope c. France et affaire X c. France', *Cahiers du CREDHO* No. 1, 1994, pp. 129–134.

303. Case of Farmakopoulos v. Belgium

Appeal against an order rendering foreign arrest warrants enforceable

325. *Georgios Farmakopoulos, a Greek national, was apprehended by the police on 11 January 1985 while he was passing through Belgium. On the next day he was provisionally detained by order of an investigating judge in Antwerp with a view to his extradition following a radiogram from the United Kingdom authorities stating that there were two warrants out for his arrest, one for murder and one for theft. As the warrants had not been served on Mr Farmakopoulos within the statutory time-limit, the Belgian Minister of Justice ordered on 26 January that the applicant should leave Belgian territory and remain in custody pending his departure for Argentina, the country to which he had finally chosen to be deported.*

On 6 February, the day before his intended departure, the applicant was served with copies of the two British warrants and the order of the Committals Chamber of the Antwerp Court of First Instance giving them effect, and was imprisoned once more with a view to his extradition. On 19 March, the Indictments Chamber of the Antwerp Court of Appeal held that his appeal of 8 February against the order giving effect to the warrants was inadmissible as being out of time (the appeal had to be lodged within twenty-four hours). On 21 May, the Court of Cassation dismissed his appeal. He was extradited to the United Kingdom in August, where he was sentenced to life imprisonment, and then handed over to the Greek authorities.

326. *In his application to the Commission of 4 July 1985, Mr Farmakopoulos complained* inter alia *that he had been unable to take proceedings in accordance with Article 5 § 4 of the Convention against the Committals Chamber's order of 6 February 1985.*[1]

Judgment of 27 March 1992 *(Chamber) (Series A No. 235–A)*

327. Despite being approached by the registry on several occasions over a period of eight months, Mr Farmakopoulos had shown no interest

---

1 On 8 September 1990, the Commission declared the complaint based on Article 5 § 4 admissible and the remainder of the application inadmissible. In its report of 4 December 1990, it expressed the opinion that there had been a violation of Article 5 § 4 (unanimously).

in the proceedings pending before the Court. The Court considered that this was an implied withdrawal, constituting a 'fact of a kind to provide a solution of the matter' within the meaning of Rule 49 § 2 of the Rules of Court. In addition, it discerned no reason of *ordre public* (public policy) for continuing the proceedings (Rules of Court, Rule 49 § 4). These were concerned to a large extent with questions of fact, whose examination would furthermore require additional information on the facts of the case. The Court did not consider it necessary to seek to obtain this information of its own motion. Accordingly, it held that the case should be struck out of the list (unanimously).

328. *Summary bibliography*

COUSSIRAT-COUSTÈRE (V.).—'La jurisprudence de la Cour européenne des droits de l'homme en 1992', *A.F.D.I.* 1992, pp. 629 *et seq.*

DECAUX (E.) and TAVERNIER (P.).—'Chronique de jurisprudence de la Cour européenne des droits de l'homme (année 1992)', *J.D.I.* 1993, pp. 728 and 729.

LAMBERT (P.).—'La présomption de désistement', *J.T.* 1992, p. 726.

MERRILLS (J.G.).—'Decisions on the European Convention on Human Rights during 1992', *B.Y.B.I.L.* 1992, p. 576.

SUDRE (F.), LEVINET (M.), PEYROT (B.) and ECOCHARD (B.).—'Chronique de la jurisprudence de la Cour européenne des droits de l'homme—1992', *R.U.D.H.* 1993, Nos 1–2, pp. 1 *et seq.*

SWART (B.).—'The case-law of the European Court of Human Rights in 1992', *E.J.C.* 1993, pp. 167 *et seq.*

304. Case of X v. France

Length of compensation proceedings brought first before the administrative authorities and then in the administrative courts

329. *Mr X, a haemophiliac, underwent several blood transfusions between September 1984 and January 1985 in a public hospital in Paris. On 21 June 1985, it was discovered that he had been infected with the AIDS virus. After an association of haemophiliacs had unsuccessfully tried to obtain compensation from the State for the damage suffered by its members who had been so infected, Mr X addressed a claim for compensation on 1 December 1989 to the Minister of Health as a preliminary to bringing an action in the administrative courts. He sought compensation on the ground that he had been infected as a result of the negligent delay of the Minister in implementing appropriate rules for the supply of blood products. The Director General for Health rejected Mr X's claim on 30 March 1990. On 30 May, Mr X filed an application for compensation in the Paris Administrative Court. On 20 December 1991, the court dismissed his application. Mr X appealed to the Paris Administrative Court of Appeal on 20 January 1992. He died on 2 February 1992.*

330. *In his application to the Commission of 19 February 1991, Mr X complained about the length of the proceedings which he had brought and relied on Article 6 § 1 of the Convention.*[1]

Judgment of 31 March 1992 *(Chamber) (Series A No. 234–C)*

331. Although Mr X had died, his parents expressed the wish to continue the proceedings. In accordance with its case law, the Court accepted that his father and mother were entitled to take his place.

332. Unlike the Government, the Court considered that the outcome of the proceedings was decisive for private rights and obligations and that hence Article 6 § 1 was applicable.

333. The period to be taken into consideration had already lasted more than two years. It had begun on 1 December 1989, when the

1 In its report of 17 October 1991, the Commission expressed the opinion that there had been a violation of Article 6 § 2 (thirteen votes to two).

applicant had filed his preliminary claim with the Minister of Health and Social Protection, and had not yet ended.

In the Court's opinion, the case was one of some complexity and investigations could have been necessary to determine the State's liability and its extent. However, the Government had probably been aware for a long time that proceedings were imminent. It would have been possible for them to obtain much of the relevant information and they ought to have commissioned an objective report on the question of liability immediately after the commencement of the cases against them.

The applicant's conduct could not be reproached. Already in his memorial of 11 July 1990, Mr X had emphasized the consequences for him of the discovery that he was HIV positive and of the 'idea that he was potentially afflicted with an incurable disease'; in his supplementary memorial of 29 October 1990 he had stated that his condition had deteriorated. Even before the disclosure on 10 September 1991 that he had developed full-blown AIDS, he had therefore drawn the administrative court's attention to the worsening of his condition and the immediacy of the grave risks with which he was confronted. The Court added that the choice of the means of redress for obtaining compensation had fallen to the applicant alone.

As regards the conduct of the national authorities, the Court took the view that what had been at stake in the contested proceedings had been of crucial importance for the applicant, having regard to the incurable disease from which he had been suffering and his reduced life expectancy. Any delay had been liable to render the question to be resolved by the court devoid of purpose. In short, exceptional diligence had been called for in this instance in particular as it was a controversy the facts of which the Government had been familiar with for some months and the seriousness of which must have been obvious to them. Yet the administrative court had not used its powers to make orders for the speeding up of the progress of the proceedings, although from 29 October 1990 it had been aware of the deterioration in Mr X's health. In particular, it had been under a duty, as soon as the case had been referred to it, to conduct inquiries into the liability of the State and either to enjoin forcefully the Minister to produce his defence memorial or to give judgment without it.

A reasonable time had already been exceeded when the judgment had been delivered on 18 December 1991. There had therefore been a violation of Article 6 § 1 (held unanimously).

334. With regard to the application of Article 50, the Court found that the applicant had undeniably sustained non-pecuniary damage. It awarded his parents the whole of the 150,000 French francs claimed (unanimously).

It accepted (unanimously) the whole of Mr X's claims for costs and expenses incurred at Strasbourg (30,000 French francs).

335. *Summary bibliography*

APOSTOLIDIS (A.).—'Note', *La semaine juridique* 1992, jurisprudence, No. 21896, pp. 262–264.

COUSSIRAT-COUSTÈRE (V.).—'La jurisprudence de la Cour européenne des droits de l'homme en 1992', *A.F.D.I.* 1992, pp. 629 *et seq.*

DECAUX (E.) and TAVERNIER (P.).—'Chronique de jurisprudence de la Cour européenne des droits de l'homme', *J.D.I.* 1993, pp. 729–731.

LAMBERT (P.).—'En bref de Strasbourg. Le drame du sang contaminé', *J.T.* 1993, p. 13.

MÉRAL (C.).—'L'arrêt X . . . c. France ou une nouvelle approche du "délai raisonnable"', *G.P.* 9–10 April 1993, doctrine, pp. 56–62.

MERRILLS (J.G.).—'Decisions on the European Convention on Human Rights during 1992', *B.Y.B.I.L.* 1992, pp. 576–578.

RENUCCI (J.-F.).—'Droit européen des droits de l'homme', *D.* 1993, sommaires commentés, pp. 325 and 326.

SUDRE (F.), LEVINET (M.), PEYROT (B.) and ECOCHARD (B.).—'Chronique de la jurisprudence de la Cour européenne des droits de l'homme—1992', *R.U.D.H.* 1993, Nos 1–2, pp. 1 *et seq.*

TAMION (E.).—'Affaire Editions Périscope c. France et affaire X c. France', *Cahiers du CREDHO* No. 1, 1994, pp. 129–134.

305. Rieme v. Sweden

Prohibition on a father removing his daughter, who had been placed in public care, from a foster home

336. *Antero Rieme, a Finnish citizen, resided at Tumba, Sweden. He had a daughter, Susanne, whose mother Ms J., cohabited with him from January 1976 until March 1977 and had legal custody of Susanne from the time of her birth on 28 October 1976.*

In September 1977, the Southern Social District Council of Södertälje decided that Susanne should be taken into public care pursuant to the Child Welfare Act 1960 because of her mother's alcohol problems. Shortly afterwards, the child was placed in a foster home.

After an order of the District Court of Södertälje of September 1983, confirmed by the Svea Court of Appeal, transferring the custody of Susanne to Mr Rieme, the latter asked the Social Council on 11 October 1983 to terminate the public care of Susanne and to grant him access to her at regular intervals. The Social Council granted his first request on 16 October 1984, but decided, pursuant to section 28 of the Social Services Act 1980, to prohibit him from removing the child from the foster home on the ground that there was a risk 'which was not of a minor nature' that her mental health could be harmed. It did not rule on the question of visits. On 25 January 1985, the Stockholm County Administrative Court dismissed Mr Rieme's appeal against the order prohibiting him from removing the child. On 2 August 1985, the Administrative Court of Appeal dismissed his appeal against that judgment and, on 26 March 1986, the Supreme Administrative Court refused him leave to appeal.

Mr Rieme and his daughter met from time to time at the foster home and at his home. As from May 1986, she stayed overnight every second weekend with the applicant and his wife and spent parts of her summer holiday with them. In August 1989, she moved in with her father. The prohibition remained in force until 20 November 1989, when it was terminated by the Social Council at the father's request. However, the child returned to the foster home around Christmas 1989.

337. *In his application of 28 July 1986 to the Commission, Mr Rieme invoked Articles 6, 8 and 17 of the Convention.*[1]

---

1 On 5 July 1989, the Commission declared the complaints under Article 6 inadmissible and the remainder of the application admissible. In its report of 2 October 1990, the Commission expressed the opinion that there had been a violation of Article 8 (eight votes to five).

Judgment of 22 April 1992 *(Chamber) (Series A No. 226–B)*

338. The Court rejected the Government's preliminary objection to the effect that, since Mr Rieme had not exhausted domestic remedies, the Convention institutions' examination under Article 8 should not extend beyond 26 March 1986, which was the date of the last decision by a domestic court (unanimously).

339. The implementation of the public care order and the subsequent prohibition on removal had clearly constituted an interference with the applicant's right to respect for family life.

The Court went on to consider whether it was justified. The Court held that it was 'in accordance with the law': there was no indication that the social welfare authorities had acted in a manner inconsistent with Swedish law or with a view to hindering reunion. Taking the safeguards against arbitrary interferences into consideration, the scope of the discretion conferred on the authorities by relevant Swedish legislation appeared to the Court to be reasonable and acceptable for the purposes of Article 8. The access arrangements had been the result of co-operation and it had not been established that access arrangements had been imposed upon the applicant contrary to Swedish law.

In addition, the Court found that the interference was aimed at protecting the 'health' and 'the rights and freedoms' of the child.

Lastly, the interference was held to be necessary in a democratic society. The reasons for the decision of 16 October 1984 prohibiting removal and the court rulings confirming that decision were relevant and sufficient; they provided a valid justification for the prohibition on removal and its maintenance in force, at least up to 26 March 1986.

In sum, there had been no violation of Article 8 (held unanimously).

340. *Summary bibliography*

COUSSIRAT-COUSTÈRE (V.).—'La jurisprudence de la Cour européenne des droits de l'homme en 1992', *A.F.D.I.* 1992, pp. 629 *et seq.*

DECAUX (E.) and TAVERNIER (P.).—'Chronique de jurisprudence de la Cour européenne des droits de l'homme (année 1992)', *J.D.I.* 1993, pp. 715–718.

MERRILLS (J.G.).—'Decisions on the European Convention on Human Rights during 1992', *B.Y.B.I.L.* 1992, pp. 578–579.

SUDRE (F.), LEVINET (M.), PEYROT (B.) and ECOCHARD (B.).—'Chronique de la jurisprudence de la Cour européenne des droits de l'homme—1992', *R.U.D.H.* 1993, Nos 1–2, pp. 1 et seq.

WARBRICK (C.).—'The European Convention on Human Rights', *Y.E.L.* 1992, pp. 706–713.

306. Case of Vidal v. Belgium

Failure by a court of appeal, hearing a case remitted to it by the Court of Cassation, to call witnesses proposed by the defence

341. *In February 1983, Frans Vidal, a warder in a Belgian prison, was charged with helping a prisoner to escape by providing him with a revolver. In 1984, he was acquitted by the Namur Criminal Court and then sentenced to three years' imprisonment by the Liège Court of Appeal. The Court of Cassation subsequently quashed the judgment on grounds relating to the composition of the Court of Appeal. In December 1985, the Brussels Court of Appeal, to which the case had been remitted, sentenced Mr Vidal to four years' imprisonment. It had invited the applicant to gather the testimony of four defence witnesses, but had not summoned them to appear. An appeal to the Court of Cassation was ultimately dismissed.*

342. *In his application to the Commission of 7 July 1986, Mr Vidal complained of breaches of paragraphs 1, 2 and 3(d) of Article 6 of the Convention.*[1]

Judgment of 22 April 1992 *(Chamber) (Series A No. 235–B)*

343. The applicant had originally been acquitted after several witnesses had been heard. When the appellate judges had substituted a conviction, they had no fresh evidence; apart from the oral statements of Mr Vidal and the prisoner, they had based their decision entirely on the documents in the case-file. Moreover, the Brussels Court of Appeal had given no reasons for its rejection, which had been merely implicit, of the submissions requesting it to call the four witnesses.

To be sure, it was not the function of the Court to express an opinion on the relevance of the evidence thus offered and rejected, nor more generally on Mr Vidal's guilt or innocence, but the complete silence of the judgment of the Brussels Court of Appeal on the point in question was not consistent with the concept of a fair trial which was the basis of Article 6. This was all the more the case as the Brussels Court of

---

1 On 14 May 1990, the Commission declared one of the complaints admissible. In its report of 14 January 1991, it expressed the opinion that there had been a violation of paragraph 1 of Article 6, in conjunction with paragraph 3(d) (twelve votes to one).

Appeal had increased the sentence which had been passed at first instance. The Court therefore held that there had been a violation of Article 6 (eight votes to one).

344. At the applicant's request, the Court reserved the question of just satisfaction (unanimously).

Judgment of 28 October 1992 *(Chamber)—Application of Article 50 (Series A No. 235–E)*

345. The Court held that the applicant had suffered non-pecuniary damage and also a loss of real opportunities. It awarded him 250,000 Belgian francs under this head (unanimously).

346. The Court awarded Mr Vidal 300,000 Belgian francs for costs and expenses relating to the proceedings before the Court of Cassation and the Convention institutions (unanimously).

347. *Summary bibliography*

COUSSIRAT-COUSTÈRE (V.).—'La jurisprudence de la Cour européenne des droits de l'homme en 1992', *A.F.D.I.* 1992, pp. 629 *et seq.*

MERRILLS (J.G.).—'Decisions on the European Convention on Human Rights during 1992', *B.Y.B.I.L.* 1992, pp. 579 and 580.

PETTITI (L.-F.).—'Droits de l'homme', *R.S.C.D.P.C.* 1992, pp. 798 and 799.

SUDRE (F.), LEVINET (M.), PEYROT (B.) and ECOCHARD (B.).—'Chronique de la jurisprudence de la Cour européenne des droits de l'homme—1992', *R.U.D.H.* 1993, Nos 1–2, pp. 1 *et seq.*

SWART (B.).—'The case-law of the European Court of Human Rights in 1992', *E.J.C.* 1993, pp. 167 *et seq.*

307. Case of Castells v. Spain

Conviction of a member of Parliament for insulting the Government

348. *In 1979, Miguel Castells, a lawyer and a senator elected on the list of Herri Batasuna, a political grouping supporting independence for the Basque country, published an article in the weekly magazine* Punto y Hora de Euskalherria *in which he drew to the attention of the public the attacks made by armed groups against Basques. In his opinion, those groups acted with impunity and the Government was responsible.*

The prosecuting authorities instituted criminal proceedings against Mr Castells. Following the withdrawal of his parliamentary immunity by the Senate, the Supreme Court charged him on 7 July 1981 with having proffered serious insults against the Government contrary to Article 161 of the Criminal Code. In May 1982, the Supreme Court refused to admit evidence put forward by the defence intended to establish that the information contained in the article was true and common knowledge, on the ground that those grounds did not constitute a defence to the offence in question.

On 31 October 1983, the Criminal Division of the Supreme Court sentenced Mr Castells to a year's imprisonment and to an accessory penalty of disqualification from holding any public office and exercising a profession during that period. It considered that, as a senator, Mr Castells was bound to confine himself to the means provided for in the Senate's rules of procedure for criticizing the Government, and he had not done so. The article also exhibited an intention to defame.

On 10 April 1985, the Constitutional Court dismissed an appeal (amparo) *which Mr Castells had brought on 22 November 1983. However, it stayed the accessory penalty (the term of imprisonment had been suspended by the Supreme Court on 6 December 1983).*

349. *In his application of 17 September 1985 to the Commission, Mr Castells relied on Articles 6, 7, 10 and 14 of the Convention.*[1]

---

1 On 9 May 1989, the Commission dismissed the complaints based on Articles 6 and 7 as inadmissible. On 7 November 1989, it found the remainder of the application admissible. In its report of 8 January 1991, it expressed the opinion that there had been a violation of Article 10 (nine votes to three) and that no separate question arose under Article 14 in conjunction with Article 10 (unanimously).

Judgment of 23 April 1992 *(Chamber) (Series A No. 236)*

350.   In the first place, the Court reaffirmed that it had jurisdiction to entertain the preliminary objection raised by the Government to the effect that Mr Castells had failed to exhaust domestic remedies (unanimously).

The Government contended that the applicant had failed specifically to raise in the Constitutional Court the complaint concerning the alleged breach of the right to freedom of expression.

The Court dismissed the objection on the ground that the applicant had invoked before the Constitutional Court, at least in substance, the complaints relating to Article 10 of the Convention (unanimously). He had done so both before the Supreme Court and subsequently before the Constitutional Court. In the first place, the applicant had claimed the right, in his capacity as a senator, to criticize the Government's action, a right which was manifestly inherent in the freedom of expression in the specific case of elected representatives. The applicant had also invoked both his right to be presumed innocent and his right to adduce evidence capable of establishing the accuracy of his statements. In so doing, he had formulated a complaint which was plainly linked to the alleged violation of Article 10 of the Convention. Lastly, Mr Castells had cited Article 20 of the Constitution (enshrining the right to freedom of expression) in summarizing his complaints and had referred in a number of written communications to the Constitutional Court, in connection with the defence of truth, to his right to receive and communicate true information.

351.   As regards the merits of the complaint, the Court held that the penalties of which Mr Castells complained were an 'interference' with the exercise of freedom of expression. The legal basis for that interference was Articles 161 and 162 of the Criminal Code. In addition, the Supreme Court's rejection of the defence of truth had been foreseeable having regard to the wording of the relevant provision, despite the absence of precedents. In the circumstances obtaining in Spain in 1979, the proceedings instituted against the applicant had been brought for the 'prevention of disorder' and not only for the 'protection of the reputation of others'.

Were the restrictions necessary? Freedom of expression was especially important for an elected representative of the people, since he represented his electorate, drew attention to their preoccupations and defended their interests. As Mr Castells had expressed his views in a periodical, the Court pointed to the pre-eminent role of the press in a State governed by the rule of law. Freedom of the press afforded the public one of the best means of discovering and forming an opinion of the ideas and attitudes of their political leaders, gave politicians the opportunity to reflect and comment on the preoccupations of public opinion and enabled everyone to participate in free political debate. Freedom of political debate was not absolute in nature. The limits of permissible criticism were wider with regard to the Government than in relation to a private citizen, or even a politician. The dominant position which the Government occupied made it necessary for it to display restraint in resorting to criminal proceedings. Nevertheless it remained open to the competent State authorities to adopt measures, even of a criminal law nature, intended to react appropriately and without excess to defamatory accusations devoid of foundation or formulated in bad faith.

The applicant could not, in the criminal proceedings brought against him for insulting the Government, plead the defences of truth and good faith. Although Mr Castells had offered on several occasions to establish that the facts recounted by him were true and well known, the Supreme Court had declared such evidence inadmissible and the Constitutional Court had taken the view that it was a question of ordinary statutory interpretation and as such fell outside its jurisdiction. The Court considered that many of the assertions were susceptible to an attempt to establish their truth, just as Mr Castells could reasonably have tried to demonstrate his good faith. Consequently, the interference was not necessary in a democratic society. In sum, there had been a violation of Article 10 (held unanimously).

352. Mr Castells also claimed that he had been a victim of discrimination because other persons had expressed similar views without any criminal sanctions having been imposed on them. As this question was not a fundamental aspect of the case, the Court did not consider it necessary to deal with it separately (held unanimously).

353. With regard to Article 50, the Court observed that it did not have jurisdiction to order Governments, for instance, to publish a summary of the Court's judgment in the press or to remove any reference to the applicant's conviction in the central criminal records.

The Court dismissed Mr Castells' claims for compensation (unanimously) on the grounds that the existence of pecuniary damage had not been made out and the finding of a violation set out in the judgment constituted in itself sufficient just satisfaction for any non-pecuniary damage.

The Court awarded Mr Castells 1,000,000 pesetas for costs and expenses incurred in the Spanish courts and 2,000,000 pesetas for those incurred in Strasbourg (unanimously).

354. *Summary bibliography*

COUSSIRAT-COUSTÈRE (V.).—'La jurisprudence de la Cour européenne des droits de l'homme en 1992', *A.F.D.I.* 1992, pp. 629 *et seq.*

DECAUX (E.) and TAVERNIER (P.).—'Chronique de jurisprudence de la Cour européenne des droits de l'homme', *J.D.I.* 1993, pp. 731–733.

MERRILLS (J.G.).—'Decisions on the European Convention on Human Rights during 1992', *B.Y.B.I.L.* 1992, pp. 581–583.

PETTITI (L.-E.).—'Droits de l'homme', *R.S.C.D.P.C.* 1992, pp. 796–798.

SUDRE (F.), LEVINET (M.), PEYROT (B.) and ECOCHARD (B.).—'Chronique de la jurisprudence de la Cour européenne des droits de l'homme—1992', *R.U.D.H.* 1993, Nos 1–2, pp. 1 *et seq.*

SWART (B.).—'The case-law of the European Court of Human Rights in 1992', *E.J.C.* 1993, pp. 167 *et seq.*

VELDE (J. van der).—'Noot', *NJCM–Bulletin* 1993, pp. 431–435.

VELDE (J. van der).—'Het publieke debat en de vrijheid van meningsuiting', *NJCM–Bulletin* 1993, pp. 418–439.

WARBRICK (C.).—'The European Convention on Human Rights', *Y.E.L.* 1991, pp. 720–727.

308. Case of Megyeri v. Germany

Failure to appoint a lawyer to assist a mental patient in proceedings concerning his possible release from detention in a psychiatric hospital

355. *Zoltan Itsvan Megyeri, a Hungarian citizen, had been living in Germany since 1975. In March 1983, the Cologne Regional Court ordered that he be detained in a psychiatric hospital: he had performed acts constituting criminal offences, but could not be held responsible because he was suffering from a schizophrenic psychosis with signs of paranoia. The court further held that Mr Megyeri posed a danger to the general public because it had to be expected that he would commit further serious unlawful acts.*

Mr Megyeri subsequently made applications to several other authorities concerning his confinement. On 7 July 1986, the Aachen Regional Court decided against releasing him on probation on the basis of a written report by three experts, according to which his state of mental health had further deteriorated, and of its own impression of him. It considered that the applicant's continued detention was proportionate to the aim pursued of protecting the public. On 2 September 1986, the Cologne Court of Appeal dismissed an appeal brought by Mr Megyeri. On 10 February 1987, the Federal Constitutional Court declined to accept for adjudication the applicant's constitutional complaint on the ground that it did not offer sufficient prospects of success. The applicant was not represented by counsel in the 1986 proceedings before the Aachen and Cologne courts.

After the 1987 court decision Mr Megyeri was placed under guardianship and in 1989 he was released on probation. Thereafter he lived in an open ward of a psychiatric hospital.

356. *In his application to the Commission of 22 October 1986, Mr Megyeri raised complaints concerning a number of different sets of proceedings relating to his detention in a mental institution; he invoked Articles 2 to 14 and 17 and 18 of the Convention, Articles 1 and 2 of Protocol No. 1 and Article 2 of Protocol No. 4.*[1]

---

1 On 12 October 1988, the Commission adjourned its examination of the complaint about the 1986 proceedings and declared the remainder of the application inadmissible. On 10 July 1989, the Commission decided to strike it off its list. However, on 13 February 1990 it restored the complaint to the list and declared it admissible. In its report of 26 February 1991, it expressed the opinion that there had been a violation of Article 5 § 4 (unanimously).

Judgment of 12 May 1992 *(Chamber) (Series A No. 237–A)*

357. The Court concluded from the principles which emerged from its case law that where a person was confined in a psychiatric institution on the ground of the commission of acts which constituted criminal offences but for which he could not be held responsible on account of mental illness, he should—unless there were special circumstances—receive legal assistance in subsequent proceedings relating to the continuation, suspension or termination of his detention.

It went on to analyse Mr Megyeri's case in the light of the underlying facts and the issues which fell for determination in the 1986 proceedings relating to his possible release. Nothing in that analysis revealed that this was a case in which legal assistance had been unnecessary. Nor did the Court perceive any other special circumstances which would lead it to a different conclusion. Consequently, the failure to appoint a lawyer to assist the applicant in those proceedings constituted a breach of Article 5 § 4 (held unanimously).

358. Under Article 50, the Court dismissed a claim made on behalf of the applicant by his guardian for compensation for pecuniary damage, on the ground that no causal link had been established between the violation of Article 5 § 4 and the alleged pecuniary damage (held unanimously). In contrast, it awarded the applicant 5,000 Deutsche Mark in respect of non-pecuniary damage (unanimously).

The Court awarded in respect of lawyer's fees for the proceedings before the Strasbourg institutions the sum claimed (21,000 Deutsche Mark) less the amount granted by way of legal aid (6,900 French francs) (held unanimously).

359. *Summary bibliography*

COUSSIRAT-COUSTÈRE (V.).—'La jurisprudence de la Cour européenne des droits de l'homme en 1992', *A.F.D.I.* 1992, pp. 629 *et seq.*

MERRILLS (J.G.).—'Decisions on the European Convention on Human Rights during 1992', *B.Y.B.I.L.* 1992, pp. 583 and 584.

SUDRE (F.), LEVINET (M.), PEYROT (B.) and ECOCHARD (B.).—'Chronique de la jurisprudence de la Cour européenne des droits de l'homme—1992', *R.U.D.H.* 1993, Nos 1–2, pp. 1 *et seq.*

SWART (B.).—'The case-law of the European Court of Human Rights in 1992', *E.J.C.* 1993, pp. 167 *et seq.*

309. Case of Lüdi v. Switzerland

Telephone interception combined with the intervention of an undercover agent in the Canton of Berne

360. *On 15 March 1984, the investigating judge in Laufen (Canton of Berne), acting on information received from the German police to the effect that Ludwig Lüdi was planning to buy drugs in Switzerland, opened a preliminary investigation into him and ordered his telephone conversations to be monitored. The police decided that one of their officers should pass himself off as a potential purchaser of cocaine. After five meetings with this undercover agent, the applicant was arrested on 1 August 1984 and charged with unlawful trafficking in drugs.*

On 4 June 1985, the Laufen District Court sentenced the applicant to three years' imprisonment on seven charges under the Federal Drugs Law. In order to preserve the undercover agent's anonymity, the court declined to call him as a witness on the ground that the records of the telephone interception and the undercover agent's reports showed clearly that, even without the agent's intervention, Mr Lüdi had had the intention of acting as an intermediary in the supply of large quantities of narcotics. On 24 October 1985, the Berne Court of Appeal dismissed Mr Lüdi's appeal against his conviction on two of the charges; it also declined to call the undercover agent as a witness. On 8 April 1986, the Federal Court dismissed a public law appeal brought by Mr Lüdi; in contrast, the Cassation Division of the Federal Court granted his application for a declaration of nullity on the grounds, inter alia, that in sentencing him sufficient account had not been taken of the effect on his behaviour of the actions of the undercover agent. Subsequently, the Berne Court of Appeal reduced the sentence to eighteen months' imprisonment, suspended for three years, and ordered him to continue with out-patient treatment.

361. *Mr Lüdi applied to the Commission on 30 September 1986. He complained of the interception of his telephone conversations combined with his manipulation by an undercover agent; he claimed that this had infringed his right to respect for his private life (Convention, Article 8). He also maintained that his conviction had been based solely on the reports drawn up by the said agent, who had not been summoned to appear as a witness; he alleged that his right to a fair trial (Article 6 § 1) had been infringed, and also his right to examine or have examined witnesses against him (Article 6 § 3(d)).[1]*

Judgment of 15 June 1992 *(Chamber) (Series A No. 238)*

362. The Court dismissed the preliminary objection raised by the Government (unanimously): despite the attenuation of the penalty imposed by the Berne Court of Appeal, the applicant could claim to be a victim within the meaning of Article of 25 of the Convention.

363. As regards Article 8, there was no doubt that the telephone interception had been an interference with Mr Lüdi's private life and correspondence. The Court held however that, albeit 'in accordance with the law'—Articles 171b and 171c of the Berne Code of Criminal Procedure—, the interference was 'necessary in a democratic society' for the 'prevention of crime'.

On the other hand, the Court considered that in the present case the use of an undercover agent had not, either alone or in combination with the telephone interception, affected private life. The undercover agent's actions had taken place within the context of a deal relating to 5 kg of cocaine and the aim had been to arrest the dealers. Mr Lüdi must therefore have been aware that he had been engaged in a criminal act punishable under the Drugs Law and that consequently he had been running the risk of encountering an undercover police officer whose task would in fact be to expose him. In short, there had been no violation of Article 8 (held unanimously).

364. From the point of view of Articles 6 §§ 1 and 3(d), the Court started by recalling what it had consistently held: the evidence must normally be produced in the presence of the accused at a public hearing with a view to adversarial argument. There were exceptions to this principle, but they must not infringe the rights of the defence.

However, the accused's conviction had been based, not on statements made by anonymous witnesses, but, in particular, on written statements by a sworn police officer whose function had been known to the investigating judge. Moreover, the applicant had known the said agent, if not by his real identity, at least by his physical appearance, as a result of having met him.

However, neither the investigating judge nor the trial courts had been able or willing to hear the undercover agent as a witness and carry out a confrontation which would have enabled his statements to be contrasted with Mr Lüdi's allegations; moreover, neither Mr Lüdi

---

1 In its report of 6 December 1990, the Commission expressed the opinion that there had been a violation of Article 8 (ten votes to four) and of paragraph 3(d) in conjunction with paragraph 1 of Article 6 (thirteen votes to one).

nor his counsel had had at any time during the proceedings an opportunity to question him and cast doubt on his credibility. Yet it would have been possible to do this in a way which took into account the legitimate interest of the police authorities in a drug trafficking case in preserving the anonymity of their agent so that they could protect him and also make use of him again in the future.

In short, the rights of the defence had been restricted to such an extent that the applicant had not had a fair trial. There had therefore been a violation of paragraph 3(d) in conjunction with paragraph 1 of Article 6 (eight votes to one).

365. Mr Lüdi claimed 30,180.60 Swiss francs by way of costs and expenses incurred before the Federal Court and the Convention institutions. The Court considered it equitable to award 15,000 Swiss francs (unanimously).[1]

366. *Summary bibliography*

COUSSIRAT-COUSTÈRE (V.).—'La jurisprudence de la Cour européenne des droits de l'homme en 1992', *A.F.D.I.* 1992, pp. 629 *et seq.*

DECAUX (E.) and TAVERNIER (P.).—'Chronique de jurisprudence de la Cour européenne des droits de l'homme', *J.D.I.* 1993, pp. 733–735.

DE VALKENEER (C.).—'L'infiltration et la Convention européenne des droits de l'homme', *R.T.D.H.* 1993, pp. 313 and 314.

MERRILLS (J.G.).—'Decisions on the European Convention on Human Rights during 1992', *B.Y.B.I.L.* 1992, pp. 584–587.

SUDRE (F.), LEVINET (M.), PEYROT (B.) and ECOCHARD (B.).—'Chronique de la jurisprudence de la Cour européenne des droits de l'homme—1992', *R.U.D.H.* 1993, Nos 1–2, pp. 1 *et seq.*

SWART (B.).—'The case-law of the European Court of Human Rights in 1992', *E.J.C.* 1993, pp. 167 *et seq.*

WARBRICK (C.).—'The European Convention on Human Rights', *Y.E.L.* 1991, pp. 730 and 731.

1 In a judgment of 7 August 1992, the Federal Court, citing Article 6 of the Convention and the judgment in Lüdi, declared the evidence of an undercover agent inadmissible where the accused had not had an opportunity to question him during the trial.

310. Case of Thorgeir Thorgeirson v. Iceland

Writer convicted of defamation of the police

367. *From 1979 to 1983 a number of incidents occurred in Iceland involving allegations of police brutality, about ten of which were reported to the police. The last such complaint was made in the autumn of 1983 by a journalist, Mr Skafti Jónsson, and it led to the prosecution of three members of the Reykjavik police, of whom two were acquitted and one convicted. His case received extensive coverage in the press and gave rise to considerable discussion on relations between the public and the police. This caused Thorgeir Thorgeirson, a writer, to publish two articles on police brutality in the daily newspaper* Morgunblaóió *on 7 and 20 December 1983. He called for a new, more effective system for investigating accusations brought against the police. On account of certain passages in those articles he was charged with defamation of civil servants (Article 108 of the Penal Code).*

The Reykjavik Criminal Court held a number of hearings on the case. At some of those hearings—mostly preparatory or dealing with procedural questions—the applicant and his counsel appeared in the absence of the public prosecutor. In contrast, the latter was represented at all hearings at which evidence was adduced and witnesses heard, with the exception of a hearing when a video-taped television programme was shown to the court. The applicant was found guilty on 16 June 1986 and sentenced to a fine of 10,000 Icelandic crowns. On an appeal brought by Thorgeir Thorgeirson and the public prosecutor, the Supreme Court upheld the guilty verdict and the penalty on 20 October 1987.

368. *In his application of 19 November 1987 to the Commission, Thorgeir Thorgeirson invoked Article 6 §§ 1 and 3(c) and Article 10 of the Convention.*[1]

Judgment of 25 June 1992 *(Chamber) (Series A No. 239)*

369. As regards Article 6 § 1, the Court referred to its case law: the impartiality of a court had to be determined according to a subjective

---

1 On 14 March 1990, the Commission declared the application admissible in part. In its report adopted on 11 December 1990, it expressed the opinion that there had been no violation of Article 6 § 1 (unanimously) and that there had been a violation of Article 10 (thirteen votes to one).

test and an objective test. As to the subjective test, the applicant had adduced no evidence to suggest that the judge in question had been personally biased. As to the objective test, at those sittings at which the Public Prosecutor had been absent, the Reykjavik Criminal Court had not been called upon to conduct any investigation into the merits of the case, let alone to assume any functions which might have been fulfilled by the prosecutor had he been present. In those circumstances, such fears as the applicant might have had, on account of the prosecutor's absence, as regards the Reykjavik Court's lack of impartiality could not be held to be objectively justified. Accordingly, there had been no violation of Article 6 § 1 (held unanimously).

370. As far as Article 10 was concerned, the applicant's conviction had undoubtedly constituted an interference with his right to freedom of expression.

Was that interference prescribed by law? The Court rejected the applicant's argument that Article 108 of the Penal Code could not provide a proper basis for his conviction: the manner in which the Icelandic courts had interpreted and applied that article in the present case was not excluded by its wording and was, moreover, supported by precedent.

Did the interference have a legitimate aim or aims? The Court held that it did: protection of the reputation of others.

Was the interference 'necessary in a democratic society'? The Court observed that there was no warrant in its case law for distinguishing, in the manner suggested by the Government, between political discussion and discussion of other matters of public concern. As regards the specific circumstances of the case, the Court noted the following points: the applicant had reported on an undisputed case of police brutality; he had essentially reported what had been being said by others about police brutality and he had been convicted partly because of his failure to justify what they had considered to be his own allegations; in so far as the applicant had been required to establish the truth of his statements, he had been faced with an unreasonable, if not impossible, task; the principal aim of the applicant's articles had not been to damage the reputation of the police, but to urge the setting up of an independent and impartial body to investigate complaints of police brutality; the articles bore on a matter of serious public concern; having regard to their purpose, the language used could not be regarded as excessive; and the contested measures were capable of discouraging open discussion of matters of public concern. The interference had therefore not been necessary in a democratic society and there had been a violation of Article 10 (eight votes to one).

371. Applying Article 50, the Court awarded Mr Thorgeir Thorgeirson 530,000 Icelandic crowns for his costs and expenses in connection with the Strasbourg proceedings, but dismissed his claims in relation to the fine and legal costs in the domestic proceedings (which he had never paid), work which he had carried out himself in this case and loss of earnings (unanimously).

372. *Summary bibliography*

COUSSIRAT-COUSTÈRE (V.).—'La jurisprudence de la Cour européenne des droits de l'homme en 1992', *A.F.D.I.* 1992, pp. 629 *et seq.*

DECAUX (E.) and TAVERNIER (P.).—'Chronique de jurisprudence de la Cour européenne des droits de l'homme', *J.D.I.* 1993, pp. 735 and 736.

MERRILLS (J.G.).—'Decisions on the European Convention on Human Rights during 1992', *B.Y.B.I.L.* 1992, pp. 587–589.

SUDRE (F.), LEVINET (M.), PEYROT (B.) and ECOCHARD (B.).—'Chronique de jurisprudence de la Cour européenne des Droits de l'Homme—1992', *R.U.D.H.* 1993, nos. 1–2, pp. 1 *et seq.*

SWART (B.).—'The case-law of the European Court of Human Rights in 1992', *E.J.C.* 1993, pp. 167 *et seq.*

VELDE (J. van der).—'Noot', *NJCM–Bulletin* 1993, pp. 431–435.

WARBRICK (C.).—'The European Convention on Human Rights', *Y.E.L.* 1992, pp. 720–727.

311. Case of Drozd and Janousek v. France and Spain

Criminal proceedings before the *Tribunal de Corts* of the Principality of Andorra and imprisonment in France after convictions by that court

373. *Jordi Drozd, a Spanish citizen, and Pavel Janousek, a citizen of Czechoslovakia, were tried and convicted on 26 May 1986 by the* Tribunal de Corts *of the Principality of Andorra for an armed robbery committed in Andorra la Vella. The court gave judgment on the same day in Catalan; the Spanish text was served on them on the next day. The applicants were sentenced to fourteen years' imprisonment. The court was composed of two former French judges, nominated by the French Co-Prince (the President of the French Republic), and a Spanish jurist appointed by the episcopal Co-Prince (the Bishop of Urgel, in Spain).*

Mr Drozd and Mr Janousek then lodged the only appeal open to them, an appeal to the same judges to reconsider their ruling. After the Tribunal de Corts *dismissed their appeal on 3 July 1986, they elected to serve their sentences in France, in accordance with Andorran law, which allowed persons given a custodial sentence of over three months in Andorra to choose to serve it in France or Spain.*

374. *In their application to the Commission of 26 November 1986, Mr Drozd and Mr Janousek put forward two series of complaints.*

(a) The first series of complaints, based on Article 6 of the Convention, were directed against France and Spain, which were regarded as being responsible at the international level for the conduct of the Andorran authorities.

i. Certain complaints were common to both applicants, in reliance on Article 6 §§ 1 and 3(d). These were that they had not had a fair trial before the Tribunal de Corts *because two of the judges were the representatives of the Co-Princes in Andorra and the superior officers of the police; the judge in charge of the investigation was present at the court's deliberations in chambers; one of the judges knew little Spanish and less Catalan, Catalan being the language of the proceedings; the witnesses had not been 'isolated' before giving evidence and the victim of the theft had heard the defendants' statements before he gave evidence.*

> ii. The other complaints were made by Mr Janousek alone, in reliance on sub-paragraphs (b), (d) and (e) of Article 6 § 3. He complained that he had not received the assistance of an interpreter or a lawyer during the investigation, nor a complete translation during the trial.
>
> (b) The second group of complaints, based on Article 5 § 1 of the Convention, were directed against France alone. Both applicants considered that their imprisonment in France after being convicted by an Andorran court was 'unlawful', as there was no provision of French law relating to the enforcement of such judgments, and contrary to French public policy since there was no review by the French courts.[1]

Judgment of 26 June 1992 *(Plenary Court) (Series A No. 240)*

375. The Court started by considering its jurisdiction to examine the matter from the point of view of Article 6. The French and Spanish Governments had raised several preliminary objections in this regard, as they had before the Commission, whilst the Commission declared the application admissible, but then decided that it did not have jurisdiction to examine the merits of the case from the point of view of the article in question.

As regards the objection that the Court had no jurisdiction *ratione loci*, the Court agreed in substance with the Governments' arguments and the opinion of the Commission, which took the view that the Convention was inapplicable in Andorra, despite the fact that it had been ratified by France and Spain. It also took several circumstances into account: the Principality was not one of the members of the Council of Europe, and this prevented it being a party to the Convention in its own right, and it appeared never to have taken any steps to be admitted as an 'associate member' of the Organization; the territory of Andorra was not an area which was common to the French Republic and the Kingdom of Spain, nor was it a Franco-Spanish condominium; the relations between the Principality and France and Spain did not follow the normal pattern of relations between sovereign States and did not take the form of international agreements, although, according to the French Co-Prince, the development of the institutions of Andorra, if

---

1 In its report of 11 December 1990, the Commission expressed the opinion that there had not been a violation of Article 6 either by France (ten votes to six) or by Spain (twelve votes to four); nor had there been a violation of Article 5 § 1 by France (eight votes to eight, with the President's casting vote).

continued, might allow Andorra to 'join the international community'. In sum, the Court held that the objection was well-founded (unanimously).

376. That finding did not dispense the Court from examining whether the applicants had come under the 'jurisdiction' of France or Spain within the meaning of Article 1 of the Convention by reason of their conviction by an Andorran court.

It therefore considered the objection of lack of jurisdiction *ratione personae*. The term 'jurisdiction' was not limited to the national territory of the High Contracting Parties; their responsibility could be involved because of acts of their authorities producing effects outside their own territory. In common with the Commission, the Court associated itself with the arguments deployed by the defendant Governments: whilst it was true that judges from France and Spain sat as members of Andorran courts, they did not do so in their capacity as French or Spanish judges; those courts, in particular the *Tribunal de Corts*, exercised their functions in an autonomous manner; and their judgments were not subject to supervision by the authorities of France or Spain. Moreover, there was nothing in the case-file which suggested that the French or Spanish authorities had attempted to interfere with the applicants' trial. Finally, the secondment of judges or their placing at the disposal of foreign countries was also practised between member States of the Council of Europe. In short, the Court also upheld that objection (unanimously).

377. There remained the complaint relating to Article 5 § 1. The French Government argued that the applicants had neglected two remedies which had been available to them before the French courts: bringing criminal proceedings, joining in as civil parties, against the officials or judges who had been responsible for their detention or bringing an action for a flagrantly unlawful act by the said officials or judges. The Court found that the aim of the remedies in question was to obtain compensation for damage caused by deprivation of liberty and to impose sanctions on public officials. While they might have the indirect effect of putting an end to a person's detention, they had not hitherto brought about such a result where the detention originated from a decision by an Andorran court, because the French courts declined jurisdiction to assess the lawfulness of such decisions. The objection therefore had to be dismissed (held unanimously).

378. With regard to the merits, the Court considered whether there was a sufficient legal basis for the detention at issue. The Court considered that it did not have jurisdiction to review the observance of

Andorran legal procedures, or more generally to review the lawfulness of the applicants' deprivation of liberty in terms of the laws of the Principality. As for compliance with French law, the Court considered this to have been shown. The Franco-Andorran custom, dating back several centuries, according to which persons sentenced by Andorran courts could elect to serve their sentence in French prisons, had sufficient stability and legal force to serve as a basis for the detention in issue, notwithstanding the particular status of the Principality in international law.

Did the French courts have to review the conviction in issue? The Court considered that in this case the *Tribunal de Corts* was the 'competent court' referred to in Article 5 § 1(a). As the Convention did not require the Contracting Parties to impose its standards on third States or territories, France had not been obliged to verify whether the proceedings which had resulted in the conviction were compatible with all the requirements of Article 6. To require such a review would also thwart the current trend towards strengthening international co-operation in the administration of justice, a trend which was in principle in the interests of the persons concerned. The Contracting States were, however, obliged to refuse their co-operation if it emerged that the conviction was the result of a flagrant denial of justice.

The Court took note of the declaration made by the French Government to the effect that they could and in fact would refuse their customary co-operation if it was a question of enforcing an Andorran judgment which was manifestly contrary to the provisions of Article 6 or the principles embodied therein. It found confirmation of this assurance in the decisions of some French courts. In the Court's opinion, it had not been shown that in the circumstances of the case France was required to refuse its co-operation in enforcing the sentences. In short, no violation of Article 5 § 1 had been established (twelve votes to eleven).

379. *Summary bibliography*

Cohen-Jonathan (G.) and Flauss (J.-F.).—'Convention européenne des droits de l'homme et exécution des condamnations pénales prononcées à l'étranger', *R.T.D.H.* 1994, pp. 98–115.

Coussirat-Coustère (V.).—'La jurisprudence de la Cour européenne des droits de l'homme en 1992', *A.F.D.I.* 1992, pp. 629 *et seq.*

Decaux (E.) and Tavernier (P.).—'Chronique de jurisprudence de la Cour européenne des droits de l'homme (année 1992)', *J.D.I.* 1993, pp. 737–740.

Landais (R.).—'L'affaire Drozd et Janousek c. France et Espagne', *Cahiers du CREDHO* No. 1, 1994, pp. 97–108.

LUSH (C.).—'The territorial application of the European Convention on Human Rights: recent case law', *I.C.L.Q.* 1993, pp. 897–906.

MERRILLS (J.G.).—'Decisions on the European Convention on Human Rights during 1992', *B.Y.B.I.L.* 1992, pp. 589–592.

SUDRE (F.), LEVINET (M.), PEYROT (B.) and ECOCHARD (B.).—'Chronique de la jurisprudence de la Cour européenne des droits de l'homme—1992', *R.U.D.H.* 1993, Nos 1–2, pp. 1 *et seq.*

SWART (B.).—'The case-law of the European Court of Human Rights in 1992', *E.J.C.* 1993, pp. 167 *et seq.*

WARBRICK (C.).—'The European Convention on Human Rights', *Y.E.L.* 1992, pp. 733–735.

312. Case of Tomasi v. France

Treatment suffered during police custody, length of the proceedings instituted in respect of such treatment and length of detention on remand

380. *Félix Tomasi, a French national, was arrested by the police on 23 March 1983 at Bastia (Haute-Corse). He was suspected him of having been involved in a murder and an attempted murder carried out by the 'ex-FLNC' (Corsican National Liberation Front) on 11 February 1982. He was placed in police custody until 25 March 1983, when he was charged and remanded in custody. Ultimately, he was acquitted by a specially composed bench of the Gironde assize court on 22 October 1988 and the Compensation Board at the Court of Cassation awarded him 300,000 French francs on 8 November 1991. During his detention on remand, he made twenty-three applications to be released, all of which were rejected.*

The applicant, who orally complained to the investigating judge at the end of his period in custody that he had been maltreated, brought a complaint against person unknown and claimed damages on 29 March 1983. He was examined by several doctors, who found he had minor injuries. He was heard again by the investigating judge on 24 June and 1 July 1983. On 20 March 1985, the Court of Cassation declared the earlier investigative measures void on the ground that they had been carried out by a judge who had no jurisdiction. It appointed an investigating judge from Bordeaux, who issued an order finding that there was no case to answer. On an appeal by Mr Tomasi, the indictments division of the Court of Appeal ordered further inquiries on 3 November 1987, but ultimately confirmed on 12 July 1988 that there was no case to answer. The Court of Cassation dismissed an appeal from the applicant on 6 February 1989.

381. *In his application to the Commission of 10 March 1987, Mr Tomasi relied on Articles 3, 6 § 1 and 5 § 3 of the Convention. He claimed that during his police custody he had suffered inhuman and degrading treatment; he also criticized the length of the proceedings which he had brought in respect of such treatment; he maintained finally that his detention on remand had exceeded a 'reasonable time'.*[1]

---

1 In its report of 11 December 1990, the Commission expressed the view that there had been a violation of Article 3 (twelve votes to two), Article 6 § 1 (thirteen votes to one) and Article 5 § 3 (unanimously).

178

Judgment of 27 August 1992 *(Chamber) (Series A No. 241–A)*

382. The Court found that it had jurisdiction to examine the Government's two preliminary objections, despite the Commission's view to the contrary in respect of the first objection.

The Government contended that the applicant had lodged his application with the Commission even before he had submitted a claim to the Compensation Board. The Court dismissed the objection (unanimously): first, the right to secure the ending of a deprivation of liberty was to be distinguished from the right to receive compensation for such deprivation; secondly, Article 149 of the Code of Criminal Procedure made the award of compensation subject to the fulfilment of specific conditions not required under Article 5 § 3 of the Convention; and, thirdly, Mr Tomasi had lodged his application in Strasbourg after four years spent in detention.

In the Government's contention, the applicant had lost the status of a 'victim' within the meaning of Article 25 § 1 of the Convention because the Compensation Board had acknowledged that a 'reasonable time' had been exceeded and had made good the resulting damage. The Court held that the submission could not be regarded as being out of time but was unfounded (unanimously), since it was open to the same objections as the plea based on failure to exhaust domestic remedies.

383. The complaint based on Article 5 § 3 related to the length of the detention on remand. It had lasted five years and seven months. In order to reject Mr Tomasi's applications for release, the investigating authorities had put forward—separately or together—four main grounds.

The first ground was the seriousness of the alleged offences. The existence and persistence of serious indications of the guilt of the person concerned undoubtedly constituted relevant factors, but the Court considered that they could not alone justify such a long period of pretrial detention.

The second ground was protection of public order. The investigating judges and the indictments divisions had assessed the need to continue the deprivation of liberty from a purely abstract point of view, merely stressing the gravity of the offences or noting their effects. However, the attack in question had been a premeditated act of terrorism. It was therefore reasonable to assume that there had been a risk of prejudice to public order at the beginning, but it must have disappeared after a certain time.

The third ground was the risk of pressure being brought to bear on the witnesses and of collusion between the co-accused. There had been, from the outset, a genuine risk that pressure might be brought to bear on the witnesses. It had gradually diminished, without however disappearing completely.

The last ground was the danger of the applicant's absconding. The decisions of the judicial investigating authorities contained scarcely any reason capable of explaining why they had considered the risk of his absconding to be decisive and why they had not sought to counter it by, for instance, requiring the lodging of a security and placing him under court supervision.

Overall, the Court concluded that some of the reasons for dismissing Mr Tomasi's applications were both relevant and sufficient, but with the passing of time they had become much less so, and it was thus necessary to consider the conduct of the proceedings.

The evidence showed that the French courts had not acted with the necessary promptness. Moreover, the principal public prosecutor at the Court of Cassation had acknowledged this in his opinion before the Compensation Board. Accordingly, the length of the contested detention would not appear to have been essentially attributable either to the complexity of the case or to the applicant's conduct. There had therefore been a violation of Article 5 § 3 (held unanimously).

384.   Relying on Article 3, Mr Tomasi claimed to have suffered ill-treatment during his period of custody.

The Government argued that he could have brought an action for damages in the civil courts against the State alleging culpable conduct on the part of its officials in the performance of their duties. Since the plea that domestic remedies had not been exhausted had not been raised before the Commission, the Court considered that the Government was estopped (unanimously).

The Court therefore considered the merits of the complaint by examining, first, whether there had been a causal connection between the treatment which the applicant had allegedly suffered during his police custody and the injuries noted. The Government acknowledged that they could give no explanation as to the cause of the injuries, but maintained that they had not resulted from the treatment complained of by Mr Tomasi. That was not the view taken by the Court, having regard to several considerations. First, no one had claimed that the marks on the applicant's body could have dated from a period prior to his being taken into custody or originated in an act carried out by the applicant against himself or again as a result of an escape attempt. Secondly, at his first appearance before the investigating judge, he had drawn attention to the marks on his body. Thirdly, four different doctors had examined the accused in the days following the end of his police custody. Their certificates contained precise and concurring medical observations and indicated dates for the occurrence of the injuries which corresponded to the period spent in custody on police premises.

There remained the question of the gravity of the treatment complained of. The Court did not consider that it had to examine the system of police custody in France and the rules pertaining thereto, or, in this case, the length and the timing of the applicant's interrogations. It found it sufficient to observe that the medical certificates and reports, drawn up in total independence by medical practitioners, attested to the large number of blows inflicted on Mr Tomasi and their intensity; these were two elements which were sufficiently serious to render such treatment inhuman and degrading. The requirements of the investigation and the undeniable difficulties inherent in the fight against crime, particularly with regard to terrorism, could not result in limits being placed on the protection to be afforded in respect of the physical integrity of individuals. There had accordingly been a violation of Article 3 (held unanimously).

385. With regard to Article 6 § 1, the applicant complained of the time taken to examine his complaint against persons unknown, lodged together with an application to join the proceedings as a civil party, in respect of the ill-treatment which he had suffered.

The Government contended that the applicant had failed to exhaust his domestic remedies, in so far as he had not brought an action against the State for compensation pursuant to Article 781–1 of the Code of Judicial Organization. The Court held (unanimously) that this submission was out of time, having been made for the first time before it at the hearing.

386. With regard to the merits of the complaint, the Government argued that an investigation opened upon the filing of an application to join the proceedings as a civil party concerned the existence of an offence and not that of a right. The Court could not accept this view. The right to compensation claimed by Mr Tomasi depended on the conviction of the perpetrators of the treatment complained of. It was a civil right, notwithstanding the fact that the criminal courts had jurisdiction. Consequently, Article 6 § 1 was applicable.

Had Article 6 § 1 been complied with? The period to be taken into consideration had begun on the date on which Mr Tomasi had filed his complaint; it had ended with the delivery of the Court of Cassation's judgment: it had therefore lasted for more than five years and ten months. A reading of the decisions given in those proceedings showed that the case was not a particularly complex one. In addition, Mr Tomasi had hardly contributed to delaying the outcome of the proceedings by challenging in the Bordeaux indictments division the decision finding no case to answer. Responsibility for the delays found lay essentially with the judicial authorities, in particular, the Bastia public prosecutor and the Bordeaux investigating judge. There had therefore been a violation of Article 6 § 1 (held unanimously).

387. Under Article 50, the applicant claimed 2,600,000 French francs compensation for damage. The Court found that the applicant had sustained undeniable non-pecuniary and pecuniary damage. Taking into account the various relevant considerations, including the Compensation Board's decision, it awarded him 700,000 francs (unanimously).

Mr Tomasi claimed 513,700 French francs for costs and expenses incurred before the French courts and the Convention institutions. Making an assessment on an equitable basis, the Court awarded him a total of 300,000 French francs (unanimously).

388. *Summary bibliography*

COUSSIRAT-COUSTÈRE (V.).—'Jurisprudence de la Cour européenne des droits de l'homme en 1992', *A.F.D.I.* 1992, pp. 629 *et seq.*

DECAUX (E.) and TAVERNIER (P.).—'Chronique de jurisprudence de la Cour européenne des droits de l'homme (année 1992)', *J.D.I.* 1993, pp. 740–744.

KOERING-JOULIN (R.).—'Les affaires Birou et Tomasi et la détention avant jugement', in *Le droit français et la Convention européenne des droits de l'homme. 1974–1992*, Kehl, Engel, 1994. pp. 185–195.

MERRILLS (J.G.).—'Decisions on the European Convention on Human Rights during 1992', *B.Y.B.I.L.* 1992, pp. 592 and 593.

PETTITI (L.-E.).—'Droits de l'homme', *R.S.C.D.P.C.* 1993, pp. 142–146.

RENUCCI (J.-F.).—'Droit européen des droits de l'homme', *D.* 1993, sommaires commentés, pp. 383 and 384.

SÉDILLOT (R.).—'L'affaire Tomasi c. France', *Cahiers du Credho* No. 2, 1994, pp. 109–116.

SUDRE (F.).—'L'arrêt de la Cour européenne des droits de l'homme, du 27 août 1992, Tomasi c. France: mauvais traitements et délai raisonnable', *R.S.C.D.P.C.* 1993, pp. 33–43.

SUDRE (F.), LEVINET (M.), PEYROT (B.) and ECOCHARD (B.).—'Chronique de la jurisprudence de la Cour européenne des droits de l'homme—1992', *R.U.D.H.* 1993, Nos 1–2, pp. 1 *et seq.*

SWART (B.).—'The case-law of the European Court of Human Rights in 1992', *E.J.C.* 1993, pp. 167 *et seq.*

VORMS (D.).—'Note', *G.P.* 4–6 October 1992, pp. 28 and 29.

WARBRICK (C.).—'The European Convention on Human Rights', *Y.E.L.* 1992, pp. 694 and 695.

313. Case of Vijayanathan and Pusparajah v. France

Direction to two Sri Lankan asylum seekers to leave French territory

389. *Ampalam Vijayanathan and Nagalingam Pusparajah, Sri Lankans of Tamil origin, entered France clandestinely in 1989. They applied for political asylum but the French Office for the Protection of Refugees and Stateless Persons and, on appeal, the Refugee Appeals Board dismissed their applications in 1990: those bodies took the view that the facts and fears of persecution on which the applications were based had not been proved. In December 1990 and January 1991, respectively, Mr Vijayanathan and Mr Pusparajah were directed to leave the country within a month, failing which they would be liable to expulsion, but they failed to comply with this direction. At the date of the Commission's report, that administrative measure—against which an appeal would lie to the administrative courts—had not been carried out and the applicants were still living in France unlawfully.*

390. *Mr Vijayanathan and Mr Pusparajah lodged their applications with the Commission on 10 December 1990 and 10 January 1991, respectively. They alleged that their imminent repatriation to Sri Lanka would expose them to persecution and treatment prohibited by Article 3 of the Convention.*[1]

Judgment of 27 August 1992 *(Chamber) (Series A No. 241–B)*

391. The Government's principal arguments, as before the Commission, were that the applicants were not 'victims' and had not exhausted domestic remedies.

The Court pointed in the first place to the difference between this case and the cases of *Soering v. the United Kingdom*[2] (where the Home Secretary had already signed the warrant for Mr Soering's extradition to the United States) and *Vilvarajah and Others v. the United Kingdom*[3] (where the deportation of the applicants to Sri Lanka had taken place

---

1 In its report of 5 September 1991, the Commission expressed the opinion that there had not been a violation of Article 3 (nine votes to six).
2 Series A No. 16; see Vol. II of this work, 248–262.
3 Series A No. 215; see Chapter 235, above.

during the proceedings before the Commission). It also noted that despite the direction to leave French territory, which was not enforceable in itself, and the rejection of the application for exceptional leave to remain brought by Mr Pusparajah, no expulsion order had been made with respect to the applicants. If the Commissioner of Police were to decide that they should be removed, the appeal provided for in section 22 bis of the order of 2 November 1945, as amended, would be open to them, with all its attendant safeguards. In sum, Mr Vijayanathan and Mr Pusparajah could not, as matters stood, claim to be the victims of a violation within the meaning of Article 25 § 1 of the Convention. The Court therefore upheld the Government's objection (unanimously).

392. In view of this conclusion, it was not necessary to examine the Government's other submissions.

393. *Summary bibliography*

COUSSIRAT-COUSTÈRE (V.).—'Jurisprudence de la Cour européenne des droits de l'homme en 1992', *A.F.D.I.* 1992, pp. 629 *et seq.*

DECAUX (E.) and TAVERNIER (P.).—'Chronique de jurisprudence de la Cour européenne des droits de l'homme (année 1992)', *J.D.I.* 1993, pp. 745 and 746.

LESCÈNE (P.).—'Affaires Beldjoudi c. France et Vijayanathan et Pusparajah c. France', *Cahiers du CREDHO* No. 1, 1994, pp. 81–84.

MERRILLS (J.G.).—'Decisions on the European Convention on Human Rights during 1992', *B.Y.B.I.L.* 1992, pp. 594–595.

PEDRAZZI (F.).—'Corte europea dei diritti dell'uomo, richiendenti asilo e procedura di riconoscimento dello status di rifugiato. Considerazioni critiche sulla sentenza Vilvarajah', *Riv. I.D.U.* 1992, pp. 187–202.

SUDRE (F.), LEVINET (M.), PEYROT (B.) and ECOCHARD (B.).—'Chronique de la jurisprudence de la Cour européenne des droits de l'homme—1992', *R.U.D.H.* 1993, Nos 1–2, pp. 1 *et seq.*

WARBRICK (C.).—'The European Convention on Human Rights', *Y.E.L.* 1992, pp. 697 and 698.

314. Case of Artner v. Austria

Criminal conviction based in part on statements made to the police and the investigating judge by a witness and then read out at the trial following the disappearance of the witness

394. *On 16 December 1986, the Vienna Regional Court sentenced Josef Artner to three years' imprisonment on, inter alia, two counts of usury. In one of the two cases of usury, the court relied on statements made by the victim, Miss L., to the police and to the investigating judge and on documents which she had produced. She did not appear at the trial and her address was sought in vain in order that she might testify. Finally, her statements were read out at the trial. The Court found, inter alia, that the account of the events was very similar to that which the victim had given in the other case of usury.*

On 26 May 1987, the Supreme Court dismissed an appeal and an application for a declaration of nullity brought by Mr Artner in so far as they related to the proceedings of relevance to the Court of Human Rights.

395. *In his application to the Commission of 6 July 1987, Mr Artner complained that he had been convicted solely on the basis of the statements of Miss L., whom the Regional Court had not heard; he relied on Article 6 §§ 1 and 3(d) of the Convention.*[1]

Judgment of 28 August 1992 *(Chamber) (Series A No. 242–A)*

396. The Court found that from June 1983 to June 1986 the applicant's absence had made it impossible to organize a confrontation between him and Miss L: from the moment when the proceedings had first been instituted, he had proved impossible to trace, so much so that in July 1983 the investigating judge had directed that he be placed on the list of wanted persons. The investigating judge had had to wait until he was extradited on 19 June 1986 before he could question him.

Shortly afterwards Miss L. had disappeared in her turn. The Regional Court had twice instructed the police to make every effort to find her, even adjourning the hearing in order to allow the inquiries sufficient time to bear fruit, but to no avail. It would of course have

1 In its report of 8 January 1991, the Commission expressed the opinion that there had been no violation of Article 6 §§ 1 and 3(d) (nine votes to seven).

been preferable if she could have testified in court, but her failure to appear had not in itself made it necessary to halt the prosecution—the appropriateness of which, moreover, fell outside the scope of the Court's review—provided that the authorities had not been negligent in their efforts to find the persons concerned. As it had been impossible to secure Miss L.'s attendance at the hearing, it had been open to the national court, subject to the rights of the defence being respected, to have regard to the statements obtained by the police and the investigating judge, in particular in view of the fact that it could consider those statements to be corroborated by other evidence before it.

There had therefore been no breach of paragraphs 1 and 3(d) of Article 6, taken together (five votes to four).

397. *Summary bibliography*

COUSSIRAT-COUSTÈRE (V.).—'Jurisprudence de la Cour européenne des droits de l'homme en 1992', *A.F.D.I.* 1992, pp. 629 *et seq.*

MERRILLS (J.G.).—'Decisions on the European Convention on Human Rights during 1992', *B.Y.B.I.L.* 1992, pp. 595 and 596.

SUDRE (F.), LEVINET (M.), PEYROT (B.) and ECOCHARD (B.).—'Chronique de la jurisprudence de la Cour européenne des droits de l'homme—1992', *R.U.D.H.* 1993, Nos 1–2, pp. 1 *et seq.*

SWART (B.).—'The case-law of the European Court of Human Rights in 1992', *E.J.C.* 1993, pp. 167 *et seq.*

315. Case of Schwabe v. Austria

Politician's conviction for defamation and for having reproached a person with an offence for which he had already served his sentence

398. *On 26 September 1986, the Klagenfurt Regional Court fined Karl Thomas Uwe Schwabe 3,000 schillings for defamation (Criminal Code, Article 111 §§ 1 and 2) and for having reproached a person with an offence for which he had already served his sentence (Article 113).*

Mr Schwabe had drawn up and published in a newspaper on 20 August 1985 a press release mentioning a criminal conviction of the Deputy Head of the Carinthian Provincial Government, dating from 1967, for a traffic accident which had left one person dead and several injured. Headed 'Different standards?', the press release criticized the Head of the Provincial Government for having reproached a mayor of a city in Carinthia with not having resigned after he had been convicted for drunk driving.

After appealing unsuccessfully to the Graz Court of Appeal on 29 April 1987, Mr Schwabe requested the Attorney General to file a plea of nullity for the preservation of the law. On 27 October 1987, he was informed that the Attorney General did not intend to take any action.

399. *In his application to the Commission of 1 February 1988, Mr Schwabe relied on Article 10 of the Convention.*[1]

Judgment of 28 August 1992 *(Chamber) (Series A No. 242–B)*

400. The Court observed in the first place that the fact that the sanction complained of clearly constituted an interference with the applicant's exercise of his freedom of expression, was prescribed by law and had the legitimate aim of protecting the reputation or rights of others was not disputed.

It tackled the main question—that of necessity—in the light of its case law on freedom of expression and, in particular, on the limits of acceptable criticism in the context of public debate on a political question of general interest. To that end, the Court considered the impugned judicial decisions in the light of the case as a whole, including the applicant's press release and the context in which it had been written.

---

1 In its report of 8 January 1991, the Commission expressed the opinion that there had been a violation of Article 10 (ten votes to six).

Mr Schwabe had been seeking above all to make a statement about political morality: he had not been trying to compare the two traffic accidents from a legal point of view and the reference to the first accident had been merely incidental. This had triggered a general debate on political morals between the two rival parties (the People's Party and the Socialist Party).

A politician's previous criminal convictions of the kind at issue here might be relevant factors in assessing his fitness to exercise political functions. In addition, the applicant had based his statements on an article already published in a magazine, verified the facts with the author and used substantially the same words as the 1967 judgment.

The applicant's conviction for defamation stemmed, according to the Austrian courts, from the fact that he had failed to prove the truth of his statements. However, the applicant had concluded that the accidents had enough features in common to warrant the resignation of both the politicians concerned; this comparison essentially amounted to a value-judgment, for which no proof of truth was possible. He could not therefore be considered to have exceeded the limits of freedom of expression: the facts on which the applicant had based his value-judgment were substantially correct and his good faith did not give rise to serious doubts. There had, accordingly, been a violation of Article 10 of the Convention (seven votes to two).

401. With regard to the application of Article 50, the Court accepted the applicant's claim for reimbursement of the fine imposed on him and for the costs awarded against him by the Regional Court (35,242.42 schillings), but dismissed the remainder of his claim for compensation for pecuniary damage (unanimously).

The finding of a violation of Article 10 constituted sufficient just satisfaction for any non-pecuniary damage (held unanimously).

The Court awarded the whole of the sums claimed for costs and expenses incurred in Austria and before the Convention institutions (130,402.20 schillings) (unanimously).

402. *Summary bibliography*

COUSSIRAT-COUSTÈRE (V.).—'La jurisprudence de la Cour européenne des droits de l'homme en 1992', *A.F.D.I.* 1992, pp. 629 *et seq.*

CREMONA (J.J.).—'The thick hide of politicians and Article 10 of the European Convention on Human Rights', in *Présence du droit public et des droits de l'homme. Mélanges offerts à Jacques Velu*, Brussels, Bruylant, Vol. III, 1992, pp. 1799–1811.

MERRILLS (J.G.).—'Decisions on the European Convention on Human Rights during 1992', *B.Y.B.I.L.* 1992, pp. 596–598.

SUDRE (F.), LEVINET (M.), PEYROT (B.) and ECOCHARD (B.).—'Chronique de jurisprudence de la Cour européenne des droits de l'homme—1992', *R.U.D.H.* 1993, Nos 1–2, pp. 1 *et seq.*

SWART (B.).—'The case-law of the European Court of Human Rights in 1992', *E.J.C.* 1993, pp. 167 *et seq.*

VELDE (J. van der).—'Noot', *NJCM–Bulletin* 1993, pp. 431–435.

WARBRICK (C.).—'The European Convention on Human Rights', *Y.E.L.* 1992, pp. 720–727.

316. Case of F.M. v. Italy

Length of proceedings brought by a disabled person to obtain an attendance allowance

403. *On 5 February 1986, Mrs F.M., a disabled person, instituted proceedings against the Minister of the Interior before the Rome magistrate's court for the payment of an attendance allowance which the Latium social security authorities had refused her. On 13 October 1986, the court found against the Minister, whose appeal to the Rome District Court was dismissed on 25 January 1989.*

404. *In her application of 2 March 1987 to the Commission, Mrs F.M. complained of the length of the proceedings brought by her and relied on Article 6 § 1 of the Convention.*[1]

Judgment of 23 September 1992 *(Chamber) (Series A No. 245–A)*

405. The Court considered that the applicant's death and the failure of the attempts made to discover any heirs constituted facts 'of a kind to provide a solution of the matter' (Rules of Court, Rule 49 § 2). In addition, the Court discerned no reason of *ordre public* (public policy) for continuing the proceedings (Rule 49 § 4). It therefore decided that the case should be struck out of the list (unanimously).

406. *Summary bibliography*

COUSSIRAT-COUSTÈRE (V.).—'La jurisprudence de la Cour européenne des droits de l'homme en 1992', *A.F.D.I.* 1992, pp. 629 *et seq.*
MERRILLS (J.G.).—'Decisions on the European Convention on Human Rights during 1992', *B.Y.B.I.L.* 1992, p. 598.
SUDRE (F.), LEVINET (M.), PEYROT (B.) and ECOCHARD (B.).—'Chronique de la jurisprudence de la Cour européenne des droits de l'homme—1992', *R.U.D.H.* 1993, Nos 1–2, pp. 1 *et seq.*

---

1 In its report of 20 February 1992, the Commission expressed the opinion that there had been a breach of Article 6 § 1 (thirteen votes to eight).

317. Case of Herczegfalvy v. Austria

Detention and psychiatric treatment of a person of unsound mind

407. *Istvan Herczegfalvy, a Hungarian citizen, arrived in Austria in 1964; at the time of the proceedings, he lived in Vienna. In 1976, when he was serving a sentence of imprisonment, new criminal proceedings were brought against him for assaults on warders and fellow prisoners and for serious threats against judges. After completing his first sentence on 13 May 1977, he remained in prison and, on 9 January 1978, he was placed in an institution for mentally ill offenders, at times provisionally, at times definitively. He remained there until 28 November 1984, when his conditional release was ordered.*

408. *In his application to the Commission of 27 November 1978, Mr Herczegfalvy brought a series of complaints relating to the lawfulness, length and conditions of his detention and the medical treatment carried out during it.*[1]

Judgment of 24 September 1992 *(Chamber) (Series A No. 244)*

409. None of the periods in detention at issue, some of which came under paragraph 1(c) of Article 5, others under paragraph 1(e), had infringed those provisions (held unanimously): national law had been complied with and the decisions of the competent authorities had not been tainted by arbitrariness.

410. The duration of the detention on remand (27 May 1978 to 10 January 1979 and 30 October 1979 to 9 April 1980) had not exceeded a 'reasonable time' within the meaning of Article 5 § 3 (held unanimously). The Court did not find any negligence on the part of the

---

1 On 10 March 1988, the Commission declared several of the complaints inadmissible. On 4 October 1989, it declared certain of the other complaints admissible and the remainder of the application inadmissible. In its report of 1 March 1991, it expressed the opinion that there had been violations of Article 3 (unanimously), Article 5 § 1(e) for the periods from 11 December 1981 to 8 February 1982 and from 8 February 1983 to 16 February 1984 (unanimously), Article 5 § 4 (unanimously), Article 8 (unanimously), Article 10 (unanimously) and Article 13 (eighteen votes to two), but not of Article 5 § 1(c) (eleven votes to nine), Article 5 § 1(e) (for the other periods) (eleven votes to nine) or Article 5 § 3 (unanimously).

authorities during the first period such as to delay the proceedings to the point of violating the Convention; it considered that the applicant himself had contributed to the prolongation of the proceedings. Neither did the second period appear excessive, bearing in mind *inter alia* the different composition of the court to which the case had been remitted.

411. The Court recalled its case law on the scope of paragraphs 1 and 4 of Article 5, according to which, in order to satisfy the requirements of the Convention, judicial review of detention must comply with both the substantive and procedural rules of the national legislation and be conducted in conformity with the aim of Article 5: protecting the individual against arbitrariness. The latter condition implied, not only that the competent courts must decide 'speedily', but also that their decisions must follow at reasonable intervals. Two of the three decisions at issue could not be regarded as having been taken at reasonable intervals, especially as the numerous requests for release submitted at that time by Mr Herczegfalvy had brought no response. Those conclusions meant that there was no need for the Court to examine whether the decisions in issue complied with national law. In short, there had been a violation of Article 5 § 4 (held unanimously).

412. Mr Herczegfalvy also complained of his medical treatment in that he had been subjected to brutal treatment incompatible with Article 3.

In the Court's view, the position of inferiority and powerlessness which was typical of patients confined in psychiatric hospitals called for increased vigilance in reviewing whether the Convention had been complied with. Whilst it was for the medical authorities to decide, on the basis of the recognized rules of medical science, on the therapeutic methods to be used (if necessary by force) to preserve the physical and mental health of patients who were entirely incapable of deciding for themselves and for whom they were therefore responsible, such patients nevertheless remained under the protection of Article 3, whose requirements permitted of no derogation. It was above all the length of time during which the handcuffs and security bed had been used which exercised the Court. However, the evidence before the Court was not sufficient to disprove the Government's argument that, according to the psychiatric principles generally accepted at the time, medical necessity justified the treatment in issue. Moreover, certain of the applicant's allegations were not supported by the evidence. No violation of Article 3 had thus been shown (held unanimously).

413. By administering food to Mr Herczegfalvy by force and imposing on him the treatment considered under Article 3, the hospital authorities had not violated Article 8 (held unanimously): the Court had no information capable of shaking the Government's view that the hospital authorities had been entitled to regard the applicant's psychiatric illness as rendering him entirely incapable of taking decisions for himself.

In contrast, the practice of sending all the applicant's letters to the curator for him to select which ones to pass on had violated Article 8 (held unanimously), since the interference with the right guaranteed by that article had not been 'in accordance with the law' within the meaning of Article 8 § 2: in the absence of any detail at all as to the kind of restrictions permitted or their purpose, duration and extent or the arrangements for their review, the Austrian legislation did not offer the minimum degree of protection against arbitrariness required by the rule of law in a democratic society.

414. Article 10, which the applicant relied on in order to contest the restrictions on his access to information, had been violated (held unanimously) for the same reasons which had led the Court to hold that Article 8 had been infringed.

415. As regards the complaints under Article 13, the Court did not consider it necessary to rule on this point in view of its decision with respect to Articles 8 and 10 (held unanimously).

416. Taking a decision on an equitable basis, the Court awarded Mr Herczegfalvy 100,000 schillings for the damage resulting from the violations found (unanimously). It ordered the costs to be reimbursed in full, namely 8,000 Deutsche Mark and 12,000 schillings, less 22,971 French francs already paid by the Council of Europe as legal aid (unanimously).

417. *Summary bibliography*

CALLEWAERT (J.).—'L'affaire Herczegfalvy ou le traitement psychiatrique à l'épreuve de l'article 3 . . . et vice versa', *R.T.D.H.* 1993, pp. 433 and 443.

COUSSIRAT-COUSTÈRE (V.).—'La jurisprudence de la Cour européenne des droits de l'homme en 1992', *A.F.D.I.* 1992, pp. 629 *et seq.*

DECAUX (E.) and TAVERNIER (P.).—'Chronique de jurisprudence de la Cour européenne des droits de l'homme (année 1992)', *J.D.I.* 1993, pp. 748 and 749.

GERBRANDA (T.).—'Noot', *NJCM–Bulletin* 1993, pp. 444–448.

SUDRE (F.), LEVINET (M.), PEYROT (B.) and ECOCHARD (B.).—'Chronique de jurisprudence de la Cour européenne des droits de l'homme—1992', *R.U.D.H.* 1993, Nos 1–2, pp. 1 *et seq.*

SWART (B.).—'The case-law of the European Court of Human Rights in 1992', *E.J.C.* 1993, pp. 167 *et seq.*

WARBRICK (C.).—'The European Convention on Human Rights', *Y.E.L.* 1991, pp. 740–742.

318. Case of Kolompar v. Belgium

Lawfulness and length of detention with a view to extradition

418.   *In May 1981, Djula Kolompar, a Yugoslav national, was sentenced* in absentia *by the Florence Assize Court of Appeal to ten years' imprisonment for attempted rape and attempted murder. In May 1983, Italy requested the Belgian authorities to extradite him. On 22 January 1984, Mr Kolompar was arrested in Belgium on suspicion of offences committed in that country and on the following day an Antwerp investigating judge remanded him in custody in respect of those charges. On 7 March 1984, the judgment of the Florence Assize Court of Appeal was served on the applicant; the bailiff's writ stated that he would be detained with a view to his extradition. The applicant's detention on remand ended on 11 April but he remained in custody in connection with the extradition proceedings. On 2 May, the Belgium Minister of Justice authorized Mr Kolompar's extradition to Italy following a favourable opinion from the indictments chamber of the Antwerp Court of Appeal.*

On 4 January 1985, the Antwerp Criminal Court sentenced him to one year's imprisonment for the offences committed in Belgium. That judgment was upheld by the Antwerp Court of Appeal on 25 April 1985. On 4 June, the Minister of Justice informed the applicant that, on account of the period that he had spent in detention since 22 January 1984, the prison term was to be deemed to have been completed on 20 January 1985.

On 15 June, the applicant applied for his release to the committals chamber of the Antwerp First-Instance Court; the Minister stayed execution of the extradition order pending the decision. On 21 June, the committals chamber declared the application inadmissible. On 5 July, the indictments chamber of the Antwerp Court of Appeal confirmed the committals chamber's order on the ground that it had no power to order the applicant's release. An appeal brought by the applicant in the Court of Cassation was dismissed on 8 October. In the meantime, on 17 September, Mr Kolompar had applied to the President of the Brussels First-Instance Court seeking an urgent order prohibiting his extradition and requiring him to be released forthwith; the extradition procedure was suspended pending the outcome of that application. On 21 March 1986, the President of the court dismissed the application and, on 12 June, the applicant contested his decision in the Brussels Court of Appeal; those proceedings were still pending.

On 13 September 1987, Mr Kolompar informed the Minister of Justice that he no longer opposed his extradition to Italy and that he waived his right to rely on the Minister's undertaking not to hand him over to Italy pending the outcome of the appeals lodged in Belgium. He was extradited on 25 September 1987 and released on 27 December 1990 under an amnesty.

419. *In his application to the Commission of 10 June 1985, Mr Kolompar alleged violations of Article 5 §§ 1, 2 and 4 of the Convention by Belgium and of Articles 3 and 6 § 1 by Italy.*[1]

Judgment of 24 September 1992 *(Chamber) (Series A No. 235–C)*

420. As regards Article 5 § 1, the Government criticized the applicant for having failed to take to their conclusion the urgent application proceedings instituted by him. However, as the defendant in those proceedings, the Belgian State had contested the jurisdiction of the President of the Brussels First-Instance Court. The Court dismissed that objection on the ground that the Government could not put to the Court arguments which were inconsistent with the position that they had adopted before the national courts (unanimously).

421. The Court considered that the detention in respect of the offences committed in Belgium had satisfied the requirements of sub-paragraphs (a) and (c) of Article 5 § 1.

As far as the detention with a view to extradition was concerned, it was in principle justified under sub-paragraph (f), but as it had lasted for over two years and eight months, it was necessary to determine whether it had remained compatible with that provision to the end.

The Court noted that the period spent in detention pending extradition had been unusually long. However, the extradition proceedings properly so-called had been completed less than one month after the decision to revoke the order remanding the applicant in custody in respect of his alleged offences in Belgium. The detention had been continued as a result of the applicant's successive applications for a stay of execution or for release as well as the time which the Belgian authorities had required to verify the applicant's alibi in Denmark.

1 On 16 May 1990, the Commission declared the complaints based on Article 5 §§ 1 and 4 admissible; it found the remainder of the application inadmissible and in particular the complaints concerning Italy. In its report of 26 February 1991, it expressed the opinion that there had been a breach of Article 5 § 1 (eight votes to three) and Article 5 § 4 (ten votes to one).

The authorities and courts before which the case had come prior to the beginning of the urgent application proceedings had given their decisions within a normal time. To that extent it appeared beyond doubt that the requirements of Article 5 § 1(f) had been complied with.

For the subsequent period, the Belgian State could not be held responsible for the delays to which the applicant's conduct had given rise. The Court accordingly concluded that there had been no violation of Article 5 § 1 (held unanimously).

422. The Court then considered whether the remedies available in Belgium had afforded the guarantees laid down in Article 5 § 4.

Although, in the urgent application proceedings, the applicant had contested the lawfulness of his initial detention with a view to extradition, he had not sought to argue, even in the alternative, that the passing of time had rendered his detention unlawful. In addition, the extradition request had not been issued in connection with court proceedings which had still been pending; it had been intended to secure the execution of a sentence imposed in Italy by a decision having final effect. In so far as the length of the deprivation of liberty none the less gave rise to a problem under paragraph 4 of Article 5 ('speedily'), it was in this instance a problem which the Court had already dealt with in relation to paragraph 1. Consequently, there had been no violation of Article 5 § 4 (held unanimously).

423. *Summary bibliography*

DECAUX (E.) and TAVERNIER (P.).—'Chronique de jurisprudence de la Cour européenne des droits de l'homme', *J.D.I.* 1993, pp. 746 and 747.

COUSSIRAT-COUSTÈRE (V.).—'La jurisprudence de la Cour européenne des droits de l'homme en 1992', *A.F.D.I.* 1992, pp. 629 *et seq.*

SUDRE (F.), LEVINET (M.), PEYROT (B.) and ECOCHARD (B.).—'Chronique de la jurisprudence de la Cour européenne des droits de l'homme—1992', *R.U.D.H.* 1993, Nos 1–2, pp. 1 *et seq.*

SWART (B.).—'The case-law of the European Court of Human Rights in 1992', *E.J.C.* 1993, pp. 167 *et seq.*

319. Case of Croissant v. Germany

Order directing a convicted person to pay the fees of three court-appointed defence counsel, two designated at his request and the third against his will

424. *On 16 February 1979, Klaus Croissant was sentenced to two years and six months' imprisonment by the Stuttgart Regional Court for supporting a criminal organization. Initially the applicant was represented by two court-appointed defence counsel. On 11 January 1978, the Regional Court had appointed a third lawyer in view of the complexity of the case and the impossibility of predicting the exact duration of the proceedings. Mr Croissant contested the appointment of a third counsel. In the alternative, he asked that that counsel be replaced by a lawyer of his choice. The initial appointment was confirmed by the Stuttgart Court of Appeal on 6 March 1978.*

On 27 December 1979, the costs office of the Stuttgart Regional Court asked Mr Croissant to pay the costs and expenses of the three court-appointed defence counsel. On 30 April 1987, the Stuttgart Court of Appeal dismissed an appeal against the costs order. Likewise, on 23 June 1987, the Constitutional Court refused to entertain a constitutional appeal brought by the applicant. However, the enforcement of the costs order was suspended at the time of the European Court's judgment.

425. *In his application of 3 December 1987 to the Commission, Mr Croissant complained that he had been ordered to pay the fees and expenses of three court-appointed lawyers. He relied on Article 6 §§ 1 and 3(c) of the Convention.*[1]

Judgment of 25 September 1992 *(Chamber) (Series A No. 237–B)*

426. The Court held that neither the requirement that a defendant be assisted by counsel at all stages of the Regional Court's proceedings nor the appointment of more than one defence counsel was inconsistent

---

1 In its report of 7 March 1991, the Commission expressed the opinion that there had been no violation of Article 6 §§ 1 and 3(c) either in respect of the fees and expenses of the two lawyers appointed at his request (unanimously) or in respect of those of the third lawyer appointed against the applicant's will (seven votes to four).

with the Convention. However, in the absence of relevant, sufficient grounds, before nominating more than one counsel a court should pay heed to the accused's views as to the number needed, especially where, as in Germany, he would in principle have to bear the consequent costs if he were convicted.

The appointment of the first two lawyers did not raise any problems in this regard. In contrast, Mr Croissant regarded the appointment of the third as unnecessary. The Court considered that the grounds on which the national courts had based, and confirmed, their appointment of the third lawyer were relevant and sufficient: in particular, his qualifications, the location of his chambers within the Regional Court's jurisdiction and the fact that the accused had already chosen two court-appointed counsel himself. It also pointed to the active role played by the third counsel in conducting Mr Croissant's defence. Consequently, there had been no violation of Article 6 §§ 1 and 3(c) (eight votes to one).

427. In a system such as the one operating in Germany, a convicted person was in principle always bound to pay the fees and disbursements of his court-appointed lawyers, it being only in the enforcement procedure that the financial situation of the convicted person played a role. Such a system would not be compatible with Article 6 of the Convention if it adversely affected the fairness of the proceedings. That had not been the case here, since the national courts were entitled to consider it necessary to appoint counsel and the amounts claimed for them were not excessive. The courts had granted several extensions of the time-limit for payment and had reserved their decision on the cancellation of the debt. There was no reason to doubt that, should the applicant be able to establish that he could not afford to pay the entire amount owed, the relevant legislation and practice of the *Land* would be applied. The Court concluded that the reimbursement order was therefore not incompatible with Article 6 § 3(c) (unanimously).

428. *Summary bibliography*

COUSSIRAT-COUSTÈRE (V.).—'La jurisprudence de la Cour européenne des droits de l'homme en 1992', *A.F.D.I.* 1992, pp. 629 *et seq.*

SUDRE (F.), LEVINET (M.), PEYROT (B.) and ECOCHARD (B.).—'Chronique de la jurisprudence de la Cour européenne des droits de l'homme—1992', *R.U.D.H.* 1993, Nos 1–2, pp. 1 *et seq.*

SWART (B.).—'The case-law of the European Court of Human Rights in 1992', *E.J.C.* 1993, pp. 167 *et seq.*

320. Case of Pham Hoang v. France

Conviction on appeal for a customs offence and presumptions created by the Customs Code; refusal to make an official assignment of counsel for an appeal on points of law

429. *On 25 March 1985, Tuan Tran Pham Hoang, a French national, was committed for trial on a charge under drugs legislation (a criminal offence) and on a charge of smuggling prohibited goods (a customs offence). On 31 May, he was acquitted by the Paris criminal court. On 10 March 1986, however, the Paris Court of Appeal overturned that judgment in part: it held the applicant guilty of the second offence as a person in possession or having an interest in customs evasion and ordered him to pay, jointly and severally with others, penalties totalling 5,670,000 French francs, his personal liability being limited to the sum of 2,000,000 French francs. The Court of Cassation dismissed the applicant's appeal on 9 March 1987; he unsuccessfully applied for legal aid.*

430. *In his application to the Commission of 20 August 1987, Mr Pham Hoang complained that he had been convicted on the basis of statutory presumptions of guilt which were incompatible with the rights of the defence and with the presumption of innocence (Article 6 §§ 1 and 2 of the Convention). He also complained that he had not been assisted by a lawyer during the hearing of his appeal on points of law (Article 6 § 3(c)).*[1]

Judgment of 25 September 1992 *(Chamber) (Series A No. 243)*

431. With regard to Article 6 §§ 1 and 2, the Government maintained that Mr Pham Hoang had not put the Court of Cassation in a position to try his appeal.

Although the Commission maintained the contrary, the Court held that it had jurisdiction to entertain the objection. It dismissed it (unanimously) on the ground that the refusal of an official assignment of counsel had rendered the remedy in question ineffective.

---

1 In its report of 26 February 1991, the Commission expressed the opinion that there had been no violation of Article 6 §§ 1 and 2 (seven votes to five) and that there had been a violation of Article 6 § 3(c) (unanimously).

432. In the Court's view, Mr Pham Hoang had not been deprived of all means of defending himself before the Paris Court of Appeal since he had been entitled to try to show that he had acted from necessity or as a result of unavoidable mistake. That court had taken account of a cumulation of facts. It had duly weighed the evidence before it, assessed it carefully and based its finding of guilt on it. It had refrained from any automatic reliance on the presumptions created in the relevant provisions of the Customs Code and had not applied them in a manner incompatible with Article 6 §§ 1 and 2 (held unanimously).

433. The Court then had to rule on the question of compliance with Article 6 § 3(c). The applicant had, it appeared, met with the refusal during a transitional period, as the authority of the Legal Aid Office at the Court of Cassation had since been extended by legislation to cover criminal proceedings. Nevertheless, the proceedings had clearly been fraught with consequences for the applicant, who had been acquitted at first instance but found guilty on appeal. In addition, and above all, Mr Pham Hoang had intended to challenge in the Court of Cassation the compatibility of several provisions of the Customs Code with Article 6 §§ 1 and 2 of the Convention. He did not, however, have the legal training essential to enable him to present and develop the appropriate arguments on such complex issues himself. The interests of justice accordingly required a lawyer to be officially assigned to the case. Since he had been unable to secure this, the applicant had been the victim of a breach of Article 6 § 3(c) (held unanimously).

434. Under Article 50, the Court dismissed the applicant's claim for compensation for pecuniary damage, since it could not speculate as to the outcome of the appeal if legal assistance had been granted (held unanimously).

The Court held—and Mr Pham Hoang agreed—that the finding of a violation of Article 6 § 3(c) constituted reasonable compensation for the non-pecuniary damage which he had suffered (unanimously).

It awarded a total net sum of 30,000 French francs for costs and expenses incurred before the Convention institutions, since the applicant had received legal aid at Strasbourg (unanimously).[1]

---

1 Law No 91–647 of 10 July 1991 on legal aid amended the system for its grant. In addition, it set up at each *tribunal de grande instance*, the Court of Cassation, the *Conseil d'Etat* and the Appeals Board for Refugees legal aid boards to rule on applications for legal aid. An appeal will lie against their decisions.

435. *Summary bibliography*

Coussirat-Coustère (V.).—'La jurisprudence de la Cour européenne des droits de l'homme en 1992', *A.F.D.I.* 1992, pp. 629 *et seq.*

Decaux (E.) and Tavernier (P.).—'Chronique de jurisprudence de la Cour européenne des droits de l'homme', *J.D.I.* 1993, pp. 749 and 750.

Renucci (J.-F.)—'Droit européen des droits de l'homme', *D.* 1993, sommaires commentés, p. 386.

Sudre (F.), Levinet (M.), Peyrot (B.) and Ecochard (B.).—'Chronique de la jurisprudence de la Cour européenne des droits de l'homme—1992', *R.U.D.H.* 1993, Nos 1–2, pp. 1 *et seq.*

Swart (B.).—'The case-law of the European Court of Human Rights in 1992', *E.J.C.* 1993, pp. 167 *et seq.*

321. Case of Boddaert v. Belgium

Length of criminal proceedings

436. *On 20 July 1980, a warrant was issued for the arrest of Jean-Claude Boddaert on suspicion of the murder of one Jehin. It was issued in his absence as he had fled to Spain, but was confirmed on 30 July when Mr Boddaert was handed over to the Belgian authorities. On 2 February 1982 he was released. On 6 September 1985, the indictment division of the Liège Court of Appeal committed the applicant and his co-accused, Mr Piron, for trial in the Liège assize court. On 11 February 1986, the President of the assize court ordered the joinder of the case and the proceedings brought against Mr Boddaert's co-accused for the murder of one Thérèse Hemeleers and decided that the proceedings relating to the two murders should be dealt with at the same hearing. On 14 March 1986, the assize court found Mr Boddaert guilty of murder and sentenced him to ten years' imprisonment; Mr Piron was found guilty of two murders and sentenced to death. The Court of Cassation dismissed Mr Boddaert's appeal on 22 October 1986.*

437. *In his application to the Commission of 13 February 1986, Mr Boddaert relied on Article 6 § 1 ('reasonable time') and Article 6 § 3(b) of the Convention.*[1]

Judgment of 12 October 1992 *(Chamber) (Series A No. 235–D)*

438. The period to be taken into consideration had extended over six years, two months and twenty-two days; it had run from 19 July 1980, the date on which the warrant had been issued for the applicant's arrest, until 22 October 1986, when the Court of Cassation had delivered its judgment, with a brief interruption owing to Mr Boddaert's flight to Spain.

The Court noted at the outset that the present case originated in a murder following shortly after another murder committed in the same place. A number of persons, including the applicant, coming from the same circle had been implicated.

---

1 On 2 July 1990, the Commission declared the complaint based on Article 6 § 3(b) admissible. In its report of 17 April 1991, it expressed the opinion that there had been a violation of Article 6 § 1 (nine votes to two).

The inquiry had been a difficult one. Initially this had been because of the lack of witnesses and because Mr Boddaert and Mr Piron had accused each other of having committed the crime of which they were both suspected. The investigation, which had been pursued without interruption until 2 February 1982, had failed to shed light on the motives for the murder and to establish the personalities of the accused. It had however revealed the existence of possible links with other offences.

In addition to this, the criminal conduct of Mr Piron had had to be taken into account. This had led the investigating judge to shelve the investigation in case there were any further developments. When on 1 June 1983 Mr Piron had been accused of the murder of Thérèse Hemeleers, the authorities had considered that that murder and the crime with which Mr Boddaert was charged were closely linked; they had then decided to await the outcome of the investigation of the second case in order to complete the file on the first and to hold a joint trial of all the charges brought against Mr Piron.

The Court held that the gravity of the offences in question and the interdependence of the charges, which had been noted by the assize court itself, could reasonably appear to make it necessary for such a 'parallel progression' of the two cases. The conduct of the authorities had been consistent with the fair balance which had to be struck between the principle that judicial proceedings should be expeditious and the more general principle of the proper administration of justice. Consequently, there had been no violation of Article 6 § 1 (held unanimously).

439. *Summary bibliography*

COUSSIRAT-COUSTÈRE (V.).—'La jurisprudence de la Cour européenne des droits de l'homme en 1992', *A.F.D.I.* 1992, pp. 629 *et seq.*

LAMBERT (P.).—'A la Cour européenne des droits de l'homme—Un critère supplémentaire dans l'appréciation du délai raisonnable?', *J.T.* 1993, p. 154.

SUDRE (F.), LEVINET (M.), PEYROT (B.) and ECOCHARD (B.).—'Chronique de la jurisprudence de la Cour européenne des droits de l'homme—1992', *R.U.D.H.* 1993, Nos 1–2, pp. 1 *et seq.*

SWART (B.).—'The case-law of the European Court of Human Rights in 1992', *E.J.C.* 1993, pp. 167 *et seq.*

322. Case of T. v. Italy

Trial *in absentia* of an 'untraceable' accused

440. *T., an Italian national, was living abroad when, in February 1983, the Italian judicial authorities sent him 'judicial notification' that criminal proceedings had been commenced against him for raping his daughter, who was a minor aged fourteen years at the time of the alleged offence. He claimed that he had not received the notification in question, although he admitted that he had had indirect knowledge of the proceedings in June 1982. In November 1983 the investigating judge in Genoa declared the applicant untraceable; similar declarations were made, following police inquiries, at later stages in the proceedings. In October 1984, the Genoa District Court convicted T. in* absentia *and sentenced him,* inter alia, *to seven years' imprisonment. The officially-appointed lawyer appealed against the judgment, but the Genoa Court of Appeal upheld it,* again in absentia, *in October 1986. In August 1987 he was arrested in Copenhagen and on 29 October extradited to Italy. He lodged an objection to the execution of the warrant and brought two further appeals after his return to Italy, but was unsuccessful. He completed his sentence in 1991.*

441. *The applicant lodged his application with the Commission on 1 April 1988; he relied on Articles 5 § 1(a), 6 §§ 1, 2 and 3(a) to (d), 8, 9, 10, 13 and 14 of the Convention.*[1]

Judgment of 12 October 1992 *(Chamber) (Series A No. 245–C)*

442. The Court considered T.'s complaint only from the point of view of Article 6 § 1. In this case, the question as to whether and in what circumstances an accused could waive his right to appear and defend himself did not arise, since T. denied having received the 'judicial notification'.

The Court considered that to inform someone of a prosecution brought against him was a legal act of such importance that it must be carried out in accordance with procedural and substantive requirements capable of guaranteeing the effective exercise of the accused's rights. Vague and informal knowledge could not suffice.

---

1 On 3 December 1990, the Commission declared the complaint based on Article 6 admissible and found the remainder of the application inadmissible. In its report of 4 July 1991, it expressed the opinion that there had been a breach of Article 6 § 1 (unanimously).

From the outset it had been clear that the applicant had been living abroad. Notwithstanding this, the Italian judicial authorities had declared him untraceable and then convicted and sentenced him on 9 October 1984 and 1 October 1986, without having ordered more thorough investigations.

In conclusion, T. had not received a fair trial. As the legislation in force at the time had not afforded him any means of redress in this respect, there had been a violation of Article 6 § 1 (held unanimously).

443. With regard to Article 50, the Court was of the opinion that the finding of a violation constituted in itself sufficient just satisfaction for any non-pecuniary damage (held unanimously).

It dismissed T.'s claim for costs and expenses, since he had received legal aid before the Commission and the Court.[1]

444. *Summary bibliography*

COUSSIRAT-COUSTÈRE (V.).—'La jurisprudence de la Cour européenne des droits de l'homme en 1992', *A.F.D.I.* 1992, pp. 629 *et seq.*

SUDRE (F.), LEVINET (M.), PEYROT (B.) and ECOCHARD (B.).—'Chronique de la jurisprudence de la Cour européenne des droits de l'homme—1992', *R.U.D.H.* 1993, Nos 1–2, pp. 1 *et seq.*

SWART (B.).—'The case-law of the European Court of Human Rights in 1992', *E.J.C.* 1993, pp. 167 *et seq.*

---

1 The new Code of Criminal Procedure, which entered into force on 24 October 1989, amended the former provisions relating to the re-opening of time-limits for appealing against a judgment given *in absentia* so as to bring them into line with the requirements of the Convention (Article 175, formerly Article 183 bis). Moreover, the Court of Cassation construed the Code in this way in its judgment of 12 May 1993 in the *Medrano* case.

323. Case of Cesarini v. Italy

Length of civil proceedings

445. *On 10 September 1982, Franco Cesarini, an Italian national, instituted proceedings against his employer before the Rome magistrate's court seeking a ruling that his lay-off on 14 June 1982 had been unlawful and that he was entitled to payment of his wages as from that date. On 9 February 1984 the magistrate's court dismissed the applicant's suit and on 18 November 1986 the Rome District Court rejected his appeal of 29 March 1985. On 25 March 1988, he appealed to the Court of Cassation, but the parties reached a friendly settlement on 19 January 1989. On 7 February, the applicant withdrew his appeal. On 22 February 1989 the Court of Cassation noted the applicant's withdrawal of his action and closed the proceedings.*

446. *In his application of 11 September 1985 to the Commission, Mr Cesarini complained of the length of the civil proceedings brought by him and relied on Article 6 § 1 of the Convention.*[1]

Judgment of 12 October 1992 *(Chamber) (Series A No. 245–B)*

447. The period to be taken into consideration had started, not on 10 September 1982, when proceedings had been instituted against Mr Cesarini's employer, but on 10 June of that year, when the applicant had requested the Rome magistrate's court to adopt an emergency measure. It had ended on 22 February 1989, when the Court of Cassation had noted that the applicant had withdrawn the action and closed the proceedings. It had thus lasted for more than six years and eight months.

The Court effected an overall assessment and found that there had been several periods of inactivity on the part of the judicial authorities. Nevertheless, having regard to the applicant's attitude, to the fact that the case had come before three different courts and to the friendly settlement, the delays that had occurred did not appear substantial enough for the total length of the proceedings to be able to be regarded as excessive. There had therefore been no breach of Article 6 § 1 (held unanimously).

1 In its report of 10 July 1991, the Commission expressed the opinion that there had been a breach of Article 6 § 1 (fourteen votes to five).

448. *Summary bibliography*

COUSSIRAT-COUSTÈRE (V.).—'La jurisprudence de la Cour européenne des droits de l'homme en 1992', *A.F.D.I.* 1992, pp. 629 *et seq.*

SUDRE (F.), LEVINET (M.), PEYROT (B.) and ECOCHARD (B.).—'Chronique de la jurisprudence de la Cour européenne des droits de l'homme—1992', *R.U.D.H.* 1993, Nos 1–2, pp. 1 *et seq.*

324. Case of Salerno v. Italy

Length of proceedings brought to obtain repayment of old-age pension contributions

449. *Vincenzo Salerno, an Italian national, had worked as an auxiliary notary for nineteen years. By proceedings which ended in 1980 in the Court of Cassation, he sought unsuccessfully to establish his right to join the notaries' pension fund* (Cassa Nazionale di Notariato) *and to draw the pension payable to its members. On 8 April 1982, the applicant instituted further proceedings in the Rome magistrate's court to have the notaries' pension fund repay old-age pension contributions he had paid into it. On 12 May 1983, the court dismissed the applicant's claim and his appeal to the Rome District Court of 21 July 1983 was dismissed by a judgment of 14 November 1984 (filed with the registry on 22 January 1985). In turn, the Court of Cassation dismissed an appeal of 10 April 1985 by a judgment of 12 June 1986 (filed with the registry on 1 April 1987), on the ground that it was based on a claim which had been rejected definitively in the earlier proceedings.*

450. *In his application of 18 January 1986 to the Commission, Mr Salerno relied on Article 6 § 1 of the Convention on the basis of the complaint that the proceedings that he had brought had taken too long and that the courts that had heard the case had not been impartial.*[1]

Judgment of 12 October 1992 *(Chamber) (Series A No. 245–D)*

451. The Court ruled first on the applicability of Article 6 § 1, which was contested by the Government. The Court noted that the second proceedings which Mr Salerno had brought on 8 April 1982 related to a disputed issue, on which only the competent courts could rule. The two sets of proceedings had had different purposes: the first action had been brought to secure recognition of a right to old-age benefits, whereas the second action had been for the repayment of pension contributions. Above all, the courts to which the fresh application had been made in 1982 had acknowledged that the applicant's arguments

1 On 5 March 1990, the Commission declared the second complaint inadmissible but found the application to be admissible in respect of the first complaint. In its report of 5 September 1991, the Commission expressed the opinion that there had been a breach of Article 6 § 1 (sixteen votes to four).

were sufficiently tenable, since they had held the action to be admissible. Since, furthermore, the claimed right was undoubtedly a civil one, Article 6 § 1 was applicable (held unanimously).

452. The period to be considered had begun on 8 April 1982, with the institution of proceedings against the notaries' pension fund in the Rome magistrate's court, and had ended on 1 April 1987, when the Court of Cassation's judgment had been filed. It had therefore lasted for nearly five years.

The Court made an overall assessment and found that there had been several periods of inactivity on the part of the judicial authorities. Nevertheless, having regard to the fact that the case had come before three different courts, the delays that had occurred did not appear substantial enough for the total length of the proceedings to have exceeded an acceptable limit. There had accordingly been no breach of Article 6 § 1 (held unanimously).

453. *Summary bibliography*

COUSSIRAT-COUSTÈRE (V.).—'La jurisprudence de la Cour européenne des droits de l'homme en 1992', *A.F.D.I.* 1992, pp. 629 *et seq.*

SUDRE (F.), LEVINET (M.), PEYROT (B.) and ECOCHARD (B.).—'Chronique de la jurisprudence de la Cour européenne des droits de l'homme—1992', *R.U.D.H.* 1993, Nos 1–2, pp. 1 *et seq.*

325. Case of Mlynek v. Austria

Length of criminal proceedings

454. *On 21 May 1980 criminal proceedings were brought against Hannes Mlynek. They culminated, on 30 May 1984, in his conviction by the Vienna Regional Court for misappropriation of funds and fraud. On 30 January 1987 the Supreme Court quashed the judgment of the Regional Court. Proceedings were re-opened in that court on 11 January 1988.*

On 19 September 1989, following an initial application to the European Commission in Strasbourg, the Committee of Ministers of the Council of Europe considered that the length of the proceedings had exceeded a 'reasonable time' contrary to Article 6 § 1 of the Convention, and recommended that the applicant should be paid a sum by way of just satisfaction. In the meantime, on 23 March 1988, he had been sentenced by the Vienna Regional Court. However, its judgment was quashed by the Supreme Court on 1 June 1990, which sent the case back yet again to the Regional Court. The proceedings were still pending but confined to a prosecution for negligent bankruptcy.

455. *In his application to the Commission of 21 March 1989, Mr Mylnek complained of the length of the proceedings after 10 March 1988 and relied on Article 6 § 1 of the Convention.*[1]

Judgment of 27 October 1992 *(Chamber) (Series A No. 242–C)*

456. The Court took note of the agreement reached between the Austrian Government and Mr Mylnek: the former undertook to uphold a claim which the applicant would make once the decision in the proceedings which were the subject of the complaint had become final, so as to exonerate him from the obligation to pay the costs and expenses relating to those proceedings; the Government and the applicant—who declared that his applications pending in Strasbourg (the one before the Court and another before the Commission) were to be regarded as settled—agreed that they would not bring before an authority, whether Austrian or international, claims arising in any way from the subject-

---

1 In its report of 9 December 1991, the Commission expressed the unanimous opinion that there had been a violation of Article 6 § 1.

matter of the human rights applications, namely the criminal proceedings at issue.

457. The Court discerned no reason of public policy militating against striking the case out of the list (Rules of Court, Rule 49 §§ 2 and 4) (held unanimously).

458. *Summary bibliography*

COUSSIRAT-COUSTÈRE (V.).—'La jurisprudence de la Cour européenne des droits de l'homme en 1992', *A.F.D.I.* 1992, pp. 629 *et seq*.

SUDRE (F.), LEVINET (M.), PEYROT (B.) and ECOCHARD (B.).—'Chronique de jurisprudence de la Cour européenne des droits de l'homme—1992', *R.U.D.H.* 1993, Nos 1–2, pp. 1 *et seq*.

SWART (B.).—'The case-law of the European Court of Human Rights in 1992', *E.J.C.* 1993, pp. 167 *et seq*.

326. Case of Open Door and Dublin Well Woman v. Ireland

Injunction granted by the Supreme Court restraining counselling agencies *inter alia* from providing pregnant women with information concerning abortion facilities abroad

459.   *Open Door Counselling Ltd and Dublin Well Woman Centre Ltd were Irish non-profit-making companies which provided* inter alia *counselling services for pregnant women in Ireland; if the women so wished, they would inform them about opportunities for obtaining abortions in clinics in Great Britain.*

Proceedings were brought against the two companies by the Attorney General at the request of the Society for the Protection of Unborn Children (Ireland) Ltd (S.P.U.C.). On 16 March 1988, the Supreme Court held that non-directive counselling provided by the two companies assisted in the destruction of the life of the unborn guaranteed by Article 40, s.3, subs.3 of the Constitution. The court granted an injunction prohibiting the companies, their servants or agents 'from assisting pregnant women within the jurisdiction to travel abroad to obtain abortions by referral to a clinic, by the making for them of travel arrangements, or by informing them of the identity and location of and the method of communication with a specified clinic or clinics or otherwise'.

460.   *Open Door applied to the Commission on 19 August 1988, Dublin Well Woman on 22 September 1988, likewise two of its trained counsellors (Bonnie Maher, an American, and Ann Downes, an Irish national) and two Irish women (Mrs X and Maeve Geraghty). They complained that the injunction in question constituted an unjustified interference with their right to impart or receive information contrary to Article 10 of the Convention. Open Door, Mrs X and Ms Geraghty further claimed that the restrictions amounted to an interference with their right to respect for private life in breach of Article 8. Open Door argued, in addition, that the restrictions constituted discrimination contrary to Article 14 in conjunction with Articles 8 and 10.*[1]

1   In its report of 7 March 1991, the Commission expressed the opinion that:
    (a) there had been a violation of Article 10 in respect of the Supreme Court injunction as it affected the applicant companies and counsellors (eight votes to five);

212

Judgment of 29 October 1992 *(Plenary Court) (Series A No. 246–A)*

461. Before the Court, Dublin Well Woman and the two counsellors complained for the first time that there had been a violation of Article 8. The Court pointed out that the scope of the Court's jurisdiction was determined by the Commission's decision declaring the originating application admissible. As the complain based on Article 8 was a new and separate complaint, the Court had no jurisdiction to entertain it.

462. The Government raised three preliminary objections.

In the first place, it submitted that only the corporate applicants could claim to be 'victims' of an infringement of their Convention rights. In contrast, the Court held that that was also the case with Ms Maher and Ms Downes (unanimously), since they were directly affected by the Supreme Court injunction, and with Mrs X and Ms Geraghty (fifteen votes to eight), since they belonged to a class of women of child-bearing age which might be adversely affected by the restrictions imposed by the injunction.

Secondly, the Government submitted that the application should be rejected under Article 26 for failure to comply with the six-month rule. The Court rejected this plea as being out of time (unanimously).

Thirdly, the Government also submitted that domestic remedies had not been exhausted by Open Door as regards its complaints under Articles 8 and 14; by both Open Door and Dublin Well Woman in so far as they sought to introduce in their complaint under Article 10 evidence and submissions concerning abortion and the impact of the Supreme Court injunction on women's health that had not been raised before the Irish courts; and by the four individuals on the grounds that they had made no attempt to exhaust domestic remedies under Irish law. The Court rejected that plea (unanimously): having regard to the reasoning of the Supreme Court, Open Door's complaints would have had no prospect of success; Open Door and Dublin Well Woman were not introducing a fresh complaint but were merely developing their submissions in respect of complaints which had already been examined by the Irish courts; and any action brought by the four individual applicants would have had no prospects of success.

    (b) there had been a violation of Article 10 in respect of the Supreme Court injunction as it affected Mrs X and Ms Geraghty (seven votes to six);

    (c) it was not necessary to examine further the complaints of Mrs X and Ms Geraghty under Article 8 (seven votes to two, with four abstentions); and

    (d) there had been no violation of Articles 8 and 14 in respect of Open Door (unanimously).

463.   As regards Article 10, the Court noted that the injunction had interfered with the corporate applicants' freedom to impart information, and that there had also been an interference with the rights of the applicant counsellors to impart information and with the rights of Mrs X and Ms Geraghty to receive information in the event of their being pregnant.

The Court went on to consider whether the interference was 'prescribed by law'. Taking into consideration the high threshold of protection of the unborn provided under Irish law generally and the manner in which the courts had interpreted their role as the guarantors of constitutional rights, the possibility that action might be taken against the corporate applicants must have been, with appropriate legal advice, reasonably foreseeable. This conclusion was reinforced by the legal advice that had actually been given to Dublin Well Woman that, in the light of Article 40.3.3 of the Irish Constitution, an injunction could be sought against its counselling activities. The restriction was accordingly 'prescribed by law'.

Did the interference have legitimate aims? The protection afforded under Irish law to the right to life of the unborn was based on profound moral values concerning the nature of life which were reflected in the stance of the majority of the Irish people against abortion as expressed in the 1983 referendum. The restriction thus pursued the legitimate aim of the protection of morals of which the protection in Ireland of the right to life of the unborn was one aspect. It was not necessary in the light of this conclusion to decide whether the term 'others' under Article 10 § 2 extended to the unborn.

The Court then determined whether the restriction was 'necessary in a democratic society'. The Court observed that it was not called upon to examine whether a right to abortion was guaranteed under the Convention or whether the foetus was encompassed by the right to life as contained in Article 2. The applicants had not claimed that the Convention contained a right to abortion, as such, their complaint being limited to that part of the injunction which restricted their freedom to impart and receive information concerning abortion abroad.

The State's discretion in the field of the protection of morals was not unfettered and unreviewable. Admittedly, the national authorities did enjoy a wide margin of appreciation in matters of morals, particularly in an area such as the present, which touched on matters of belief concerning the nature of human life. However, that power of appreciation was not unlimited and it was for Court to supervise whether a restriction was compatible with the Convention. As regards the application of the 'proportionality' test, whilst it was, in principle, open to the national authorities to take such action as they considered necessary to respect the rule of law or to give effect to constitutional rights, they had to do so in a manner which was compatible with their obligations under the Convention and subject to review by the Convention institutions.

As for the 'necessity' of the restrictions, the Court pointed out that freedom of expression was also applicable to 'information' or 'ideas' that offended, shocked or disturbed the State or any sector of the population. Limitations on information concerning activities which, notwithstanding their moral implications, had been and continued to be tolerated by national authorities, called for careful scrutiny by the Convention institutions as to their conformity with the tenets of a democratic society.

The Court was first struck by the absolute nature of the Supreme Court injunction, which imposed a 'perpetual' restraint on the provision of information to pregnant women concerning abortion facilities abroad, regardless of age or state of health or their reasons for seeking counselling on the termination of pregnancy. On that ground alone the restriction appeared over broad and disproportionate. Moreover, that assessment was confirmed by other factors. In the first place, the corporate applicants had been engaged in the counselling of pregnant women in the course of which counsellors had neither advocated nor encouraged abortion, but had confined themselves to an explanation of the available options. The decision as to whether or not to act on the information so provided had been for the woman concerned to take. Secondly, information concerning abortion facilities abroad could be obtained from other sources in Ireland, such as magazines and telephone directories, or by persons with contacts in Great Britain. Accordingly, information that the injunction sought to restrict was already available elsewhere, although in a manner which was not supervised by qualified personnel and thus less protective of women's health. Lastly, the available evidence, which had not been disputed by the Government, suggested that the injunction had created a risk to women's health: women were now seeking abortions at a later stage in their pregnancy, due to lack of proper counselling, and were not availing themselves of customary medical supervision after the abortion had taken place. Moreover, the injunction might have had more adverse effects on women who were not sufficiently resourceful or had not the necessary level of education to have access to alternative sources of information.

The Government, invoking Articles 17 and 60 of the Convention, submitted that Article 10 should not be interpreted in such a manner as to limit, destroy or derogate from the right to life of the unborn, which enjoyed special protection under Irish law. Without calling into question under the Convention the regime of protection of unborn life that existed under Irish law, the Court recalled that the injunction had not prevented Irish women from having abortions abroad and that the information it had sought to restrain was available from other sources. Accordingly, it was not the interpretation of Article 10 but the position in Ireland as regards the implementation of the law that made possible the continuance of the current level of abortions obtained by Irish women abroad.

In sum, the restraint imposed on the applicants was disproportionate to the aims pursued. Accordingly there had been a breach of Article 10 (fifteen votes to eight).

464. Having regard to that finding, the Court held that it was not necessary to examine the complaints made by Dublin Well Woman, Open Door, Mrs X and Ms Geraghty under Articles 8 and 14 (unanimously).

465. Under Article 50, the Court awarded Dublin Well Woman IR£25,000 in respect of loss of income due to the injunction (seventeen votes to six).

It accepted Open Door's claim for costs and expenses incurred in the domestic proceedings and before the Strasbourg institutions in full and that of Dublin Well Woman in part. The former was awarded IR£68,985.75 and the latter IR£100,000, less the amounts received by way of legal aid (unanimously).

466. *Summary bibliography*

COUSSIRAT-COUSTÈRE (V.).—'La jurisprudence de la Cour européenne des droits de l'homme en 1992', *A.F.D.I.* 1992, pp. 629 *et seq.*

DECAUX (E.) and TAVERNIER (P.).—'Chronique de jurisprudence de la Cour européenne des droits de l'homme (année 1992)', *J.D.I.* 1993, pp. 751–755.

DUBOUIS (L.).—'La liberté d'information sur les possibilités d'IVG à l'étranger au regard de la CEDH', *Revue de droit sanitaire et social* 1993, pp. 32–41.

HOGAN (G.).—'The right to life and the abolition question under the European Convention on Human Rights', in Hefferman (L.) (ed.), *Human rights. A European perspective*, The Round Hall Press, Blackrock, Dublin, 1994, pp. 104–116.

RIGAUX (F.).—'La diffusion d'informations relatives aux interruptions médicales de grossesse et la liberté d'expression', *R.T.D.H.* 1993, pp. 345–358.

SUDRE (F.).—'L'interdiction de l'avortement: le conflit entre le juge constitutionnel irlandais et la Cour européenne des droits de l'homme', *Revue française de droit constitutionnel* 1993, pp. 216–222.

SUDRE (F.), LEVINET (M.), PEYROT (B.) and ECOCHARD (B.).—'Chronique de jurisprudence de la Cour européenne des droits de l'homme—1992', *R.U.D.H.* 1993, Nos 1–2, pp. 1 *et seq.*

WARBRICK (C.).—'The European Convention on Human Rights', *Y.E.L.* 1992, pp. 713–720.

327. Case of Y v. the United Kingdom

Corporal punishment in an independent school in England

467. *In 1983, Y, then aged fifteen, was a day pupil at an independent school in England. On 29 September he was knocked over at the school by a fellow pupil who was chasing a younger boy. The applicant subsequently defaced the cover of the fellow pupil's file. He was sent for punishment to the headmaster who caned him four times on his bottom through his trousers. On his return from school, his mother took him straight to the family doctor, who found that he had four wheals across both buttocks, each wheal approximately 15cm in length and 1.23cm in width. There was heavy bruising and swelling of both buttocks.*

The police initially advised that the injuries amounted to evidence of assault occasioning actual bodily harm, but after further investigation decided not to prosecute the headmaster. In July 1986, a County Court judge dismissed a civil action brought by the parents for, inter alia, damages for assault: the parents had entered into a binding contract with the school in which it had been agreed that the school was authorized to cane pupils as a disciplinary punishment; the force used in such punishment, which would inevitably leave marks and bruising, had nevertheless to be reasonable; there had been nothing unusual or excessive in the caning and the parents had overreacted to the incident. The parents did not appeal against the County Court decision as they were advised by counsel that such an appeal had no prospects of success.

468. *In their application to the Commission of 2 September 1986, Mrs X and her son Y invoked Articles 3, 8, 13 and 14 of the Convention. The complaint under Article 14 was subsequently withdrawn.*[1]

Judgment of 29 October 1992 *(Chamber) (Series A No. 247–A)*

469. The Court took formal note of the friendly settlement reached by the Government and Y: without any admission by the Government that a breach of the Convention had occurred and on condition that the

---

1 On 13 December 1990, the Commission declared the mother's complaints inadmissible and the son's admissible. In its report of 8 October 1991, the Commission expressed the opinion (by eleven votes to two) that there had been a violation of Articles 3 and 13, and that no separate issue arose under Article 8.

case was withdrawn from the Court and no further cases were instituted against the Government in respect of this matter in any national or international court, the Government proposed to pay the applicant £8,000 plus his costs.

470. The Court discerned no reason of public policy (*ordre public*) why the case should not be struck out of the list (Rules of Court, Rule 49 §§ 2 and 4) (held unanimously).

471. *Summary bibliography*

COUSSIRAT-COUSTÈRE (V.).—'Jurisprudence de la Cour européenne des droits de l'homme en 1992', *A.F.D.I.* 1992, pp. 629 *et seq.*
PHILLIPS (B.).—'The case for corporal punishment in the United Kingdom. Beaten into submission in Europe?', *I.C.L.Q.* 1994, pp. 153–163.
SUDRE (F.), LEVINET (M.), PEYROT (B.) and ECOCHARD (B.).—'Chronique de jurisprudence de la Cour européenne des droits de l'homme—1992', *R.U.D.H.* 1993, Nos 1–2, pp. 1 *et seq.*

328. Case of Abdoella v. the Netherlands

Length of criminal proceedings

472. *On 18 January 1983, Abodel Aliem Klan Abdoella was arrested and charged with incitement to murder on the ground that he had promised money and heroin to another person who had been asked to help him kill a third party. On the same day, he was detained on remand. On 17 May 1983, the Regional Court at The Hague sentenced him to twelve years' imprisonment. On an appeal brought by the applicant, the Court of Appeal at The Hague upheld the Regional Court's judgment on 29 August 1983. Mr Abdoella then appealed to the Supreme Court, which, on 15 January 1985, quashed the Hague Court of Appeal's judgment on technical grounds and referred the case to the Amsterdam Court of Appeal. The hearing of 28 June 1985 before the latter court was adjourned at the applicant's request and resumed, with his consent, on 20 September 1985. On 4 October 1985, the Court of Appeal sentenced the applicant to ten years' imprisonment. Mr Abdoella appealed for a second time to the Supreme Court, but his appeal was dismissed on 19 May 1987. Subsequently, the Deputy Minister of Justice refused a request for a pardon and the Supreme Court declared an application for review brought by Mr Abdoella inadmissible.*

473. *In his application of 9 February 1987 to the Commission, Mr Abdoella complained,* inter alia, *of the length of the criminal proceedings against him and relied on Article 6 § 1 of the Convention.*[1]

Judgment of 25 November 1992 *(Chamber) (Series A No. 248–A)*

474. At the hearing, the Government argued that domestic remedies had not been exhausted with regard to the periods preceding the second appeal on points of law before the Supreme Court.

The Court observed, that under the Rules of Court, that objection ought to have been raised at an earlier stage in the proceedings; it therefore dismissed it as time-barred (unanimously).

---

1 On 10 April 1991, the Commission declared the application admissible in respect of this complaint and inadmissible as to the remainder. In its report of 14 October 1991, it expressed the unanimous opinion that there had been a violation of Article 6 § 1.

475. With regard to the merits, in view of the fact that five court examinations had been involved, the total period (five years, four months and one day) was not unreasonable.

However, after the applicant had filed his first appeal on points of law, more than ten months had elapsed between the date of the judgment of the Hague Court of Appeal and the date when the documents had been sent to the Supreme Court; as for the second appeal on points of law, nearly eleven and a half months had elapsed after the judgment of the Amsterdam Court of Appeal. Totalling more than twenty-one months of the fifty-two which it had taken to deal with the case, those delays were unacceptable, especially where, as in the present case, the accused was detained. There had accordingly been a violation of Article 6 § 1 (held unanimously).

476. The Court held that the finding of a violation constituted sufficient just satisfaction for any non-pecuniary damage which Mr Abdoella might have suffered (unanimously).

It awarded the applicant 10,901.88 guilders for costs and expenses, less 8,825 French francs paid by way of legal aid at Strasbourg (unanimously).

477. *Summary bibliography*

Coussirat-Coustère (V.).—'La jurisprudence de la Cour européenne des droits de l'homme en 1992', *A.F.D.I.* 1992, pp. 629 *et seq.*

Myjer (E.).—'Het lange wachten van Abdoella', *NJCM–Bulletin* 1993, pp. 169–174.

Sudre (F.), Levinet (M.), Peyrot (B.) and Ecochard (B.).—'Chronique de jurisprudence de la Cour européenne des droits de l'homme—1992', *R.U.D.H.* 1993, Nos 1–2, pp. 1 *et seq.*

Swart (B.).—'The case-law of the European Court of Human Rights in 1992', *E.J.C.* 1993, pp. 167 *et seq.*

329. Case of Brincat v. Italy

Possible successive exercise of the functions of investigation and prosecution by the same public prosecutor in the same proceedings

478. *Joseph Brincat was a lawyer and a member of the Maltese Parliament and the Assembly of the Council of Europe. On 19 November 1987, one of his clients, Mr S., was seriously injured in a road accident in Italy and Mr Brincat was instructed by an insurance company to report on it. On 5 December, accompanied by the victim's wife, he went to a scrapyard where the vehicle had been taken. Mrs S. having attempted to recover personal property concealed in the petrol tank, the owner of the scrapyard alerted the police, who discovered in her possession items and banknotes; one of which formed part of a ransom paid for the release of a person who had been kidnapped.*

The police took them to the police station, where they were placed under arrest on that very day. On the following day, they were transferred to Lagonegro prison (Potenza). On 7 December, the deputy public prosecutor questioned the applicant, who was assisted by two lawyers, and decided that he should remain in custody. Mr Brincat contested that decision, but in the meantime the Lagonegro deputy public prosecutor declared that he did not have territorial jurisdiction. He sent the file by post to the public prosecutor's office which did have jurisdiction, that of Paola, and which received it on 18 December. The Paola public prosecutor issued a new warrant for Mr Brincat's arrest that day and ordered him to be transferred to Cosenza Prison. On the following day, Mr Brincat contested that warrant in the Cosenza District Court on the basis, inter alia, *of Article 5 §§ 3 and 4 of the Convention. On 28 December, the District Court vacated the arrest warrant and ordered the applicant's immediate release, as there was insufficient evidence against him.*

479. *In his application of 8 January 1988 to the Commission, Mr Brincat relied on Article 3 and Article 5 § 3 of the Convention.*[1]

---

1 On 13 July 1990, the Commission declared the first complaint admissible, but declared the remainder of the application inadmissible. In its report of 28 May 1991, it expressed the opinion that there had been a violation of Article 5 § 3 (unanimously).

Judgment of 26 November 1992 *(Chamber) (Series A No. 249–A)*

480. The complaints raised by the applicant before the Court under Article 3 and Article 5 § 4 of the Convention were outside the scope of the case.

The only matter in dispute was the objective impartiality of the Lagonegro deputy public prosecutor. The Court saw no reason for departing from its case law, despite the Government's suggestion that it should do so. Only the objective appearances at the time of the decision on detention were material. At that time, the deputy public prosecutor could intervene in the subsequent proceedings as a representative of the prosecuting authority; the mere fact that it had become clear afterwards that he lacked territorial jurisdiction was immaterial. On the same grounds, the Paola public prosecutor—who had jurisdiction— had not fulfilled the conditions required by Article 5 § 3 either and, moreover, had not heard Mr Brincat 'promptly'. There had therefore been a violation of Article 5 § 3 (held unanimously).

481. The Court dismissed the applicant's claim for loss of earnings, but, taking its decision on an equitable basis, awarded him 1,000 Maltese liri for non-pecuniary damage (unanimously).

The Court awarded part of Mr Brincat's claim for costs and expenses incurred before the Italian courts to a total of 821.43 Maltese liri. As regards the proceedings before the Strasbourg institutions, it awarded him only his travel expenses (£400) (unanimously).

482. *Summary bibliography*

COUSSIRAT-COUSTÈRE (V.).—'La jurisprudence de la Cour européenne des droits de l'homme en 1992', *A.F.D.I.* 1992, pp. 629 *et seq.*

LAMBERT (P.).—'A la Cour européenne des droits de l'homme—L'exercice successif de functions d'instruction et de poursuite', *J.T.* 1993, p. 234.

SUDRE (F.), LEVINET (M.), PEYROT (B.) and ECOCHARD (B.).—'Chronique de jurisprudence de la Cour européenne des droits de l'homme—1992', *R.U.D.H.* 1993, Nos 1–2, pp. 1 *et seq.*

SWART (B.).—'The case-law of the European Court of Human Rights in 1992', *E.J.C.* 1993, pp. 167 *et seq.*

330. Case of Francesco Lombardo v. Italy
331. Case of Giancarlo Lombardo v. Italy

Length of civil proceedings in the Court of Audit seeking the grant of, or an increase in, retirement pensions

483. *Francesco Lombardo served in the* Carabinieri *from 1946 to March 1974, when he was invalided out of the service because as a result of two illnesses. Since January 1975 the applicant had been in receipt of an ordinary retirement pension. In June 1974 he applied for an 'enhanced ordinary pension' on the ground that the illnesses which had caused his disablement were due to his service. In May 1977, the Ministry of Defence granted him payment at the enhanced rate on account of only one of his illnesses, thereby partly rejecting his application. In a letter received on 22 December 1977, the applicant appealed to the Court of Audit. The appeal was upheld by a judgment of 15 February 1989 and the text of the judgment was deposited with the registry on 7 July 1989.*

484. *On 11 November 1980, Giancarlo Lombardo appealed to the Italian Court of Audit against a decree of the Minister of Justice rejecting his application for the amount of his pension as a retired judge to be increased. He argued that the provisions of the legislation on which disparities between pensions paid to persons of the same grade and with the same seniority were based were unconstitutional. The proceedings were adjourned pending the outcome of an appeal in an analogous case which gave rise to judgments of the Constitutional Court in 1984 and 1988. In a judgment dated 13 March 1989, filed with the registry on 20 March, the Court of Audit ordered the readjustment of the applicant's pension, re-evaluation of the sums due and payment of interest on those sums.*

485. *In their applications of 3 October 1984 and 29 July 1986 to the Commission, Francesco and Giancarlo Lombardo complained of the length of the proceedings brought by them in the Court of Audit (Article 6 § 1 of the Convention). Giancarlo Lombardo also complained that there had been breaches of Article 1 of Protocol No. 1 and of Articles 2, 10 and 14 of the Convention.*[1]

---

1 The Commission held that the first application was admissible in its entirety (5 March 1990) and that the second was admissible in part (9 November 1990). In its reports of 10 July and 14 October 1991, it expressed the

Judgments of 26 November 1992 *(Chamber) (Series A No. 249–B and C)*

486. The Court recalled that there was no common uniform European notion in regard to entitlement to insurance benefits under social security schemes. However, even though disputes relating to the recruitment, employment and retirement of civil servants (Francesco Lombardo) and judges (Giancarlo Lombardo) were as a general rule outside the scope of Article 6 § 1, State intervention by means of a statute or delegated legislation had not prevented the Court from finding the right in issue to have a civil character.

Notwithstanding public law aspects, what was concerned here in each case was essentially an obligation on the State to pay pensions in accordance with the legislation in force. In performing that obligation, the State was not using discretionary powers and might be compared with an employer who was a party to a contract of employment governed by private law. Consequently, a *carabiniere*'s entitlement to an 'enhanced ordinary pension' (Francesco Lombardo) and a judge's right to obtain an adjustment of the amount of his pension (Giancarlo Lombardo) were to be regarded as 'civil rights' within the meaning of Article 6 § 1, which was therefore applicable in this case (held unanimously).

487. The periods to be taken into consideration extended, in the case of Francesco Lombardo, from 22 December 1977, when proceedings had been instituted in the Court of Audit, to 7 July 1989, when the judgment had been filed (approximately eleven and a half years), and, in the case of Giancarlo Lombardo, from 11 November 1980, when proceedings had been instituted in the Court of Audit, to 20 March 1989, when the judgment had been filed (approximately eight years and four months).

The Court found that there had been difficulties which did not in themselves justify the length of the proceedings. The Government's arguments based on the heavy workload of the Court of Audit (Francesco Lombardo) and of the Constitutional Court (Giancarlo Lombardo) together with the time necessary to carry out certain formalities (Giancarlo Lombardo) could not be taken into account. The delays had been so substantial that the overall length of the proceedings had to be regarded as excessive and hence Article 6 § 1 had been violated in both cases (held unanimously).

opinion that Article 6 § 1 had been violated (Francesco Lombardo: thirteen votes to one; Giancarlo Lombardo: unanimously).

488. Francesco Lombardo sought nothing under Article 50; it was not necessary for the Court to consider this question of its own motion (held unanimously). As for Giancarlo Lombardo, he might have sustained a degree of non-pecuniary damage, but the finding of a violation provided in itself sufficient just satisfaction (held unanimously).

489. *Summary bibliography*

COUSSIRAT-COUSTÈRE (V.).—'La jurisprudence de la Cour européenne des droits de l'homme en 1992', *A.F.D.I.* 1992, pp. 629 *et seq.*

LAMBERT (P.).—'Observations', *J.T.* 1993, pp. 280 and 281

SUDRE (F.), LEVINET (M.), PEYROT (B.) and ECOCHARD (B.).—'Chronique de jurisprudence de la Cour européenne des droits de l'homme—1992', *R.U.D.H.* 1993, Nos 1–2, pp. 1 *et seq.*

332. Case of Olsson v. Sweden (no. 2)

Prohibition on parents from removing from foster homes their children who had been taken into public care

490. *Stig and Gun Olsson had three children, Stefan, Helena and Thomas, who were born in June 1971, December 1976 and January 1979 respectively. In September 1980, the children were taken into care by the social services and placed in separate foster homes. In February 1987 the Administrative Court of Appeal directed that the public care of Stefan should be terminated. He was then returned to his parents. A similar decision was taken by the Supreme Administrative Court with regard to Helena and Thomas in June 1987. Those measures were the subject of the judgment in* Olsson v. Sweden (no. 1).[1]

Following the decision of the Supreme Administrative Court and a number of administrative and judicial decisions, the applicants were refused leave to remove Helena and Thomas from their foster homes on the ground that there was a not insignificant risk of harming the children's mental health thereby (Social Services Act 1980, section 28); this therefore restricted their access to their children. A series of proceedings were brought before the administrative courts, during which guardians ad litem *were appointed for the children on two occasions. In August 1987, Mr and Mrs Olsson also applied, unsuccessfully, for Helena and Thomas to be returned to them in accordance with the rules set out in Chapter 21 of the Parental Code. In January 1991, following an application from the District Social Council, the District Court of Alingsås transferred custody of the two children to their respective foster parents. That decision was upheld by the Court of Appeal for Western Sweden in January 1992. No decision had yet been taken on the applicant's appeals against that decision or against a new prohibition on recovering their children and the restrictions on access.*

491. *In their application lodged with the Commission of 23 October 1987, Mr and Mrs Olsson alleged a series of violations of Article 8 of the Convention on the ground that the Swedish social welfare authorities had hindered their reunion with Helena and Thomas and had prevented the applicants from having access to them. They also relied on Articles 6, 13 and 53.*[2]

1 Series A No. 130; see Vol. II of this work, 25–33.
2 In its report of 17 April 1991, the Commission expressed the opinion that:
   (a) there had been a violation of Article 8 on the ground that the restrictions on access were not "in accordance with the law" (unanimously);

Judgment of 27 November 1992 *(Chamber) (Series A No. 250)*

492. The Court held in the first place that the application concerned solely the complaints as to the prohibition on removal, its maintenance in force and the restrictions on the applicants' access to the children while the prohibition had been in force; the length of certain specific domestic proceedings and the lack of a hearing on appeal; and the alleged violations of the right of access to a court or to an effective remedy with respect to certain decisions.

493. As regards Article 8, the prohibition on removal and its maintenance in force, as well as the restrictions on access, had clearly constituted, and this had not been disputed, interferences with the applicants' right to respect for family life.

The prohibition on removal and its maintenance in force had been 'in accordance with the law', since they were based on the relevant provisions of Swedish legislation and there was no evidence that those measures had been taken in order to prevent the children from being reunited with their parents. On the other hand, the imposition of restrictions on access imposed between 23 June 1987 and 1 July 1990, but not that imposed subsequently, had lacked any legal basis.

- (b) there had been a violation of Article 8 with regard to the prohibition on removal (seventeen votes to three);
- (c) there had been a violation of Article 6 § 1 on the ground that the applicants did not have access to court to challenge the restrictions on access to the children (unanimously);
- (d) there had been no violation of Article 6 § 1 as a result of the duration of the proceedings concerning the termination of the public care of Stefan, Helena and Thomas (fourteen votes to six);
- (e) there had been no violation of Article 6 § 1 with regard to the duration of the proceedings under Chapter 21 of the Parental Code (nineteen votes to one);
- (f) there had been no violation of Article 6 § 1 on the ground that the Supreme Administrative Court did not hold a hearing on the applicants' appeal concerning the prohibition on removal (nineteen votes to one);
- (g) there had been no violation of Article 6 § 1 in relation to the first appointment of a guardian *ad litem* (unanimously);
- (h) there had been no violation of Article 6 § 1 as a result of the duration of the proceedings relating to the second appointment of a guardian *ad litem* (unanimously);
- (i) it was not necessary to examine whether there had been a violation of Article 13 in respect of the restrictions on access (unanimously); and
- (j) there had been no violation of Article 13 in respect of the first appointment of a guardian *ad litem* (unanimously).

The prohibition on removal and the restrictions on access (imposed before or after 1 July 1990) had had the legitimate aim of protecting the children's 'health' and 'rights and freedoms'.

The Court held that the reasons underlying the initial decision to prohibit the children's removal from their respective foster homes were relevant and sufficient within the meaning of Article 8.

Since the various factors invoked by the Swedish authorities had not essentially changed during the period under review, the reasons put forward for the maintenance in force of the prohibition on removal were also relevant. In order to establish whether they were also sufficient, it had to be examined why the preparatory contacts between the parents and the children had remained insufficient. In that connection, the Court considered the reasons invoked to justify the restrictions on access imposed throughout the period: in like manner to the reasons underlying the prohibition of removal, they were relevant and it had not been established that the national authorities, having regard to their margin of appreciation, had failed to fulfil their obligation to take the steps which they reasonably could have been expected to take with a view to the family's being reunited. Hence the maintenance in force of the prohibition of removal and the restrictions on access were also based on sufficient reasons too.

The Court held that there had been a violation of Article 8 in so far as concerned the restrictions on access between 23 June 1987 and 1 July 1990 (unanimously) but not as regards the prohibition on removal and the restrictions on access imposed after 1 July 1990 (six votes to three).

494.   The Court held that no separate issue arose under Article 53 (seven votes to two). After considering the wording of Resolution DH (88)18 of the Committee of Ministers concerning the execution of the judgment in *Olsson (no. 1)*, the Court further noted that the facts and circumstances underlying the applicants' complaint under Article 53 raised a new issue which had not been determined by the judgment in *Olsson (no. 1)* and was essentially the same as the issues which it had considered under Article 8.

495.   With regard to Article 6 § 1, the Court held—and this point had not been disputed before the Court—that the fact that it had not been possible to have the restrictions on access imposed between 23 June 1987 and 1 July 1990 reviewed by a court constituted a violation of that provision (unanimously).

In contrast, the Court held that there had been no violation of Article 6 § 1 with regard to the length of certain proceedings (unanimously).

The overall duration of the proceedings relating to one of the requests made by the applicants for termination of public care could not be regarded as being excessive. Although the proceedings relating to the applicants' request under Chapter 21 of the Parental Code to have their children returned to them had concerned the enforcement of existing rights, the Court took the view that, whereas Article 6 § 1 was applicable, it had not been breached. As for the proceedings relating to the second appointment of a guardian *ad litem*, they had been concluded within a reasonable time.

496. Various other complaints based on Article 6 § 1 and Article 13, which in the Commission's opinion were unfounded or did not need examination, had not been mentioned by the applicants before the Court, which did not consider it necessary to examine them of its own motion (held unanimously).

497. Under Article 50, the applicants were awarded 50,000 Swedish kronor for non-pecuniary damage and 55,000 konor for costs and expenses, less 6,900 French francs which had been received from the Council of Europe by way of legal aid (unanimously).[1]

498. *Summary bibliography*

COUSSIRAT-COUSTÈRE (V.).—'La jurisprudence de la Cour européenne des droits de l'homme en 1992', *A.F.D.I.* 1992, pp. 629 *et seq.*
DECAUX (E.) and TAVERNIER (P.).—'Chronique de jurisprudence de la Cour européenne des droits de l'homme', *J.D.I.* 1993, pp. 715–718.
SUDRE (F.), LEVINET (M.), PEYROT (B.) and ECOCHARD (B.).—'Chronique de jurisprudence de la Cour européenne des droits de l'homme—1992', *R.U.D.H.* 1993, Nos 1–2, pp. 1 *et seq.*
WARBRICK (C.).—'The European Convention on Human Rights', *Y.E.L.* 1992, pp. 706–713.

1 By virtue of the Law containing Special Provisions on the Care of Young Persons, which was passed on 8 March 1990 and entered into force on 1 July 1990, the County Administrative Court now has the power to prohibit the removal of a child from a foster home and to review decisions of the Social Council concerning parental access to a child subject to a prohibition of removal from a foster home.

333. Case of M.R. v. Italy

Length of proceedings before a regional administrative court

499. *On 19 October 1984, Mrs M.R. brought an action in the Lazio Regional Administrative Court for the recalculation of the salary due to her husband (who had died in the meantime) following the career restructuring ordered by the Ministry of Finance on 14 April 1980. The court upheld her claim on 29 October 1985; the text of the judgment was filed in the registry on 24 September 1987.*

500. *In her application of 10 June 1987 to the Commission, Mrs M.R. complained of the length of the proceedings brought by her, and relied on Article 6 § 1 of the Convention.[1]*

Judgment of 27 November 1992 *(Chamber) (Series A No. 245–E)*

501. The Court considered that Mrs M.R.'s silence despite several attempts by the registry to contact her over a period of nearly five months, constituted a fact 'of a kind to provide a solution of the matter' (Rules of Court, Rule 49 § 2). In addition, the Court discerned no reason of public policy for continuing the proceedings (Rule 49 § 4). Accordingly, it decided to strike the case out of the list (unanimously).

502. *Summary bibliography*

Coussirat-Coustère (V.).—'La jurisprudence de la Cour européenne des droits de l'homme en 1992', *A.F.D.I.* 1992, pp. 629 *et seq.*
Sudre (F.), Levinet (M.), Peyrot (B.) and Ecochard (B.).—'Chronique de jurisprudence de la Cour européenne des droits de l'homme—1992', *R.U.D.H.* 1993, Nos 1–2, pp. 1 *et seq.*

1 In its report of 8 April 1992, the Commission expressed the opinion that there had been a breach of Article 6 § 1 (unanimously).

334. Case of Hennings v. Germany

Shortness of the time-limit for lodging an objection and failure to effect personal service of a penal order

503. *On 15 April 1984, Hans-Dieter Hennings, a German national, had an altercation with a ticket collector on a train journey from Kufstein in Austria to Munich. He refused to pay a fine of 300 Deutsche Mark and proceedings were brought against him. By a penal order issued on 7 November 1984 after summary proceedings, the Rosenheim District Court sentenced him to a fine of 40 Deutsche Mark per day for twenty-five days for coercion and for the further offence of dangerous assault, which had not been not mentioned previously.*

The order was served by way of a notification in his letter-box on 12 November 1984 to collect a letter deposited at the Oberaudorf post office. However, Mr Hennings, who was absent when the postman visited, did not have the key to the letter-box. The parties disagreed whether the letter was collected on 19 or 20 November. On 26 November, although the legal two-week time-limit had expired, Mr Hennings lodged an objection to the order and applied for the proceedings to be reinstated. On 6 December, the applicant's objection was dismissed by the Rosenheim District Court on the ground that he could have filed the objection within the time-limit on 19 November, and that he had not submitted the application for reinstatement within the time-limit of one week of the cessation of the impediment. Two subsequent appeals, brought on 24 January 1985 before the Traunstein Regional Court and on 17 October 1985 before the Federal Constitutional Court, were unsuccessful.

504. *In his application of 16 April 1986 to the Commission, Mr Hennings complained about the short time-limit for filing an objection against the penal order and that it was not served on him personally. He relied on Article 6 of the Convention, taken in isolation and in conjunction with Article 14.*[1]

---

1 In its report of 30 May 1991, the Commission expressed the opinion that there had been no violation of Article 6 § 1 (nine votes to four) or of Article 14 taken together with Article 6 § 1 (twelve votes to one).

Judgment of 16 December 1992 *(Chamber) (Series A No. 251–A)*

505. The Court recalled that the guarantees contained in paragraph 3 of Article 6 were constituent elements of the general notion of a fair trial. It was of the opinion that the complaint should be examined under paragraph 1 having regard to those guarantees.

The authorities could not be held responsible for barring Mr Hennings' access to a court, because he had failed to take the necessary steps to ensure receipt of his mail and had thereby been unable to comply with the requisite time-limits laid down under German law. Since the applicant had not been denied his right of access to a court, there had been no violation of Article 6 § 1 of the Convention (eight votes to one).

506. Even if it had jurisdiction to entertain the complaint based on Article 14 in conjunction with Article 6, the Court saw no reason to examine this claim since it was subsumed in his general complaint that he had been denied access to a court (held unanimously).

507. *Summary bibliography*

COUSSIRAT-COUSTÈRE (V.).—'La jurisprudence de la Cour européenne des droits de l'homme en 1992', *A.F.D.I.* 1992, pp. 629 *et seq.*

MEIJERS (L.C.M.).—'Kort (nader) commentaar', *NJCM–Bulletin* 1993, pp. 568 and 569.

SUDRE (F.), LEVINET (M.), PEYROT (B.) and ECOCHARD (B.).—'Chronique de jurisprudence de la Cour européenne des droits de l'homme—1992', *R.U.D.H.* 1993, Nos 1–2, pp. 1 *et seq.*

SWART (B.).—'The case-law of the European Court of Human Rights in 1992', *E.J.C.* 1993, pp. 167 *et seq.*

335. Case of Niemietz v. Germany

Search of a lawyer's office in the course of criminal proceedings against a third party

508. *On 9 December 1985, a letter was sent by telefax from the Freiburg post office to Judge Miosga of the Freising District Court. It related to criminal proceedings for insulting behaviour pending before that court against an employer who refused to deduct from his employees' salaries and pay over to the tax office the Church tax to which they were liable. The letter bore the signature of one Klaus Wegner—possibly a fictitious person—followed by the words 'on behalf of the Anti-clerical Working Group of the Freiburg* Bunte Liste *[multicoloured group]' and a post-office box number. The applicant, Gottfried Niemietz, had been chairman for some years of the Freiburg* Bunte Liste, *a local political party, and a colleague of his, with whom he shared Chambers, had also been active on behalf of that party.*

Criminal proceedings were then instituted against Klaus Wegner. The Munich District Court issued, on 8 August 1986, a warrant to search, inter alia, *the applicant's law office and to seize any document which might reveal the identity of Klaus Wegner; the warrant gave the following reason: until 1985 mail addressed to the* Bunte Liste *had been sent to a box number and from there to the applicant's law-office. The search took place on 13 November 1986; four filing cabinets with data concerning clients and six individual files were examined, but no relevant document was found.*

On 27 March 1987, the Munich I Regional Court declared an action brought by Mr Niemietz against the search warrant inadmissible on the ground that it had already been carried out. On 18 August 1987, the Federal Constitutional Court declared an appeal against the search warrant and the judgment of the Regional Court inadmissible on the ground that it had no prospects of succeeding.

509. *In his application lodged with the Commission on 15 February 1988, Mr Niemietz alleged that the search had violated his right to respect for his home and correspondence, guaranteed by Article 8 of the Convention, and had also, by impairing the goodwill of his law office and his reputation as a lawyer, constituted a breach of his rights under Article 1 of Protocol No. 1. In addition, he submitted that, contrary to Article 13 of the Convention, he had no effective remedies before German authorities in respect of those complaints.*[1]

Judgment of 16 December 1992 *(Chamber) (Series A No. 251–B)*

510. The Government contested that there had been an interference, on the ground that Article 8 drew a clear distinction between private life and home, on the one hand, and professional premises, on the other.

The Court did not consider it possible or necessary to attempt an exhaustive definition of the notion of 'private life'. However, it would be too restrictive to limit the notion to an 'inner circle' in which the individual could live his own personal life as he chose and to exclude therefrom entirely the outside world not encompassed within that circle. Respect for private life must also comprise to a certain degree the right to establish and develop relationships with other human beings. There appeared, furthermore, to be no reason of principle why this understanding of the notion of 'private life' should be taken to exclude activities of a professional or business nature since it was, after all, in the course of their working lives that the majority of people had a significant, if not the greatest, opportunity of developing relationships with the outside world. This was confirmed by the fact that it was not always possible to distinguish clearly which of an individual's activities formed part of his professional or business life and which did not. Thus, especially in the case of a person exercising a liberal profession, his work in that context might form part and parcel of his life to such a degree that it became impossible to know in what capacity he was acting at a given moment of time. Moreover, there might be inequality of treatment if the protection of Article 8 were denied on the ground that the measure complained of related only to professional activities: such protection would remain available to a person whose professional and non-professional activities were so intermingled that there was no means of distinguishing between them. In fact, the Court had not previously drawn such distinctions.

As regards the word 'home', appearing in the English text of Article 8, the Court observed that in certain Contracting States, notably Germany, it had been accepted as extending to business premises. Such an interpretation was, moreover, fully consonant with the French text, since the word *'domicile'* had a broader connotation than the word 'home' and might extend, for example, to a professional person's office. In this context also, it might not always be possible to draw precise distinctions:

---

1 On 5 April 1990, the Commission declared the complaints under Article 8 of the Convention and Article 1 of Protocol No. 1 admissible and the remainder of the application inadmissible. In its report of 29 May 1991, it expressed the unanimous opinion that there had been a violation of Article 8 of the Convention and that no separate issue arose under Article 1 of Protocol No. 1.

activities related to a profession or business might well be conducted from a person's private residence and activities which were not so related might well be carried on in an office or commercial premises. A narrow interpretation of the words 'home' and '*domicile*' could therefore give rise to the same risk of inequality of treatment as a narrow interpretation of the notion of 'private life'.

More generally, to interpret the words 'private life' and 'home' as including certain professional or business activities or premises would be consonant with the essential object and purpose of Article 8, namely to protect the individual against arbitrary interference by the public authorities. Such an interpretation would not unduly hamper the Contracting States, for they would retain their entitlement to 'interfere' to the extent permitted by paragraph 2 of Article 8; that entitlement might well be more far-reaching where professional or business activities or premises were involved than would otherwise be the case.

To those general considerations must be added a further factor pertaining to the particular circumstances of the case. The warrant issued by the Munich District Court had ordered a search for, and seizure of, 'documents'—without qualification or limitation—revealing the identity of Klaus Wegner. Furthermore, those conducting the search had examined four cabinets with data concerning clients as well as six individual files; their operations must have covered 'correspondence' and materials that could properly be regarded as such for the purposes of the Convention. It sufficed to note in this context that the word 'correspondence' in Article 8, unlike the word 'life', was not qualified by any adjective. Taken together, those reasons led the Court to find that the search of the applicant's office constituted an interference.

511. The Court went on to consider whether the interference had been justified. It was 'in accordance with the law', since both the Munich I Regional Court and the Federal Constitutional Court had considered that the search was lawful in terms of Article 103 of the Code of Criminal Procedure.

The interference had legitimate aims, namely the prevention of crime and the protection of the rights of others, viz. the honour of Judge Miosga.

As to whether the interference had been necessary, the Court held it was not proportionate. It was true that the offence in connection with which the search had been effected, involving as it had not only an insult to, but also an attempt to bring pressure on, a judge, could not be classified as no more than minor. On the other hand, the warrant had been drawn in broad terms: it ordered a search for and seizure of 'documents', without any limitation, revealing the identity of the author of the offensive letter; this point was of special significance where, as in Germany, the search of a lawyer's office was not accompanied by any special procedural safeguards, such as the presence of an independent observer. More importantly, having regard to the materials that had in fact been inspected, the search had impinged on professional secrecy to an extent that appeared disproportionate; where a lawyer was involved, an encroachment on professional secrecy might have repercussions on the proper administration of justice and hence on the rights guaranteed by Article 6. In addition, the attendant publicity must have been capable of having an adverse effect on the applicant's professional reputation, in the eyes both of his existing clients and of the public at large.

In sum, there had been a violation of Article 8 (held unanimously).

512. As it had already taken into consideration, in the context of Article 8, the potential effects of the search on the applicant's professional reputation, the Court held that no separate issue arose under Article 1 of Protocol No. 1 (unanimously).

513. It rejected the applicant's claim for compensation under Article 50 (unanimously): the applicant had not established that the breach of Article 8 had caused him pecuniary damage; if and in so far as it might have occasioned non-pecuniary damage, the Court's finding of a violation constituted of itself sufficient just satisfaction. The applicant had supplied no particulars of his costs and expenses.

514. *Summary bibliography*

COUSSIRAT-COUSTÈRE (V.).—'La jurisprudence de la Cour européenne des droits de l'homme en 1992', *A.F.D.I.* 1992, pp. 629 *et seq.*

DECAUX (E.) and TAVERNIER (P.).—'Chronique de jurisprudence de la Cour européenne des droits de l'homme', *J.D.I.* 1993, pp. 755–758.

HANGARTNER (Y.).—'Durchsuchung einer Anwaltskanzlei. Anwendung von Art. 8 EMRK auf Geschätsräume und geschäftliche Tätigkeiten', *A.J.P./P.J.A.* 1993, pp. 724–725.

JAKHIAN (E.) AND LAMBERT (P.).—'Les perquisitions dans les cabinets d'avocats', *J.T.* 1994, pp. 66–68.

JUNOSZA-ZDROJEWSKI (G.).—'Perquisitions au cabinet d'un avocat (arrêt de la Cour européenne des Droits de l'Homme)', *G.P.*, 23–24 June 1993, pp. 2 and 3.

LAMBERT (P.) and RIGAUX (F.).—'Perquisitions au cabinet d'un avocat et droit au respect de la vie privée, de la correspondence et du domicile', *R.T.D.H.* 1993, pp. 470–481.

MYJER (E.).—'De getergde rechter en het advocatenkantoor', *NJCM–Bulletin* 1993, pp. 320–329.

RENUCCI (J.-F.).—'Droit européen des droits de l'homme', *D.* 1993, sommaires commentés, pp. 386 and 387.

SUDRE (F.), LEVINET (M.), PEYROT (B.) and ECOCHARD (B.).—'Chronique de jurisprudence de la Cour européenne des droits de l'homme—1992', *R.U.D.H.* 1993, Nos 1–2, pp. 1 *et seq.*

WARBRICK (C.).—'The European Convention on Human Rights', *Y.E.L.* 1992, pp. 735–737.

336. Case of Hadjianastassiou v. Greece

Obstacles to substantiating an appeal on points of law and conviction of an air force officer for disclosing information of minor importance but classified secret

515. *Constantinos Hadjianastassiou, a Greek aeronautical engineer, was a captain in the air force. On 22 October 1984, the Athens Permanent Air Force Court found him guilty of disclosing military secrets because he had communicated to a private company a technical study on guided missiles, which he had prepared himself for the air force.*

He appealed to the Courts-Martial Appeal Court, which, after holding a hearing, deliberated in private and answered a series of questions by 'yes' or 'no'. Giving judgment in Mr Hadjianastassiou's presence on 22 November 1985, it sentenced him for disclosure of military secrets of minor importance to five months' imprisonment.

On 26 November 1985, the applicant appealed to the Court of Cassation, alleging 'the erroneous application and interpretation' of the relevant provisions of the Military Criminal Code, but it was not until January 1986 that he received a copy of the record of the proceedings of the Courts-Martial Appeal Court setting out the exact reasons why he had been found guilty. In a memorial addressed to the Court of Cassation, he claimed that he had been unable in the five days which he had had to lodge his appeal to substantiate his claims further, since he had not received the text of the judgment until the time-limit had expired and had, therefore, not been able to ascertain the grounds on which it was based. The Court of Cassation considered that his ground of appeal was too vague, and declared the appeal inadmissible on 18 June 1986.

516. *In his application to the Commission of 4 October 1990, Mr Hadjianastassiou relied on Articles 6 and 10 of the Convention, complaining that he had been prevented from further substantiating his appeal to the Court of Cassation and from exercising freedom of expression.*[1]

---

1 In its report of 6 June 1991, the Commission expressed the opinion that there had been a violation of Article 6 §§ 1 and 3(b), but not of Article 10 (unanimously).

Judgment of 16 December 1992 *(Chamber) (Series A No. 252)*

517. The Court noted at the outset that, pending the adoption of the law referred to in Article 96 § 5 of the Constitution, the Court of Cassation could review the proper application of the criminal law by the military courts only through the questions put by the presidents of those courts and the replies given by their colleagues, from which the reasoning was elicited.

Whilst the Contracting States enjoyed considerable freedom in the choice of the appropriate means to ensure that their judicial systems complied with the requirements of Article 6, the courts had to indicate with sufficient clarity the grounds on which they based their decisions. It was this, for example, which made it possible for the accused to exercise usefully the rights of appeal available to him.

In this instance, the judgment read out by the President of the Courts-Martial Appeal Court had contained no mention of the questions as they appeared in the record of the hearing and had not been based on the same grounds as the decision of the Permanent Air Force Court. In his appeal on points of law, filed within the five-day time-limit laid down in Article 425 § 1 of the Military Criminal Code, Mr Hadjianastassiou had been able to rely only on what he had been able to hear or gather during the hearing. In accordance with a consistent line of cases, it had moreover been impossible for him to expand upon his appeal by making additional submissions. The rights of the defence had been subject to such restrictions that the applicant had not had the benefit of a fair trial. There had therefore been a violation of paragraph 3(b) of Article 6, taken in conjunction with paragraph 1 (held unanimously).

518. Of course, the freedom of expression guaranteed by Article 10 applied to servicemen just as it did to other persons within the jurisdiction of the Contracting States. Accordingly, the sentence imposed by the Permanent Air Force Court, then reduced by the Courts-Martial Appeal Court, had constituted an interference with the exercise of the applicant's right to the freedom of expression.

It had been 'prescribed by law', since the manner in which the Courts-Martial Appeal Court had interpreted and applied Articles 97 and 98 of the Military Criminal Code had not conflicted with their wording.

Clearly the contested sentence was intended to punish the disclosure of information on an arms project classified as secret, and therefore to protect 'national security'.

Was the interference 'necessary in a democratic society'? The air force's programme for the manufacture of a guided missile had been classified as a 'military secret'. The Court took the view that the disclosure of the State's interest in a given weapon and that of the corresponding technical knowledge, which might give some indication of the state of progress in its manufacture, were capable of causing considerable damage to national security. It was also necessary to take into account the special conditions attaching to military life and the specific 'duties' and 'responsibilities' incumbent on members of the armed forces. The applicant, as the officer in charge of an experimental missile programme, had been bound by an obligation of discretion in relation to anything concerning the performance of his duties. As the limits of the margin of appreciation to be left to the domestic authorities in matters of national security had not been overstepped, there had been no violation of Article 10 (held unanimously).

519. As regards the application of Article 50, the Court took the view that only the costs and expenses referable to the Court of Cassation and to the proceedings in Strasbourg qualified for reimbursement. It therefore awarded the applicant 29,260 French francs and 520,000 drachmas (unanimously).

520. *Summary bibliography*

COUSSIRAT-COUSTÈRE (V.).—'La jurisprudence de la Cour européenne des droits de l'homme en 1992', *A.F.D.I.* 1992, pp. 629 *et seq.*

DECAUX (E.) and TAVERNIER (P.).—'Chronique de jurisprudence de la Cour européenne des droits de l'homme (année 1992)', *J.D.I.* 1993, p. 758.

MYJER (E.).—'Een soort Griese kop—staart', *NJCM–Bulletin* 1993, pp. 318 and 319.

SUDRE (F.), LEVINET (M.), PEYROT (B.) and ECOCHARD (B.).—'Chronique de jurisprudence de la Cour européenne des droits de l'homme—1992', *R.U.D.H.* 1993, Nos 1–2, pp. 1 *et seq.*

SWART (B.).—'The case-law of the European Court of Human Rights in 1992', *E.J.C.* 1993, pp. 167 *et seq.*

337. Case of Sainte-Marie v. France

Successive exercise by the same appellate judges in respect of the same accused of the functions of judge responsible for hearing applications for release from detention on remand in one criminal case and trial judge in another related case, which had been conducted in parallel

521. *On 31 January 1985, following bomb attacks carried out in November 1984 and January 1985 against police stations, responsibility for one of which was subsequently claimed by Iparretarrak, a clandestine Basque separatist movement, Jean-Pierre Sainte-Marie was charged under two heads: unauthorized possession of weapons and criminal conspiracy and, secondly, causing criminal damage to immoveable property. The two sets of proceedings were conducted in parallel, as regards both the review of the detention on remand and the investigation and trial.*

An application for release in the case concerning the possession of weapons was dismissed at first instance by an investigating judge on 8 March 1985 and on appeal by the Indictment Division of the Pau Court of Appeal. On 4 July 1985, the Bayonne Criminal Court declared void the proceedings brought against the applicant. That decision was overturned by the Criminal Appeals Division of the Pau Court of Appeal on 14 August 1985. It heard the case on the merits and, on 29 October 1985, sentenced the applicant to four years' imprisonment.

In the meantime, on 8 July 1985, the investigating judge dismissed an application for Mr Sainte-Marie to be released on remand in the proceedings concerning the charge of criminal damage on 8 July 1985. That decision was upheld on 8 August 1985 by the Indictment Division, two members of which—Mr Bataille and Mr Biecher—were subsequently to sit in the Criminal Appeals Division which sentenced the applicant on the charge of possession of weapons on 29 October 1985. On 10 April 1986, the Bayonne Criminal Court sentenced Mr Sainte-Marie to five years' imprisonment on the charge of criminal damage.

522. *In his application to the Commission of 29 April 1987, Mr Sainte-Marie alleged a violation of Article 6 § 1 of the Convention in so far as the Criminal Appeals Division of the Pau Court of Appeal had not constituted an impartial tribunal when it convicted him on 29 October 1985, because two of its members had previously ruled on an application for release.*[1]

Judgment of 16 December 1992 *(Chamber) (Series A No. 253–A)*

523. The Government contended that the applicant had failed to exhaust his domestic remedies on the ground that he had never challenged in the French courts the participation of Judges Bataille and Biecher in the adoption of the decision of 14 August 1985 (in the proceedings relating to the possession of arms).

The Court held that that preliminary objection was devoid of purpose because the applicant's complaint before the Convention organs had been directed at something completely different, namely those judges' participation in the adoption of the judgment of 8 August 1985 (in the criminal damage proceedings). It therefore dismissed the objection (unanimously).

524. As regards Article 6 § 1, the main thrust of the applicant's argument, namely that the fact of those judges' having ruled on the question of detention on remand necessarily entailed a lack of objective impartiality, ran counter to the Court's case law (judgment of 24 May 1989 in *Hauschildt v. Denmark*[2]). Only special circumstances might warrant fears as to the impartiality of a judge who had already taken pre-trial decisions in the case.

There had been nothing of that nature in the present case. On 8 August 1985, the Indictment Division had made express reference to the facts which it had already examined in the decision of 5 April 1985, given by a division composed to a large extent differently, and setting out extremely precise findings. The Indictment Division had thus based its decision of 8 August 1985 on the applicant's own statements, which he had not retracted and had never claimed that they had been obtained under duress. They had moreover been corroborated by uncontested physical evidence. The Indictment Division had confined itself to making a brief assessment of the available facts in order to establish whether *prima facie* the police suspicions had some substance and gave ground for fearing that there was a risk of the accused's absconding.

The participation of Judges Bataille and Biecher in the adoption of the judgment of 29 October 1985 had not undermined the impartiality of the Criminal Appeals Division, since the applicant's misgivings could not be regarded as objectively justified. There had therefore been no violation of Article 6 § 1 (eight votes to one).

1 In its report of 10 July 1991, the Commission expressed the opinion that there had been no violation of Article 6 § 1 (fourteen votes to five).
2 Series A No. 154; see Vol. II of this work, 191–196.

525. *Summary bibliography*

COUSSIRAT-COUSTÈRE (V.).—'La jurisprudence de la Cour européenne des droits de l'homme en 1992', *A.F.D.I.* 1992, pp. 629 *et seq.*

DECAUX (E.) and TAVERNIER (P.).—'Chronique de jurisprudence de la Cour européenne des droits de l'homme (année 1992)', *J.D.I.* 1993, pp. 758 and 759.

PETTITI (L.-E.).—'Droits de l'homme', *R.S.C.D.P.C.* 1993, pp. 367–369.

PRADEL (J.).—'Procédure pénale', *D.* 1993, sommaires commentés, pp. 204 and 205.

RENUCCI (J.-F.).—'Droit européen des droits de l'homme', *D.* 1993, sommaires commentés, pp. 384 and 385.

SUDRE (F.), LEVINET (M.), PEYROT (B.) and ECOCHARD (B.).—'Chronique de jurisprudence de la Cour européenne des droits de l'homme—1992', *R.U.D.H.* 1993, Nos 1–2, pp. 1 *et seq.*

SWART (B.).—'The case-law of the European Court of Human Rights in 1992', *E.J.C.* 1993, pp. 167 *et seq.*

338. Case of de Geouffre de la Pradelle v. France

Access to the *Conseil d'Etat* to challenge the lawfulness of a decree designating an area as being of outstanding beauty

526.   *In 1980, the Minister for the Environment set in motion proceedings to designate the Montane valley in the* département *of Corrèze as an area of outstanding beauty. Raymond de Geouffre de la Pradelle, a French lawyer, owned an estate in the valley. He received formal notification that the procedure had been initiated and availed himself of his right to inform the authorities of his objections to the proposal.*

The valley was designated an area of outstanding beauty by ministerial decree of 4 July 1983, an extract from which, mentioning that the full text could be consulted at the prefecture of Corrèze, was published in the Official Gazette on 12 July. On 13 September 1983, the Prefect of Corrèze served the full text of the decree at the applicant's Paris home.

On 27 October 1986, the applicant applied to the Conseil d'Etat *for judicial review of the decree. On 7 November 1986, the* Conseil d'Etat *declared the application inadmissible for being out of time (the time-limit was two months): in the case of a decree which, like the one at issue, did not put the proprietor on notice to change the state or use of the land, time began to run as from the publication of the designation decision in the Official Gazette.*

527.   *In his application to the Commission of 2 February 1987, Mr de Geouffre de la Pradelle invoked Articles 6 and 13 of the Convention and Article 1 of Protocol No. 1.*[1]

Judgment of 16 December 1992 *(Chamber) (Series A No. 253–B)*

528.   The Government maintained that Mr de Geouffre de la Pradelle had not exhausted domestic remedies, since in his appeal to the *Conseil d'Etat* he had raised only points of French law without pleading, even in substance, the appropriate provisions of the Convention.

---

1 On 5 October 1990, the Commission declared the complaint based on Article 1 of Protocol No. 1 inadmissible, but declared the other allegations admissible. In its report of 4 September 1991, the Commission expressed the opinion that there had been a breach of Article 6 § 1 (seven votes to five) and that it was unnecessary to examine the application under Article 13 (unanimously).

The Court considered that the applicant had drawn the *Conseil d'Etat'*s attention to requirements of legal certainty and non-discrimination that were also reflected in the Convention. He had derived arguments from national law that amounted to complaining, in substance, of an infringement of the rights secured in Articles 6 and 13. The objection should therefore be dismissed (held unanimously).

529. French law undoubtedly gave the applicant the possibility of challenging the relevant decree in court and he had taken advantage of this. It remained to be ascertained whether the procedure for making such an application, in particular as regards the calculation of the time-limit to be complied with, had been such as to ensure that the right to a court had been effective as required by Article 6.

The rule in Article 6 of the decree of 13 June 1969 that designation decisions should be published nationally offered undeniable advantages. However, the Court could not but be struck by the extreme complexity of the positive law resulting from the legislation on the conservation of places of interest taken together with the case law on the classification of administrative acts. In view also of the proceedings that had actually taken place in respect of the applicant, such complexity had been likely to create legal uncertainty as to the exact nature of the decree designating the Montane valley and as to how to calculate the time-limit for bringing an appeal.

The Court noted in the first place the numerous methods of publication provided for in the decree of 13 June 1969. Furthermore, the scheme in issue had covered a limited area and affected eight identifiable property owners in all. Mr de Geouffre de la Pradelle and the other seven had, moreover, been individually informed that designation proceedings had been set in motion and that a public inquiry was being opened. The property owners could have reasonably inferred from those notifications that the outcome of the proceedings, whether favourable or unfavourable, would likewise have been communicated to each of them without their having had to peruse the Official Gazette for months or years on end.

The applicant had been entitled to expect a coherent system that would achieve a fair balance between the authorities' interests and his own; in particular, he should have had a clear, practical and effective opportunity to challenge an administrative act that had been a direct interference with his right of property. In sum, since the applicant had not had a practical, effective right of access to the *Conseil d'Etat*, there had been a breach of Article 6 § 1 (held unanimously).

530. In view of that decision, the Court considered that it did not have to examine the case under Article 13 (held unanimously).

531. Applying Article 50, it considered it reasonable to hold that the applicant had suffered a loss of opportunities justifying an award of 100,000 French francs. It awarded him 75,000 French francs in respect of costs and expenses incurred at Strasbourg (unanimously).

532. *Summary bibliography*

BENOIT-ROHMER (F.).—'Note', *D.* 1993, jurisprudence, pp. 562–566.

COUSSIRAT-COUSTÈRE (V.).—'La jurisprudence de la Cour européenne des droits de l'homme en 1992', *A.F.D.I.* 1992, pp. 629 *et seq.*

DECAUX (E.) and TAVERNIER (P.).—'Chronique de jurisprudence de la Cour européenne des droits de l'homme (année 1992)', *J.D.I.* 1993, pp. 759–761.

GONZALEZ (G.).—'A propos de quelques "incohérences" du contentieux de l'annulation en droit administratif français', *L.P.A.* No. 76, 25 June 1993, pp. 25–29.

LEPAGE-JESSUA (C.).—'La Cour européenne des droits de l'homme affirme sa suprématie sur les juridictions nationales administratives', *G.P.* 11–13 July 1993, doctrine, pp. 914–917.

SUDRE (F.), LEVINET (M.), PEYROT (B.) and ECOCHARD (B.).—'Chronique de jurisprudence de la Cour européenne des droits de l'homme—1992', *R.U.D.H.* 1993, Nos 1–2, pp. 1 *et seq.*

TAMION (E.).—'L'affaire de Geouffre de la Pradelle c. France', *Cahiers du CREDHO* No. 1, 1994, pp. 117–127.

VELDE (J. van der).—'Noot', *NJCM–Bulletin* 1993, pp. 333–336.

339. Case of Edwards v. the United Kingdom

Failure on the part of the police to disclose certain facts to the defence

533. *On 9 November 1984, Derek Edwards was convicted at Sheffield Crown Court of one count of robbery and two counts of burglary. He received a sentence of imprisonment of ten years for the robbery, and two sentences of eight years each for the burglary offences. All three sentences were to be served concurrently.*

On 21 March 1986, the Secretary of State for the Home Department referred the applicant's case to the Court of Appeal (Criminal Division) under section 17(1)(a) of the Criminal Appeal Act 1968, after an independent police report (the Carmichael report) revealed that certain police witnesses had withheld information at the trial. In particular, the police had not stated that one of the victims, who said she could probably recognize her assailant, had not picked the applicant out from volumes of police photographs, or that fingerprints (not the applicant's) had been found at the scene of the crime. The prosecution evidence had consisted of detailed oral admissions that the applicant had allegedly made to the police concerning his alleged involvement in the offences. After examining the deficiencies in the police evidence, the Court of Appeal held that there was not anything unsafe or unsatisfactory about the convictions.

534. *In his application to the Commission of 29 September 1986, Mr Edwards invoked Articles 6 § 1 and 13 of the Convention.*[1]

Judgment of 16 December 1992 *(Chamber) (Series A No. 247–B)*

535. The guarantees in paragraph 3 of Article 6 were specific aspects of the right to a fair trial. It was unnecessary to examine the relevance of paragraph 3(d) to the case since the applicant's allegations, in any event, amounted to a complaint that the proceedings had been unfair. The Court would therefore confine its examination to this point.

---

1 The application was initially rejected by the Commission on 7 December 1987 for failure to comply with the six months' rule. But, on 13 July 1988, the President of the Commission restored the case to the list when the applicant showed that he had in fact complied with that rule. In its report of 10 July 1991, it concluded that there had been no violation of paragraph 1, read in conjunction with paragraph 3(d), of Article 6 (by eight votes to six), and that no separate issue arose under Article 13 (twelve votes to two).

In so doing, the Court had to consider the proceedings as a whole, including the decision of the appellate court. It was not within the Court's province to substitute its own assessment of the facts for that of the domestic courts and, as a general rule, it was for those courts to assess the evidence before them.

The Court considered that it was a requirement of fairness—indeed one which was recognized under English law—that the prosecution authorities should disclose to the defence all material evidence for or against the accused and that the failure to do so in the present case had given rise to a defect in the trial proceedings.

However, the Court of Appeal had examined the transcript of the trial, including the applicant's alleged confession, and considered in detail the impact of the new information on the conviction. Admittedly the police officers who had given evidence at the trial had not been heard by the Court of Appeal, but it had been open to counsel for the applicant to make an application to the Court—which they had chosen not to do—that the police officers be called as witnesses. Likewise, Mr Edwards could have applied to the Court of Appeal for the production of the Carmichael report but had not done so. He claimed that he had not made such an application because the Crown might have resisted it by claiming public interest immunity. That argument was untenable since such a claim would have been for the Court of Appeal to determine. The Court concluded that the defects of the original trial had been remedied by the subsequent procedure before the Court of Appeal; there was no indication that the appellate proceedings had been in any respect unfair. Accordingly there had been no breach of Article 6 § 1 (seven votes to two).

536. As the applicant had abandoned his complaint under Article 13, the Court had no need to examine it (held unanimously).

537. *Summary bibliography*

Coussirat-Coustère (V.).—'La jurisprudence de la Cour européenne des droits de l'homme en 1992', *A.F.D.I.* 1992, pp. 629 *et seq.*

Myjer (E.).—'Edwards en de achtergehouden gegevens', *NJCM–Bulletin* 1993, pp. 449–453.

Pettiti (L.-E.).—'Droits de l'homme', *R.S.C.D.P.C.* 1993 pp. 369–371.

Sudre (F.), Levinet (M.), Peyrot (B.) and Ecochard (B.).—'Chronique de jurisprudence de la Cour européenne des droits de l'homme—1992', *R.U.D.H.* 1993, Nos 1–2, pp. 1 *et seq.*

Swart (B.).—'The case-law of the European Court of Human Rights in 1992', *E.J.C.* 1993, pp. 167 *et seq.*

Warbrick (C.).—'The European Convention on Human Rights', *Y.E.L.* 1992, pp. 727-730.

340. Case of W. v. Switzerland

Length of detention on remand in the Canton of Berne

538. *Suspected of a series of economic offences, W. was arrested on 27 March 1985 and placed in detention on remand, on the grounds that there was a risk of absconding, collusion and repetition of offences. The charges related to some sixty Swiss and foreign companies managed by W. and to events some of which went back to 1977. Eleven other persons were accused alongside W. The investigation, which was conducted by two ad hoc investigating judges, looked into about 200 bank accounts, included the questioning of W. and his co-accused on around 350 occasions and resulted in a principal case-file consisting of 711 binders, plus the original documents, which alone took up more than 120 metres of shelving. The losses sustained in the case were put at a conservative estimate at 50,000,000 Swiss francs. Between March 1985 and May 1988, W. made eight applications for release on bail, all of them unsuccessful. On 2 September 1988, he was committed for trial to the Berne Economic Criminal Court, which, on 30 March 1989, following a trial lasting almost six weeks, found him guilty, inter alia, of offences including fraud on a professional basis, fraudulent bankruptcy, forgery of documents and aggravated criminal mismanagement. He was sentenced to eleven years' imprisonment and a fine of 10,000 Swiss francs. The 1,465 days spent in detention on remand were deducted from the main sentence.*

539. *In his application to the Commission of 20 September 1988, W. complained of the length of his detention on remand and relied on Article 5 § 3 of the Convention.*[1]

Judgment of 26 January 1993 *(Chamber) (Series A No. 254–A)*

540. The period to be taken into consideration had begun on 27 March 1985, the date of W.'s arrest, and ended on 30 March 1989 with his conviction by the Berne Economic Criminal Court. It had thus lasted for four years and three days.

In refusing to release W., the Swiss courts had relied on three main grounds, apart from the serious suspicion against him.

---

1 In its report of 10 September 1991, the Commission expressed the opinion that there had been a violation of Article 5 § 3 (nineteen votes to one).

First, there was the danger of his absconding. In their carefully reasoned decisions, the Bernese courts had based themselves on specific characteristics of the applicant's situation. The Federal Court had examined those reasons carefully on 7 November 1985, 25 August 1986 and 25 April 1988. It had considered that the factors specified by the indictments chamber left no real doubt as to W.'s intention of absconding and could legitimately suffice to demonstrate that such a danger still existed. There was no reason for the Court to reach a different conclusion.

Secondly, there was the danger of collusion. In order to demonstrate that a substantial risk of collusion had existed and continued to exist until the beginning of the trial, the indictments chamber had referred essentially to the exceptional extent of the case, the extraordinary quantity of documents seized and their intentionally confused state, and the large number of witnesses to be questioned, including witnesses abroad. It had based a secondary argument on the applicant's personality. The Federal Court, on each occasion, had examined scrupulously whether those considerations did indeed make continued detention necessary. At no time had it excluded the existence of a danger of collusion. On the contrary, it had confirmed that such a risk had been present even during the period following the close of the investigation and the committal for trial (2 September 1988). Here too, the Court saw no reason for disagreeing with the Federal Court's opinion.

Lastly, there was the danger of repetition of offences. The Federal Court had not examined the impugned decisions on this point, as the dangers of absconding and collusion in themselves justified the continued detention. The Court shared that view.

There remained the question of the conduct of the proceedings, as W. complained that the investigating judges had caused substantial delays in the investigation. Having regard to the intensive continuous review carried out by the Federal Court, the Court agreed in substance with the Government's arguments. It found no period during which the investigators had not carried out their inquiries with the necessary promptness, nor had there been any delay caused by possible shortage of personnel or equipment. The length of the detention in issue appeared therefore to have been essentially attributable to the exceptional complexity of the case and W.'s conduct.

In conclusion, there had not been a violation of Article 5 § 3 (five votes to four).

541. *Summary bibliography*

JUNOSZA-ZDROJEWSKI (G.).—'La durée prolongée de la détention provisoire (un arrêt de la Cour européenne)', *G.P.* 11–12 June 1993, doctrine, pp. 9–11.

SCHÜRMANN (F.).—'Europäischer Gerichtshof für Menschenrechte—Chronik der Rechtsprechung (1.1.–30.6.1993)', *A.J.P./P.J.A.* 1993, pp. 1136–1145 and 1282–1293.

SUDRE (F.) and others.—'Chronique de la jurisprudence de la Cour européenne des droits de l'homme. Première partie : janvier-mai 1993', *R.U.D.H.* 1993, pp. 217 *et seq.*

341. Case of Fey v. Austria

Criminal case tried by the District Court which had taken certain pre-trial measures, including preliminary inquiries, in the same case

542. *During January 1988, Hans Jürgen Fey, a German pensioner, rented a room in Mayrhofen in Austria. After he had told his landlady that his wife was very ill and was undergoing treatment in an Innsbruck hospital and that he was expecting to receive pension payments from Germany, she handed over 2,500 schillings to him and waived the rent of 1,500 schillings. Subsequently, she reported the matter to the police, whereupon the Innsbruck Public Prosecutor's Office asked the investigating judge of the Innsbruck Regional Court to institute a preliminary investigation into the applicant on suspicion of fraud. In addition, the prosecutor requested the judge to order his detention on remand. The judge granted those requests on 9 February 1988. The judge questioned Mr Fey further and sent letters rogatory to the Zell am Ziller District Court asking it to put some questions to the landlady. The District Court judge, Andrea Kohlegger, did so on 25 February 1988.*

On 1 March 1988, the Innsbruck Public Prosecutor's Office dropped one of the fraud charges against the applicant and, on jurisdictional grounds, transferred the case to the District Court. Subsequently, Judge Kohlegger carried out various investigations into the payment of the pension at an Austrian bank and two German insurance companies and arranged for the landlady to be questioned by the Innsbruck District Court. On 18 March, the trial hearing was set down for 24 March. It took place on that date before the District Court, with Judge Kohlegger sitting as a single judge. The court heard the applicant and the landlady and all the evidence was produced. By judgment of 24 March, the District Court convicted him and sentenced him to three months' imprisonment.

On 13 May, the Innsbruck Regional Court dismissed Mr Fey's appeal against that judgment.

543. *In his application of 10 November 1988 to the Commission, Mr Fey relied on Article 6 § 1 of the Convention: he alleged that the District Court judge had not been impartial and that the Regional Court judges who had rejected his request for release had subsequently been called upon to rule on his appeal.*[1]

---

1 On 9 October 1990, the Commission declared the first of these complaints admissible and the second inadmissible. In its report of 15 October 1991,

Judgment of 24 February 1993 *(Chamber) (Series A No. 255–A)*

544. The Court referred to its case law, according to which the impartiality of a court had to be determined according to a subjective and an objective test. As to the subjective test, the applicant did not dispute the personal impartiality of District Judge Kohlegger.

As to the objective test, before the case had been referred to the District Court, a preliminary investigation had already been carried out by the Innsbruck Regional Court. It was true that the interrogation of the landlady had been conducted by Judge Kohlegger, but this had been done under a rogatory letter; in the limited capacity in which she had acted it had not been for her to examine the merits of the accusations against the applicant, nor did it appear from the case-file that she had actually done so; and there was no indication that at the time when the questioning had taken place there had been any prospect of Judge Kohlegger later trying the case. Following referral of the case to the Zell am Ziller District Court, Judge Kohlegger had undertaken certain pre-trial measures of a preparatory character, being designed to complete the case-file before the hearing. The decision to set the case down for trial could not be regarded as being the equivalent of a formal decision to commit an accused for trial. It was not until the hearing on 24 March 1988 that Judge Kohlegger had been faced with the applicant for the first time; she had then heard both him and the landlady and all the evidence in the case had been presented. It was only at that stage that she had been in a position to form any opinion as to the applicant's guilt. In the light of the extent and nature of the pre-trial measures taken by Judge Kohlegger, the Court did not find that such fears as the applicant might have had as to her impartiality could be held to have been objectively justified. Accordingly, there had been no violation of Article 6 § 1 (seven votes to two).

545. *Summary bibliography*

SCHÜRMANN (F.).—'Europäischer Gerichtshof für Menschenrechte—Chronik der Rechtsprechung (1.1.–30.6.1993)', *A.J.P./P.J.A.* 1993, pp. 1136–1145 and 1282–1293.

SUDRE (F.) and others.—'Chronique de la jurisprudence de la Cour européenne des droits de l'homme. Première partie : janvier–mai 1993', *R.U.D.H.* 1993, pp. 217 *et seq.*

the Commission expressed the opinion that there had been a violation of Article 6 § 1 (sixteen votes to three).

342. Case of Funke v. France

House searches and seizures made by customs officers; conviction for refusing to produce documents at the request of the administration

343. Case of Crémieux v. France
344. Case of Miailhe v. France

House searches and seizures made by customs officers

546. *Jean-Gustave Funke, a German national, worked as a sales representative and lived in France. In the course of a investigation into possible offences under the legislation governing financial relations with countries abroad, customs officers, assisted by a senior police officer* (officier de police judiciaire), *searched his home on 14 January 1980 and seized a number of documents and items. They also asked Mr Funke to produce certain foreign bank statements. In April 1982, the customs authorities obtained from the Strasbourg District Court an order, which was confirmed on appeal, attaching Mr Funke's property to the value of 100,220 French francs by way of security for the customs fines. As a result, Mr Funke's bank accounts were frozen in August 1982 and a charge was registered on a building which he owned; those measures were discharged in July 1990 at Mrs Funke's request.*

Since Mr Funke did not fulfil his undertaking to produce the bank statements, the customs authorities summoned him before the Strasbourg police court, which, on 27 September 1982, fined him 1,200 French francs and ordered him to produce the bank statements on penalty of 20 francs per day's delay. On 14 March 1983, the Colmar Court of Appeal upheld the judgment of the court below with the exception of one point, and increased the pecuniary penalty to 50 francs per day's delay. On 21 November 1983, the Court of Cassation dismissed an appeal brought by Mr Funke. Lastly, in January 1985, the customs authorities served a garnishee notice on the applicant's bank requiring it to pay a sum representing the amount of the penalties outstanding for the non-production of the bank statements. After the Strasbourg District Court upheld the notice in question in March 1985, the Colmar Court of Appeal delivered a judgment in February 1989 reversing the lower court's judgment. The customs authorities then unsuccessfully appealed to the Court of Cassation. At the time of his death on 22 July 1987, Mr Funke had still not been tried for the relevant offences.

547. *In the course of an investigation into possible offences contrary to legislation on financial relations with countries abroad, involving a company of which Paul Crémieux, a French citizen, was chairman and managing director, customs officers, assisted by a senior police officer* (officier de police judiciaire), *made numerous searches of Mr Crémieux's home and residences between January 1977 and February 1980 during which they seized a large quantity of documents. Mr Crémieux was charged in November 1982, but the customs authorities agreed to compound with him and the criminal proceedings were discharged in June 1987. When the proceedings were pending, Mr Crémieux contested the legality and constitutionality of the house searches, the validity of the reports made on the searches and the compatibility with the Convention of the relevant provisions of the Customs Code. In particular, the Court of Cassation dismissed an appeal in January 1985.*

548. *On 5 and 6 January 1983, customs officers accompanied by a senior police officer* (officier de police judiciaire), *made searches of premises in Bordeaux occupied by William Miailhe, his mother Victoria and his wife Brigitte and which also served as the Philippines consulate, and seized approaching 15,000 documents, some of which they later returned. The operation was part of an investigation into the applicants' residential status—they were French citizens but one also had Philippine nationality—and into whether they had contravened the legislation on financial dealings with foreign countries.*

Mr and Mrs Miailhe instituted proceedings against the Director-General of Customs and Excise in the Paris District Court in which they asked the court to declare the seizures null and void. On 20 December 1983, the court declined jurisdiction on the ground that the ordinary courts had no jurisdiction over such disputes unless there had been a violation of a personal freedom or a flagrantly unlawful act. The applicants then applied to the Paris tribunal de grande instance which, on 16 May 1984, in turn declined jurisdiction. The Paris Court of Appeal confirmed that ruling on 23 October 1984; there had been no manifest, deliberate violation of a personal freedom. On 17 June 1986, the Court of Cassation dismissed an appeal brought by Mr and Mrs Miailhe.

A local investigating judge in Bordeaux charged them on 20 June 1985. By orders of 3 July 1991, he discharged Victoria Miailhe and committed Mr and Mrs Miailhe for trial at the Bordeaux Criminal Court, which ruled on 2 December 1992 that the public prosecution and the proceedings for imposition of customs penalties were barred.

549. *In his application of 13 February 1984 to the Commission, Mr Funke raised several complaints. He claimed that his criminal conviction for refusal to produce the documents requested by the customs had violated his right to a fair trial (Article 6 § 1 of the Convention) and disregarded the principle of presumption of innocence (Article 6 § 2); that his case had not been heard within a reasonable time (Article 6 § 1); and that the search and seizures effected at his home by customs officers had infringed his right to respect for his private and family life, his home and his correspondence (Article 8).*

For his part, Mr Crémieux applied to the Commission on 11 March 1985, complaining of the searches and seizures made by customs officers at his home and at other addresses of his. He relied on Article 8 (infringement of his right to respect for his private life, his home and his correspondence), Article 6 § 3 (non-compliance with mandatory formalities) and Article 10 (failure to respect his freedom of expression).

As for Mr and Mrs Miailhe, they applied to the Commission on 11 December 1986. They complained of the searches and seizures made on their premises by customs officers. They relied on Article 8 of the Convention (infringement of their right to respect for their private life, their home and their correspondence) and Article 13 (lack of any effective remedy before a national authority).[1]

Judgments of 25 February 1993 *(Chamber) (Series A No. 256–A, B and C)*

550. Only in the Funke case, did questions arise as to fairness of the proceedings and the presumption of innocence.

According to the Government, Mr Funke did not have the status of a victim, since no criminal proceedings had been taken against him for contravening the regulations governing financial dealings with foreign countries. The Court dismissed the objection (unanimously), since the applicant's complaints related to quite different proceedings, those concerning the production of documents.

1 In its reports of 8 October 1991, the Commission expressed the following opinion:
  (a) *in the Funke case*: there had been no violation of Article 6 § 1 either as regards the principle of a fair trial (seven votes to five) or on account of the length of the proceedings (eight votes to four), of Article 6 § 2 (nine votes to three) or of Article 8 (six votes to six, with the President's casting vote);
  (b) *in the Crémieux case*: there had been no violation of Article 8 (eleven votes to seven), Article 6 § 3 (unanimously) or Article 10 (unanimously); and
  (c) *in the Miailhe case*: there had been no violation of Article 8 (eleven votes to seven) or Article 13 (unanimously).

551. The customs had secured Mr Funke's conviction in order to obtain certain documents which they believed must exist, although they had not been certain of the fact. Being unable or unwilling to procure them by some other means, they had attempted to compel the applicant himself to provide the evidence of offences he had allegedly committed. The special features of customs law could not justify such an infringement of the right of anyone 'charged with a criminal offence', within the autonomous meaning of this expression in Article 6, to remain silent and not to contribute to incriminating himself. Since the applicant had not had a fair trial, there had been a breach of Article 6 § 1 (eight votes to one).

552. That conclusion made it unnecessary for the Court to ascertain whether Mr Funke's conviction had also contravened the principle of the presumption of innocence guaranteed by Article 6 § 2 (eight votes to one).

553. The Court considered it likewise unnecessary to examine the complaint that the proceedings relating to the making and discharge of the interim orders had lasted for more than a 'reasonable time' as required by Article 6 § 1 (eight votes to one).

554. As regards Article 8, the Government raised preliminary objections in the Crémieux and Miailhe cases: Mr Crémieux had not exhausted domestic remedies in that he had not complained in the ordinary courts of a flagrantly unlawful act (*voie de fait*) on the part of the customs officers and had not sought compensation for it, and Mr and Mr Miailhe had lodged their application to Strasbourg prematurely, as, at the onset of their trial at the Bordeaux Criminal Court, they could have complained that the customs' action forming the basis of the prosecution had been unlawful. The Court dismissed the objections of inadmissibility (unanimously) on the ground that the applicants had brought proceedings to have customs reports on the facts and on the seizures declared null and void and pursued them to a conclusion, without omitting to plead Article 8.

555. As for the merits of the complaint, the Court found that there had been an interference with all the applicants' private life and correspondence and, in the case of Mr Funke and Mr Crémieux, also with their right to respect for their home. It therefore considered whether the interferences in question fulfilled the conditions of Article 8 § 2.

The applicants contended that the interferences had had no legal basis. As worded at the time, Article 64 of the Customs Code was, they claimed, contrary to the 1958 Constitution because it did not make house searches and seizures subject to judicial authorization. The Court did not consider it necessary to determine the issue in this instance, as at all events the interferences complained of were incompatible with Article 8 in other respects.

Notwithstanding the applicant's arguments to the contrary, the Court was of the view that the interferences were in pursuit of at any rate the interests of 'the economic well-being of the country'.

The Court then considered whether the interferences were necessary in a democratic society. In the field of the prevention of capital outflows and tax evasion, States encountered serious difficulties owing to the scale and complexity of banking systems and financial channels and to the immense scope for international investment, made all the easier by the relative porousness of national borders. The Court therefore recognized that they might consider it necessary to have recourse to measures such as house searches and seizures in order to obtain physical evidence of exchange-control offences and, where appropriate, to prosecute those responsible. Nevertheless, the relevant legislation and practice must afford adequate and effective safeguards against abuse.

This had not been so here. At the material time—and the Court did not have to express an opinion on the legislative reforms of 1986 and 1989, which were designed to afford better protection for individuals—the customs authorities had had very wide powers; in particular, they had exclusive competence to assess the expediency, number, length and scale of inspections. Above all, in the absence of any requirement of a judicial warrant the restrictions and conditions provided for in law appeared too lax and full of loopholes for the interferences with the applicant's rights to have been strictly proportionate to the legitimate aim pursued. In addition, the customs authorities had never lodged a complaint against Mr Funke alleging an offence against the regulations governing financial dealings with foreign countries and the seizures made on the Miailhes' premises had been wholesale and, above all, indiscriminate. In sum, there had been a breach of Article 8 (eight votes to one).

556. Since the infringements of the rights of the defence (Article 6 § 3) and of freedom of expression (Article 10) alleged by Mr Crémieux related to the same facts as those which the Court had held to have contravened Article 8, the Court held that it was unnecessary to consider them separately (unanimously).

557. As Mr and Mrs Miailhe had not pressed before the Court their complaint relating to the lack of any effective remedy before a national authority (Article 13), the Court did not consider it necessary to examine it of its own motion (held unanimously).

558. The Court considered that two of the applicants must have suffered non-pecuniary damage: it awarded Mr Funke 50,000 French francs and considered that the judgment afforded Mr Crémieux sufficient compensation (unanimously).

It awarded Mr Funke 70,000 French francs and Mr Crémieux 50,000 French frances for costs and expenses incurred before the French courts and the Convention institutions (unanimously).

In the Court's opinion, the question of the application of Article 50 was not ready for decision in the *Miailhe* case although the criminal proceedings against the couple had ended. The question should therefore be reserved (held unanimously).

Judgments of 29 November 1993 *(Miailhe) (Chamber)—Application of Article 50 (Series A No. 277–C)*

559. The Court discerned no causal link between, on the one hand, the lack of judicial authorization for the house searches and the seizures—a lack it had held to be contrary to Article 8—and, on the other hand, the pecuniary damage alleged by Mr and Mrs Miailhe, and it accordingly disallowed that part of their claim (unanimously). In contrast, the Court considered that the applicants must have sustained non-pecuniary damage, for which it awarded Mr Miailhe 50,000 French francs and Mrs Victoria Miailhe and Brigitte Miailhe 25,000 francs each (unanimously).

560. Although the applicants had not provided any detailed statements of costs or any vouchers, the Court considered that it should, on an equitable basis, take into account the costs incurred at Strasbourg and part of those incurred before the national courts. It awarded each of the three applicants a lump sum of 60,000 French francs (unanimously).

561. *Summary bibliography*

DECAUX (E.) and TAVERNIER (P.).—'Chronique de jurisprudence de la Cour européenne des droits de l'homme (année 1993)', *J.D.I.* 1994, pp. 780–781.

DUGRIP (O.).—'La conformité du droit des visites domiciliaires en matière de concurrence, douanière et fiscale avec l'article 8 CEDH', in *Le droit français et la Convention européenne des droits de l'homme. 1974–1992,* Kehl, Engel, 1994, pp. 143–163.

FROMMEL (S.N.).—'The European Court of Human Rights and the right of the accused to remain silent: can it be invoked by taxpayers?', *Intertax* 1993, pp. 520–549, and *Rivista di diritto e pratica tributaria* 1993, pp. 2149–2198.

FROMMEL (S.N.).—'La Corte europea dei diritti dell'uomo e il diritto dell'accusato di mantenere il silenzio', *Forum* No. 6, 1993, pp. 22–40.

FROMMEL (S.N.).—'The right to silence and the Serious Fraud Office', *International Corporate Law*, April 1994, pp. 21–24.

GARNON (R. et A.).—'Note', *J.C.P.*, édition générale, II. jurisprudence, 1993, No. 2073, pp. 243 and 244.

GOY (R.).—'Les affaires Funke c. France et Crémieux c. France', *Cahiers du CREDHO*, no. 2, 1994, pp. 115–126.

HUET (I).—'Note', *G.P.* 15-19 July 1994, pp. 33 and 34.

JAVET (M.).—'L'affaire Miailhe c. France', *Cahiers du CREDHO*, no. 2, 1994, pp. 129–147.

KINSCH (P.).—'Le droit de ne pas contribuer à sa propre incrimination', *B.D.H.* 1993, pp. 51–54.

MELLO (X.A. de).—'Droit de la concurrence et droits de l'homme', *R.T.D.E.* 1993, pp. 601–633.

MYJER (E.).—'Zwijgen op aangeven van de douane', *NJCM–Bulletin* 1993, pp. 584–592.

PANNIER (J.).—'Note', *D.* 1993, jurisprudence, pp. 460–462.

PETTITI (L.-E.).—'Droits de l'homme', *R.S.C.D.P.C.* 1993, pp. 581–584.

RENUCCI (J.-F.).—'Droit européen des droits de l'homme', *D.* 1993, sommaires commentés, pp. 387 and 388.

SCHÜRMANN (F.).—'Europäischer Gerichtshof für Menschenrechte—Chronik der Rechtsprechung (1.1.—30.6.1993)', *A.J.P./P.J.A.* 1993, pp. 1136–1145 and 1282–1293.

SPIELMANN (D.).—'Cour européenne des droits de l'homme (premier semestre 1993)', *B.D.H.* 1993, pp. 60 and 61.

SUDRE (F.) and others.—'Chronique de la jurisprudence de la Cour européenne des droits de l'homme. Première partie : janvier–mai 1993', *R.U.D.H.* 1993, pp. 217 *et seq.*

SUDRE (F.) and others.—'Chronique de la jurisprudence de la Cour européenne des droits de l'homme. Deuxième partie: juin–décembre 1993', *R.U.D.H.* 1993, pp. 377 *et seq.*

VAN OVERBEEK (W.B.J.).—'The right to remain silent in competition investigations. The Funke decision of the Court of Human Rights makes revision of the ECJ's case law necessary', *European Competition Law Review* 1994, pp. 127–233.

VIRIOT-BARRIAL (D.).—'La preuve en droit douanier et la Convention européenne des droits de l'homme (à propos de trois arrêts du 25 février 1993 à la Cour européenne des droits de l'homme)', *R.S.C.D.P.C.* 1994, pp. 537–547.

YERNAULT (D.).—'Les pouvoirs d'investigation de l'administration face à la délinquance économique : les locaux professionnels et l'article 8 de la Convention européenne', *R.T.D.H.* 1994, pp. 121–136.

345. Case of Dobbertin v. France

Length of criminal proceedings

562. *Rolf Dobbertin, a national of the German Democratic Republic, was a plasma physicist and was working in Paris as a research assistant under contract to the French National Scientific Research Centre. On 19 January 1979, he was arrested by the police and held in custody until 25 January, when he was brought before the investigating judge at the National Security Court* (Cour de sûreté de l'Etat), *who charged him with being in communication with agents of a foreign power (the German Democratic Republic) and remanded him in custody. The investigation ended in May 1981 but, as a result of the abolition of the National Security Court that year, the case was transferred to the Military Court. Other inquiries were made, but in 1983, following the abolition of the Military Court in peacetime, the case was transferred once again, this time to the ordinary courts.*

A series of procedural developments then occurred, including five appeals on points of law to the Court of Cassation and a decision, in 1986, of the Indictment Division of the Amiens Court of Appeal quashing the greater part of the proceedings subsequent to May 1979. In September 1989, Mr Dobbertin was committed for trial at the Paris special Assize Court, which, on 15 June 1990, sentenced him to twelve years' imprisonment. However, on appeal, the Court of Cassation set aside that judgment on 6 March 1991 and remitted the case to a differently constituted bench of the Paris special Assize Court.

On 29 November 1991, that court acquitted the applicant. The prosecution did not appeal within the five-day period laid down in Article 568 of the Code of Criminal Procedure.

563. *In his application of 19 June 1987 to the Commission, Mr Dobbertin complained that the length of the criminal proceedings had exceeded a 'reasonable time' (Article 6 § 1 of the Convention), that he had not had the benefit of the presumption of innocence (Article 6 § 2) or of the safeguards of a fair trial (Article 6 § 3(a) and (d)) and that his right to freedom of expression (Article 10) had been infringed.*[1]

---

1 On 12 July 1988 the Commission declared the application inadmissible as being manifestly ill-founded, with the exception of the first complaint, which it declared admissible on 1 October 1990. In its report of 10 September 1991, it expressed the opinion that there had been a breach of Article 6 § 1 (unanimously).

Judgment of 25 February 1993 *(Chamber) (Series A No. 256–D)*

564. The period to be considered had begun on 19 January 1979, when Mr Dobbertin had been arrested, and ended on 4 December 1991, when the period during which the prosecution could have appealed on points of law against the acquittal of the applicant had expired.

While Mr Dobbertin's case had presented real difficulties arising from the highly sensitive nature of the offences charged, those difficulties could not on their own justify the total length of the proceedings.

On the other hand, several of the applicant's appeals had achieved their purpose of remedying certain procedural irregularities.

It was apparent from the file that for various reasons the course taken by the proceedings had left a great deal to be desired. Once the National Security Court and the Paris Military Court had been abolished, the authorities had taken no steps to ensure that the cases still pending were dealt with swiftly. For their part, the ordinary courts had been slow to resolve two essential procedural issues. Whilst the final stages of the proceedings had been conducted at an acceptable speed, the total length of the proceedings had nevertheless exceeded a 'reasonable time'.

There had therefore been a breach of Article 6 § 1 (held unanimously).

565. Under Article 50, Mr Dobbertin claimed 5,000,000 French francs for non-pecuniary damage. The Court awarded him 200,000 francs (unanimously).

Mr Dobbertin also sought 507,014.54 French francs for the fees of the lawyers who had assisted him during the trial, 107,000 francs representing the cost of three libel actions he had brought and 92,508 francs in respect of the costs and expenses incurred in the proceedings before the Convention institutions. The Court awarded him 50,000 French francs for the first item, dismissed the second and awarded him all the whole of the sum claimed in respect of the third.

566. *Summary bibliography*

DECAUX (E.) and TAVERNIER (P.).—'Chronique de jurisprudence de la Cour européenne des droits de l'homme (année 1993)', *J.D.I.* 1994, pp. 781–782.

RENUCCI (J.-F.).—'Droit européen des droits de l'homme', *D.* 1993, sommaires commentés, p. 384.

SCHÜRMANN (F.).—'Europäischer Gerichtshof für Menschenrechte—Chronik der Rechtsprechung (1.1.–30.6.1993)', *A.J.P./P.J.A.* 1993, pp. 1136–1145 and 1282–1293.

SUDRE (F.) and others.—'Chronique de la jurisprudence de la Cour européenne des droits de l'homme. Première partie : janvier–mai 1993', *R.U.D.H.* 1993, pp. 217 *et seq.*

346. Case of Padovani v. Italy

Magistrate successively carrying out functions of investigation and judgment *vis-à-vis* the same accused

567. *Alessandro Padovani was arrested on 21 February 1987 by the Bergamo police, who had found certain items of stolen property in his possession. On the same day the police brought him before the local magistrate (*pretore*), who immediately after questioning him confirmed his arrest. On 26 February the magistrate issued a warrant for the applicant's arrest and set the hearing down for 2 March, the charge being receiving stolen goods. On 2 March, the magistrate imposed a suspended sentence of one year's imprisonment on the applicant and fined him 250,000 lire. Mr Padovani did not appeal.*

568. *In his application to the Commission of 1 July 1987, Mr Padovani complained that the magistrate had not been an impartial tribunal and relied on Article 6 § 1 of the Convention.*[1]

Judgment of 26 February 1993 (Chamber) (Series A No. 257–B)

569. The Government argued that the applicant had not exhausted domestic remedies, as he had not appealed against the judgment of the *pretore* and asked the appellate court to appeal to the Constitutional Court.

The Court found that the first argument was unfounded, since the District Court would not have been able to quash the judgment. As for the second, the Government was estopped from raising it as it had not been put forward before the Commission. Consequently, the Court dismissed the objection (unanimously).

570. The Court pointed out that the existence of impartiality for the purposes of Article 6 § 1 must be determined according to a subjective and an objective test.

As to the subjective test, no evidence had been produced which might suggest bias on the part of the magistrate.

As to the objective test, the applicant's fear on account of the measures taken by the magistrate before the trial could not be regarded as

1 In its report of 6 June 1991, the Commission expressed the opinion that there had been a breach of Article 6 § 1 (sixteen votes to two).

objectively justified. The summary investigative measures had consisted merely of questioning the applicant and his two co-accused. In addition, in issuing the arrest warrant of 26 February 1987, the magistrate had relied *inter alia* on Mr Padovani's own statements. In addition, the *pretore* had followed specific rules applicable to *flagrante delicto* cases within his jurisdiction. *Giudizio direttissimo* (immediate proceedings) was a flexible procedure which sought to satisfy the 'reasonable time' requirement. There had therefore not been a violation of Article 6 § 1 (held unanimously).

571. *Summary bibliography*

LAMBERT (P.).—'Vers un assouplissement de la notion d'impartialité objective?', *J.T.* 1993, p. 390.

SCHÜRMANN (F.).—'Europäischer Gerichtshof für Menschenrechte—Chronik der Rechtsprechung (1.1.–30.6.1993)', *A.J.P./P.J.A.* 1993, pp. 1136–1145 and 1282–1293.

SUDRE (F.) and others.—'Chronique de la jurisprudence de la Cour européenne des droits de l'homme. Première partie : janvier–mai 1993', *R.U.D.H.* 1993, pp. 217 *et seq.*

347. Case of Pizzetti v. Italy
348. Case of De Micheli v. Italy

Length of civil proceedings

572. *Bartolomeo Pizzetti and Roberta de Micheli were Italian citizens. Mr Pizzetti brought an action for damages against Mr G. before the Bergamo District Court in respect of the injuries he sustained when he was assaulted during an argument. Mrs de Micheli appealed to the Udine District Court against an injunction ordering her to pay a sum of money to the Z. company.*

573. *In their applications to the Commission made on 28 July 1986 and 27 February 1987, the applicants complained chiefly or solely of the length of the civil proceedings in question and relied on Article 6 § 1 of the Convention.*[1]

Judgments of 26 February 1993 *(Chamber) (Series A No. 257–C and D)*

574. The Court started by determining in each case the period to be taken into consideration for assessing whether the length of the proceedings had been reasonable:

Pizzetti: approximately nine years and five months (from the date when the defendant had been summoned until the date of the Strasbourg judgment, since the proceedings before the Bergamo District Court were still pending);

De Micheli: approximately four years and five months (from the date when the defendant had been summoned until the date when the judgment of the Udine District Court had become final).

The Court went on to find that there had been a period of inactivity of almost four years (Pizzetti) and phases amounting to over two years during which the proceedings had stagnated (De Micheli). Hence there had been a violation of Article 6 § 1 (held unanimously).

---

1 In its reports of 10 December 1991 and 13 January 1992, the Commission expressed the opinion that there had been violations of Article 6 § 1 (unanimously) but not—in the *Pizzetti* case—of Article 13 (fourteen votes to six).

575. In view of that decision, the Court did not consider it necessary also to examine the Pizzetti case under Article 13 (held unanimously).

576. As regards Article 50, Mr Pizzetti claimed nothing in respect of pecuniary damage and Mrs De Micheli's claim was dismissed (unanimously) on the ground that there was no causal connection with the violation found.

The Court awarded Mr Pizzetti 10,000,000 lire for non-pecuniary damage and Mrs De Micheli 25,000,000 (unanimously).

The Court accepted in full the applicants' claims for costs and expenses incurred before the Strasbourg institutions, namely 3,175,800 lire in the case of Mr Pizzetti and 4,271,300 in the case of Mrs De Micheli (unanimously).

577. *Summary bibliography*

SCHÜRMANN (F.).—'Europäischer Gerichtshof für Menschenrechte—Chronik der Rechtsprechung (1.1.–30.6.1993)', *A.J.P./P.J.A.* 1993, pp. 1136–1145, 1282–1293 and 1530–1531.

SUDRE (F.) and others.—'Chronique de la jurisprudence de la Cour européenne des droits de l'homme. Première partie : janvier–mai 1993', *R.U.D.H.* 1993, pp. 217 *et seq.*

349. Case of Salesi v. Italy

Length of proceedings seeking payment of a disability allowance by the State

578. *Enrica Salesi, an Italian national, lived at Pomezia (province of Rome). On 28 February 1986, the applicant instituted proceedings against the Minister of the Interior before the Rome magistrate's court, seeking payment of a monthly disability allowance which the Lazio social security department had refused her. On 21 May, the court ordered an expert medical opinion. The expert appointed took the oath at the hearing of 17 June 1986. At the end of the hearing held on 2 December, the court ordered the Minister of the Interior to pay the allowance requested. The text of this decision was deposited with the registry on 16 December.*

On 21 April 1987, the Minister of the Interior appealed against that decision and, on 5 May, the President of the Rome District Court arranged for the appeal to be heard by the competent division of the court on 24 May 1989. On that date the court dismissed the appeal. The judgment was filed in the registry on 27 January 1990. The Minister appealed on points of law on 20 July, but the Court of Cassation dismissed the appeal in a judgment of 5 June 1991 that was filed in the registry on 10 March 1992.

579. *Article 38 of the Italian Constitution provided as follows:*

'All citizens who are unfit for work and lack the basic wherewithal to live shall be entitled to means of subsistence and welfare assistance.
(. . .)
The bodies and institutions set up or supported by the State shall be responsible for discharging the functions provided for in this article.
(. . .)'

Under section 13 of Law No. 118/71, enacted pursuant to Article 38 of the Constitution, the State paid a monthly disability allowance to disabled ex-servicemen and civilians aged 18–64 who had been found to be more than two-thirds disabled and who were destitute.

As this was a compulsory welfare benefit, disputes over the existence of a right to the allowance came within the magistrate's labour jurisdiction, and trial procedure was governed by the provisions laid down for labour proceedings (Articles 442 and 444 of the Code of Civil Procedure).

580. *In her application to the Commission of 12 June 1987, Mrs Salesi complained of the length of proceedings she had brought and relied on Article 6 § 1 of the Convention.*[1]

Judgment of 26 February 1993 *(Chamber) (Series A No. 257–E)*

581. The Government maintained that the case presented features of public law only. First, the right claimed derived from an ordinary statute, not from a contract of employment. Secondly, the State met the entire cost of financing the scheme. Thirdly, entitlement to disability allowance was not dependent on the payment of contributions.

The Court took the view that the general rule today was that Article 6 § 1 applied in the field of social insurance. However, this case was concerned with welfare assistance. There were differences between the two, but they could not be regarded as fundamental at the present stage of development of social security law.

State intervention was not sufficient to establish that Article 6 § 1 was inapplicable. Mrs Salesi had not been affected in her relations with the administrative authorities as such, acting in the exercise of discretionary powers; she had suffered an interference with her means of subsistence and was claiming an individual, economic right flowing from specific rules laid down in a statute giving effect to the Constitution. Indeed, disputes about that basic right came within the jurisdiction of the ordinary court, the labour magistrate's court. In sum, the Court saw no convincing reason to distinguish between the right to welfare benefits and the right to social insurance and therefore held that Article 6 § 1 was applicable in this case (unanimously).

582. The period to be considered had begun on 28 February 1986, when proceedings had been instituted against the Minister of the Interior in the Rome magistrate's court, and had ended on 10 March 1992, when the Court of Cassation's judgment had been filed. It had therefore lasted a little over six years.

The case was not complex and Mrs Salesi's conduct had not substantially contributed to the length of the proceedings. These had followed their course at a normal speed in the magistrate's court but not thereafter. On appeal the case had remained dormant for over two years. It was difficult to understand also why it had taken more than eight months and ten months respectively to make known the reasons

---

1 In its report of 20 February 1992, the Commission expressed the opinion that there had been a breach of Article 6 § 1 (thirteen votes to eight).

supporting the District Court's and the Court of Cassation's judgments by filing the judgments in the relevant registries. That being so, and in view of what had been at stake for the applicant, there had been a breach of Article 6 § 1 (held unanimously).

583. The Court took the view that the applicant had undoubtedly sustained damage and that her claims (7,000,000 Italian lire in respect of pecuniary damage and 4,000,000 lire in respect of non-pecuniary damage) were in no way excessive. The Court upheld those claims (unanimously).

In the absence of any objections on the part of the Government, the Court awarded the applicant 7,140,000 lire in respect of her costs and expenses relating to the proceedings before the Convention institutions.

584. *Summary bibliography*

SCHÜRMANN (F.).—'Europäischer Gerichtshof für Menschenrechte—Chronik der Rechtsprechung (1.1.–30.6.1993)', *A.J.P./P.J.A.* 1993, pp. 1136–1145 and 1282–1293.

SUDRE (F.) and others.—'Chronique de la jurisprudence de la Cour européenne des droits de l'homme. Première partie : janvier–mai 1993', *R.U.D.H.* 1993, pp. 217 *et seq.*

350. Case of Trevisan v. Italy
351. Case of Billi v. Italy

Length of civil proceedings

585. *Paolo Trevisan and Emma Billi were Italian nationals. Mr Trevisan instituted proceedings against the AMP company before the Treviso magistrate's court seeking an order requiring AMP to pay him the arrears of salary to which he claimed entitlement, together with damages in respect of the company's premature termination of his contract of employment. Mrs Billi instituted proceedings before the Perugia District Court as the heir of her father, a member of the governing body of a friendly society, some of whose property had been seized as an interim measure at the request of the municipality of Perugia.*

586. *In their applications to the Commission made on 2 February 1988 and 20 January 1989, the applicants complained of the length of the civil proceedings in question and relied on Article 6 § 1 of the Convention.*[1]

Judgments of 26 February 1993 *(Chamber) (Series A No. 257–F and G)*

587. The Court started by determining in each case the period to be taken into consideration for assessing whether the length of the proceedings had been reasonable:

Trevisan: approximately five years (from 9 June 1987—the Commission had declared the application inadmissible as out of time as regards the period prior to that date—to the date on which the Treviso magistrate's court's decision had become final);

Billi: somewhat more than sixteen years (from the date when Italy's declaration recognizing the right of individual petition took effect to the date on which the judgment of the Perugia District Court had become final).

The Court went on to find that there had been several periods of inactivity in excess of two years in the Trevisan case and that it had

---

1 In its reports of 9 December 1991, the Commission expressed the opinion that there had been a violation of Article 6 § 1 (Trevisan: ten votes to one; Billi: unanimously).

taken more than twelve years to draw up the expert reports in the Billi case. Hence there had been a violation of Article 6 § 1 (held unanimously).

588. As regards Article 50, the Court dismissed Mr Trevisan's claim in respect of pecuniary damage because it dated from a period prior to 9 June 1987, but it awarded him 10,000,000 lire for non-pecuniary damage and 6,477,130 lire for costs and expenses incurred before the Strasbourg institutions (unanimously).

Mrs Billi was awarded 20,000,000 lire for damage, to cover all the heads of claim (including costs and expenses) (unanimously).

589. *Summary bibliography*

SCHÜRMANN (F.).—'Europäischer Gerichtshof für Menschenrechte—Chronik der Rechtsprechung (1.1.–30.6.1993)', *A.J.P./P.J.A.* 1993, pp. 1136–1145 and 1282–1293.

SUDRE (F.) and others.—'Chronique de la jurisprudence de la Cour européenne des droits de l'homme. Première partie : janvier–mai 1993', *R.U.D.H.* 1993, pp. 217 *et seq.*

352. Case of Messina v. Italy

Length of criminal proceedings; inspection of the applicant's correspondence during his detention on remand

590. *On 18 October 1985, Antonio Messina was arrested under an arrest warrant issued the previous day by the investigating judge attached to the Marsala District Court and charged with membership of a criminal organization and with drugs offences. Mr Messina remained in detention on remand until 25 May 1987, when he was released on condition that, for a specified period, he resided in a certain sector and reported every day to the police station. The investigation closed on 8 July 1992, but the case was still pending in the Marsala District Court.*

591. *In his application to the Commission of 27 October 1987, Mr Messina complained of the length of his detention on remand and that of the criminal proceedings brought against him and of interferences with his right to respect for his correspondence. He relied on Article 5 § 3, Article 6 § 1 and Article 8 of the Convention.*[1]

Judgment of 26 February 1993 *(Chamber) (Series A No. 257–H)*

592. As far as Article 6 § 1 was concerned, the period to be taken into consideration had begun on 18 October 1985, the date on which Mr Messina had been arrested, and had not yet ended, since the proceedings were still pending.

In view of the nature of the charges preferred against the applicant, the Court accepted that the judicial authorities must have encountered some difficulties in investigating the case. The Court could not however regard as 'reasonable' in this instance a lapse of time which was already more than seven years. There had therefore been a violation of Article 6 § 1.

593. As regards Article 8, the very existence of an 'interference by a public authority' was a matter of dispute in this case. Mr Messina

---

1 On 4 March 1991, the Commission declared the applicant's second complaint and part of the third admissible. It declared the remainder of the application inadmissible. In its report of 20 February 1992, it expressed the opinion that there had been a violation of Article 6 § 1 and Article 8 (unanimously).

claimed that he had never received some of his mail, whereas the Government maintained that it had on the contrary been delivered.

Confronted with that dispute, the Court had to reach its decision on the basis of the available evidence. As the Commission had emphasized, a Contracting State could not claim to have discharged its obligations under Article 8 merely by supplying a record of a prisoner's incoming mail. In the absence of evidence such as might establish the contrary, the Court could not be certain that the items in question had reached their addressee. It accordingly had to conclude that there had been a violation of Article 8 (seven votes to two).

594. The applicant claimed 3,000 million lire for pecuniary and non-pecuniary damage. The Court considered that Mr Messina had adduced no evidence of any pecuniary damage deriving from the violations found, but that he had suffered some non-pecuniary damage, for which it awarded him 5,000,000 lire (unanimously).

595. *Summary bibliography*

HUET (I.).—'Note', *G.P.* 15–19 July 1994, pp. 34 and 35.

SCHÜRMANN (F.).—'Europäischer Gerichtshof für Menschenrechte—Chronik der Rechtsprechung (1.1.–30.6.1993)', *A.J.P./P.J.A.* 1993, pp. 1136–1145, 1282–1293 and 1528–1529.

SUDRE (F.) and others.—'Chronique de la jurisprudence de la Cour européenne des droits de l'homme. Première partie : janvier–mai 1993', *R.U.D.H.* 1993, pp. 217 *et seq.*

353. Case of Costello-Roberts v. the United Kingdom

Corporal punishment in an independent school in England

596. *In 1985, Jeremy Costello-Roberts, then aged seven, was attending an independent boarding preparatory school in England. On 3 October 1985, the applicant was reprimanded for talking in the corridor and was given a demerit mark. He already had four demerit marks for similar conduct and for being late for bed on one occasion. Having discussed the matter with his colleagues, the headmaster decided that corporal punishment should be administered, this being the penalty for incurring five demerit marks. Consequently, three days later, eight days after Jeremy had received his fifth demerit mark, the headmaster disciplined him by giving him three 'whacks' on the bottom through his shorts with a rubber-soled gym shoe. No other persons were present. In the first half of November, Jeremy's mother complained to the police and the National Society for the Protection of Children, but they both told her that there was no action they could take without any visible bruising on the child's buttocks. Jeremy entered a new school in January 1986.*

597. *Mrs Costello-Roberts and her son applied to the Commission on 17 January 1986: they submitted that his corporal punishment had constituted a breach of Article 3 of the Convention and also violated the right of each of them to respect for their private and family life guaranteed by Article 8; in addition, they alleged that, contrary to Article 13, they had no effective domestic remedies for these Convention complaints. A complaint under Article 14 was subsequently withdrawn.*[1]

Judgment of 25 March 1993 *(Chamber) (Series A No. 247–C)*

598. The Court first considered whether the facts complained of by the applicant were such as might engage the responsibility of the United Kingdom under the Convention. The Court pointed out that the

---

1 On 13 December 1990, the Commission declared the mother's complaints inadmissible and the son's admissible. In its report of 8 October 1991, the Commission expressed the opinion that there had been a violation of Article 8 (private life), but not of Article 3 (nine votes to four) and that there had been a violation of Article 13 (eleven votes to two).

responsibility of a State was engaged if a violation of one of the rights and freedoms defined in the Convention was the result of non-observance of Article 1. Several factors had to be taken into account in this regard. First, the State had an obligation to secure to children their right to education (Article 2 of Protocol No. 1). A school's disciplinary system fell within the ambit of the right to education and this had been recognized in Article 28 of the United Nations Convention on the Rights of the Child of 20 November 1989. Secondly, the fundamental right of everyone to education was a right guaranteed equally to pupils in State and independent schools. Thirdly, the State could not absolve itself from responsibility by delegating its obligations to private bodies or individuals.

599.   As far as Article 3 was concerned, the circumstances of the applicant's punishment could be distinguished from the facts of *Tyrer v. the United Kingdom*,[1] where the Court had found the punishment to be degrading. The applicant had adduced no evidence of any severe or long-lasting effects as a result of the treatment complained of beyond the consequences to be expected from measures taken on a purely disciplinary plane. A punishment which did not occasion such effects might fall within the ambit of Article 3, provided that in the particular circumstances of the case it might be said to have reached the minimum threshold of severity required. That minimum level of severity had not been attained in this case, even though the Court had certain misgivings about the automatic nature of the punishment and the three-day wait before its imposition. Accordingly, no violation of Article 3 had been established (five votes to four).

600.   As regards Article 8, the Court agreed that the notion of 'private life' was a broad one which was not susceptible of exhaustive definition. Measures taken in the field of education might, in certain circumstances, affect the right to respect for private life but not every act or measure which might be said to affect adversely the physical or moral integrity of a person necessarily gave rise to such an interference. Article 3 provided a first point of reference for examining a case concerning disciplinary measures in a school. The Court did not exclude the possibility that Article 8 could be regarded as sometimes affording in relation to disciplinary measures protection going beyond that given by Article 3. Nevertheless, it considered that, having regard to the purpose and aim of the Convention taken as a whole, and bearing in mind that sending a child to school necessarily involved some degree of

1   Series A No. 26; see Vol. I of this work, 166–173.

interference with his or her private life, the treatment complained of had not entailed adverse effects sufficient to bring it within the scope of the prohibition contained in Article 8. While not wishing to be taken to approve in any way the retention of corporal punishment as part of the disciplinary regime of a school, the Court therefore held there had been no violation of that article (unanimously).

601. In the Court's opinion, Jeremy had had an effective remedy as regards his complaints based on Articles 3 and 8. Consequently, there had been no violation of Article 13 (held unanimously). This was because he could have instituted civil proceedings for assault and, had they succeeded, the English courts would have been in a position to grant him appropriate relief. The effectiveness of a remedy did not depend on the certainty of a favourable outcome; in any event, it was not for the Court to speculate as to the outcome of such proceedings. Lastly, Article 13 did not go so far as to guarantee a remedy allowing a Contracting State's laws as such to be challenged before a 'national authority' on the ground of being contrary to the Convention or to equivalent domestic legal norms.

602. *Summary bibliography*

DECAUX (E.) and TAVERNIER (P.).—'Chronique de jurisprudence de la Cour européenne des droits de l'homme (année 1993)', *J.D.I.* 1994, pp. 775–778.

EMMERIK (M.L. van).—'Noot', *NJCM–Bulletin* 1993, pp. 578–583.

MAZIÈRE (P.).—'Interprétation des articles 3, 8 et 13 de la Convention européenne des droits de l'homme à propos d'un châtiment corporel dans une école privée britannique', *La Semaine juridique*, 25 May 1994, II, No. 22262, pp. 204–209.

PHILLIPS (B.).—'The case for corporal punishment in the United Kingdom. Beaten into submission in Europe?', *I.C.L.Q.* 1994, pp. 153–163.

SCHÜRMANN (F.).—'Europäischer Gerichtshof für Menschenrechte—Chronik der Rechtsprechung (1.1.–30.6.1993)', *A.J.P./P.J.A.* 1993, pp. 1136–1145, 1282–1293, 1529–1530 and 1535–1536.

SUDRE (F.) and others.—'Chronique de la jurisprudence de la Cour européenne des droits de l'homme. Deuxième partie : juin–décembre 1993', *R.U.D.H.* 1993, pp. 377 *et seq.*

354. Case of Kraska v. Switzerland

Failure of a member of the Federal Court to read thoroughly the whole file concerning a public-law appeal

603. *Martin Kraska obtained his diploma in medicine in 1981 and had since practised mostly as an assistant doctor. In 1982, he received authorization to practise independently in the Canton of Zürich, but it was withdrawn by the Zürich Health Authority in the following year on the ground that he no longer lived in the canton. An application for a new authorization in January 1985 was turned down in September 1985 because he was not 'trustworthy' within the meaning of the Zürich Public Health Act as criminal proceedings—in which he was subsequently acquitted—were pending against him.*

Appeals to the Cantonal Government and the Zürich Administrative Court were dismissed, as was, by a majority verdict on 22 October 1987, a public-law appeal to the Federal Court in which Mr Kraska asked the court to quash the Administrative Court's judgment requiring him to wait before re-applying for authorization. At the Federal Court's discussions, which were held in public, one of the judges in the majority complained that the file had not been available long enough and that he had been able to read only about half of the memorial in depth. Subsequently, the Federal Court dismissed four applications from Mr Kraska seeking the re-opening of the proceedings.

On 8 December 1987, the Health Authority granted Mr Kraska the authorization he sought.

604. *In his application to the Commission of 2 April 1988, Mr Kraska relied on Article 6 §§ 1 and 2 and Article 3 of the Convention.*[1]

Judgment of 19 April 1993 *(Chamber) (Series A No. 254–B)*

605. The Government contested the applicability of Article 6 § 1. For its part, the Court took the view that the dispute concerned the very existence of a right which could be said, on arguable grounds, to be recognized under Swiss law: Article 31 of the Swiss Constitution guar-

---

1 On 4 October 1990, the Commission declared the complaint based on Article 6 § 1 admissible, but found the remainder of the application inadmissible. In its report of 15 October 1991, the Commission expressed the opinion that there had been a violation of that provision (fourteen votes to five).

anteed the freedom of professional activity, which embraced the medical profession. In addition, as Mr Kraska had obtained a medical diploma in 1981, he had been entitled to apply for an authorization to practise independently in Zürich once he had satisfied the conditions laid down by law. On the question of whether the right in issue was a 'civil right', the Court referred to its case law on the medical profession; although in Switzerland the profession had features which were undeniably of a public-law nature, the applicant wished to work in the private sector, on the basis of contracts concluded between him and his patients. Lastly, it pointed out that proceedings came within the scope of Article 6 § 1, even if they were conducted before a constitutional court, where their outcome was decisive for civil rights and obligations. That was the case with the public-law appeal which Mr Kraska had brought before the Federal Court in view of the impact of the judgment of 22 October 1987 on the recognition of the right asserted. Consequently, Article 6 § 1 was applicable (held unanimously).

606. The effect of Article 6 § 1 was to place the tribunal having jurisdiction under a duty to conduct a proper examination of the submissions, arguments and evidence adduced by the parties, without prejudice to its assessment of whether they were relevant to its decision.

The Health Authority, the Cantonal Government and the Administrative Court of Zürich had carefully studied Mr Kraska's application for an authorization. Once the matter had been brought before the Federal Court, the judges assigned to sit in the case had all had access to the 'cantonal' file and the rapporteur had communicated to them his opinion a few days before the deliberations. They had also been able, in principle, to consult their own court's file.

All things considered, and in particular the fact that the judge in question had actively participated in the deliberations and the way in which the proceedings had been conducted, there had been no violation of Article 6 § 1 (six votes to three).

607. *Summary bibliography*

CAMBI (A.).—'Le droit à l'examen des moyens de défense', *R.T.D.H.* 1994, pp. 230–238.

SCHÜRMANN (F.).—'Europäischer Gerichtshof für Menschenrechte—Chronik der Rechtsprechung (1.1.–30.6.1993)', *A.J.P./P.J.A.* 1993, pp. 1136–1145 and 1282–1293.

SUDRE (F.) and others.—'Chronique de la jurisprudence de la Cour européenne des droits de l'homme. Première partie : janvier–mai 1993', *R.U.D.H.* 1993, pp. 217 *et seq.*

355. Case of Sibson v. the United Kingdom

Obligation imposed on a lorry driver to be a member of a particular trade union or to move to another depot

608. *Dennis Sibson was employed by Courtaulds Northern Spinning Ltd from November 1973 as a heavy goods vehicle driver. He was based at its depot at Greengate, Lancashire. His terms of employment specified that he had the right to be a member of no trade union and, at the time, no closed shop agreement was in force in the depot.*

In July 1985, the adjudication panel of the local branch of the Transport and General Workers Union ('the TGWU') dismissed a complaint brought by Mr Sibson concerning an accusation made by Mr D., another driver, to the effect that he had 'milked the funds' of the union. Mr Sibson was so dissatisfied with that decision that he resigned from the TGWU and joined the United Road Transport Union. Some of his fellow drivers at Greengate immediately ostracized him and others obstructed him in the performance of his work.

Courtaulds attempted in vain to resolve the dispute. In October 1985, the TGWU members at Greengate voted in favour of industrial action unless Mr Sibson rejoined the TGWU or was transferred elsewhere. On 8 November, at the last of a series of meetings, the applicant declined to rejoin the TGWU on the ground that he would not accept as an apology a statement to be signed by Mr D. He also declined Courtaulds' offer of a transfer to Chadderton depot, about 1 1/2 miles away from Greengate. Although the personnel manager assured him that it would be the case, he considered that the conditions at Chadderton would be less advantageous and would result in him earning less. On the same date, the applicant, who had been informed that if he reported to Greengate for work, he would be sent home without pay, resigned.

On 21 July 1986, the Industrial Tribunal upheld Mr Sibson's complaint that he had been 'constructively dismissed' and that his dismissal had been unfair. It held that the request that he move to Chadderton was not reasonable since it was not made for genuine operational reasons and its only motive was his exercise of his right not to belong to a trade union. On 16 January 1987, the Employment Appeal Tribunal dismissed an appeal by Courtaulds.

Courtaulds then appealed to the Court of Appeal, which held on 25 March 1988 that Mr Sibson had not been constructively dismissed and that it must be considered that he had resigned; Courtaulds had acted within its contractual rights in requiring the applicant to transfer to another depot, since there was an implied term in his contract that his employer could—for genuine operational or non-operational reasons—direct him to work at any place within reasonable daily reach of his home. On 19 August 1988, legal aid to appeal to the House of Lords was refused because counsel advised that there were no reasonable prospects of success.

609. *In his application lodged with the Commission on 17 October 1988, Mr Sibson relied on Article 11 of the Convention.*[1]

Judgment of 20 April 1993 *(Chamber) (Series A No. 258–A)*

610. The Government pleaded that Mr Sibson had not exhausted domestic remedies. In the first place, he had not raised in the domestic proceedings the allegation to the effect that his conditions of employment at Chadderton depot would have been less favourable than those at Greengate. Secondly, he had not contended in the English courts, as an alternative to his plea of unfair dismissal, that he had been subjected to 'action short of dismissal'. He had thereby decided to forgo any right to compensation if the domestic tribunal held that he had not been dismissed.

As the two preliminary objections raised issues that were closely linked to the merits, the Court joined them for that purpose.

611. In the Court's opinion, the facts of the case were such that it could be distinguished from that of *Young, James and Webster*.[2] Mr Sibson had not objected to rejoining the TGWU on account of any specific convictions as regards trade union membership (and he had in fact joined another union instead). It was clear that he would have rejoined the TGWU had he received a form of apology acceptable to him, and that accordingly his case did not also have to be considered in the light of Articles 9 and 10 of the Convention. Furthermore, a closed shop agreement had not been in force. Above all, Mr Sibson had not been faced with a threat of dismissal involving loss of livelihood: he had had the possibility of going to work at the nearby Chadderton depot, to which his employers were contractually entitled to move him; their offer to him in this respect had not been conditional on his rejoining the TGWU; and it had not been established that his working conditions there would have been significantly less favourable than those at

---

1 In its report of 10 December 1991, the Commission expressed the opinion that there had been no violation of Article 11 (eight votes to six).
2 Series A No. 44; see Vol. I of this work, 395–305.

Greengate. Having regard to those various factors, the Court came to the conclusion that Mr Sibson had not been not subjected to a form of treatment striking at the very substance of the freedom of association. There had accordingly been no violation of Article 11 (seven votes to two).

612. It was therefore unnecessary to rule on the Government's preliminary objections.

613. *Summary bibliography*

DECAUX (E.) and TAVERNIER (P.).—'Chronique de jurisprudence de la Cour européenne des droits de l'homme (année 1993)', *J.D.I.* 1994, pp. 782 and 783.

LECLERCQ (M.).—'Les aspects positif et négatif de la liberté d'association syndicale', *R.T.D.H.* 1993, pp. 589–593.

PETTITI (C.).—'Le droit de ne pas s'affilier à un syndicat en droit européen', *Droit social* 1993, pp. 999–1002.

SCHÜRMANN (F.).—'Europäischer Gerichtshof für Menschenrechte—Chronik der Rechtsprechung (1.1.–30.6.1993)', *A.J.P./P.J.A.* 1993, pp. 1136–1145 and 1282–1293.

SUDRE (F.) and others.—'Chronique de la jurisprudence de la Cour européenne des droits de l'homme. Première partie : janvier–mai 1993', *R.U.D.H.* 1993, pp. 217 *et seq.*

356. Case of Modinos v. Cyprus

Prohibition of homosexual relations in private between consenting adults

614. *Alecos Modinos, a Cypriot, was a homosexual who, at the time of the proceedings, was involved in a sexual relationship with another male adult. He was the President of the 'Liberation Movement of Homosexuals in Cyprus'. He stated that he suffered great strain, apprehension and fear of prosecution by reason of the legal provisions which criminalized certain homosexual acts.*

615. *In his application of 22 May 1989 to the Commission, Mr Modinos relied on Article 8 of the Convention.[1]*

Judgment of 22 April 1993 *(Chamber) (Series A No. 259)*

616. The Government submitted that neither the applicant nor any other person in his situation could be lawfully prosecuted under the relevant sections of the Cypriot Criminal Code, since, to the extent that those provisions concerned homosexual relations in private between consenting male adults, they were in conflict with the Cypriot Constitution and the Convention.

The Court first observed that the prohibition of male homosexual conduct in private between adults still remained on the statute book. Moreover, the Supreme Court of Cyprus in the case of *Costa v. The Republic* had considered that the relevant provisions of the Criminal Code violated neither the Convention nor the Constitution notwithstanding the European Court's judgment in *Dudgeon v. the United Kingdom*.[2] In the Court's view, whatever the status in domestic law of the Government's remarks, it could not fail to take into account such a statement from the highest court in the land on matters so pertinent to the issue before it. The Attorney-General's consistent policy of not bringing criminal proceedings in respect of private homosexual conduct on the basis that the relevant law was a dead letter provided no guarantee that action would not be taken by a future Attorney-General to enforce the law, particularly when regard was had to statements by

1 In its report of 3 December 1991, the Commission concluded that there had been a breach of Article 8 (unanimously).
2 Series A No. 45; see Vol. I of this work, 306–315.

282

Government ministers which appeared to suggest that the relevant provisions of the Criminal Code were still in force. Consequently, the existence of the prohibition continuously and directly affected the applicant's private life.

617. The Government had limited their submissions to maintaining that there had been no interference with the applicant's rights, and had not sought to argue that there existed a justification under paragraph 2 of Article 8 for the impugned legal provisions. In the light of this concession and having regard to the Court's case law, a re-examination of that question was not called for. Accordingly, there had been a breach of Article 8 (eight votes to one).

618. The Court considered that the finding of a breach of Article 8 constituted sufficient just satisfaction.

The Court awarded Mr Modinos 4,000 Cyprus pounds in respect of fees together with the full amount claimed by way of expenses (2,836 Cyprus pounds) (unanimously).

619. *Summary bibliography*

DECAUX (E.) and TAVERNIER (P.).—'Chronique de jurisprudence de la Cour européenne des droits de l'homme (année 1993)', *J.D.I.* 1994, pp. 788–790.

SCHÜRMANN (F.).—'Europäischer Gerichtshof für Menschenrechte—Chronik der Rechtsprechung (1.1.–30.6.1993)', *A.J.P./P.J.A.* 1993, pp. 1136–1145, 1282–1293 and 1530–1531.

SUDRE (F.) and others.—'Chronique de la jurisprudence de la Cour européenne des droits de l'homme. Première partie : janvier–mai 1993', *R.U.D.H.* 1993, pp. 217 *et seq.*

357. Case of Kokkinakis v. Greece

Conviction of a Jehovah's Witness for proselytism

620. *Minos Kokkinakis, a retired businessman of Greek nationality, was born into a Greek Orthodox family in 1919. After becoming a Jehovah's Witness in 1936, he was arrested more than sixty times for proselytism. He was also interned and imprisoned on several occasions.*

On 2 March 1986, he and his wife called at the home of Mrs Kyriakaki, an Orthodox Christian, in Sitia (Crete) and engaged in a discussion with her in the course of which Mr Kokkinakis attempted to convert her, in particular by reading her passages from several books and giving her others. Mrs Kyriakaki's husband informed the police, who arrested Mr and Mrs Kokkinakis and took them to the local police station, where they were detained. They were both charged of the offence of proselytism contrary to section 4 of Law No. 1363/1938, which had been adopted under the dictatorship of Metaxas (1936-1940). On 20 March 1986, they were each sentenced by the Lasithi Criminal Court to four months' imprisonment, convertible into a pecuniary penalty of 400 drachmas per day's imprisonment, and a fine of 10,000 drachmas. On 17 March 1987, the Crete Court of Appeal, to which Mr and Mrs Kokkinakis had appealed, quashed Mrs Kokkinakis' conviction and upheld her husband's, but reduced his prison sentence to three months and converted it into a pecuniary penalty of 400 drachmas per day. Mr Kokkinakis appealed on points of law, but his appeal was dismissed in April 1988.

621. *The Christian Eastern Orthodox Church, which during nearly four centuries of foreign occupation had symbolized the maintenance of Greek culture and the Greek language, had taken an active part in the Greek people's struggle for emancipation, to such an extent that Hellenism was to some extent identified with the Orthodox faith. Greece's successive Constitutions had referred to the Church as being 'dominant'. The overwhelming majority of the population were members of it, and, according to Greek conceptions, it represented* de jure *and* de facto *the religion of the State itself, a good number of whose administrative and educational functions it moreover carried out. The Constitutions of 1844, 1864, 1911 and 1952 contained a clause forbidding 'proselytism and any other action against the dominant religion'. The 1975 Constitution prohibited proselytism in general: the ban covered all 'known religions', meaning those whose doctrines were not apocryphal and in which no secret initiation was required of neophytes.*

622. *In his application to the Commission of 22 August 1988, Mr Kokkinakis claimed that his conviction for proselytism was in breach of the rights secured in Articles 7, 9 and 10 of the Convention. He also relied on Article 5 § 1 and Article 6 §§ 1 and 2.*[1]

Judgment of 25 May 1993 *(Chamber) (Series A No. 260–A)*

623. As enshrined in Article 9, freedom of thought, conscience and religion was one of the foundations of a 'democratic society' within the meaning of the Convention. It was one of the most vital elements that went to make up the identity of believers and their conception of life, but it was also a precious asset for atheists, agnostics, sceptics and the unconcerned. In particular, religious freedom implied freedom to 'manifest [one's] religion', not only in community with others, 'in public' and within the circle of those whose faith one shared, but also 'alone' and 'in private'; it included in principle the right to try to convince one's neighbour, for example through 'teaching'.

The fundamental nature of the rights guaranteed in Article 9 was also reflected in the wording of the paragraph providing for limitation on them. Unlike the second paragraphs of Articles 8, 10 and 11, which covered all the rights mentioned in the first paragraphs of those articles, that of Article 9 referred only to 'freedom to manifest one's religion or belief'.

624. Having set out those general principles, the Court considered their application. The sentence passed by the Lasithi Criminal Court and subsequently reduced by the Crete Court of Appeal amounted to an interference with the exercise of Mr Kokkinakis' right to 'freedom to manifest [his] religion or belief'.

Was that interference 'prescribed by law'? The Court had already noted that the wording of many statutes was not absolutely precise. The need to avoid excessive rigidity and to keep pace with changing circumstances meant that many laws were inevitably couched in terms which, to a greater or lesser extent, were vague and whose interpretation and application depended on practice. In this instance, section 4 of Law No. 1363/1938 had been supplemented by a body of settled national case law, which had been published and was accessible.

1   The Commission declared the application admissible on 7 December 1990 except for the complaints based on Articles 5 and 6. In its report of 3 December 1991, the Commission expressed the opinion that there had been no violation of Article 7 (eleven votes to two), there had been a violation of Article 9 (unanimously) and no separate issue arose under Article 10 (twelve votes to one).

The impugned measure was in pursuit of a legitimate aim under Article 9 § 2, namely the protection of the rights and freedoms of others.

As for its necessity in a democratic society, a distinction had to be made between bearing Christian witness and improper proselytism: the former corresponded to true evangelism; the latter represented a corruption or deformation of it and was not compatible with respect for the freedom of thought, conscience and religion of others. The criteria for identifying proselytism which had been adopted by the Greek legislature could be regarded as acceptable in so far as they were designed only to punish improper proselytism, which did not have to be defined in the abstract in this case.

The Court noted, however, that the Greek courts had established the applicant's liability by merely reproducing the wording of section 4 and had not sufficiently specified in what way the accused had attempted to convince his neighbour by improper means. None of the facts they set out warranted that finding. That being so, it had not been shown that the applicant's conviction was justified by a pressing social need. In conclusion, there had been a breach of Article 9 (six votes to three).

625. Article 7 § 1 of the Convention was not confined to prohibiting the retrospective application of the criminal law to an accused's disadvantage. It also embodied, more generally, the principle that only the law could define a crime and prescribe a penalty and the principle that the criminal law must not be extensively construed to an accused's detriment, for instance by analogy; it followed from this that an offence must be clearly defined in law.

In this case, the applicant could know from the wording of section 4 of Law No. 1363/1938 and, if need be, with the assistance of the courts' interpretation of it, what acts and omissions would make him liable. There had therefore been no breach of Article 7 (eight votes to one).

626. Having regard to its decision on Article 9, the Court considered it unnecessary to examine the complaints based on Article 10 and Article 14 in conjunction with Article 9 (held unanimously).

627. Under Article 50, the Court awarded Mr Kokkinakis 400,000 drachmas for non-pecuniary damage (unanimously).

It awarded him 2,789,500 drachmas in respect of costs and expenses incurred in Greece and before the Strasbourg institutions (unanimously).

628. Summary bibliography

DECAUX (E.) and TAVERNIER (P.).—'Chronique de jurisprudence de la Cour européenne des droits de l'homme (année 1993)', *J.D.I.* 1994, pp. 790–792.

JORION (B.).—'Jurisprudence de la Cour européenne des droits de l'homme en matière de droit de famille et l'exercice du culte', *L.P.A.* 10 August 1994, pp. 35–56.

JUNOSZA-ZDROJEWSKI (G.).—'La Cour européenne et les activités des sectes', *G.P.* 15–19 July 1994, pp. 41–43.

LABUSCHAGNE (B.).—'Noot', *NJCM–Bulletin* 1994, pp. 706–709.

RIGAUX (F.).—'L'incrimination du prosélytisme face à la liberté d'expression', *R.T.D.H.* 1994, pp. 144–150.

ROUVIÈRE-PERRIER (I.).—'Les témoins de Jéhovah devant la Cour européenne des droits de l'homme', *L.P.A.*, 17 November 1993, No. 138, pp. 24–26.

SCHÜRMANN (F.).—'Europäischer Gerichtshof für Menschenrechte—Chronik der Rechtsprechung (1.1.–30.6.1993)', *A.J.P./P.J.A.* 1993, pp. 1136–1145, 1282–1293 and 1531–1533.

SUDRE (F.) and others.—'Chronique de la jurisprudence de la Cour européenne des droits de l'homme. Première partie : janvier-mai 1993, *R.U.D.H.* 1993, pp. 217 *et seq.*

358. Case of Brannigan and McBride v. the United Kingdom

Arrest and detention of suspects under legislation on the prevention of terrorism and validity of the United Kingdom derogation under Article 15 of the Convention (Northern Ireland)

629. *Peter Brannigan lived in Northern Ireland. He was arrested on 9 January 1989 and removed to the Interrogation Centre at Gough Barracks (Armagh). His arrest was effected pursuant to section 12(1)(b) of the Prevention of Terrorism (Temporary Provisions) Act 1984, under which a person in relation to whom there were reasonable grounds for suspecting to be a person who was or had been concerned in the commission, preparation or instigation of acts of terrorism could be arrested without warrant. A two-day extension of his detention was granted by the Secretary of State on 10 January and a further three-day extension was granted on 12 January. The applicant was released on 15 January after having spent a total period of six days, fourteen hours and thirty minutes in detention.*

630. *As for Patrick McBride, he was arrested on 5 January 1989 pursuant to the same section of the 1984 Act and removed to Castlereagh Interrogation Centre. A three-day extension of his period of detention was granted by the Secretary of State on 6 January. He was released on 9 January 1989 having spent a total period of four days, six hours and twenty-five minutes in detention. Mr McBride was shot dead on 4 February 1992 by a policeman who had run amok and attacked Sinn Fein Headquarters.*

631. *On 23 December 1988, the United Kingdom informed the Secretary General of the Council of Europe that the Government had availed itself of the right of derogation conferred by Article 15 § 1 of the Convention to the extent that the exercise of powers under section 12 of the 1984 Act might be inconsistent with the obligations imposed by Article 5 § 3 of the Convention.*

632. *In their applications lodged with the Commission on 19 January 1989, Mr Brannigan and Mr McBride complained that they had not been brought promptly before a judge, in breach of Article 5 § 3. They also alleged that they had not had an enforceable right to compensation in breach of Article 5 § 5 and that there was no effective remedy in* *respect of their complaints contrary to Article 13.*[1] *They subsequently withdrew other complaints that they had made under Articles 3, 5 §§ 1 and 4, 8, 9 and 10.*

Judgment of 28 May 1993 *(Plenary Court) (Series A No. 258–B)*

633. Having regard to its judgment in the case of *Brogan and Others*,[2] the Court found that Article 5 §§ 3 and 5 had not been respected. As the Government had invoked their derogation under Article 15 of the Convention, the Court had to examine its validity. Referring to its judgment in *Ireland v. the United Kingdom*,[3] the Court recalled that it fell to each Contracting State, with its responsibility for 'the life of [its] nation', to determine whether that life was threatened by a 'public emergency' and, if so, how far it was necessary to go in attempting to overcome the emergency. By reason of their direct and continuous contact with the pressing needs of the moment, the national authorities were in principle in a better position than the international judge to decide both on the presence of such an emergency and on the nature and scope of derogations necessary to avert it. Accordingly, in this matter a wide margin of appreciation should be left to the national authorities. The Court nevertheless was competent to rule on whether the States had gone beyond the 'extent strictly required by the exigencies' of the crisis. At the same time, in exercising its supervision, the Court had to give appropriate weight to such relevant factors as the nature of the rights affected by the derogation and the circumstances leading to, and the duration of, the emergency situation.

634. In the light of all the material before it as to the extent and impact of terrorist violence in Northern Ireland and elsewhere in the United Kingdom, the Court considered there could be no doubt that a public emergency threatening the life of nation existed.

635. The Court went on to consider whether the measures were strictly required by the exigencies of the situation.

1 In its report of 3 December 1991, the Commission expressed the opinion that there had been no violation of Article 5 §§ 3 and 5 of the Convention in view of the United Kingdom's derogation of 23 December 1988 under Article 15 (eight votes to five) and that no separate issue arose under Article 13 (unanimously).
2 Series A No. 145–B; see Vol. II of this work, 122–135.
3 Series A no. 25; see Vol. I of this work, 156–165.

Was the derogation a genuine response to an emergency situation? The Court first observed that the power of arrest and extended detention had been considered necessary by the Government since 1974 in dealing with the threat of terrorism. Following the judgment in *Brogan and Others*, the Government had been faced with the option of either introducing judicial control of the decision to detain or lodging a derogation from their Convention obligations in this respect. Since the power of extended detention without judicial control and the notice of 23 December 1988 were clearly linked to the persistence of the emergency situation, there was no indication that the derogation was other than a genuine response.

Was the derogation premature? The validity of the derogation could not be called into question for the sole reason that the Government had decided to examine whether in the future a way could be found of ensuring greater conformity with Convention obligations. Indeed, such a process of continued reflection was not only in keeping with Article 15 § 3, which required permanent review of the need for emergency measures, but was also implicit in the very notion of proportionality.

Was the absence of judicial control of extended detention justified? According to the various reports reviewing the operation of the prevention of terrorism legislation, the difficulties of investigating and prosecuting terrorist crime gave rise to the need for an extended period of detention which would not be subject to judicial control. Furthermore, it remained the view of the respondent Government that it was essential to prevent the disclosure to the detainee and his legal adviser of information on the basis of which decisions on the extension of detention were made; in the adversarial system of the common law, the independence of the judiciary would be compromised if judges or other judicial officers were to be involved in the granting or approval of extensions. The introduction of a 'judge or other officer authorized by law to exercise judicial power' into the process of extension of periods of detention would not of itself necessarily bring about a situation of compliance with Article 5 § 3. As to what measures were most appropriate or expedient at the relevant time in dealing with a continuing emergency situation, it was not the Court's role to substitute its view for that of the Government, which had direct responsibility for establishing the balance between the taking of effective measures to combat terrorism on the one hand, and respecting individual rights on the other. In the context of Northern Ireland, where the judiciary was small and vulnerable to terrorist attacks, public confidence in the independence of the judiciary was understandably a matter to which the Government attached great importance.

Were there safeguards against abuse? The remedy of habeas corpus was available to test the lawfulness of the original arrest and detention. There was no dispute that this remedy had been open to Mr Brannigan and Mr McBride and their legal advisers and that it provided an important measure of protection against arbitrary detention. Secondly, detainees had an absolute and legally enforceable right to consult a solicitor after forty-eight hours from the time of arrest. Both of the applicants had, in fact, been free to consult a solicitor after this period. It was also not disputed that detainees were entitled to inform a relative or friend about their detention and to have access to a doctor. In addition to those basic safeguards, the operation of the legislation in question had been kept under regular independent review.

636. Were the derogating measures inconsistent with 'other obligations under international law'? The applicants contended that it was an essential requirement for a valid derogation under Article 4 of the 1966 United Nations International Covenant on Civil and Political Rights that a public emergency must have been 'officially proclaimed'. The Court noted that, in his statement of 22 December 1988 to the House of Commons, the Secretary of State for the Home Department had explained in detail the reasons underlying the Government's decision to derogate and had announced that steps were being taken to give notice of derogation under both Article 15 of the European Convention and Article 4 of the Covenant. Such a statement was well in keeping with the notion of an official proclamation.

637. In sum, the derogation lodged by the United Kingdom satisfied the requirements of Article 15 and therefore the applicants could not validly complain of a violation of Article 5 § 3 (twenty-two votes to four). It followed that there was no obligation under Article 5 § 5 to provide the applicants with an enforceable right to compensation.

638. It had been open to the applicants to challenge the lawfulness of their detention by way of proceedings for habeas corpus and the Court in *Brogan and Others* had found that that remedy satisfied Article 5 § 4. Since the requirements of Article 13 were less strict than those of Article 5 § 4, Article 13 had not been violated (twenty-two votes to four).

639. *Summary bibliography*

DECAUX (E.) and TAVERNIER (P.).—'Chronique de jurisprudence de la Cour européenne des droits de l'homme (année 1993)', *J.D.I.* 1994, pp. 783–788.
LOOF (J.-P.).—'Noot', *N.J.C.M.–Bulletin* 1993, pp. 803–810.

PETTITI (L.-E.).—'Droits de l'homme', *R.S.C.D.P.C.* 1993, pp. 818–820.

SCHÜRMANN (F.).—'Europäischer Gerichtshof für Menschenrechte—Chronik der Rechtsprechung (1.1.–30.6.1993)', *A.J.P./P.J.A.* 1993, pp. 1136–1145 and 1282–1293.

SUDRE (F.) and others.—'Chronique de la jurisprudence de la Cour européenne des droits de l'homme. Première partie : janvier–mai 1993', *R.U.D.H.* 1993, pp. 217 *et seq.*

359. Case of Bunkate v. the Netherlands

Length of criminal proceedings

640. *On 12 September 1983, Johannes Maria Clemens Bunkate was arrested on suspicion of having committed forgery. He remained in detention on remand until 16 December 1983, on which date the Public Prosecutor ordered his release on the ground of a shortage of cells. The preliminary investigation lasted from 16 September to 19 October 1983. On 5 January 1984, the Regional Court in the Hague sentenced him to one year's imprisonment. Both the Public Prosecutor and the applicant filed an appeal on that same day. The applicant was allowed to remain at liberty pending the appeal. Two days later, the applicant travelled to the Dominican Republic. While there, his death was announced in the Netherlands by means of certificate issued by the competent Dominican authorities. The applicant's death was registered in The Hague on 18 May 1984. He returned to the Netherlands on 19 November 1984. The register of deaths was rectified on 25 June 1986 in accordance with an order of the District Court at The Hague, to which an application had been made by Mr Bunkate's mother on 3 December 1984.*

Following a hearing on 14 May 1985, the Court of Appeal in the Hague upheld the guilty verdict on 28 May 1985, but increased the sentence to one year and four months. The applicant appealed to the Supreme Court on 10 June 1985. The registry of the Court of Appeal forwarded the case-file to the Supreme Court on 23 September 1986, that is to say, fifteen and a half months later. The Procurator-General filed his opinion on 17 February 1987, and the Supreme Court dismissed his appeal on 26 May 1987.

641. *In his application of 24 November 1987 to the Commission, Mr Bunkate complained of the length of the criminal proceedings against him and relied on Article 6 § 1 of the Convention.*[1]

Judgment of 26 May 1993 *(Chamber) (Series A No. 248–B)*

642. The Government, being the party which had brought the case before the Court, notified the Registrar of their intention not to proceed with the case (Rules of Court, Rule 49 § 1).

---

1 In its report of 1 April 1992, the Commission expressed the unanimous opinion that there had been a violation of Article 6 § 1.

The Court observed there had been no friendly settlement, arrangement or other fact of a kind to provide a solution of the matter; the applicant's entitlement to a formal and binding decision on the merits and as to just satisfaction, if any, overrode any interest the Government might have in discontinuance of the case. Accordingly, the Court decided not to strike the case out of its list (unanimously).

643. The period to be taken into consideration had begun on 12 September 1983, the date of the applicant's arrest, and ended on 26 May 1987, the date of the decision of the Supreme Court by which the sentence of sixteen months' imprisonment had become final. However, the period from 7 January to 19 November 1984, during which the applicant had been in the Dominican Republic and thus effectively out of reach of the Netherlands authorities, should be deducted from the overall period.

The applicant had directed no particular complaint against the proceedings at first instance and on appeal. However, although the applicant had filed his appeal on 10 June 1985, the registry of the Supreme Court had not received the case-file from the Court of Appeal until 23 September 1986. The Government had offered no satisfactory explanation for this period of fifteen and a half months. The Court could not accept such a period of total inactivity and held that there therefore had been a violation of Article 6 § 1 (unanimously).

644. With regard to the application of Article 50, the applicant assumed that a finding by the Court that a criminal charge had not been decided within a reasonable time automatically resulted in the extinction of the right to execute the sentence and that consequently, if the sentence had already been executed when the Court gave judgment, such execution became unlawful with retroactive effect. That assumption was, however, incorrect. As the Court could discern no other basis for the claims, it dismissed them (unanimously).

645. *Summary bibliography*

SCHÜRMANN (F.).—'Europäischer Gerichtshof für Menschenrechte—Chronik der Rechtsprechung (1.1.–30.6.1993)', *A.J.P./P.J.A.* 1993, pp. 1136–1145 and 1282–1293.

SUDRE (F.) and others.—'Chronique de la jurisprudence de la Cour européenne des droits de l'homme. Première partie : janvier–mai 1993', *R.U.D.H.* 1993, pp. 217 *et seq.*

360. Case of K. v. Austria

Accused sentenced on account of his refusal to give evidence in another trial for fear of incriminating himself

646. *K., an Austrian national, was accused of buying three grammes of heroin from a couple, who were facing a separate prosecution for drug trafficking. He pleaded not guilty and on 19 May 1989 his trial was adjourned. He was then summoned to appear on 30 May 1989 to give evidence in the trial of the couple, also for drug trafficking. At the hearing, K. refused to testify because of the proceedings pending against him. The court then decided not to give him leave to remain silent (Article 153 of the Code of Criminal Procedure). Nevertheless, K. refused to answer a question and was fined 3,000 schillings. As he persisted in his refusal to testify, he was sentenced to five days' imprisonment. On 2 June 1989, the Court of Appeal dismissed his appeal. On 25 January 1990, the applicant admitted having purchased heroin from the couple on two occasions. In the intervening period, the Attorney General's Office had filed an appeal in the interests of the law against the order imprisoning the applicant. The Supreme Court dismissed this appeal on 19 December 1990.*

647. *In his application of 27 November 1989 to the Commission, K. claimed that the proceedings resulting in the imposition of the fine had infringed Article 6 of the Convention, in particular sub-paragraphs (a) to (c) of paragraph 3, and that the obligation to make a statement liable to incriminate himself had been contrary to Article 6 § 1. He also complained of his detention and the lack of any possibility of judicial review thereof (Article 5 §§ 1 and 4).*[1]

---

1 The Commission declared the application admissible on 18 February 1992; it decided to examine the complaint relating to the obligation to testify also under Article 10. In its report of 13 October 1992, it expressed the opinion that:
  (a) Article 6 was inapplicable to the proceedings imposing the fine (seven votes to five);
  (b) there had been a violation of Article 10 as regards the refusal to allow the applicant to remain silent (ten votes to two);
  (c) there had been no violation of Article 6 § 1 on the same point (eleven votes to one);
  (d) there had been a violation of Article 5 §§ 1 and 4 (ten votes to two).

Judgment of 2 June 1993 *(Chamber) (Series A No. 255–B)*

648. The agreement concluded between the Austrian Government and K. provided for the payment of certain sums as compensation for the detention plus costs. For his part, K. agreed to waive his right to pursue any further claims arising out of the case.

649. Despite the objections of the Commission's Delegate, the Court considered that the possibility of a breach of the Convention, deriving from the manner in which the national authorities had applied a provision of national law or might have applied it in a specific case, could not in itself justify a refusal to strike a case out of the list. It noted in addition that the Austrian Government had laid before Parliament a bill intended, *inter alia*, to amend Articles 152, 153 and 160 of the Code of Criminal Procedure. The new draft provisions would eliminate any public policy reason for requiring a decision on the merits of the case. Consequently, the Court struck the case from the list (unanimously).[1]

650. *Summary bibliography*

KINSCH (P.).—'Le droit de ne pas contribuer à sa propre incrimination', *B.D.H.* 1993, pp. 47–51.

SCHÜRMANN (F.).—'Europäischer Gerichtshof für Menschenrechte—Chronik der Rechtsprechung (1.1.–30.6.1993)', *A.J.P./P.J.A.* 1993, pp. 1136–1145 and 1282–1293.

SUDRE (F.) and others.—'Chronique de la jurisprudence de la Cour européenne des droits de l'homme. Deuxième partie : juin–décembre 1993', *R.U.D.H.* 1993, pp. 377 *et seq.*

---

1 A law, which was passed by Parliament on 30 July 1993 and entered into force on 1 January 1994, amended the Code of Criminal Procedure so as to remove the obligation to testify of persons whose statements were liable to incriminate them.

361. Case of Melin v. France

Obstacles preventing a convicted person from putting forward arguments in support of his appeal on points of law

651. *On 6 May 1985, the Nanterre Criminal Court convicted Pierre-André Melin of fraud and sentenced him to a suspended term of sixteen months' imprisonment, combined with an order requiring him to compensate the victim for the damage which he had sustained. On an appeal brought by Mr Melin, the Versailles Court of Appeal upheld the lower court's guilty verdict on 15 January 1986, but deferred pronouncement of sentence. On 17 January, Mr Melin lodged an appeal on points of law with the registry of the Court of Appeal. According to the applicant, he requested a copy of the contested judgment on the same occasion and deferred preparing his grounds of appeal until he had received the judgment. On 18 June 1986, the procureur général at the Versailles Court of Appeal informed him that the Court of Cassation had dismissed his appeal by a judgment delivered on 27 May 1986. In the course of a subsequent exchange of letters, the Chief Registrar of the Court of Cassation informed him that, as the judgment of the Court of Cassation was final, he could not appeal against it.*

652. *Mr Melin applied to the Commission on 21 November 1986. Relying on paragraphs 1 and 3(b) and (c) of Article 6, he complained that he had not received in good time a copy of the judgment of the Versailles Court of Appeal and that he had been informed neither of the time-limit for submitting a memorial to the Court of Cassation nor of the date of the hearing at which his appeal was examined.*[1]

Judgment of 22 June 1993 *(Chamber) (Series A No. 261–A)*

653. The Court observed that the requirements of fairness included the right of every accused to be informed of the grounds for his conviction, the right to have adequate time and facilities for the preparation of his appeal on points of law and the right to have the opposing party's observations communicated to him.

Mr Melin, a former lawyer, had known that in accordance with the legislation in force the authorities had been under no obligation to

1 In its report of 9 April 1992, the Commission expressed the opinion that there had been a violation of paragraph 1 of Article 6, taken in conjunction with paragraph 3(b) and (c) thereof (unanimously).

serve the Court of Appeal's judgment on him. It had thus been reasonable to expect him to have adopted one of the following three courses of action. First, he could have consulted the original of the judgment in question at the registry of the Versailles Court of Appeal. Secondly, assuming that he had unsuccessfully requested a copy, he could and should have repeated that request. A third possibility remained open to him: he could have made enquiries at the Court of Cassation's registry as to the date on which the court was to give judgment and sought an adjournment so as to be able to file a memorial in good time and to have the opportunity to present his case. Being well versed in the routines of judicial procedure, he must have known that the latter was subject to relatively short time-limits, especially as the relevant rules were sufficiently coherent and clear.

In conclusion, the applicant could not claim that the authorities had made it impossible for him to produce a memorial. As he had deliberately waived his right to be assisted by a lawyer, he had been under a duty to show diligence himself. Accordingly, there had been no violation of Article 6 (five votes to four).

654. *Summary bibliography*

DECAUX (E.) and TAVERNIER (P.).—'Chronique de jurisprudence de la Cour européenne des droits de l'homme (année 1993), *J.D.I.* 1994, pp. 796 and 797.

LAURENT (T.).—'L'affaire Melin c. France', *Cahiers du CREDHO*, no. 2, 1994, pp. 149–155.

PETTITI (L.-E.).—'Droits de l'homme', *R.S.C.D.P.C.* 1994, pp. 816–818.

SCHÜRMANN (F.).—'Europäischer Gerichtshof für Menschenrechte—Chronik der Rechtsprechung (1.1.–30.6.1993)', *A.J.P./P.J.A.* 1993, pp. 1136–1145 and 1282–1293.

SUDRE (F.) and others.—'Chronique de la jurisprudence de la Cour européenne des droits de l'homme. Deuxième partie : juin–décembre 1993', *R.U.D.H.* 1993, pp. 377 *et seq.*

362. Case of Ruiz-Mateos v. Spain

Length of proceedings for the restitution of expropriated property and proceedings in the Constitutional Court

655. *José María Ruiz-Mateos, a businessman, Zoilo Ruiz-Mateos, Rafael Ruiz-Mateos, Isidoro Ruiz-Mateos, Alfonso Ruiz-Mateos and Maria Dolores Ruiz-Mateos were brothers and sister. They were all of Spanish nationality. They held 100% of the shares in RUMASA S.A., the parent company of the RUMASA group, comprising several hundred undertakings in which RUMASA S.A.'s holding varied from one to the other.*

By a legislative decree of 23 February 1983 (subsequently replaced by Law No. 7/1983), the Government ordered the expropriation in the public interest and the immediate possession of all the shares in the companies comprising the RUMASA group, including those of the parent company.

On 9 and 27 May 1983, the six applicants brought proceedings (which were subsequently joined) in the civil courts. They argued that the expropriation was illegal and sought restitution of their shares. They subsequently asked Madrid First-Instance Court No. 18 to refer to the Constitutional Court a question on the conformity of Law No. 7/1983 with certain articles of the Constitution. On 5 October 1984, Court No. 18 acceded to that request in part, and asked the Constitutional Court whether Articles 1 and 2 of the Law were compatible with the constitutional guarantee for the right to effective judicial protection. On 19 December 1986, the Constitutional Court, by a majority, answered the question in the affirmative. It had previously received written observations from the Attorney General and the Counsel for the State. A number of applications made by the first applicant were rejected on the ground that he lacked locus standi. After the judgment had been communicated to Court No. 18, it dismissed the action for restitution on 23 December 1986.

On 27 December, the applicants appealed to the Audiencia provincial of Madrid. By decision of 13 February 1989, which was confirmed on 7 July, that court rejected their request that the proceedings should be stayed pending the outcome of their application to the European Commission in Strasbourg. On 9 July 1989, acting, moreover, on the applicant's alternative request, it asked the Constitutional Court whether the above-mentioned two articles of the 1983 Law were compatible with the constitutional guarantees of the right to equal treatment and the right of property. On 15 January 1991, after receiving the observations of the Attorney General and the Counsel for the State, the Constitutional Court held, by a majority, that the question should be answered in the affirmative. The Audiencia provincial *was notified on 25 January 1991; it dismissed the applicants' appeal on 25 February 1991.*

656. *The Ruiz-Mateos applied to the Commission on 5 May 1987. They alleged in the first place that their case had not been given a fair hearing conducted within a reasonable time by an impartial tribunal (Article 6 § 1 of the Convention). They claimed in addition that they had been deprived of their right of access to the courts to challenge the public interest justification for the expropriation and the necessity of the immediate transfer of their property (Articles 6 § 1 and 13). Finally, they complained of discrimination in relation to other Spanish citizens in that the latter were subject to the ordinary law on expropriations and could therefore institute proceedings in the administrative courts (Article 14 read in conjunction with Articles 6 § 1 and 13).*[1]

Judgment of 23 June 1993 *(Plenary Court) (Series A No. 262)*

657. The judgment started with several preliminary observations. Although the application mentioned solely the first set of proceedings in the Constitutional Court, the Court decided to examine all the proceedings in issue, including those which had been held after the application had been lodged with the Commission. It noted that the applicability of Article 6 § 1 to the applicants' civil actions for the restitution of their assets was not open to dispute, but that the Government maintained that the proceedings in the Constitutional Court should not be taken into account.

658. As regards compliance with the 'reasonable time' requirement, the period to be taken into consideration had begun on 27 May 1983, when five of the applicants had brought their action in respect of half the capital of RUMASA, thereby supplementing the action brought by José María Ruiz-Mateos on 9 May 1983. It had ended on 25 February 1991, the date of the judgment of the *Audiencia provincial* of Madrid. It covered the duration of the two sets of proceedings before the

---

1 On 6 November 1990, the Commission declared the first complaint admissible and the remainder of the application inadmissible. In its report of January 1992, the Commission expressed the opinion that there had been a violation of Article 6 § 1 inasmuch as the applicants had not been given a fair hearing (thirteen votes to two) and the relevant proceedings had not been conducted within a reasonable time (eleven votes to four).

Constitutional Court. That conclusion was based on well-established case law of the Court according to which proceedings in a constitutional court were to be taken into account for calculating the relevant period where the result of such proceedings was capable of affecting the outcome of the dispute before the ordinary courts. It was applicable *a fortiori* to proceedings relating to preliminary issues. As a result, the period to be taken into account had lasted nearly seven years and nine months.

The Court considered that although the main civil action had not been complex at the outset, it had subsequently given rise to constitutional questions which were undeniably difficult. However, the procedure for resolving such questions did not involve steps liable to lead to prolongations.

By asking for the appeal proceedings to be adjourned and the proceedings before the *Audiencia provincial* to be stayed pending the decision of the European Commission in Strasbourg, the applicants, for their part, had delayed the decision in the appeal proceedings by more than eight months.

As regards the conduct of the competent authorities, the Court noted the interruption during the proceedings at first instance to resolve the constitutionality issue (more than twenty-five months) and two others during the appeal proceedings: (a) the delay between the decision on admissibility and the court's starting to consider the appeal (more than sixteen months) and (b) the delay caused by the examination of the second question (almost fourteen months). The remedial action taken in June 1988 by the public authorities to lighten the workload of the *Audiencia provincial* had been too late to have any effect in this case. In spite of the special features of the Constitutional Court, the relevant proceedings had gone on too long. Lastly, what was at stake in this case was considerable, not only for the applicants but also for Spanish society in general, in view of its vast social and economic implications. The large number of persons concerned—employees, shareholders and third parties—and the amount of capital involved militated in favour of a prompt resolution of the dispute.

Article 6 § 1 had therefore been violated on this point (twenty-two votes to two).

659. As for the right to a fair trial, the Court noted that the applicants' complaint under this head was directed solely at the proceedings in the Constitutional Court, which had, however, to be placed in the context in which they had arisen, namely an action for the restitution of expropriated assets.

The Government denied that Article 6 § 1 was applicable to the proceedings before the Constitutional Court, since that court's role was not to rule on the rights and interests of individuals but to ensure that the legislature, the executive and the judiciary respected the Constitution. The Court stressed the close link between the main civil proceedings and the proceedings on constitutionality: the annulment, by the Constitutional Court, of the contested provisions would have led the civil courts to allow the claims of the Ruiz-Mateos family. It further pointed out that, by raising questions of constitutionality, the applicants had used the sole available means of complaining of an interference with their right of property: an *amparo* appeal (individual appeal for protection against violation of constitutional rights) did not lie in connection with Article 33 of the Constitution. The Court therefore took the view that Article 6 § 1 was applicable.

Had Article 6 § 1 been complied with? The Court examined the complaint in the light of the whole of Article 6 § 1 because the principle of equality of arms was only one feature of the wider concept of a fair trial, which also included the fundamental right that proceedings should be adversarial. That meant the opportunity for the parties to have knowledge of and comment on the observations filed or evidence adduced by the other party.

Admittedly, proceedings before a constitutional court had their own characteristics which took account of the specific nature of the legal rules to be applied and the implications of the constitutional decision for the legal system in force. They were also intended to enable a single body to adjudicate on a large number of cases relating to very different subjects. Nevertheless, it might happen that, as here, they dealt with a law which directly concerned a restricted circle of persons. If in such a case the question whether that law was compatible with the Constitution was referred to the Constitutional Court within the context of proceedings on a civil right to which persons belonging to that circle were a party, those persons must as a rule be guaranteed free access to the observations of the other participants in those proceedings and a genuine opportunity to comment on those observations.

The Court saw no reason to depart from that rule in this case. It would be artificial to dissociate the role of the executive (on whose authority the decision to expropriate had been taken) from that of the Directorate General for National Assets (the beneficiary of the measure), and even more so to purport to identify a real difference between their respective interests. The opportunity which the Constitutional Court had had to examine the applicants' arguments addressed to the civil courts in favour of a reference to the Constitutional Court was not enough. The Counsel for the State, representing the Government, had submitted to the Constitutional Court observations to which the applicants had had no opportunity to reply; moreover, he had had advance knowledge of their arguments and had been able to comment on them in the last instance. There had accordingly been a violation of Article 6 § 1 (eighteen votes to six).

660. As regards the application of Article 50, the Court dismissed the applicants' claim for compensation for damage amounting to 2,000 billion pesetas (unanimously) on the ground that no causal connection between the alleged damage and the violations found had been established: there was nothing to suggest that, in the absence of those violations, the Constitutional Court would have declared the impugned law void.

661. *Summary bibliography*

COHEN-JONATHAN (G.).—'Justice constitutionnelle et Convention européenne des droits de l'homme. L'arrêt Ruiz-Mateos contre Espagne', *Revue française de droit constitutionnel* 1994, pp. 175–183.

DECAUX (E.) and TAVERNIER (P.).—'Chronique de jurisprudence de la Cour européenne des droits de l'homme (année 1993)', *J.D.I.* 1994, pp. 799–804.

KLEIN (V.) and MESTRE (C.).—'La Cour européenne, le juge constitutionnel et le droit à un procès équitable: *ad minorem juris gloriam*', *Europe*, February 1994, chronique No. 2, pp. 1–5.

SCHÜRMANN (F.).—'Europäischer Gerichtshof für Menschenrechte—Chronik der Rechtsprechung (1.1.–30.6.1993)', *A.J.P./P.J.A.* 1993, pp. 1136–1145 and 1282–1293.

SUDRE (F.) and others.—'Chronique de la jurisprudence de la Cour européenne des droits de l'homme. Deuxième partie : juin–décembre 1993', *R.U.D.H.* 1993, pp. 377 *et seq.*

VERDUSSEN (M.).—'Le juge constitutionnel face à l'article 6, 1°, de la Convention européenne des droits de l'homme', *Revue belge de droit constitutionnel* 1994, p. 131–134.

363. Case of Hoffmann v. Austria

Parental rights after divorce refused to the mother in view of her membership of the Jehovah's Witnesses

662. *Ingrid Hoffmann married in 1980. At the time, she and her husband were Roman Catholics. Their two children, born to them in 1980 and 1982, were baptised as Roman Catholics. Subsequently, Mrs Hoffmann became a Jehovah's Witness; her husband and the children remained Catholics. In August 1984, following the breakdown of their marriage, Mrs Hoffmann left the marital home with the children; they were divorced in June 1966.*

During the divorce proceedings, each of the parents claimed custody of the children; the father was opposed to the grant of custody to the mother, essentially on account of her membership of the Jehovah's Witnesses and the practices and principles which they followed. On 8 January 1986, the Innsbruck District Court granted custody to the applicant. The husband appealed, but the appeal was dismissed by the Innsbruck Regional Court on 14 March 1986. However, on 3 September 1986 the Supreme Court allowed the father's appeal on the ground that the lower courts' decisions were manifestly wrong in law: to bring up children in accordance with the principles of the Jehovah's Witnesses infringed the provisions of the Law on the Religious Education of Children and the lower courts had not taken those provisions into account; the lower courts had also disregarded the children's welfare, since their membership of the religious sect would very likely cause them to become social outcasts; in addition, their lives could be threatened if the mother refused to allow them to receive blood transfusions.

663. *In her application of 20 February 1987 to the Commission, Mrs Hoffmann complained that she had been denied custody of the children on the ground of her religious convictions. She invoked her right to respect for her family life (Article 8 of the Convention), her right to freedom of religion (Article 9) and her right to ensure the education of her children in conformity with her own religious convictions (Article 2 of Protocol No. 1); she further claimed that she had been discriminated against on the ground of religion (Article 14 of the Convention).*[1]

1 In its report of 16 January 1992, the Commission expressed the opinion that there had been a violation of Article 8 read in conjunction with Article 14 (eight votes to six); that no separate issue arose in regard to Article 9 taken separately or in conjunction with Article 14 (twelve votes to two) and that there had been no violation of Article 2 of Protocol No. 1 (unanimously).

Judgment of 23 June 1993 *(Chamber) (Series A No. 255–C)*

664. The Court noted at the outset that the children had lived with the applicant for two years after she had left the marital home with them before the judgment of the Supreme Court had compelled the applicant to give them up to their father. That decision therefore constituted an interference with the applicant's right to respect for her family life and the case thus fell within the ambit of Article 8. The fact relied on by the Government in support of the opposite view, namely that the Supreme Court's decision had been taken in the context of a dispute between private individuals, made no difference in this respect.

In view of the nature of the allegations made, the Court considered it appropriate to examine the case under Article 8 taken in conjunction with Article 14.

Depending on the circumstances, the factors relied on by the Austrian Supreme Court in support of its decision—the practical consequences of the mother's membership of the Jehovah's Witnesses, namely the possible effects on the children's social life of being associated with a particular religious minority and the hazards attaching to the applicant's total rejection of blood transfusions not only for herself but, in the absence of a court order, for her children as well—might in themselves be capable of tipping the scales in favour of one parent rather than the other. However, the Supreme Court had also introduced a new element, namely the Federal Act on the Religious Education of Children. This factor had clearly been decisive for the Supreme Court. Consequently there had been a difference in treatment and that difference was on the ground of religion; this conclusion was supported by the tone and phrasing of the Supreme Court's considerations regarding the practical consequences of the applicant's religion.

The aim pursued by the judgment of the Supreme Court was a legitimate one, namely the protection of the health and rights of the children.

In so far as the Austrian Supreme Court had not relied solely on the Law on the Religious Education of Children, it had weighed the facts differently from the courts below, whose reasoning was moreover supported by psychological expert opinion. Notwithstanding any possible arguments to the contrary, a distinction based essentially on a difference in religion alone was not acceptable. Given the absence of a reasonable relationship of proportionality between the means employed and the aim pursued, there had been a violation of Article 8 taken in conjunction with Article 14 (five votes to four).

665. In view of that conclusion, the Court considered it unnecessary to rule on the allegation of a violation of Article 8 taken alone, since the arguments advanced in this respect were the same (held unanimously).

666. The Court held (unanimously) that no separate issue arose under Article 9 either taken alone or read in conjunction with Article 14, since the circumstances relied on as the basis of this complaint were the same as those at the root of the complaint under Article 8 taken in conjunction with Article 14.

667. The applicant's complaint under Article 2 of Protocol No. 1 had not been pursued before the Court and it found no reason to examine it of its own motion (held unanimously).

668. The Court awarded Mrs Hoffmann 75,000 schillings in respect of costs and expenses incurred before the Convention organs and not covered by legal aid (eight votes to one).

669. *Summary bibliography*

BLOIS (M. de).—'Opvoedingsvrijheid voor godstienstige minderheden', *NJCM–Bulletin* 1994, pp. 710–715.

DECAUX (E.) and TAVERNIER (P.).—'Chronique de jurisprudence de la Cour européenne des droits de l'homme (année 1993)', *J.D.I.* 1994, pp. 778–780.

JORION (B.).—'Jurisprudence de la Cour européenne des droits de l'homme en matière de droit de la famille et d'exercice public du culte', *L.P.A.* 10 August 1994, pp. 53–56.

HAUSER (J.).—'Note', *D.* 1994, jurisprudence, pp. 327–329.

JUNOSZA-ZDROJEWSKI (G.).—'La Cour européenne des droits de l'homme et les activités des sectes', *G.P.* 15–19 July 1994, pp. 41–43.

NORANGE (J.).—'Liberté religieuse et garde d'enfants', *R.T.D.H.* 1994, pp. 414–428.

ROUVIÈRE-PERRIER (I.).—'Les témoins de Jéhovah devant la Cour européenne des droits de l'homme', *L.P.A.*, 17 November 1993, No. 138, pp. 24–26.

SCHÜRMANN (F.).—'Europäischer Gerichtshof für Menschenrechte—Chronik der Rechtsprechung (1.1.–30.6.1993)', *A.J.P./P.J.A.* 1993, pp. 1136–1145, 1282–1293 and 1533–1534.

SPIELMANN (D.).—'Cour européenne des droits de l'homme (premier semestre 1993)', *B.D.H.* 1993, pp. 61 and 62.

SUDRE (F.) and others.—'Chronique de la jurisprudence de la Cour européenne des droits de l'homme. Deuxième partie : juin–décembre 1993', *R.U.D.H.* 1993, pp. 377 *et seq.*

364. Case of Schuler-Zgraggen v. Switzerland

Access to the file of a cantonal invalidity-insurance appeals board; no hearing in the Federal Insurance Court; reasoning in support of a judgment by that court based on sex

670. *In 1976, the Compensation Office of the Swiss Machine and Metal Industry decided to grant half an invalidity pension to Margrit Schuler-Zgraggen, an employee of a business who had paid in to the federal invalidity-insurance scheme, because she had contracted tuberculosis. As from 1979, she lost her job on account of her illness; she was subsequently granted a full pension, which was confirmed in 1981 and 1982. In May 1984, she gave birth to a son.*

Following an examination, during which the medical centre and two doctors drew up reports, the Invalidity Insurance Board cancelled Mrs Schuler-Zgraggen's pension on 21 March 1986 on the ground that her family circumstances had radically changed with the birth of her child, her health had improved, and she was 60–70% able to look after her home and her child.

On 8 May 1987, the applicant's appeal to the Canton of Uri Appeals Board for Invalidity Insurance was dismissed; she had claimed a full pension or, in the alternative, a half-pension.

On 21 June 1988, the Federal Insurance Court partly upheld her administrative-law appeal. It held that she was entitled to a half-pension if she was in financial difficulties. It remitted the case to the Compensation Office, which was instructed to ascertain whether that condition was met. It examined to what extent she had been restricted in her activities as a housewife, but not her aptitude to perform her former job, on the assumption that, since she had a young child, she would have given up her job even if she had not had health problems.

On 17 July 1989, the Compensation Office decided that Mrs Schuler-Zgraggen could not claim a half-pension since her income in 1986, 1987 and 1988 had greatly exceeded the maxima applicable in those years to 'cases of hardship'.

671. *In her application to the Commission of 29 December 1988, Mrs Schuler-Zgraggen complained, firstly, that her right to a fair trial (Convention, Article 6 § 1) had been infringed in that she had had insufficient access to the file of the Appeals Board and there had been no hearing in the Federal Insurance Court. She also claimed that the assumption made by that court, that she would have given up working* *even if she had not had health problems, amounted to discrimination on the ground of sex (Article 14 taken together with Article 6 § 1).*[1]

Judgment of 24 June 1993 *(Chamber) (Series A No. 263)*

672. The Court pointed out that State intervention was not sufficient to establish that Article 6 § 1 was inapplicable, as the Government maintained. Although the case exhibited public-law features, the applicant, who had suffered an interference with her means of subsistence, was claiming an individual, economic right flowing from specific rules laid down in a federal statute. The Court saw no convincing reason to distinguish between Mrs Schuler-Zgraggen's right to an invalidity pension and the rights to social-insurance benefits asserted by the applicants in *Feldbrugge v. the Netherlands*[2] and *Deumeland v. Germany*.[3] Consequently, Article 6 § 1 was applicable (held unanimously).

673. The applicant alleged that Article 6 § 1 had not been observed. She complained in the first place that she had been given insufficient access to the Appeals Board's file.

The Government argued that she lacked of victim status in that she had not availed herself of the opportunity of examining the file at the Appeals Board's registry. The Court noted that the applicant's complaint related rather to having the documents in the file handed over or, at any rate, securing photocopies of them. The objection must therefore be dismissed (held unanimously).

With regard to the merits, the Court found that the proceedings before the Appeals Board had not enabled Mrs Schuler-Zgraggen to have a complete, detailed picture of the particulars supplied to the Board. It considered, however, that the Federal Insurance Court had remedied this shortcoming by requesting the Board to make all the documents available to the applicant—who had been able, among other things, to make copies—and then forwarding the file to the applicant's lawyer. It also noted that neither the Appeals Board nor the Federal Insurance Court had had the lung specialist's report. Since, taken as a whole, the impugned proceedings had therefore been fair,

---

1 In its report of 7 April 1992, the Commission expressed the opinion that there had been no breach of Article 6 § 1 either on account of the failure to hold a hearing (ten votes to five) or in respect of access to the file (thirteen votes to two) and that there had been no breach of Article 14 taken together with Article 6 § 1 (nine votes to six).
2 Series A No. 99; see Vol. I of this work, 632–639.
3 Series A No. 100; see Vol. I of this work, 640–645.

there had not been a breach of Article 6 § 1 in this respect (eight votes to one).

674. Mrs Schuler-Zgraggen also complained that there had been no hearing before the Federal Insurance Court.

According to the Government, she had not exhausted domestic remedies, as she had failed to apply for the proceedings to be oral and public. The Court held that there was an estoppel (unanimously), as the Government had only raised the objection before the Commission after the decision on admissibility.

In the Court's view, the applicant had unequivocally waived her right to a public hearing in the Federal Insurance Court, despite the possibility afforded her by that court's Rules of Procedure. Above all, it did not appear that the dispute raised issues of public importance such as to make a hearing necessary. Since it was highly technical, it had been better dealt with in writing than in oral argument. Lastly, it was understandable that in this sphere the national authorities should have regard to the demands of efficiency and economy: systematically holding hearings could be an obstacle to the particular diligence required in social-security cases. There had accordingly been no breach of Article 6 § 1 in this respect (eight votes to one).

As for the independence of the medical experts, which the applicant disputed, this was a new complaint which had not been raised before the Commission. The Court had no jurisdiction to consider it (held unanimously).

675. As regards Article 14 in conjunction with Article 6 § 1, the Government maintained that the applicant had not made to the Federal Insurance Court a precise complaint relating to discrimination in the exercise of a right secured by the Convention. The Court dismissed the objection that domestic remedies had not been exhausted (unanimously): no appeal lay against the Federal Insurance Court's judgment and the applicant had already criticized the Appeals Board decision.

It then turned to the applicant's complaint. The Federal Insurance Court had adopted in its entirety the Appeals Board's assumption that women gave up work when they gave birth to a child; it had not attempted to probe the validity of that assumption itself by weighing arguments to the contrary. The assumption in question constituted the sole basis for the reasoning, thus being decisive, and introduced a difference of treatment based on the ground of sex only. The advancement of the equality of the sexes was today a major goal in the Member States of the Council of Europe and very weighty reasons would have to be put forward before such a difference of treatment could be regarded as compatible with the Convention. The Court discerned no such reason in this case. It therefore concluded that, for want of any reasonable and objective justification, there had been a breach of Article 14 taken together with Article 6 § 1 (eight votes to one).

676. The question of the applicant's claims under Article 50 remained to be considered. The Court held that the applicant might have suffered non-pecuniary damage but that its judgment provided her with sufficient satisfaction for it (held unanimously). It reserved the question of pecuniary damage, since it was possible under Swiss law for the applicant to ask for the proceedings to be re-opened (held unanimously).

Mrs Schuler-Zgraggen sought 21,426.60 Swiss francs in respect of costs and expenses for the proceedings in Switzerland and in Strasbourg. Making its assessment on an equitable basis, the Court awarded the applicant 7,500 Swiss francs under this head as matters stood (eight votes to one).

677. *Summary bibliography*

DECAUX (E.) and TAVERNIER (P.).—'Chronique de jurisprudence de la Cour européenne des droits de l'homme (année 1993)', *J.D.I.* 1994, pp. 804–808.

SCHÜRMANN (F.).—'Europäischer Gerichtshof für Menschenrechte—Chronik der Rechtsprechung (1.1.–30.6.1993)', *A.J.P./P.J.A.* 1993, pp. 1136–1145, 1282–1293 and 1534–1535.

SPIELMANN (D.).—'Cour européenne des droits de l'homme (premier semestre 1993)', *B.D.H.* 1993, pp. 62 and 63.

SUDRE (F.) and others.—'Chronique de la jurisprudence de la Cour européenne des droits de l'homme. Deuxième partie : juin–décembre 1993', *R.U.D.H.* 1993, pp. 377 *et seq.*

365. Case of Papamichalopoulos and Others v. Greece

Land belonging to private individuals occupied by the Navy since 1967

678. *By a Law of 20 August 1967 which was passed some months after the dictatorship was established, the Greek State transferred a huge area of land near Agia Marina beach in Attica to the Navy Fund. However, part of the land transferred consisted of parcels of agricultural land belonging to the fourteen applicants or to persons from whom the applicants had inherited it. In 1968, in respect of three of them, orders were made restoring their property, but the Navy kept the whole of the area, on which it intended to construct a naval base and a holiday resort for officers. In 1976, the father of two of the applicants obtained a judgment, which was upheld by the Court of Cassation in 1978, recognizing that he owned part of the land, but his efforts to have it restored to him came to naught.*

In 1980, the Minister of Defence informed the applicants that the construction of the naval base prevented the return of the land in question, but that proceedings were under way with a view to a grant of other plots of land in Attica. In 1982, a committee of experts of the Ministry of Agriculture designated the land to be transferred, but the transfer did not take place. Subsequently, using a procedure provided for by Law No. 1341/1983 designed to produce a swifter settlement of the 1967 problem, the applicants obtained a decision from the Expropriation Board, which the Court of Cassation upheld at last instance in 1988, recognizing their title to the agricultural land situated at Agia Marina. In the meantime, the Minister of Agriculture informed them that there was no land available for exchange and suggested that they should take land in the prefecture of Pieria instead, four hundred and fifty kilometres from the land occupied by the Navy. However, at the date of the Commission's report that transfer had not taken place given the lack of availability of State-owned land. Two actions for the recovery of land and several for damages were brought against the Navy by the applicants and were still pending at that date.

679. *The applicants applied to the Commission on 7 November 1988. They relied on Article 1 of Protocol No. 1, alleging that their land had been unlawfully occupied by the Navy Fund since 1967 and that to date they had not been able either to enjoy their possessions or to obtain compensation.*[1]

Judgment of 24 June 1993 *(Chamber) (Series A No. 260–B)*

680.   In the Greek Government's contention, the applicants could not claim to be victims of a violation of the Convention nor had they exhausted domestic remedies, since their actions for the recovery of the land were still pending before the Athens Court of First Instance.

The Court held that the Government was estopped from raising the two preliminary objections (unanimously). It had not raised the first at all before the Commission and had made the second only in respect of the compensation proceedings.

681.   As regards Article 1 of Protocol No. 1, the Government disputed that the applicants—other than the heirs of Petros Papamichalopoulos— had the status of owners, since this had not been acknowledged in any judicial decision and the proceedings brought by the applicants in 1977 had still not ended. The Court held that, for the purposes of this dispute, the applicants must be regarded as being the owners of the land in issue.

The breach claimed by the applicants had begun in 1967. At that time, Greece had already ratified the Convention and Protocol No. 1. The fact that Greece had denounced them under the military dictatorship (from 13 June 1970 to 28 November 1974) did not release it from its obligations under them 'in respect of any act which, being capable of constituting a violation of such obligations, [might] have been performed by it' earlier (Convention, Article 65 § 2). Admittedly, Greece had not recognized the Commission's competence to receive individual petitions until 20 November 1985 and then only in relation to acts, decisions, facts or events subsequent to that date, but the Government had not in this instance raised any preliminary objection in this regard and the question did not call for consideration by the Court of its own motion. The Court noted merely that the applicants' complaints related to a continuing situation, which still obtained at the time of these proceedings.

The occupation of the land by the Navy Fund represented a clear interference with the applicants' exercise of their right to the peaceful enjoyment of their possessions, but it had not been for the purpose of controlling the use of property nor had it been a formal expropriation. However, from 1967 the applicants had been unable either to make use of their property or to sell, bequeath or mortgage it or make a gift of it. The steps taken by the authorities, after the restoration of democracy, with a view to exchanging the land for other parcels of equal value had not been successful.

---

1   In its report of 9 April 1992, the Commission expressed the unanimous opinion that there had been a violation of Article 1 of Protocol No. 1.

The loss of all ability to dispose of the land in issue, taken together with the failure of the attempts made so far to remedy the situation complained of, had entailed sufficiently serious consequences for the applicants to have been expropriated *de facto* in a manner incompatible with their right to the peaceful enjoyment of their possessions. Therefore, there had been and continued to be a breach of Article 1 of Protocol No. 1 (held unanimously).

682. The applicants claimed compensation for pecuniary and non-pecuniary damage and reimbursement of the costs and expenses which they had incurred in Greece and before the Convention institutions.

Since the Court considered that the question of the application of Article 50 was not ready for decision, it reserved it and also asked the applicants and the Government to choose experts by agreement to value the land at issue (held unanimously).

683. *Summary bibliography*

DECAUX (E.) and TAVERNIER (P.).—'Chronique de jurisprudence de la Cour européenne des droits de l'homme (année 1993)', *J.D.I.* 1994, pp. 792–796.

SAPIENZA (R.).—'Su un caso di illegitima occupazione di terreni in Grecia', *Riv.D.I.* 1994, pp. 465–473.

SUDRE (F.) and others.—'Chronique de la jurisprudence de la Cour européenne des droits de l'homme. Deuxième partie: juin–décembre 1993', *R.U.D.H.* 1993, pp. 377 *et seq.*

SCHÜRMANN (F.).—'Europäischer Gerichtshof für Menschenrechte—Chronik der Rechtsprechung (1.1.–30.6.1993)', *A.J.P./P.J.A.* 1993, pp. 1136–1145 and 1282–1293.

366. Case of Lamguindaz v. the United Kingdom

Deportation of a Moroccan—who had arrived in the country at a young age—separating him from his parents

684. *Ahmed Lamguindaz was born in Morocco in 1967. He came to the United Kingdom on or about 1974 to join his father who had settled there. His mother and three brothers and sisters did likewise. He had a long criminal record for minor offences of dishonesty and certain offences involving violence. On 17 May 1985, he was convicted of wounding. On 19 February 1986, the Home Secretary decided to make a deportation order against him on the ground that such an order was 'conducive to the public good'.*

An appeal to the Immigration Appeal Tribunal, on the grounds inter alia *that he spoke no Arabic and that all his family lived in the United Kingdom, was rejected on 9 June 1986. A deportation order was signed on 22 October 1986. In February 1988, the applicant was taken by his father to Morocco and left there in an attempt to keep him out of trouble with the police. He returned to the United Kingdom in September 1989 and was eventually deported on 12 May 1990 to Morocco.*

685. *In his application lodged with the Commission on 6 February 1989, Mr Lamguindaz relied on Articles 8 and 14 of the Convention.*[1]

Judgment of 28 June 1993 *(Chamber) (Series A No. 258–C)*

686. Mr Lamguindaz accepted the following proposals for a settlement: without any admission by the Government that a breach of the Convention had occurred and on condition that the case was withdrawn from the Court and no further cases were instituted against the Government in respect of this matter in any national or international court, the Government proposed to revoke the deportation order against the applicant, allow the applicant to re-enter the United Kingdom, give the applicant indefinite leave to remain, allow the applicant to make an application for naturalization and pay the costs which the applicant had actually and necessarily incurred and which were reasonable as to quantum, namely £8,398.02.

---

1 In its report of 13 October 1992, the Commission expressed the opinion that there had been a violation of Article 8 (thirteen votes to one), and that it was unnecessary to decide whether there had been a breach of Article 14.

687. The Court discerned no reason of public policy (*ordre public*) why the case should not be struck out of the list (Rules of Court, Rule 49 §§ 2 and 4).

688. *Summary bibliography*

SCHÜRMANN (F.).—'Europäischer Gerichtshof für Menschenrechte—Chronik der Rechtsprechung (1.1.–30.6.1993)', *A.J.P./P.J.A.* 1993, pp. 1136–1145 and 1282–1293.

SUDRE (F.) and others.—'Chronique de la jurisprudence de la Cour euro-péenne des droits de l'homme. Deuxième partie : juin–décembre 1993', *R.U.D.H.* 1993, pp. 377 *et seq.*

367. Case of Colman v. the United Kingdom

Restrictions on advertising a private medical practice

689. *Dr Richard Colman was a medical practitioner in private general practice. In 1985 he established in York a practice named the 'Holistic Counselling and Education Centre'. The 'holistic' approach to health care involved not just treating patients, but trying to help them to explore the cause of their problems and to take more responsibility for their remedy. In March 1987, the applicant applied in writing to the General Medical Council ('the G.M.C.') for authorization to insert brief, factual advertisements about his practice in local newspapers.*

In May 1987, the applicant was informed by the G.M.C. that to advertise in the local press could lead to disciplinary action against him. In August 1987, Dr Colman instituted legal proceedings seeking a declaration that the G.M.C.'s decision and policy on the dissemination of information by doctors were unlawful. He was unsuccessful before the High Court in November 1988 and before the Court of Appeal in December 1989.

690. *In the meantime, in November 1987, the Government submitted to Parliament a White Paper proposing a loosening of the restraints on doctors' rights to advertise their services. A report by the Monopolies and Mergers Commission, presented to Parliament in March 1989, concluded that the G.M.C.'s rules in this respect were not in the public interest. The Government accepted this report and asked the Director General of Fair Trading to negotiate with the G.M.C. to implement the report's recommendation to relax the restrictions on the publication of factual information about medical practitioners. In May 1990, the G.M.C. revised its advertising rules to allow the publication in the press of factual information about doctors' services.*

691. *In his application lodged with the Commission on 11 May 1990, Dr Colman claimed that the G.M.C. policy had been in violation of his right to freedom of expression as guaranteed by Article 10 of the Convention. He also maintained that, contrary to Article 13, he had had no effective remedy under English law in respect of his complaint under Article 10.*[1]

1 In its report of 19 October 1992, the Commission expressed the opinion that there had been no violation of Article 10 (eleven votes to eight) or of Article 13 (eighteen votes to one).

Judgment of 28 June 1993 *(Chamber) (Series A No. 258–D)*

692. Dr Colman accepted the following proposal for a settlement: without any admission by the Government that a breach of the Convention had occurred and on the conditions that the case was withdrawn from the Court and no further cases were instituted against the Government in respect of this matter in any national or international court, the Government would pay the applicant £12,500.

693. The Court discerned no reason of public policy (*ordre public*) why the case should not be struck out of the list (Rules of Court, Rule 49 §§ 2 and 4).

694. *Summary bibliography*

SCHÜRMANN (F.).—'Europäischer Gerichtshof für Menschenrechte—Chronik der Rechtsprechung (1.1.–30.6.1993)', *A.J.P./P.J.A.* 1993, pp. 1136–1145 and 1282–1293.

SUDRE (F.) and others.—'Chronique de la jurisprudence de la Cour européenne des droits de l'homme. Deuxième partie : juin–décembre 1993', *R.U.D.H.* 1993, pp. 377 *et seq.*

368. Case of Sigurdur A. Sigurjónsson v. Iceland

Obligation imposed by law on a taxi driver to be a member of a specific organization for taxi operators

695. *On 24 October 1984, Sigurdur A. Sigurjónsson was granted a licence to operate a taxicab. He undertook to comply with the relevant ministerial regulation, which provided, inter alia, that he had to belong to Frami Automobile Association ('Frami'). At Frami's request, his operator's licence was withdrawn by the Committee for Taxicab Supervision ('the Committee') with effect from July 1986 on the ground, inter alia, that he had stopped paying membership fees; he had previously informed Frami that he wished to cease being a member of the association. He appealed to the Minister of Transport, who confirmed the decision. On 1 August 1986, while driving his taxi, the applicant was stopped by the police, who removed the plates identifying his vehicle as one for public hire.*

On 17 July 1987, the Civil Court of Reykjavik dismissed an action brought by the applicant for a declaration that the revocation of licence was null and void. On an appeal from the applicant, the Supreme Court held on 15 December 1988 that the obligation to remain a member of Frami was not unconstitutional. However, it overturned the lower court's judgment on the ground that that obligation lacked a statutory basis.

The Icelandic Parliament passed a new law on vehicles for public hire, which entered into force on 1 July 1989 and expressly made membership of the trade union in question a condition for the issue of a taxi operator's licence. Since then, the applicant had reluctantly rejoined Frami.

696. *In his application lodged with the Commission on 22 December 1989, Sigurdur A. Sigurjónsson alleged a violation of Article 11 of the Convention or, in the alternative, Articles 9, 10 and 13.*[1]

Judgment of 30 June 1993 *(Chamber) (Series A No. 264)*

697. The question whether there had been an interference was the first to be considered.

---

1 In its report adopted on 15 May 1992, the Commission expressed the opinion that there had been a violation of Article 11 (seventeen votes to one) but not of Article 13 (unanimously), and that it was not necessary to examine separately whether there had been a violation of Articles 9 and 10 (unanimously).

In the Court's view, Frami was predominantly a private-law organization and thus had to be considered an 'association' for the purposes of Article 11. It was not necessary to decide whether Frami could also be regarded as a 'trade union'.

As far as the scope of the right at issue was concerned, Article 11 had to be viewed as encompassing a negative right of association.

The Government's argument that the applicant had agreed to become a member of Frami or that an obligation to join had already existed when the applicant had obtained his licence in 1984 did not convince the Court. Membership had only become a requirement after the 1989 Law had entered into force. The applicant had since been compelled to remain a member or to lose his licence. Such a form of compulsion struck at the very substance of the right guaranteed by Article 11 and itself amounted to an interference with that right. What was more, the compulsion in question went against the applicant's opinions and thus constituted in this respect also an interference with that right, considered in the light of Articles 9 and 10.

Was the interference justified in the light of paragraph 2 of Article 11? It was not contested that at the material time (the period after 1 July 1989, when the 1989 Law had entered into force) the impugned membership was 'prescribed by law' and pursued a legitimate aim, namely the protection of the 'rights and freedoms of others'.

In contrast, there was dispute as to whether the interference was 'necessary in a democratic society'. In the Court's view, the impugned membership obligation, which was one imposed by law, on the face of it must be considered incompatible with Article 11. The Court did not doubt that Frami served the public interest, and that its performance of its functions must have been facilitated by the obligation of every licence-holder within the association's area to be a member. The reasons adduced by the Government, although they could be considered relevant, were not sufficient to show that it had been 'necessary' to compel the applicant to be a member of Frami, on pain of losing his licence and contrary to his own opinions. Consequently, there had been a violation of Article 11 (eight votes to one).

698. As it had taken account of Articles 9 and 10 in the context of Article 11, the Court held that it was unnecessary to consider separately whether there had also been breaches of those articles (unanimously).

699. The Court did not find it necessary to examine of its own motion whether Article 13 had been breached (held unanimously), since the applicant had accepted the Commission's conclusion that there had been no violation of that article.

700. The Court awarded the applicant 2,134,401 Icelandic crowns for costs and expenses incurred at Strasbourg, less payments received by way of legal aid (unanimously).

701. *Summary bibliography*

ALKEMA (E.A.).—'Noot', *N.J.* 1994, pp. 949 952.

DECAUX (E.) and TAVERNIER (P.).—'Chronique de jurisprudence de la Cour européenne des droits de l'homme (année 1993)', *J.D.I.* 1994, pp. 808–811.

MARGUENAUD (J.-P.).—'Note', *D.* 1994, jurisprudence, pp. 181–185.

SCHÜRMANN (F.).—'Europäischer Gerichtshof für Menschenrechte—Chronik der Rechtsprechung (1.1.–30.6.1993)', *A.J.P./P.J.A.* 1993, pp. 1136–1145 and 1282–1293.

SUDRE (F.) and others.—'Chronique de la jurisprudence de la Cour européenne des droits de l'homme. Deuxième partie : juin–décembre 1993', *R.U.D.H.* 1993, pp. 377 *et seq.*

369. Case of Scuderi v. Italy

Length of proceedings in a Regional Administrative Court

702. *By a decree of the Minister of Finance dated 14 April 1980, Giuseppe Scuderi, a retired civil servant, was retrospectively acknowledged as being entitled to an upgrading and, consequently, to receive the corresponding difference in remuneration.*

On 23 November 1982, the applicant brought an action against the Ministry of Finance, the Treasury and Ente Nazionale di Previdenza e Assistenza per i Dipendenti Statali *in the Lazio Regional Administrative Court. He sought a recalculation of the salary due to him. On 29 October 1985, the Lazio Regional Administrative Court allowed Mr Scuderi's application. The text of the judgment was filed in the registry on 3 March 1987.*

703. *In his application of 14 February 1987 to the Commission, Mr Scuderi relied on Article 6 § 1 of the Convention. He complained of the length of the proceedings he had instituted to assert his right to an upgrading and of the action he had brought in the Lazio Regional Administrative Court.*[1]

Judgment of 24 August 1993 *(Chamber) (Series A No. 265–A)*

704. The period to be considered had begun on 23 November 1982, the date of the application to the Regional Administrative Court, and ended on 13 May 1987, on the expiry of the time-limit for any appeal by counsel for the State.

The case was not complex and Mr Scuderi's conduct had not contributed to slowing down the proceedings. Whilst these had followed their course at a normal speed until 29 October 1985, it had thereafter taken more than sixteen months for the reasons given in the judgment delivered by the Administrative Court on that date to be made known through being filed in the registry. That being so, the Court could not consider that a period of more than four years and five months for a single level of jurisdiction had been 'reasonable' in this case. There had therefore been a breach of Article 6 § 1 (held unanimously).

---

1 On 14 October 1991, the Commission declared the application admissible as regards the second complaint and inadmissible as to the rest. In its report of 8 April 1992, the Commission expressed the opinion that there had been a violation of Article 6 § 1 (unanimously).

705.   The Court held that the applicant had not suffered any pecuniary damage as a result of the breach but that he had sustained non-pecuniary damage, for which he was awarded 3,000,000 lire (unanimously).

706.   *Summary bibliography*

SUDRE (F.) and others.—'Chronique de la jurisprudence de la Cour européenne des droits de l'homme. Deuxième partie : juin–décembre 1993', *R.U.D.H.* 1993, pp. 377 *et seq.*

370. Case of Massa v. Italy

Length of proceedings in the Court of Audit

707. *On 25 January 1980, following a judgment of the Constitutional Court holding that a Law of 9 December 1977 on equality of treatment between men and women in the field of employment had retrospective effect, Aldo Massa was entitled to claim the reversionary pension which the Ministry of Education and the Court of Audit had refused him in 1968 and 1976, respectively. On 23 April 1985, Mr Massa applied to the Court of Audit to have the relevant pension awarded to him with effect from the first day of the month following his wife's death and the ministerial decision of 16 May 1981 (holding that entitlement arose only as of the entry into force of the law in question) quashed.*

At the hearing on 11 May 1987, the Court of Audit ordered the relevant authorities to produce certain documents. Subsequently, a hearing due to be held on 21 November 1990 was postponed to 25 January 1991 at the applicant's request. On that date the Court of Audit allowed Mr Massa's application.

708. *In his application of 2 November 1988 to the Commission, Mr Massa relied on Articles 8, 13 and 6 § 1 of the Convention.*[1]

Judgment of 24 August 1993 *(Chamber) (Series A No. 265–B)*

709. The Court held that, notwithstanding the public-law aspects pointed out by the Government, the present dispute arose from an obligation on the State to pay a reversionary pension to the husband of a public servant in accordance with the legislation in force. In performing this obligation, the State was not using discretionary powers and might be compared to an employer who was a party to a contract of employment governed by private law. Accordingly, the applicant's right to a reversionary pension was a 'civil' one within the meaning of Article 6 § 1, which was therefore applicable in the instant case (unanimously).

---

1 On 8 July 1991 the Commission declared the application admissible in respect of the complaint based on the length of the proceedings brought in the Court of Audit and declared it inadmissible as to the remainder. In its report of 13 May 1992, the Commission expressed the opinion that there had been a violation of Article 6 § 1 (six votes to two).

710. The Court then turned to consider whether Article 6 § 1 had been complied with. The period to be considered had begun on 23 April 1985, when Mr Massa had applied to the Court of Audit, and ended on 18 March 1991, when that court's judgment had been filed. It had therefore covered more than five years and eleven months.

The Court noted that it was a fairly straightforward case and that the adjournment sought by Mr Massa had scarcely prolonged the proceedings; moreover, on 18 July 1986 Mr Massa had tried to expedite them. On the other hand, there had been two periods of inactivity attributable to the respondent State, which were sufficiently substantial for the overall length of the proceedings to have to be regarded as excessive. There had therefore been a breach of Article 6 § 1 (held unanimously).

711. With regard to the application Article 50, the Court considered that Mr Massa had not proved the existence of pecuniary damage resulting from the breach. In contrast, it held that he had sustained non-pecuniary damage, for which it awarded him 10,000,000 lire (unanimously).

The Court regarded the amount sought in respect of costs and expenses (8,365,000 lire) as reasonable, and awarded it in full (unanimously).

712. *Summary bibliography*

SUDRE (F.) and others.—'Chronique de la jurisprudence de la Cour européenne des droits de l'homme. Deuxième partie : juin–décembre 1993', *R.U.D.H.* 1993, pp. 377 *et seq.*

371. Case of Nortier v. the Netherlands

Successive exercise by the same juvenile judge of the functions of investigating judge and review chamber, making pre-trial decisions, and trial judge

713. *Hans Erik Nortier, a Netherlands national born in 1972, was arrested on suspicion of attempted rape on 30 September 1987. Following his arrest, he admitted the crime to the police.*

On 2 October 1987, the prosecutor asked the juvenile judge at the Middelburg Regional Court, Mr Meulenbroek, to order the applicant to be placed in detention on remand in view of the risk of his committing further offences. The judge granted this request and agreed to the opening of a preliminary investigation.

As the defence feared that the applicant's initial confession had been obtained under duress, Judge Meulenbroek was asked to authorize the hearing of certain witnesses. In accordance with the usual practice in the Netherlands, this task was given to another judge. During the applicant's detention on remand, the judge also gave leave for Mr Nortier to undergo a psychiatric examination.

The applicant was summoned to appear before Judge Meulenbroek for trial. On 5 January 1988, the applicant challenged that judge on the ground that he was not impartial, since he had taken pre-trial decisions concerning the applicant's detention on remand. The judge rejected the challenge on 6 January 1988. His decision was upheld on appeal by the Middelburg Regional Court. At the hearing on 25 January 1988, the applicant admitted the offence and Judge Meulenbroek committed him to an institution for juvenile offenders.

714. *In his application lodged with the Commission on 28 April 1988, Mr Nortier relied on Article 6 § 1 of the Convention, complaining that he had not received a hearing before an impartial tribunal because the juvenile judge who tried him had also acted as investigating judge during the preliminary investigation and, moreover, had taken several decisions regarding the prolongation of his detention on remand.* [1]

Judgment of 24 August 1993 *(Chamber) (Series A No. 267)*

715. The Court recalled that the subjective apprehensions of the suspect, however understandable, were not the decisive factor: what had

---

1 In its report of 9 July 1992, the Commission expressed the opinion that there had been a violation of Article 6 § 1 (twelve votes to three).

to be established above all was whether they could be held to be objectively justified. The mere fact that the judge had also made pre-trial decisions, including decisions relating to detention on remand, could not be taken as in itself justifying fears as to his impartiality; what mattered was the scope and nature of these decisions.

Apart from his decisions relating to the applicant's detention on remand, Judge Meulenbroek had made no other pre-trial decisions than the one allowing the application made by the prosecution for a psychiatric examination of the applicant, which the latter had not contested. He had made no other use of his powers as investigating judge.

As for his decisions on the applicant's detention on remand, they could justify fears as to the judge's impartiality only under special circumstances. The questions which the judge had had to answer when taking those decisions had not been the same as those which had been decisive for his final judgment. In finding that there were 'serious indications' against the applicant, his task had only been to ascertain summarily that the prosecution had *prima facie* grounds for the charge against the applicant. The charge had, moreover, been admitted by the applicant and had already at that stage been supported by further evidence.

As to the arguments put forward by the applicant concerning the fact that the judge had sat alone in a case involving a fifteen-year-old, the Court pointed out that the defendant's interests had been looked after by a lawyer, who had assisted him at all stages of the proceedings, and that he could have appealed, in which case there would have been a complete rehearing before three judges of the Court of Appeal.

Under those circumstances, the applicant's fear could not be regarded as objectively justified. There had therefore not been a violation of Article 6 § 1 (held unanimously).

716. In view of this conclusion, it was not necessary to go into whether Article 6 should be applied to juvenile criminal procedure in the same way as it was to adult criminal procedure.

717. *Summary bibliography*

COMPERNOLLE (J. van).—'Evolution et assouplissement de la notion d'impartialité objective', *R.T.D.H.* 1994, pp. 437–444.

DECAUX (E.) and TAVERNIER (P.).—'Chronique de jurisprudence de la Cour européenne des droits de l'homme (année 1993)', *J.D.I.* 1994, pp. 812–814.

MYJER (E.).—'De onpartijdige Kinderrechter', *NJCM–Bulletin* 1993, pp. 985–990.

SUDRE (F.) and others.—'Chronique de la jurisprudence de la Cour européenne des droits de l'homme. Deuxième partie : juin–décembre 1993', *R.U.D.H.* 1993, pp. 377 *et seq.*

372. Case of Sekanina v. Austria

Court decisions whereby the applicant, having been acquitted, was refused compensation for detention on remand

718. *Karl Sekanina, an Austrian national suspected of killing his wife, was the subject of criminal proceedings and placed in detention on remand on 1 August 1985; he remained in detention until 30 July 1986. He was tried for murder and for having threatened a fellow detainee with death if he disclosed certain admissions relating to the murder charge. On 30 July 1986, an assize court sitting at the Linz Regional Court acquitted him and he was released forthwith.*

Mr Sekanina then applied for compensation for the pecuniary damage sustained on account of his being kept in detention, but the Linz Regional Court dismissed his application on 10 December 1986: under the relevant legislation, he had no right to compensation because serious grounds for suspecting him still subsisted, in particular his numerous, repeated threats, acts of violence and aggressive behaviour, his admissions to a fellow detainee, his evident satisfaction at his wife's death and the financial pressures which he was under. On 25 February 1987, his appeal against that decision was dismissed by the Linz Court of Appeal.

719. *In his application to the Commission of 21 April 1987, Mr Sekanina alleged that there had been a violation of the principle of presumption of innocence guaranteed by Article 6 § 2 of the Convention.*[1]

Judgment of 25 August 1993 *(Chamber) (Series A No. 266–A)*

720. The Government primarily contested the applicability of Article 6 § 2. The Court considered that, even though the Linz Regional Court's decision refusing to award compensation had been given several months after the judgment acquitting the applicant, having regard to Austrian legislation and practice that decision was nonetheless a consequence and, to some extent, the concomitant thereof; in addition, the Regional Court, albeit composed differently, had relied heavily on the evidence from the Assize Court's case-file in order to justify their decision. Consequently, Article 6 § 2 was applicable in this case (held unanimously).

---

1 In its report of 20 May 1992, the Commission expressed the opinion that there had been a violation of Article 6 § 2 (eighteen votes to one).

In ensuring that Article 6 § 2 had been complied with, the Court was confronted with a different situation from those with which it had had to deal in the cases of *Englert and Nölkenbockhoff v. Germany*,[1] where the proceedings had been terminated before any final decision on the merits. In this case, the Assize Court sitting at the Linz Regional Court had acquitted Mr Sekanina by a judgment which had become final. Notwithstanding this decision, the courts empowered to grant compensation had referred, pursuant to section 2(l)(b) of the 1969 Law on Compensation in Criminal Cases, to the suspicions still hanging over Mr Sekanina, and had set out an exhaustive list of the evidence supporting those suspicions. In the Court's view, the voicing of suspicions regarding an accused's innocence was conceivable as long as the conclusion of criminal proceedings had not resulted in a decision on the merits of the accusation, but not once an acquittal had become final. There had therefore been a violation of Article 6 § 2 (held unanimously).

721. With regard to the application of Article 50, the Court dismissed the applicant's claims for compensation of approximately 1,000,000 schillings (unanimously) on the ground that there was no direct causal connection between the violation found and the alleged damage.

Making an assessment on an equitable basis, the Court awarded the applicant 110,000 schillings for costs and expenses incurred before the Austrian courts and the Strasbourg institutions (unanimously).

722. *Summary bibliography*

SUDRE (F.). and others.—'Chronique de la jurisprudence de la Cour européenne des droits de l'homme. Deuxième partie : juin–décembre 1993', *R.U.D.H.* 1993, pp. 377 *et seq.*

WAGNER (B.).—'L'indemnisation d'une détention provisoire suivie d'un acquittement', *R.T.D.H.* 1994, pp. 563–567.

---

1 Series A No. 123; see Vol. I of this work, 785–791.

373. Case of Chorherr v. Austria

Arrest and imposition of an administrative criminal fine for causing a breach of the peace during a military ceremony

723. *On 26 October 1985, a military ceremony, involving the taking of the oath and a march past, was held between 11 a.m. and about 1 p.m. in the Rathausplatz in Vienna in the presence of some 50,000 spectators and numerous dignitaries to mark the thirtieth anniversary of Austrian neutrality and the fortieth anniversary of the end of the Second World War. At the same time, Otmar Chorherr and a friend distributed leaflets calling for a referendum on the purchase of fighter aircraft by the Austrian armed forces. They wore rucksacks to the backs of which were attached placards projecting above their heads bearing the slogan 'Austria does not need any interceptor fighter planes'. As they refused to comply with police orders to stop distributing the leaflets and to remove the placards, the two men were arrested at 11.15 a.m. and taken to the police station; Mr Chorherr was released at 2.40 p.m. after questioning.*

On 28 November 1986, the Constitutional Court dismissed an appeal brought by Mr Chorherr in which he relied inter alia *on Articles 5 and 10 of the Convention. It found that his arrest and detention had complied with the relevant administrative provisions and that the order to remove the placards and cease distributing leaflets had not infringed the constitutional right to freedom of opinion, as its aim was not to prevent the applicant exercising such freedom, but rather to put an end to a breach of the peace. At the conclusion of the administrative criminal proceedings, Mr Chorherr was fined 700 schillings for the breach of the peace caused by his having obstructed the spectators' view of the ceremony.*

724. *In his application to the Commission of 14 July 1987, Mr Chorherr relied on Articles 5 and 10 of the Convention.*[1]

---

1 On 1 March 1991, the Commission declared the complaint relating to the sentence order inadmissible and the remainder of the application admissible. In its report of 21 May 1992, it expressed the opinion that there had been no breach of Article 5 (twelve votes to two), but that there had been a violation of Article 10 (seven votes to seven, with the acting President's casting vote).

Judgment of 25 August 1993 *(Chamber) (Series A No. 266–B)*

725. Since Mr Chorherr's arrest and detention were based on laws covered by the Austrian reservation in respect of Article 5, it was necessary to consider whether the reservation satisfied the conditions laid down in Article 64 of the Convention. Only two of them needed to be examined: the prohibition of reservations 'of a general character' and the requirement that the reservation should contain 'a brief statement of the law concerned'.

The Austrian reservation encompassed a limited number of laws which, taken together, constituted a well-defined and coherent body of substantive and procedural administrative provisions. Among other things, they laid down rules for the punishment of offences, setting out the punishable acts, the penalties incurred and the procedure to be followed. They had all been in force on 3 September 1958, when Austria had ratified the Convention. Therefore, the wording of the reservation in question did not attain the degree of generality prohibited by Article 64 § 1.

As for the reference to the Federal Official Gazette—preceded moreover by an indication of the subject-matter of the relevant provisions—it made it possible for everyone to identify the precise laws concerned and to obtain any information regarding them. It also provided a safeguard against any interpretation which would unduly extend the field of application of the reservation. Accordingly, the reservation complied with Article 64 § 2. As the reservation was therefore compatible with Article 64, the Court found that there had been no violation of Article 5 (unanimously).

726. None of the participants in the proceedings disputed that the deprivation of Mr Chorherr's liberty had constituted an interference with the exercise of his right to freedom of expression and the Court examined whether the requirements of paragraph 2 of Article 10 had been met.

There was nothing in the Constitutional Court's judgment to lend weight to the proposition that the wording of Article IX(1), subparagraph 1, of the Introductory Law created a situation incompatible with legal certainty. Mr Chorherr had therefore been in a position to foresee to a reasonable extent the risks inherent in his conduct. Accordingly, the interference had been 'prescribed by law'.

Having regard to all the circumstances surrounding the actions of the applicant and the police, the Court saw no grounds for doubting that the arrest in issue had pursued at least one of the legitimate aims referred to in Article 10 § 2, namely the prevention of disorder.

As regards necessity, the Court noted in the first place that the nature, importance and scale of the parade had been capable of appearing to the police to justify strengthening the forces deployed to ensure that it passed off peacefully. In addition, when he had chosen this event for his demonstration against the Austrian armed forces, Mr Chorherr must have realized that it might lead to a disturbance requiring measures of restraint, which in this instance, moreover, had not been excessive. Finally, when the Constitutional Court had approved those measures, it had expressly found that they had been intended to prevent breaches of the peace and not to frustrate the expression of an opinion. It could not be said that the authorities had overstepped the margin of appreciation which they enjoyed. In conclusion, no violation of Article 10 had been established (six votes to three).

727. *Summary bibliography*

DECAUX (E.) and TAVERNIER (P.).—'Chronique de jurisprudence de la Cour européenne des droits de l'homme (année 1993)', *J.D.I.* 1994, pp. 811 and 812.

SUDRE (F.) and others.—'Chronique de la jurisprudence de la Cour européenne des droits de l'homme. Deuxième partie : juin–décembre 1993', *R.U.D.H.* 1993, pp. 377 *et seq.*

374. Case of Pardo v. France

Nature of an appeal hearing in commercial proceedings

728. *By judgment given on 27 June 1983 following a public hearing, the Marseilles Commercial Court ordered Ernest Pardo, the* de facto *manager of a company which had just been wound up, to pay 5,000,000 French francs as a contribution to a deficiency in the company's assets. The court took the view that the company had engaged in business which was out of proportion to its assets.*

Mr Pardo appealed to the Aix-en-Provence Court of Appeal, which he subsequently asked to stay the proceedings pending the conclusion of criminal bankruptcy proceedings brought against him. At the hearing on 9 November 1984, his counsel apparently confined his pleadings to the request for the stay of proceedings. On 15 January 1985, the Court of Appeal upheld the contested judgment without holding another hearing. Mr Pardo unsuccessfully sought an interview with the First President of that court, complaining that argument had not been taken on the merits. On 15 July 1986, the Court of Cassation dismissed an appeal by Mr Pardo.

729. *In his application to the Commission of 12 November 1986, Mr Pardo alleged that there had been a violation of his right to a fair trial guaranteed under Article 6 § 1 of the Convention: he had not had an opportunity to plead his case on the merits in the Court of Appeal, although the President had said that there would be a hearing. He also claimed to have been the victim of a breach of the principle of the presumption of innocence, laid down in Article 6 § 2, on account of the application in his case of Article 99 of Law No. 67–563 of 13 July 1967 on composition proceedings, compulsory winding-up, bankruptcy and fraudulent bankruptcy.*[1]

Judgment of 20 September 1993 *(Chamber) (Series A No. 261–B)*

730. Confronted with a dispute concerning the exact course of the proceedings in the Aix-en-Provence Court of Appeal, the Court had to

1 On 1 March 1991, the Commission declared the first complaint admissible and the second complaint inadmissible. In its report of 1 April 1992, the Commission expressed the opinion that there had been a violation of Article 6 § 1 (unanimously).

reach its decision on the basis of the available evidence. The statements gathered by Mr Pardo from two lawyers who had been present at the hearing and from a third who should have been present did not provide sufficient *prima facie* evidence of the accuracy of his version of events. In addition, the record of the hearing constituted a significant element in support of the opinion that judgment had indeed been reserved, which ruled out the possibility of a further hearing. Furthermore, there was nothing to show that in the course of the sole hearing the parties had confined themselves to expanding upon their submissions concerning the stay of the proceedings or that the applicant's lawyer had not had an opportunity to lodge documents. There had therefore not been a violation of Article 6 (six votes to three).

731. *Summary bibliography*

DECAUX (E.) and TAVERNIER (P.).—'Chronique de jurisprudence de la Cour européenne des droits de l'homme (année 1993), *J.D.I.* 1994, p. 797.

SUDRE (F.) and others.—'Chronique de la jurisprudence de la Cour européenne des droits de l'homme. Deuxième partie : juin–décembre 1993', *R.U.D.H.* 1993, pp. 377 *et seq.*

375. Case of Saïdi v. France

Criminal conviction based exclusively on the statements of witnesses not confronted with the accused

732. *Fahrat Saïdi, a Tunisian national born in 1951, was a bricklayer and lived in Nice. On 29 May 1986, he was arrested in connection with an inquiry concerning two deaths caused by the use of drugs on the basis of information received from drug users and small-time dealers. Subsequently, he was identified by witnesses through a two-way mirror and from photographs. Despite his requests to that effect, he was not confronted with the witnesses during the investigation or at the trial or on appeal.*

On 3 February 1987, the Nice Criminal Court sentenced Mr Saïdi to ten years' imprisonment for possession of and dealing in drugs and involuntary homicide, and permanently excluded him from French territory. The Aix-en-Provence Court of Appeal reduced the sentence to eight years and confirmed Mr Saïdi's exclusion from France. On 19 August 1988, the Court of Cassation dismissed an appeal brought by the applicant.

733. *In his application to the Commission of 17 January 1989, Mr Saïdi complained of the refusal of the judicial authorities to organize a confrontation with the prosecution witnesses; he considered this to be incompatible with Article 6 §§ 1 and 3(d) of the Convention.*[1]

Judgment of 20 September 1993 *(Chamber) (Series A No. 261–C)*

734. The Government contended primarily that Mr Saïdi had failed to exhaust his domestic remedies inasmuch as he had not called witnesses in the Criminal Court or asked for witnesses to be summoned in the Court of Appeal.

The Court dismissed the objection (unanimously) on the ground that Mr Saïdi had provided the courts with the opportunity to prevent or to put right the violations alleged against them. At first instance, he had manifested the desire that the court should hear the persons who had denounced or identified him. On appeal, he had stressed the inadequacy of the investigation and the Aix-en-Provence Court of Appeal had gone into the substance of the matter and given detailed reasons for its

1 In its report of 14 May 1992, the Commission expressed the opinion that there had been a violation of Article 6 §§ 1 and 3(d) (thirteen votes to one).

refusal to hear the prosecution witnesses. As regards the appeal to the Court of Cassation, the applicant's sole submission had been based on Article 6 § 3(d) of the Convention and on that provision alone.

As far as the merits of the complaint were concerned, the Court referred to its case law on the taking of evidence. The testimony gathered before the trial had constituted the sole basis for the applicant's conviction, after having been the only ground for his committal for trial. Yet neither at the investigation stage nor during the trial had the applicant been able to examine the witnesses concerned or have them examined. The lack of any confrontation had deprived him in certain respects of a fair trial. The Court was fully aware of the undeniable difficulties of the fight against drug-trafficking—in particular with regard to obtaining and producing evidence—and of the ravages caused to society by the drug problem, but such considerations could not justify restricting to this extent the rights of the defence of 'everyone charged with a criminal offence'. In short, there had been a violation of Article 6 §§ and 3(d) (held unanimously).

735. Under Article 50, the Court noted that the Convention did not give it jurisdiction to direct the French State to open a new trial or to adopt one of the other measures sought by the applicant (removal of his criminal conviction from his police record or of certain extracts (*bulletins*) therefrom and regularization of his situation on French territory). It dismissed his claim (unanimously).

Mr Saïdi also claimed compensation of 1,000,000 French francs for the imprisonment which he had undergone. The Court could not speculate as to what the outcome of the proceedings in question would have been had the violation of the Convention not occurred. It held that the judgment constituted sufficient just satisfaction (unanimously).

The Court accepted most of the applicant's claims for costs and expenses incurred before the French Courts and the Convention institutions, awarding him 42,000 French francs (unanimously).

736. *Summary bibliography*

CHAMBON (P.).—'Note', *La semaine juridique*, édition générale, 23 February 1994, jurisprudence, pp. 76–78.

DECAUX (E.) and TAVERNIER (P.).—'Chronique de jurisprudence de la Cour européenne des droits de l'homme (année 1993), *J.D.I.* 1994, pp. 798 and 799.

KNIGGE (G.).—'Noot', *N.J.* 1994, pp. 1665–1667.

PETTITI (L.-E.).—'Droits de l'homme', *R.S.C.D.P.C.* 1994, pp. 142–144.

SUDRE (F.) and others.—'Chronique de la jurisprudence de la Cour européenne des droits de l'homme. Deuxième partie : juin–décembre 1993', *R.U.D.H.* 1993, pp. 377 *et seq.*

376. Case of Zumtobel v. Austria

Expropriation proceedings prior to the construction of a provincial highway

737. *F.M. Zumtobel, a commercial company incorporated under Austrian law (formerly a partnership), was based in Dornbirn. Mr Zumtobel was its manager and sole shareholder.*

On 28 February 1985, the Highways Authority of the Provincial Government of Vorarlberg initiated expropriation proceedings in respect of 2,140 square metres of land belonging to the Zumtobel company in order to build a new provincial by-pass. A hearing took place before the Office of the Provincial Government, which heard the applicants and three official experts. On 13 February 1986, the Government made an order for expropriation and awarded the applicants compensation.

On 27 November 1987, the Constitutional Court dismissed an application brought by the applicants alleging that the expropriation proceedings had not complied with Article 6 § 1 of the Convention, on the ground that it did not have sufficient prospects of success. An appeal brought in the Administrative Court was also dismissed on 22 September 1989. On 24 March 1988, the Feldkirch Regional Court fixed the compensation payable to the applicant at 4,560,000 schillings, which constituted a significant decrease on the amount which had been granted on 17 December 1987 by the District Court of Feldkirch. On 6 October 1988, the Supreme Court refused to quash that decision.

738. *In their application to the Commission of 10 June 1986, the Zumtobel company and Mr Zumtobel relied on Article 6 § 1 and Articles 13 and 14 of the Convention and Article 1 of Protocol No. 1.*[1]

Judgment of 21 September 1993 *(Chamber) (Series A No. 268–A)*

739. The Court held in the first place that the Government Office did not constitute a tribunal for the purposes of Article 6 § 1 and that the Constitutional Court had not had the requisite full jurisdiction. As for the Administrative Court, which had been responsible for ensuring that

---

1 On 15 October 1991, the Commission held that the complaint based on Article 6 § 1 was admissible. In its report of 30 June 1992, it expressed the opinion, by different majorities on the various points in issue, that there had not been a violation of Article 6 § 1

the Government Office complied with the relevant rules of the Provincial Highways Law, it had been concerned solely with the submissions made in the proceedings before the Government Office. It had considered those submissions on their merits, point by point, without ever having to decline jurisdiction in replying to them or in ascertaining various facts. Regard being had to the respect which must be accorded to decisions taken by the administrative authorities on grounds of expediency and to the nature of the complaints made by the Zumtobel partnership, the review by the Administrative Court had accordingly fulfilled the requirements of Article 6 § 1.

740. The Zumtobel partnership had not asked the Administrative Court to hold a hearing. It must be deemed to have waived unequivocally its right to a hearing and the dispute had not given rise to questions of public interest making such a hearing necessary.

741. As regards the complaints relating to the lack of independence of the experts consulted by the regional authorities and the failure to communicate documents, the Court observed that those complaints, which related to the proceedings before the Government Office, had been examined and rejected by the Administrative Court under a procedure which in this instance had been in conformity with Article 6 § 1.

742. In conclusion, no violation of Article 6 § 1 had been established (held unanimously).

743. *Summary bibliography*

CLEMENT (J.-N.).—'Note', *G.P.* 15–19 July 1994, pp. 18 and 19.
DECAUX (E.) and TAVERNIER (P.).—'Chronique de jurisprudence de la Cour européenne des droits de l'homme (année 1993)', *J.D.I.* 1994, pp. 814 and 815.
SUDRE (F.) and others.—'Chronique de la jurisprudence de la Cour européenne des droits de l'homme. Deuxième partie : juin–décembre 1993', *R.U.D.H.* 1993, pp. 377 *et seq.*

377. Case of Kremzow v. Austria

Appeal and nullity proceedings before the Supreme Court

744.   *On 16 December 1982, Friedrich Wilhelm Kremzow, a retired judge, spontaneously presented himself before the Regional Court of Korneuburg and confessed to having killed Mr P. At the hearing in June 1984, the applicant retracted his confession which he claimed was the product of a psychotic aberration. On 18 December 1984, a jury in Court of Assizes found him guilty on charges including that of murder and he was sentenced to twenty years' imprisonment and committed to an institution for mentally deranged criminals. The applicant filed a plea of nullity with the Supreme Court, complaining that he had been denied the right to defend himself and that the trial had not been fair. The public prosecutor also appealed against the sentence, requesting that a life sentence be imposed. His wife and his mother filed a further plea of nullity as well as an appeal.*

On 2 August 1985, the Attorney General's position paper (croquis), considering in detail the various grounds of nullity, was received by the Supreme Court. In September and October 1985, Mr Kremzow and his counsel sought in vain communication of that document. It was finally sent to counsel on 9 June 1986. The hearing on the plea of nullity and the appeals was put down for 2 July 1986. Before that, the judge rapporteur drew up for the Supreme Court a draft judgment which generally followed the Attorney General's position paper. On 25 June 1986, the Supreme Court dismissed the applicant's request to attend its hearing on the plea of nullity in person, to obtain a copy of the croquis and to be authorized to consult the case-file, on the ground that the fact that his counsel had been given a copy of the croquis *was sufficient. The decision was notified to the applicant on the date of the hearing (2 July 1986). The Supreme Court considered the plea of nullity and the appeals against the penalty in the applicant's absence. It upheld in particular the public prosecutor's appeal and sentenced Mr Kremzow to life imprisonment in an ordinary prison. It appeared from the original of the judgment that the dismissal of the plea of nullity was based on the judge-rapporteur's draft.*

745.   *In his application to the Commission of 1 August 1986, Mr Kremzow made numerous complaints about the proceedings in the Assize Court and in the Supreme Court. He relied on Article 5, Article 6 §§ 1, 2 and 3 and Articles 13 and 14 of the Convention.*[1]

338

Judgment of 21 September 1993 *(Chamber) (Series A No. 268–B)*

746.   The Court considered that it had jurisdiction to consider a complaint based on breach of the principle of the presumption of innocence enshrined in Article 6 § 2 which had not been examined by the Commission.

747.   The Government claimed that the applicant's complaint under Article 6 § 3(c) that he had not been permitted to attend the nullity and appeal hearings before the Supreme Court should be rejected as inadmissible for non-exhaustion of domestic remedies.

The Court observed that the Government's arguments on both points were closely linked to the well-foundedness of the applicant's complaints under Article 6 § 3(c). The plea should therefore be joined to the merits (held unanimously).

748.   With regard to Article 6, the Court first considered and then dismissed (unanimously) the three complaints based on paragraph 1 in conjunction with paragraph 3(b).

First, there was the Attorney General's *croquis*. It had consisted of forty-nine pages and had been served on counsel for the applicant on 9 June 1986, some three weeks before the date fixed for the hearing. That period had afforded the applicant and his lawyer sufficient opportunity to formulate their reply in time for the oral hearing of 2 July

1   The Commission declared the case admissible on 5 September 1990 but only as regards the complaints relating to the proceedings before the Supreme Court. In its report adopted on 20 May 1992, the Commission expressed the opinion that:
   (a) there had been a violation of Article 6 §§ 1 and 3(c) in that the applicant was not allowed to be present in person at the Supreme Court's hearing (eleven votes to three);
   (b) it was not necessary to examine the same complaint under Article 14 in conjunction with Article 6 (eleven votes to three);
   (c) there had been no violation of Article 6 § 1 on account of the fact that a draft judgment had been prepared before the Supreme Court's hearing (unanimously);
   (d) there had been a violation of Article 6 §§ 1 and 3(b) in that the applicant had not been granted sufficient opportunities to obtain, and to comment on, the Attorney General's position paper (eight votes to six);
   (e) there had been no violation of Article 6 as regards his remaining complaints concerning the fairness of the Supreme Court's proceedings (unanimously); and
   (f) there had been no violation of Article 13 or of Article 5 in conjunction with Article 14 (unanimously).

1986. In addition, it had been open to the applicant's lawyer to request the court for permission to consult the case-file with a view to examining the croquis prior to its transmission. Although the applicant might have been to some extent disadvantaged in the preparation of his defence, he nevertheless had had 'adequate time and facilities' to formulate his response to the *croquis*.

Secondly, there was the refusal to allow the applicant to inspect the file. The Court considered that restriction of the right to inspect the file to an accused's lawyer was not incompatible with the rights of the defence under Article 6.

Thirdly, there was the question of the notification of the decision relating to the applicant's appearance at the hearing. The Court observed that there was no indication that the notification of the Supreme Court's decision on the day of the hearing had unduly hampered the defence in the preparation of its case.

749. The Court then considered the complaints based on paragraph 1 in conjunction with paragraph 3(c) relating to the refusal to allow Mr Kremzow to be present at the hearings.

As regards the hearing of the pleas of nullity, the Court observed that under Austrian law the Supreme Court, in dealing with nullity proceedings, was primarily concerned with questions of law that arose in regard to the conduct of the trial and other matters. Since Mr Kremzow had been legally represented, it had not been necessary for him to be present at the hearing (held unanimously).

In the light of this conclusion, it was not necessary to deal with the question relating to the failure to exhaust domestic remedies which the Court had previously reserved (held unanimously).

As regards the hearing of the appeals against sentence, the Court observed that the Supreme Court had been called upon in the appeal proceedings to examine whether the applicant's sentence should be increased from twenty years to life imprisonment and whether the sentence should be served in a normal prison instead of a special institution for mentally deranged offenders. In the event, the Supreme Court had answered both questions in the affirmative. Unlike the jury, which had been unable to establish a motive for the offence, it had also found that the applicant had carried out the murder to cover up his own 'financial misdeeds'. These proceedings had thus been of crucial importance for the applicant and had involved not only an assessment of his character and state of mind at the time of the offence but also his motive. The applicant had failed to make a request in his appeal or counter-statement to attend the hearing. However, section 296 § 3 of the Code of Criminal Procedure provided that in the absence of a request the applicant should be brought before the court 'if his personal presence [appeared] necessary in the interest of justice'. Given the gravity of what had been at stake for the applicant, the State had been under a positive duty, notwithstanding his failure to make such a request, to ensure his presence in court. There had therefore been a breach of Article 6 § 1 in conjunction with paragraph 3(c) (held unanimously).

750. In contrast, the preparation of the draft judgment prior to the Supreme Court's hearing had not violated Article 6 § 1 (held unanimously). According to the Court, a draft judgment prepared informally in advance by members of the Chamber had not in any way bound the Supreme Court or precluded it from amending the draft and reaching a different view after hearing the parties.

751. Lastly, the Court dismissed other complaints relating to equality of arms based on Article 6 § 1 (unanimously). It was not in dispute that there was no time-limit for the submission of the Attorney General's position paper. But the Attorney General's office was required to familiarize itself with the case at a later and separate phase of the procedure than the defence, which was not in any way prejudiced by the difference in this regard. Furthermore, it was not denied by the Government that the name of the judge rapporteur had been wrongfully disclosed to the Attorney General's office. However, in itself that could not render the proceedings unfair. Lastly, there was no evidence whatsoever that a copy of the draft judgment had been forwarded to the Attorney General's office.

752. No question of a violation of the presumption of innocence arose and hence there had been no violation of Article 6 § 2 (held unanimously). Mr Kremzow had already been found guilty of murder and the Supreme Court's remarks had related solely to the question of his motive for the offence. Moreover, the reference to 'financial misdeeds' could not be construed as a finding that the applicant was guilty of a specific offence.

753. Since it had found that there had been a violation in connection with Mr Kremzow's absence from the hearing of the appeals, the Court did not deem it necessary to examine the complaint based on Article 14 in conjunction with Article 6 (held unanimously).

As for the remaining complaints, which were based on Article 14 in conjunction with Article 5 § 1(a) and Article 13, the Court pointed out that, whilst the applicant had raised them before the Commission, he had made no written or oral observation on them before the Court. It saw no reason to consider them of its own motion (held unanimously).

754. With regard to the application of Article 50, Mr Kremzow's claims were confined to costs and expenses. Taking into account the fact that, out of a multiplicity of complaints, only one had been found to be justified, it awarded him 200,000 schillings in respect of fees and 30,000 schillings for expenses (unanimously).

755. *Summary bibliography*

KNIGGE (G.).—'Noot', *N.J.* 1994, pp. 1674 and 1675.
SUDRE (F.) and others.—'Chronique de la jurisprudence de la Cour européenne des droits de l'homme. Deuxième partie : juin–décembre 1993', *R.U.D.H.* 1993, pp. 377 *et seq.*

378. Case of Klaas v. Germany

Treatment received by a woman in the course of an arrest and witnessed by her young child

756. *In the early evening of 28 January 1986, Hildegard Klaas, accompanied by her eight-year-old daughter Monika, drew up outside the back entrance to the block of flats where she lived. Two police officers who had followed her accused her of having driven through a red traffic light and of having tried to get away, which she denied. She agreed to be breathalysed, but, after several unsuccessful attempts at providing a specimen, she was told that she would have to accompany them to the local hospital in order to have a blood test. The circumstances of the arrest and the precise sequence of events were open to dispute, but Mrs Klaas claimed that the police officers inflicted serious injuries on her which were evidenced by subsequent medical examinations. She was released when the blood sample proved to have an alcohol level of 0.82 mg per ml.*

On 22 April 1986, the criminal proceedings against Mrs Klaas for driving while under the influence of alcohol and obstructing a public officer in the execution of his duties were discontinued. Instead, the competent administrative authority imposed an administrative fine of 500 Deutsche Mark and suspended her licence for a month for driving with a blood alcohol content level in excess of the legal limit of 0.80 mg per ml, which constituted a 'regulatory offence'.

Mrs Klaas laid an information against the police officers concerned alleging assault, but subsequently withdrew her allegations. On 18 September 1986, the Head of the Detmold District Administration dismissed a complaint which she had lodged against the police officers concerned on the ground that the use of force had been justified and was not disproportionate. In 1987, the Detmold Regional Court dismissed her civil action for damages which she had brought against the police officers and the Land of North-Rhine Westphalia on the grounds, inter alia, *that the arrest had not been unlawful and disproportionate force had not been used. In September 1988, the Hamm Court of Appeal dismissed Mrs Klaas's appeal against that judgment. In February 1989, a panel of three judges of the Federal Constitutional Court declined to accept for adjudication her constitutional complaint on the ground that it did not offer sufficient prospects of success.*

757. *In their application of 11 July 1989 to the Commission, Mrs Klaas and her daughter relied on Articles 3 and 8 of the Convention.*[1]

Judgment of 22 September 1993 *(Chamber) (Series A No. 269)*

758. The Court considered whether the treatment which the police officers had inflicted on Mrs Klaas in the course of her arrest had constituted inhuman and degrading treatment contrary to Article 3.

The Court noted that the parties to the national proceedings had not disputed the fact that the injuries as shown by medical evidence and illustrated by the photographs had actually arisen in the course of the arrest. However, differing versions of how those injuries had actually come about had been put forward by the applicants and the Government. The Court recalled that various proceedings had arisen out of the incident, some of which had been abandoned. In the civil proceedings brought by Mrs Klaas for compensation from the State, the Detmold Regional Court had accepted that the injuries had occurred as a result of the incident with the police, but had held that they did not give rise to a compensation claim. The Hamm Court of Appeal had confirmed this decision.

Under the Convention system, the establishment and verification of the facts fell primarily to the Commission. The Court was not, however, bound by the Commission's findings of fact and remained free to make its own appreciation in the light of all the material before it. The Court further pointed out that it was not normally within its province to substitute its own assessment of the facts for that of the domestic courts, and that, as a general rule, it was for those courts to assess the evidence before them.

The admitted injuries sustained by the first applicant were consistent with either her or the police officers' version of events. The national courts, however, had found against her. In reaching the conclusion that she could have injured herself while resisting arrest and that the arresting officers had not used excessive force, the Regional Court had had the benefit of seeing the various witnesses give their evidence and of evaluating their credibility. No material had been adduced in the course of the Strasbourg proceedings which might call into question the findings of the national courts and add weight to the applicant's allegations either before the Commission or the Court. No cogent elements had been provided which could lead the Court to depart from the national

1 In its report of 21 May 1992, the Commission expressed the opinion that:
  (a) in respect of the mother, there had been a violation of Article 3 (ten votes to five) and no separate issue had arisen under Article 8 (ten votes to five);
  (b) in respect of the daughter, there had been no violation of Article 3 (fourteen votes to one) but there had been a violation of Article 8 (eight votes to seven).

courts' findings of fact. Accordingly, no violation of Article 3 could be found to have occurred (six votes to three).

759. Mrs Klass' complaint under Article 8 (that the events had taken place on private property in the presence of her eight year-old daughter) was essentially based on the same disputed facts which had already been considered in connection with Article 3 and found not to have been established. This being so, the complaint did not call for separate examination (six votes to three).

760. As the facts on which the daughter relied had not been established, the Court considered that her complaints under Article 3 and Article 8 were likewise unfounded (unanimously and six votes to three, respectively).

761. *Summary bibliography*

DECAUX (E.) and TAVERNIER (P.).—'Chronique de jurisprudence de la Cour européenne des droits de l'homme (année 1993)', *J.D.I.* 1994, pp. 815–817.
SUDRE (F.) and others.—'Chronique de la jurisprudence de la Cour européenne des droits de l'homme. Deuxième partie : juin–décembre 1993', *R.U.D.H.* 1993, pp. 377 *et seq.*

379. Case of Istituto di Vigilanza v. Italy
380. Case of Figus Milone v. Italy
381. Case of Goisis v. Italy

Length of civil proceedings

762. *On 26 October 1978, Istituto di Vigilanza, a firm, was sued in the Turin magistrate's court* (pretore) *by Albina Figus Milone for unfair dismissal. At the first hearing, on 28 November 1978, the magistrate raised of his own motion the question whether certain legislative provisions were compatible with the constitutional principle of equality between men and women in the field of employment. On 19 December 1978, he stayed the proceedings pending the decision of the Constitutional Court. The Constitutional Court gave judgment on 16 January 1987. The plaintiff resumed the proceedings on 16 February 1987 and they ended on 28 May with a friendly settlement.*

763. *On 4 January 1989, Mario Goisis sued Mr G.N., Mr E.Q.Y. and Mrs M.T. in the Bergamo magistrate's court. He sought to have them ordered to move the low wall which enclosed their properties so that the width of the adjoining road should be not less than five metres along the whole of its length. The case was listed on 16 January 1989. Three hearings were held, in 1989, 1990 and 1991. On 20 November 1991, the magistrate reserved judgment, but on 1 December he relisted the case and commissioned an expert opinion. Three hearings were held, on 28 October 1992, 9 December 1992 and 20 January 1993. On 7 April 1993, the magistrate declined jurisdiction in favour of the Bergamo District Court. He also set a strict deadline of two months for resuming the proceedings, which recommenced on 26 May 1993.*

764. *Istituto di Vigilanza and Mrs Figus Milone applied to the Commission on 25 November 1987, Mr Goisis on 16 May 1989. All three complained of the length of the proceedings and relied on Article 6 § 1 of the Convention. Mr Goisis also claimed to be a victim of a breach of Article 13.*[1]

---

1 In its three reports of 1 July 1992, the Commission expressed the opinion that there had been a violation of Article 6 § 1 (Istituto di Vigilanza and Mrs Figus Milone: unanimously; Mr Goisis: five votes to three). It considered that there had been no breach of Article 13 in the case of Mr Goisis (unanimously).

Judgments of 22 September 1993 *(Chamber) (Series A No. 265–C to E)*

765. The Government maintained that the Commission had referred the case to the Court only on 11 December 1992, whereas its reports had been sent to the Committee of Ministers on 10 September that year.

The Court pointed out that by the terms of the French text of Article 47, it might only *'être saisie d'une affaire'* (be seised of a case) within the period of three months provided for in Article 32. The use of the verb *'saisir'* appeared to be incompatible with the interpretation of the word 'referred' that the Delegates of the Commission seemed to be advocating. In order to seise a court, it was not sufficient to decide to seise it. The decision must be implemented. Besides, any other reading of Article 32 § 1 and Article 47 would be likely to produce—as regards one of the conditions to be satisfied when applying to the Commission itself—results contrary to the letter and spirit of Article 26 *in fine* and to the case law which had been established in the matter from the very beginning.

The Commission had exceeded—albeit by only one day—the time allowed it. Furthermore, no special circumstance of a nature to suspend the running of time or justify its starting to run afresh was apparent from the file. The Court therefore held that it could not deal with the merits of the case (unanimously).

766. *Summary bibliography*

FLAUSS (J.-F.).—'Un exemple de dysfonctionnement des organes de la Convention européenne', *R.T.D.H.* 1994, pp. 571–574.

SUDRE (F.) and others.—'Chronique de la jurisprudence de la Cour européenne des droits de l'homme. Deuxième partie : juin–décembre 1993', *R.U.D.H.* 1993, pp. 377 *et seq.*

382. Case of Stamoulakatos v. Greece

Criminal trial in the accused's absence

767. *In 1979 and 1980, when he was living abroad, Nicolas Stamoulakatos was found guilty in absentia in eight sets of proceedings by the Athens Criminal Court for fraud, defamation, insulting a public officer, misappropriation, causing bodily harm, forgery and uttering. He was arrested in Brussels in 1985, extradited to Greece and imprisoned for one of those offences. He was conditionally released on 7 April 1987.*

Following his extradition, he brought several appeals against the judgments given in his absence, some of which were successful. However, on 16 July and 29 October 1986, the Athens Court of Appeal dismissed two appeals on the ground that they were out of time. In addition, on 19 March 1986, the Athens Criminal Court dismissed Mr Stamoulakatos' application to have the judgment by which he had been imprisoned set aside. Several appeals on points of law and applications for retrials made to the Court of Appeal were also unsuccessful.

768. *In his application to the Commission of 18 July 1986, Mr Stamoulakatos relied on Articles 3, 4, 5, 6 §§ 1 and 3 (he alleged that he had not been properly summoned and that he had therefore been unable to defend himself against the charges against him), 8, 9, 10, 11 and 14 of the Convention and Article 1 of Protocol No. 1.*[1]

Judgment of 26 October 1993 *(Chamber)* *(Series A No. 271)*

769. The Government's primary submission, as before the Commission, was that Mr Stamoulakatos' complaints did not come within the jurisdiction *ratione temporis* of the Convention institutions. In addition, it alleged that the applicant had not exhausted domestic remedies.

The Court found that the events which had given rise to the proceedings against the applicant, together with three judgments of the Athens Criminal Court (out of eight), were covered by the time limitation in Greece's declaration in respect of Article 25 of the Convention.

---

1 In a partial decision of 6 June 1990, the Commission declared the application inadmissible except for the complaints based on Article 6. It declared the latter admissible on 15 April 1991. In its report of 20 May 1992, the Commission expressed the opinion that there had been a violation of Article 6 §§ 1 and 3 (ten votes to four).

As for his appeals and applications against those judgments, the applicant had complained only that they had been ineffective. Although those appeals and applications had been lodged after the 'critical' date of 19 November 1985, they were closely bound up with the proceedings that had led to his conviction. Divorcing those appeals and applications from the events which had given rise to them would be tantamount to rendering Greece's declaration nugatory. As the objection was well-founded, the Court could not deal with the merits of the case (held unanimously).

770. *Summary bibliography*

DECAUX (E.) and TAVERNIER (P.).—'Chronique de jurisprudence de la Cour européenne des droits de l'homme (année 1993)', *J.D.I.* 1994, pp. 817–819.

SUDRE (F.) and others.—'Chronique de la jurisprudence de la Cour européenne des droits de l'homme. Deuxième partie : juin–décembre 1993', *R.U.D.H.* 1993, pp. 377 *et seq.*

383. Case of Darnell v. the United Kingdom

Length of civil proceedings

771. *On 16 May 1984, Dr Royce Darnell was given three months'
notice of dismissal, with effect on 19 August 1984, from his post as a
consultant microbiologist with the Trent Regional Health Authority. He
had been suspended since the opening of disciplinary proceedings in
June 1982.*

*On 23 May 1984, the applicant appealed against his dismissal to the
Secretary of State, who confirmed it on 21 February 1986. By judicial
review proceedings commenced in the High Court on 24 April 1986, Dr
Darnell challenged the fairness of the procedure leading to the Secretary
of State's decision. On 21 July 1986, the High Court granted a declaration that this decision was invalid and indicated that the Secretary of
State should reconsider the matter. The Secretary of State did so and
confirmed the decision on 18 March 1988. A further application by Dr
Darnell for judicial review of the validity of the Secretary of State's
direction was dismissed by the Divisional Court in November 1988.*

*Previously, on 10 August 1984, Dr Darnell had brought proceedings
in the Industrial Tribunal for unfair dismissal in which he sought reinstatement and re-engagement. Those proceedings had been stayed from
time to time at the applicant's request, pending the results of the appeal
to the Secretary of State and the judicial review proceedings. On 23
February 1990, the Tribunal held that the dismissal of the applicant had
not been unfair. Dr Darnell's appeal to the Employment Appeal Tribunal
was dismissed on 8 April 1993.*

772. *Dr Darnell lodged his application with the Commission on 2
December 1988. He complained of several violations of Article 6 § 1 of
the Convention and invoked Article 13.*[1]

Judgment of 26 October 1993 *(Chamber) (Series A No. 272)*

773. In view of the Government's concession that there had been a
violation of Article 6 § 1, the Court did not consider it necessary to rule

---

1 On 10 April 1991, the Commission declared the applicant's complaint concerning the length of the proceedings admissible and dismissed the remainder of his application. In its report of 13 May 1992, it expressed the
opinion that there had been a violation of Article 6 § 1 (unanimously).

on the dispute between the participants as to the starting date of the period to be taken into consideration. Even if the Court were to adopt the Government's position that, at the earliest, it should start to run from 10 August 1984 (the date of the initial application to the Industrial Tribunal), the lapse of time of nearly nine years until the Employment Appeal Tribunal had given its judgment could not be regarded as 'reasonable'. There had therefore been a violation of Article 6 § 1 (held unanimously).

774. The Court acknowledged the public apology which had been given to Dr Darnell by the Government's representative at the hearing before it, and awarded Dr Darnell £5,000 for non-pecuniary damage.

It awarded him £3,922.11 for lawyer's fees and expenses, less 6,025 French francs which he had received by way of legal aid from the Council of Europe (unanimously).

775. *Summary bibliography*

SUDRE (F.) and others.—'Chronique de la jurisprudence de la Cour euro-péenne des droits de l'homme. Deuxième partie : juin–décembre 1993', *R.U.D.H.* 1993, pp. 377 *et seq.*

384. Case of Monnet v. France

Length of civil proceedings

776. *On 15 September 1981, Claude Monnet's wife filed an application for judicial separation. By an order pronouncing the failure of the conciliation process dated 24 November 1981, the matrimonial causes judge of the Valence* tribunal de grande instance, *giving an interlocutory ruling as the judge responsible for preparing the case, awarded custody of the children to their mother, set the father's contribution to their maintenance at 2,000 French francs a month, and in addition ordered him to pay his wife 1,500 francs a month. On 30 December 1981, his wife,* née *Grosclaude, instituted judicial separation proceedings against her husband, who cross-petitioned for divorce.*

On 13 February 1985, the Valence tribunal de grande instance *pronounced the couple's divorce, finding that both were at fault; it deferred its decision on the custody of the children and the amount of maintenance.*

The applicant appealed against that judgment, asking the Grenoble Court of Appeal to pronounce the divorce with fault being attributed exclusively to his wife. On 16 March 1987, the Court of Appeal, setting aside the contested judgment, dismissed as ill-founded the petitions for judicial review of the petitions for separation and divorce. Ruling of its own motion by virtue of Article 258 of the Civil Code, it awarded custody of the children to the mother, authorized her to live apart from her husband and ordered him to pay 8,000 French francs as his monthly maintenance contribution. On 12 October 1988, the Court of Cassation dismissed the applicant's appeal.

777. *In his application of 26 November 1987 to the Commission, Mr Monnet complained of the length of the judicial separation and divorce proceedings and of criminal proceedings brought against him for wilful neglect to maintain his family. He also alleged that his case had not had a fair hearing either at first instance or in the appeal proceedings. He relied on Article 6 § 1 of the Convention.*[1]

---

1 On 6 March 1991 the Commission found only the complaint concerning the length of the civil proceedings admissible. In its report of 1 July 1992, it expressed the opinion that there had been a violation of Article 6 § 1 (seven votes to one).

Judgment of 27 October 1993 *(Chamber) (Series A No. 273–A)*

778. The period to be taken into consideration had begun on 15 September 1981, the date on which the petition for judicial separation had been filed. It had ended on 12 October 1988, when the Court of Cassation had delivered its judgment. It had therefore lasted seven years and approximately one month.

The large number of interlocutory applications filed by the parties, especially Mr Monnet, had made the case complex. The parties had hardly been diligent in filing their submissions and this had contributed considerably to prolonging the proceedings. Three of the periods might seem abnormal, but this was attributable to the applicant's conduct. As the Court did not consider the total length of the proceedings excessive, there had been no violation of Article 6 § 1 (held unanimously).

779. *Summary bibliography*

SUDRE (F.) and others.—'Chronique de la jurisprudence de la Cour européenne des droits de l'homme. Deuxième partie : juin–décembre 1993', *R.U.D.H.* 1993, pp. 377 *et seq.*

385. Case of Dombo Beheer B.V. v. the Netherlands

Application, in civil proceedings, of a rule of evidence that a party may not be heard as a witness in his own case

780. *Dombo Beheer B.V., a limited liability company incorporated under Netherlands law ('Dombo'), had its registered office in Nijmegen. A dispute arose between Dombo and its bank concerning the development of their financial relationship during the period between December 1980 and February 1981. Dombo maintained that it had concluded a contract with the bank relating to overdraft facilities. When the Bank refused to execute payment orders, Dombo sued it for damages in the Arnhem Regional Court. On 2 February 1984, the court authorized Dombo to produce evidence of the alleged contract, in particular as to the alleged extension of the credit limit. On 8 January 1985, the Arnhem Court of Appeal dismissed an appeal brought by the bank against that decision. At the request of both parties, the Court of Appeal did not refer the case back to the Regional Court, but proceeded to deal with the case itself.*

On 13 February 1985, the judge instructed to hear the witnesses refused to hear testimony from the former managing director of Dombo (Mr van Reijendam) who had negotiated the contract. In contrast, he subsequently heard a manager of a branch office, Mr van W., who had taken part in the negotiations on behalf of the bank. Although he was present at the hearing, the testimony of Dombo's former director was not heard. On 11 March 1986, the Arnhem Court of Appeal dismissed Dombo's claim for damages. On 19 February 1988, the Court of Cassation dismissed Dombo's appeal against the Court of Appeal's judgment and against the decisions of the judge who heard the witnesses; it held that the Court of Appeal had been at liberty to assess the evidence produced by the bank in the light of the observations submitted by the other party and to take into consideration the declarations made by the bank's witness.

781. *In its application lodged with the Commission on 15 August 1988, Dombo complained that the courts had heard its former managing director as a witness while the manager of the bank's branch office—the only other person present when the oral agreement had been concluded—had been so heard. They had thereby failed to observe the principle of 'equality of arms' enshrined in Article 6 § 1 of the Convention.[1]*

Judgment of 27 October 1993 *(Chamber) (Series A No. 274)*

782. The Court noted at the outset that it was not called upon to rule in general whether it was permissible to exclude the evidence of a person in civil proceedings to which he was a party. Nor was it called upon to examine the Netherlands law of evidence in civil procedure *in abstracto*. It is not within the province of the Court to substitute its own assessment of the facts for that of the national courts. The Court's task was to ascertain whether the proceedings in their entirety, including the way in which evidence had been permitted, had been 'fair' within the meaning of Article 6 § 1.

783. The requirements inherent in the concept of 'fair hearing' were not necessarily the same in cases concerning the determination of civil rights and obligations as they were in cases concerning the determination of a criminal charge. This was borne out by the absence of detailed provisions such as paragraphs 2 and 3 of Article 6 applying to cases of the former category. Thus, although those provisions had a certain relevance outside the strict confines of criminal law, the Contracting States had greater latitude when dealing with civil cases concerning civil rights and obligations than they had when dealing with criminal cases.

Nevertheless, certain principles concerning the notion of a 'fair hearing' in cases concerning civil rights and obligations emerged from the Court's case law. Thus, the requirement of 'equality of arms', in the sense of a 'fair balance' between the parties, applied in principle to such cases as well as to criminal cases; this was particularly relevant in this case. The Court considered that, in litigation involving opposing private interests, 'equality of arms' implied that each party must be afforded a reasonable opportunity to present his case—including his evidence—under conditions that did not place him at a substantial disadvantage vis-à-vis his opponent. It was left to the national authorities to ensure in each individual case that the requirements of a 'fair hearing' were met.

784. In the instant case, it had been incumbent upon the applicant company to prove that there had been an oral agreement between it and the Bank to extend certain credit facilities. Only two persons had been present at the meeting at which this agreement had allegedly been reached: Dombo's director and the manager of the bank's branch office. Yet only the latter had been permitted to be heard. The Court of Appeal had refused to grant leave to Dombo to call its own representative because the court identified him with Dombo itself.

---

1 In its report of 9 September 1992, the Commission expressed the opinion that there had been a violation of Article 6 § 1 (fourteen votes to five).

During the relevant negotiations, Dombo's director and the branch manager had acted on an equal footing, both being empowered to negotiate on behalf of their respective parties. It was therefore difficult to see why they should not both have been allowed to give evidence. The applicant company had thus been placed at a substantial disadvantage vis-à-vis the Bank and there had accordingly been a violation of Article 6 § 1 (held unanimously).

785. As regards the application of Article 50, the Court considered that Dombo's claims for pecuniary and non-pecuniary damage were based on the assumption that it would have won its case if the national courts had allowed Mr van Reijendam to testify. The Court could not accept this assumption without itself assessing the evidence. The testimony of Mr van Reijendam before the Arnhem Court of Appeal could have resulted in the existence of two opposing statements, one of which would have had to have been accepted against the other on the basis of supporting evidence. It was not for the European Court of Human Rights to say which should have been accepted. This part of the claim for just satisfaction must accordingly be dismissed (held unanimously).

The Court noted that, like the claim for compensation, the claim for reimbursement of costs and expenses incurred in the proceedings before the domestic courts was based on the assumption that the applicant company would have won its case if Mr van Reijendam had been heard. That claim must therefore be dismissed for the same reasons (held unanimously). As for the costs and expenses incurred before the Strasbourg institutions, the Court considered it reasonable, making an assessment on an equitable basis, to award the applicant company 40,000 guilders under this head, less 16,185 French francs paid in legal aid (held unanimously). In contrast, it dismissed Dombo's claim for interest (unanimously).

786. *Summary bibliography*

DE TOMBE-GROOTENHUIS (M.).—'Het Europees Hof en de partij-getuige', *N.J.B.* 1994, pp. 185–188.

KEMPEES (P.M.).—'Na Dombo Beheer: pleidooi voor aanvulling van art. 382 Rv', *N.J.B.* 1994, p. 194.

SPIELMANN (D.).—'Note d'observation sous l'arrêt de la CEDH du 27 novembre 1993 dans l'affaire Dombo Beheer B.V. c. Pays-Bas', *B.D.H.* 1993, pp. 45–46.

STERK (T.).—'De partij-getuige', *NJCM–Bulletin* 1994, pp. 695–698.

SUDRE (F.) and others.—'Chronique de la jurisprudence de la Cour européenne des droits de l'homme. Deuxième partie : juin–décembre 1993', *R.U.D.H.* 1993, pp. 377 *et seq.*

386. Case of Navarra v. France

Time taken to hear an appeal from a decision rejecting an application for release

787. *Paul Navarra, a farmer, lived in Bastia, Upper Corsica. In November 1985, he was remanded in custody on a charge of armed robbery. On 24 March 1986, an investigating judge in Nice dismissed a third application for release on bail. On 23 April 1986, the Indictment Division of the Aix-en-Provence Court of Appeal found inadmissible the appeal filed by the applicant on 25 March 1986 against that decision, which it declared void inasmuch as it had been made in respect of an application which did not comply with procedural requirements. The Court of Cassation quashed that contested decision and remitted the case to the Indictment Division of the Montpellier Court of Appeal, which, on 24 October 1986, confirmed the order of 24 March 1986 rejecting the application for release. On 24 February 1987, the Court of Cassation dismissed an appeal brought by Mr Navarra based on the claim that the Montpellier Court of Appeal had not considered the allegation that there had been a breach of Article 5 § 4 of the Convention on account of the length of the proceedings. On 27 November 1987, the applicant was released and on 17 December it was held that he had no case to answer.*

788. *In his application of 31 July 1987 to the Commission, Mr Navarra complained that his appeal of 25 March 1986 against the order made on the previous day had not been heard on its merits 'speedily' as was required under Article 5 § 4.*[1]

Judgment of 23 November 1993 *(Chamber) (Series A No. 273–B)*

789. The Government contended, as they had already done before the Commission, that Mr Navarra had failed to exhaust his domestic remedies, inasmuch as he had not brought an action for compensation against the State under Article L 781–1 of the Code of Judicial Organization.

The Court dismissed the objection (unanimously): Article L 781–1 circumscribed the State's liability very narrowly and Mr Navarra had not claimed to be the victim of a denial of justice or even of gross

---

1 In its report of 9 September 1992, the Commission expressed the opinion that there had been no violation of Article 5 § 4 (thirteen votes to six).

negligence. Besides, the right to a speedy decision on the lawfulness of detention was to be distinguished from the right to receive compensation for such detention.

790.   In order to satisfy the requirements of the Convention, a periodic judicial review must comply with both the substantive and the procedural rules of the national legislation and moreover be conducted in conformity with the aim of Article 5, namely protection of the individual against arbitrariness.

The French courts had given their decisions within the time-limits laid down by law. The information obtained at the hearing revealed a delay for which the applicant had been responsible. On the other hand, the forwarding of the file to the Court of Cassation and subsequently to the Montpellier Indictment Division had taken some time.

As for protection against arbitrariness, the Court had already ruled on the question as to how far the requirement that such proceedings be conducted 'speedily' extended. In several judgments it had taken account of the 'overall length' of proceedings, thus including the proceedings at all the different levels of jurisdiction. A State which had a second level of jurisdiction must accord to the detainees the same guarantees on appeal as at first instance. The requirement that a decision be given 'speedily' was undeniably one such guarantee; however, in order to determine whether it had been complied with, it was necessary to effect an overall assessment of the proceedings.

In this instance, the Court entertained certain doubts about the overall length of the substantive examination of the appeal of 25 March 1986. It should, however, be borne in mind that Mr Navarra had retained the right, enshrined in French law, to submit further applications for release at any time. Yet from 25 March to 24 October 1986 he had not filed any new applications. Accordingly, there had been no violation of Article 5 § 4 (held unanimously).

791.   *Summary bibliography*

SUDRE (F.) and others.—'Chronique de la jurisprudence de la Cour européenne des droits de l'homme. Deuxième partie : juin–décembre 1993', *R.U.D.H.* 1993, pp. 377 *et seq.*

387. Case of Poitrimol v. France

Judgment of a court of appeal, delivered after proceedings deemed to be *inter partes*, convicting an intentionally absent defendant and refusing to let him be represented by his counsel—Appeal on points of law held inadmissible on grounds connected with the applicant's having absconded

792. *In September 1984, Bernard Poitrimol left France for Turkey with his two children, custody over whom had been granted to his ex-wife—they had been divorced in 1982; he merely had visiting rights. In October 1984, his ex-wife lodged a complaint alleging failure to return the children. He did not return to France. In March 1986, the Marseilles Criminal Court sentenced him to a year's imprisonment and issued a warrant for his arrest.*

Counsel for Mr Poitrimol lodged an appeal against that judgment. At the hearing on 10 September 1986, the Aix-en-Provence Court of Appeal adjourned the case to 4 February 1987 and ordered that Mr Poitrimol should be summoned again, as it considered his presence in court to be necessary. The applicant did not attend the new hearing, but his counsel was present. On 25 February 1987, the Court of Appeal held that Mr Poitrimol—for whom an arrest warrant had been issued and who had absconded—was not entitled to instruct counsel to represent and defend him. Under Article 410 of the Code of Criminal Procedure, it delivered a judgment, given after proceedings deemed to be inter partes, *upholding the contested judgment.*

On 21 December 1987, the Court of Cassation dismissed an appeal brought by Mr Poitrimol on the ground that a convicted person who had not surrendered to an arrest warrant was not entitled to instruct counsel to represent him and appeal on his behalf against conviction.

793. *In his application to the Commission of 21 April 1988, Mr Poitrimol, relying on Article 6 §§ 1 and 3(c) of the Convention, alleged that he had not had a fair trial in that his counsel had not been heard by the Court of Appeal and that he had not validly been able to appeal on points of law.*[1]

---

1 In its report of 3 September 1992, the Commission expressed the opinion that there had been a violation of Article 6 §§ 1 and 3(c) taken together during the proceedings in the Court of Appeal and a violation of paragraph 1 of that article at the stage of the proceedings in the Court of Cassation (fourteen votes to one).

Judgment of 23 November 1993 *(Chamber) (Series A No. 277–A)*

794.   As the requirements of paragraph 3 of Article 6 were to be seen as particular aspects of the right to a fair trial guaranteed by paragraph 1, the Court considered that it should examine Mr Poitrimol's complaints under both provisions taken together. It considered whether an accused who deliberately avoided appearing in person, but intended to be represented by counsel, remained entitled to 'legal assistance of his own choosing' within the meaning of Article 6 § 3(c).

Although not absolute, the right of everyone charged with a criminal offence to be effectively defended by a lawyer, assigned officially if need be, was one of the fundamental features of a fair trial. A person charged with a criminal offence did not lose the benefit of this right merely on account of his not being present at the trial. It had to be determined whether the Aix-en-Provence Court of Appeal had been entitled to deprive Mr Poitrimol of this right, given that he had been summoned personally and had provided no excuse acknowledged as valid for not attending the hearing. It was of capital importance that a defendant should appear, both because of his right to a hearing and because of the need to verify the accuracy of his statements and compare them with those of the victim—whose interests needed to be protected—and of the witnesses. The legislature must accordingly be able to discourage unjustified absences. In the instant case, however, it was unnecessary to decide whether it was permissible in principle to punish such absences by ignoring the right to legal assistance, since the suppression of that right had been disproportionate in the circumstances. It had deprived Mr Poitrimol of his only chance of having arguments of law and fact presented at second instance in respect of the charge against him.

795.   The inadmissibility of the appeal on points of law, on grounds connected with the applicant's having absconded, also amounted to a disproportionate sanction. It was essential that there should have been an opportunity for review by the Court of Cassation of the legal grounds on which the Court of Appeal had rejected the excuses given by Mr Poitrimol for his absence, since whether an accused who did not appear might have arguments of law and fact presented in respect of the charge against him depended on those grounds.

796.   In sum, there had been a breach of Article 6 both in the Court of Appeal and in the Court of Cassation (five votes to four).

797.   In the absence of causal link with the breach of the Convention found in this case, the Court dismissed the applicant's claims for compensation for alleged pecuniary and non-pecuniary damage (unanimously).

The Court awarded Mr Poitrimol 109,000 French francs for costs and expenses incurred before the Court of Cassation and the Convention institutions (eight votes to one).

798. *Summary bibliography*

DECAUX (E.) and TAVERNIER (P.).—'Chronique de jurisprudence de la Cour européenne des droits de l'homme (année 1993)', *J.D.I.* 1994, pp. 821 and 822.

DELAPORTE (V.).—'Affaire Poitrimol c. France', *Cahiers du CREDHO*, no. 2, 1994, pp. 43–62.

KNIGGE (G.).—'Noot', *N.J.* 1994, pp. 1870 and 1871.

MYJER (E.).—'De verstoken vader en zijn raadsman', *NCJM–Bulletin* 1994, pp. 243–250.

SUDRE (F.) and others.—'Chronique de la jurisprudence de la Cour européenne des droits de l'homme. Deuxième partie : juin–décembre 1993', *R.U.D.H.* 1993, pp. 377 *et seq.*

388. Case of A. v. France

Recording of a telephone conversation effected clandestinely by a private citizen with the assistance of a high-ranking police officer

799. *In July or August 1980 in Paris, one Gehrling informed Chief Superintendent Aimé-Blanc, the Head of the Central Office for the Prevention of Serious Crime, of an alleged plan conceived by Mrs A., a cardiologist, to murder Pierre De Varga, who was then in custody. The police officer accepted Mr Gehrling's offer to telephone Mrs A. at her home from his office. The conversation was recorded on a cassette, which the police kept in its archives.*

On 9 November 1981, Mrs A. laid a complaint, together with an application to join the proceedings as a civil party, against Mr Gehrling and Chief Superintendent Aimé-Blanc. In her view, recording a person's conversation held in a private place without that person's consent infringed Articles 368 and 369 of the Criminal Code.

On 28 January 1985, the Paris judge assigned to the investigation of the complaint made an order finding that there was no case to answer. On 22 October 1985, the Indictment Division of the Paris Court of Appeal upheld that order. However, on 11 May 1987 the Court of Cassation quashed the Court of Appeal's judgment and remitted it to the Indictment Division, which was composed differently. On 13 January 1988, the Division upheld the order finding that there was no case to answer, on the ground, inter alia, *that the conversation in question fell outside the scope of private life. On 8 November 1988, the Court of Cassation dismissed an appeal brought by Mrs A.*

On 7 March 1991, the Paris investigating judge responsible for carrying out the investigation into Mrs A. and five other persons on suspicion of attempted murder made an order finding that there was no case to answer.

800. *In her application to the Commission of 15 February 1989, Mrs A. claimed that the recording of one of her telephone conversations had disregarded her right to respect for her private life and her correspondence, guaranteed under Article 8 of the Convention.*[1]

---

1 In its report of 2 September 1992, the Commission expressed the opinion that there had been a violation of Article 8 (nine votes to one).

Judgment of 23 November 1993 *(Chamber) (Series A No. 277–B)*

801.   The Government raised two preliminary objections.

They contended in the first place that the application had been out of time. The Court dismissed the objection (unanimously) on the ground that the appeal to the Court of Cassation against the second judgment of the Indictment Division of the Court of Appeal had not been a futile step and had had the effect at the very least of postponing the beginning of the six-month period.

In the alternative, the Government argued that Mrs A. had neglected to bring a civil action in the ordinary courts for damages against Mr Gehrling and possibly Chief Superintendent Aimé-Blanc and to institute proceedings for damages in the administrative courts in respect of the State's liability on account of the conduct of one of its officials. The Court noted that Mrs A. had laid a complaint, together with an application to join the resulting criminal proceedings as a civil party, and pursued those proceedings to their conclusion. She could not be criticized for not having had recourse to legal remedies which would have been directed essentially to the same end and would not, in any case, have offered better chances of success. The Court therefore dismissed the objection (unanimously).

802.   As far as the merits of the complaint were concerned, the Court started by establishing that there had been an interference. The recording at issue had depended on Mr Gehrling and Mr Aimé-Blanc working together; they could hardly be dissociated from each other. The former had played a decisive role in conceiving and putting into effect the plan to make the recording by going to see the Chief Superintendent and then telephoning Mrs A. Mr Aimé-Blanc, for his part, was an official of a 'public authority'. He had made a crucial contribution to executing the scheme by making available for a short time his office, his telephone and his tape recorder. Admittedly, he had not informed his superiors of his action and had not sought the prior authorization of an investigating judge, but he had been acting in the performance of his duties as a high-ranking police officer. It followed that the public authorities had been involved to such an extent that the State's responsibility under the Convention had been engaged. In any event, the recording represented an interference in respect of which the applicant had been entitled to the protection of the French legal system. Furthermore, the interference at issue had undoubtedly concerned Mrs A.'s right to respect for her 'correspondence'. Consequently, it was not necessary to consider whether it had also affected her 'private life'.

Was the interference justified? The interference had no basis in domestic law and the Government conceded this. The Court therefore held that there had been a violation of Article 8 (unanimously).

That finding made it unnecessary for the Court to rule on compliance with the other requirements of paragraph 2 of that article.

803. Under Article 50, the Court considered that the applicant may have sustained non-pecuniary damage, but that the judgment afforded her sufficient just satisfaction in that regard.

The Court accepted to a large extent Mrs A.'s claim for costs and expenses incurred before the French courts and the Strasbourg institutions, awarding her 50,000 French francs (unanimously).

804. *Summary bibliography*

DECAUX (E.) and TAVERNIER (P.).—'Chronique de jurisprudence de 1a Cour européenne des droits de l'homme (année 1993)', *J.D.I.* 1994, pp. 822 and 823.

SUDRE (F.) and others.—'Chronique de la jurisprudence de la Cour européenne des droits de l'homme. Deuxième partie : juin–décembre 1993', *R.U.D.H.* 1993, pp. 377 *et seq.*

TAMION (E.).—'L'affaire A. c. France', *Cahiers du CREDHO*, no. 2, 1994, pp. 93–104.

WACHSMANN (P.).—'Les écoutes téléphoniques', *R.T.D.H.* 1994, pp. 578–585.

389. Case of Scopelliti v. Italy

Length of civil proceedings

805. *On 10 September 1980, Antonia Scopelliti instituted proceedings against the A.N.A.S. (Azienda Nazionale Autonoma Strade—National Highways Corporation) and the Ministry of Public Works in the Catanzaro District Court. She sought compensation for damage deriving from the unauthorized occupation by the A.N.A.S. of approximately 1,000 square metres of land belonging to her, which had been used to improve a trunk road.*

The court ordered the A.N.A.S. to pay her damages by judgment of 5 October 1987. The District Court's decision, which was lodged with the registry on 14 January 1988, became final on 1 March 1989.

806. *In her application of 6 April 1989 to the Commission, Mrs Scopelliti complained of the length of the civil proceedings which she had instituted, and relied on Article 6 § 1 of the Convention.[1]*

Judgment of 23 November 1993 *(Chamber) (Series A No. 278)*

807. The period to be taken into consideration had begun on 10 December 1980, when the proceedings had been instituted against the A.N.A.S. in the Catanzaro District Court, and had ended on 1 March 1989, the date on which the District Court's judgment had become final. It had therefore lasted a little under eight years and three months.

Three periods could be distinguished. As regards the first period, the Court accepted that the drawing-up of the expert report had given rise to some difficulties. However, it found it hard to see why it should have been necessary to wait—at the very least—almost sixteen months for the report. Mrs Scopelliti had been under no obligation to request the investigating judge to replace the expert; the latter had been working in the context of judicial proceedings, supervised by a judge, who had remained responsible for the preparation and the speedy conduct of the trial. As far as the second part of the proceedings was concerned, it could be seen from the documents in the file, and in particular the records of the hearings, that the adjournments had been requested jointly by the parties. At the time Mrs Scopelliti had not challenged the

---

1 In its report of 1 July 1992, the Commission expressed the unanimous opinion that there had been a violation of Article 6 § 1.

validity of the records. Nevertheless the fact remained that considerable periods of time had elapsed between the majority of the adjournments. The respondent State could not be held responsible for the
thirteen and a half months which had elapsed until the judgment of 14
January 1988 had become final.

Considering the proceedings as a whole, the time which had elapsed
between 10 December 1980 and 14 January 1988 could not be regarded
as 'reasonable'. There had therefore been a violation of Article 6 § 1
(held unanimously).

808. There remained the question of the application of Article 50. In
the Court's view, there was no evidence of any remaining pecuniary
damage. The applicant might, however, have suffered non-pecuniary
damage, but the finding of a violation constituted adequate satisfaction
in this respect (held unanimously).

Having regard to the criteria which it applied in this field, the Court
allowed the applicant's claim for costs and expenses (11,546,310 lire)
(unanimously).

809. *Summary bibliography*

SUDRE (F.) and others.—'Chronique de la jurisprudence de la Cour européenne des droits de l'homme. Deuxième partie : juin–décembre 1993',
R.U.D.H. 1993, pp. 377 *et seq.*

390. Case of Imbrioscia v. Switzerland

Non-attendance by a lawyer at several interrogations of a suspect by the police and by the district prosecutor of the Canton of Zürich

810. *Franco Imbrioscia, an Italian national, was arrested on 2 February 1985 on suspicion of being implicated in the importation of drugs which had been seized at Zürich airport. Before being committed for trial on 10 June 1985, the Zürich district prosecutor or a police officer questioned him on seven occasions. During his first interview, he requested that a lawyer be assigned to him. Yet with the exception of the last interview by a district prosecutor on 6 June 1985, no lawyer was present at those sessions. On 25 February, his lawyer withdrew from the case, but Mr Imbrioscia had been able to communicate freely with a second lawyer, who received transcripts of the various interviews. The district prosecutor did not inform the applicant's lawyers when he was going to be questioned, although it was disputed whether or not his lawyer was told that an interview was to be held on 11 April 1985.*

The applicant was sentenced on 26 June 1985, inter alia, *to a term of seven years' imprisonment and banned from residing in Switzerland for fifteen years. On 17 January 1986, the Zürich Court of Appeal upheld the sentence. The applicant appealed to the Zürich Court of Cassation, but his appeal was dismissed on 8 October 1986. A public-law appeal to the Federal Court was dismissed on 5 November 1987.*

811. *In his application to the Commission of 5 May 1988, Mr Imbrioscia complained that his lawyer had not been present at most of his interrogations and had not attended the examination of various witnesses in Italy, and that an appeal judge had been biased; he relied on Article 6 §§ 1, 2 and 3(b), (c) and (d) of the Convention.*[1]

Judgment of 24 November 1993 *(Chamber) (Series A No. 275)*

812. The Court was unable to accept without qualification the Government's argument that preliminary investigations were not covered by

---

1 On 31 May 1991, the Commission declared the application admissible as regards the first complaint and inadmissible as regards the remainder. In its report of 14 May 1992, it expressed the opinion that there had been no breach of Article 6 §§ 1 and 3(c) (nine votes to five).

Article 6 §§ 1 and 3(c). Admittedly, the primary purpose of Article 6 as far as criminal matters were concerned was to ensure a fair trial by a 'tribunal' competent to determine 'any criminal charge', but it did not follow that the article had no application to pre-trial proceedings. The 'reasonable time' mentioned in paragraph 1 began to run from the moment a 'charge' came into being, within the autonomous meaning to be given to that term. Other requirements of Article 6—especially of paragraph 3—might also be relevant before a case was sent for trial if and in so far as the fairness of the trial was likely to be seriously prejudiced by an initial failure to comply with them.

813. The first lawyer chosen by Mr Imbrioscia had ceased to act for him on 25 February without having visited him. In the meantime, he had been interviewed three times, by the police on 13 and 15 February 1985 and by the Bülach district prosecutor on 18 February.

Even though the applicant had not at the outset had the necessary legal support, a State could not be held responsible for every short-coming on the part of a lawyer appointed for legal aid purposes or chosen by the accused. Owing to the legal profession's independence, the conduct of the defence was essentially a matter between the defendant and his representative; under Article 6 § 3(c), the Contracting States were required to intervene only if a failure by counsel to provide effective representation was manifest or sufficiently brought to their attention. However, the competent authorities had officially designated a lawyer when Mr Imbrioscia informed them on 25 February 1985 that his lawyer had withdrawn from the case.

The new lawyer had received the case file and had gone to see his client in prison, but he had not raised the issue of the non-attendance by a lawyer at the earlier interrogations, of which he had inspected the transcripts. In addition, the applicant had able to talk to his counsel before and after each interview. Counsel had not, however, attended the first two interviews, yet it was not until 17 April that he had complained that he had not been given notice that they were taking place. Thereupon the district prosecutor had allowed him to attend the last interview, which had concluded the investigation.

Lastly, the hearings in the Bülach District Court on 26 June 1985 and those in the Zürich Court of Appeal on 17 January 1986 had been attended by adequate safeguards.

That scrutiny of the proceedings as a whole therefore led the Court to hold that there had been no breach of Article 6 §§ 1 and 3(c) (six votes to three).

814. *Summary bibliography*

KNIGGE (G.).—'Noot', *N.J.* 1994, pp. 2170 and 2171.

LAMBERT (P.).—'L'article 6, 1° de la Convention européenne des droits de l'homme et les juridictions d'instruction', *J.T.* 1994, pp. 496 and 497.

PETTITI (L.-E.).—'Droits de l'homme', *R.S.C.D.P.C.* 1994, pp. 144 and 145.

SUDRE (F.) and others.—'Chronique de la jurisprudence de la Cour européenne des droits de l'homme. Deuxième partie : juin–décembre 1993', *R.U.D.H.* 1993, pp. 377 *et seq.*

391. Case of Informationsverein Lentia and Others v. Austria

Impossibility of setting up and operating private radio or television stations because of the monopoly of the Austrian Broadcasting Corporation

815. *Informationsverein Lentia was an association of co-proprietors and residents of a housing development in Linz, comprising 458 apartments and 30 businesses. On 9 June 1978, it applied to the Linz Regional Post and Telecommunications Head Office for a licence to set up and operate an internal cable television network whose programmes were to be confined to questions of mutual interest concerning members' rights. On 23 November 1979, the National Post and Telecommunications Head Office, attached to the Federal Ministry of Transport, finally turned down the application as lacking any legal basis. On 16 December 1983, the Constitutional Court dismissed the applicant's appeal against that decision: the Constitutional Law guaranteeing the independence of broadcasting had introduced a licensing system within the meaning of the last sentence of Article 10 § 1 of the Convention; that system was intended to ensure objectivity and diversity of opinions and would be ineffective if it were possible for everybody to obtain the requisite authorization; as matters stood, the right to broadcast was restricted to the Austrian Broadcasting Corporation (ORF), as no implementing legislation had been enacted in addition to the law governing that organization. The Constitutional Court then remitted the complaint to the Administrative Court, which dismissed it on 10 September 1986, essentially on the grounds relied on by the Constitutional Court.*

816. *Between 1987 and 1989, Jörg Haider elaborated a project for the setting up, with other persons, of a private radio station in Carinthia. He subsequently gave up the idea after a study had shown him that, according to the applicable law as interpreted by the Constitutional Court, he would not be able to obtain the necessary licence.*

817. *Arbeitsgemeinschaft Offenes Radio (AGORA), an Austrian association and a member of the* Fédération européenne des radios libres, *planned to establish a radio station in southern Carinthia in order to broadcast non-commercial radio programmes in German and Slovene. In 1988, AGORA applied for a licence, which was refused by the Klagenfurt Regional Post and Telecommunications Head Office on*

19 December 1989 and by the National Head Office in Vienna on 9 August 1990. On 30 September 1991, the Constitutional Court dismissed an appeal against that decision.

818. Wilhelm Weber was a shareholder in an Italian company operating a commercial radio station broadcasting to Austria and wished to operate a radio station in Austria itself. However, in view of the legislation in force, he decided not to make any application to the appropriate authorities.

819. Radio Melody GmbH was a private limited company incorporated under Austrian law. On 8 November 1988, it asked the Linz Regional Post and Telecommunications Head Office to allocate it a frequency so that it could operate a local radio station which it hoped to launch in Salzburg. On 28 April 1989, its application was rejected, a decision confirmed on 12 July 1989 by the National Head Office and on 18 June 1990 by the Constitutional Court.

820. The five applicants lodged applications with the Commission on 16 April 1987, 15 May 1989, 27 September 1989, 18 September 1989 and 20 August 1990. They complained that they were unable to set up and operate radio or, in the case of Informationsverein Lentia, television stations, and relied on Article 10 of the Convention. The first and second applicants also complained of discrimination contrary to Article 14, read in conjunction with Article 10. The fifth applicant alleged in addition a breach of Article 6 § 1, inasmuch as it had not been able to bring the dispute before a 'tribunal'.[1]

Judgment of 24 November 1993 *(Chamber) (Series A No. 276)*

821. The Court first observed that the inability to obtain an operating licence by reason of the ORF's monopoly amounted to an 'interference' with the applicants' exercise of their freedom to impart information and ideas. The only question which arose was therefore whether such interference was justified.

---

1 On 15 January 1992, the Commission found the complaints concerning Articles 10 and 14 admissible and that relating to Article 6 inadmissible. In its report of 9 September 1992, it expressed the opinion that there had been a violation of Article 10 (unanimously as regards the first applicant and by fourteen votes to one for the others) and that it was not necessary also to examine the case from the point of view of Article 14 (unanimously as regards the first applicant and by fourteen votes to one for the third applicant).

It recalled that the object and purpose of the third sentence of Article 10 § 1 and the scope of its application must be considered in the context of the article as a whole and in particular in relation to the requirements of paragraph 2, to which licensing measures remained subject. It was therefore necessary to ascertain whether the rules in question complied with both of those provisions.

822. The purpose of the third sentence of Article 10 § 1 was to make it clear that States were permitted to regulate by a licensing system the way in which broadcasting was organized in their territories, particularly in its technical aspects. Technical aspects were undeniably important, but the grant or refusal of a licence might also be made conditional on other considerations, including such matters as the nature and objectives of a proposed station, its potential audience at national, regional or local level, the rights and needs of a specific audience and the obligations deriving from international legal instruments. This might lead to interferences whose aims would be legitimate under the third sentence of paragraph 1, even though they did not correspond to any of the aims set out in paragraph 2. The compatibility of such interferences with the Convention must nevertheless be assessed in the light of the other requirements of paragraph 2. The monopoly system operated in Austria was capable of contributing to the quality and balance of programmes, through the supervisory powers over the media thereby conferred on the authorities. In the circumstances of the case it was therefore consistent with the third sentence of paragraph 1.

823. Did the interference also satisfy the requirements of paragraph 2? The interferences complained were 'prescribed by law' and this was not disputed by any of the participants in the proceedings. Their aim had already been held by the Court to be legitimate. In contrast, a problem arose in connection with the question whether the interferences were 'necessary in a democratic society'.

The Government had drawn attention in the first place to the political dimension of the activities of the audio-visual media, which was reflected in Austria in the aims fixed for such media under Article 1 § 2 of the Constitutional Broadcasting Law, namely to guarantee the objectivity and impartiality of reporting, diversity of opinions, balanced programming and the independence of persons and bodies responsible for programmes. Only the system in force, based on the monopoly of the ORF, made it possible for the authorities to ensure compliance with those requirements.

The Court recalled that it had frequently stressed the fundamental role of freedom of expression in a democratic society, in particular where, through the press, it served to impart information and ideas of general interest, which the public was moreover entitled to receive. Such an undertaking could not be successfully accomplished unless it was grounded in the principle of pluralism, of which the State was the ultimate guarantor. That observation was especially valid in relation to audio-visual media, whose programmes were often broadcast very widely. Of all the means of ensuring that those values were respected, a public monopoly was the one which imposed the greatest restrictions on freedom of expression, namely the total impossibility of broadcasting otherwise than through a national station and, in some cases, to a very limited extent through a local cable station. The far-reaching character of such restrictions meant that they could only be justified where they corresponded to a pressing need. As a result of the technical progress made over the last decades, justification for such restrictions could no longer be found today in considerations relating to the number of frequencies and channels available. Secondly, for the purposes of the present case they had lost much of their raison d'être in view of the multiplication of foreign programmes aimed at Austrian audiences and the decision of the Administrative Court to recognize the lawfulness of their retransmission by cable. Finally and above all, it could not be argued that there were no equivalent less restrictive solutions; the Court cited by way of example the practice of certain countries which either issued licences subject to specified conditions of variable content or made provision for forms of private participation in the activities of the national corporation.

The Government had also adduced an economic argument, namely that the Austrian market was too small to sustain a sufficient number of stations to avoid regroupings and the formation of 'private monopolies'.

In the Court's view, that reasoning was contradicted by the experience of several European States of comparable size to Austria in which the coexistence of private and public stations, according to rules which varied from country to country and were accompanied by measures preventing the development of private monopolies, showed the fears expressed to be groundless.

In short, the Court considered that the interferences in issue were disproportionate to the aim pursued and were, accordingly, not necessary in a democratic society. There had therefore been a violation of Article 10 (held unanimously).

824. That finding made it unnecessary for the Court to determine whether there had also been a breach of Article 14, taken in conjunction with Article 10 (held unanimously).

825. Informationsverein Lentia claimed 900,000 schillings for pecuniary damage and Radio Melody 5,444,714.66; they based their claims on the assumption that they would not have failed to obtain the licences applied for if the Austrian legislation had been in conformity with Article 10. This was, however, speculation, in view of the discretion left in this field to the authorities. No compensation was therefore recoverable under this head (held unanimously).

By way of costs and expenses, the applicants claimed respectively 136,023.54 schillings (Informationsverein Lentia), 513,871.20 schillings (Mr Haider), 390,115.20 schillings (AGORA), 519,871.20 schillings (Mr Weber) and 605,012.40 schillings (Radio Melody). Making an assessment on an equitable basis, the Court awarded 165,000 schillings each to Informationsverein Lentia, AGORA and Radio Melody for the proceedings conducted in Austria and in Strasbourg. Mr Haider and Mr Weber, who had appeared only before the Convention institutions, were entitled to 100,000 schillings each (held unanimously).

826. *Summary bibliography*

COHEN-JONATHAN (G.).—'Note', *L.P.*, no. 108, January-February 1994, VI, p. 12.

DECAUX (E.) and TAVERNIER (P.).—'Chronique de jurisprudence de la Cour européenne des droits de l'homme (année 1993)', *J.D.I.* 1994, pp. 819 and 820.

SUDRE (F.) and others.—'Chronique de la jurisprudence de la Cour européenne des droits de l'homme. Deuxième partie : juin–décembre 1993', *R.U.D.H.* 1993, pp. 377 *et seq.*

392. Case of Holm v. Sweden

Composition of a jury in defamation proceedings instituted by a private prosecutor before a District Court

827. *In 1985 a publishing house, Tidens förlag AB, published a book entitled* 'Till höger om neutraliteten' *(To the right of neutrality), the author of which, Mr Sven-Ove Hansson, had previously served as an ideological adviser to the Swedish Social Democratic Workers Party ('the SAP'). Eighty-five per cent of the shares in Tidens förlag AB were held by a company owned by the SAP. The book contained a survey of right-wing organizations and individuals, including a chapter on Carl Holm and his involvement in Contra, a foundation whose aim was to scrutinize governments of communist regimes in Eastern Europe and the activities of the SAP.*

On 15 April 1986, the applicant brought a private prosecution for aggravated libel in the District Court of Stockholm against the author of the book and the publishing house; he claimed 200,000 Swedish kronor in damages. At the defendants' request, the case was considered with a jury in accordance with the provisions of the Freedom of the Press Act.

On 10 November 1986, the applicant asked the court to exclude as disqualified those jurors who were members of the SAP. The court rejected his request on 10 November 1986. On 4 December 1986, the Court of Appeal dismissed an appeal brought by the applicant. On 14 October 1987, the District Court, sitting with a jury of nine, examined the merits of the case. Five jurymen were members of the SAP and held or had held various offices in it and on its behalf at local level. By judgment of the same date, the District Court dismissed the charges made by the applicant and his claims for damages and ordered him to pay the costs. No appeal would lie against the jury's verdict acquitting the applicant.

828. *In his application to the Commission of 24 January 1987, Mr Holm alleged a violation of Article 6 § 1 of the Convention.*[1]

Judgment of 25 November 1993 *(Chamber) (Series A No. 279–A)*

829. Only the independence and the objective impartiality of the five jurors who were affiliated to the SAP were in issue; the applicant did not contest their subjective impartiality.

---

1 In its report of 13 October 1992, the Commission expressed the opinion that there had been a violation of Article 6 § 1 (fourteen votes to one).

In Swedish law, a series of safeguards ensured the independence and impartiality of juries. In addition, under the relevant rules, the defence had been given the benefit of certain safeguards that had not been applicable to the applicant as a private prosecutor. Those features, most of which were typical of a criminal trial involving a jury and designed to enhance freedom of the press, did not as such constitute a legitimate reason to fear a lack of independence and impartiality on the part of the jurors.

There had nevertheless been links between the defendants and the jurymen in question; those jurors had been active members of the SAP and held or had held offices in or on behalf of the SAP; one of the defendants, the publishing house, was directly owned by the SAP; and the other defendant, the author, was an ideological adviser to the SAP. Furthermore, the impugned passages of the book were clearly of a political nature and had undoubtedly raised matters of concern to the SAP. The applicant's fears in this respect had been objectively justified. The defect in the first-instance proceedings could not be cured by an appeal. There had therefore been a violation of Article 6 § 1 (seven votes to two).

830. The Court dismissed the claim for compensation for non-pecuniary damage and awarded 125,000 Swedish kronor for lawyer's fees, less the amount granted by the Council of Europe by way of legal aid (unanimously).

831. *Summary bibliography*

SUDRE (F.) and others.—'Chronique de la jurisprudence de la Cour européenne des droits de l'homme. Deuxième partie : juin–décembre 1993', *R.U.D.H.* 1993, pp. 377 *et seq.*

393. Case of Zander v. Sweden

Lack of access to a court to challenge the granting of a refuse-dumping permit to a company on neighbouring land

832. *In 1979, it was discovered that refuse containing cyanide had been left on a dump adjoining land owned by Mr and Mrs Zander at Gryta and an analysis of drinking water from a nearby well showed excessive levels of cyanide. In October 1983, further analyses revealed excessive levels of cyanide in six other wells near the dump, one of which was on the applicants' property. As a result, the use of the water was prohibited and the landowners concerned were temporarily provided with municipal drinking water. However, in June 1983 the maximum permitted level of cyanide was raised and, as from February 1985, the municipality stopped supplying the landowners in question with water. On 1 July 1983, the National Licensing Board for Protection of the Environment issued a company (VAFAB) with a licence to take delivery of and treat household and industrial waste on the dump.*

In July 1986, VAFAB asked the Licensing Board to renew its permit and allow it to expand its activities on the dump. Mr and Mrs Zander together with other landowners demanded that the request should not be granted without an obligation being imposed on VAFAB by way of precautionary measure under section 5 of the 1969 Environment Protection Act: namely that VAFAB should be obliged to supply drinking water free of charge. However, on 13 March 1987, the Licensing Board granted VAFAB's request and dismissed the landowners' claim on the ground that there was no likely connection between the dump and the pollution of the well water. On 17 March 1988, the Government, as the final instance of appeal, dismissed the applicants' appeal against the Licensing Board's decision.

833. *In their application to the Commission of 2 September 1988, Mr and Mrs Zander alleged a violation of Article 6 § 1 of the Convention in that it was not possible for them to have the decision authorizing VAFAB to increase its activities on the dump reviewed by a court.*[1]

---

1 In its report of 14 October 1992, the Commission expressed the opinion that there had been a violation of Article 6 § 1 (unanimously).

Judgment of 25 November 1993 *(Chamber) (Series A No. 279–B)*

834. The request made by the applicants to the Licensing Board had been based on the 1969 Act, which laid down certain obligations incumbent upon a person who engaged or intended to engage in an environmentally hazardous activity, without however specifying who was to be the beneficiary of those obligations. The applicants could arguably maintain that they were entitled under Swedish law to protection against pollution of the well as a result of VAFAB's activities on the dump. There had been a serious disagreement between the applicants and the Licensing Board raising issues capable of going to the lawfulness of the conditions attached to VAFAB's licence. The outcome of the dispute had been directly decisive for the applicants' entitlement to the aforementioned protection. The appeal lodged by the applicants with the Government against the Licensing Board's decision had thus involved a 'determination' of one of their 'rights'.

The applicants' claim had been directly concerned with their ability to use the well water for drinking purposes, which was one facet of their right as owners of the land. The right of property was therefore a 'civil right' and Article 6 § 1 was applicable (held unanimously).

835. Under Swedish law, it had not been possible at the material time for the applicants to have the relevant decision reviewed by a court and consequently there had been a violation of Article 6 § 1 (held unanimously).

836. Under Article 50, the Court awarded each of the applicants 30,000 Swedish kronor for non-pecuniary damage and, to them both jointly, 145,860 kronor for costs and expenses, less 16,626 French francs paid by way of legal aid (unanimously).

837. *Summary bibliography*

DECAUX (E.) and TAVERNIER (P.).—'Chronique de jurisprudence de la Cour européenne des droits de l'homme (année 1993)', *J.D.I.* 1994, pp. 823 and 824.

SUDRE (F.) and others.—'Chronique de la jurisprudence de la Cour européenne des droits de l'homme. Deuxième partie : juin–décembre 1993', *R.U.D.H.* 1993, pp. 377 *et seq.*

Conclusion

838. This survey of the judgments of European Court of Human Rights would be incomplete without a brief examination of their implementation and effectiveness.

839. It goes without saying that States which have been found to have violated the Convention (the Court has found one or more violations in 262 cases out of 395—Annex D) are under a duty to comply with the judgments. The Court's judgments are final (Convention, Article 52), that is to say no appeal is possible to another authority. However, the Court may entertain two sorts of applications.

The first is the application for interpretation, which is admissible within three years of the date of the judgment. It is intended simply to clarify the operative part of the judgment, that is to say the final part containing the decision proper. This has been done only once to date, in the *Ringeisen case*.[1]

The second is the request for revision: such a request is made by a State which is party to the proceedings or the Commission when it has become aware of a fact such as to have a decisive influence which was unknown to the Court and the applicant for revision at the time when the judgment was delivered. The time-limit here is six months from the discovery of the fact in question, but the situation has yet to arise.

The Court's judgments have binding force but cannot be directly executed: they do not annul or amend any measure of the State which has been held to be at fault, be it a law, or regulation, an administrative measure or a judicial decision. Except where they grant the applicant monetary compensation, they leave the State every latitude as regards the consequences flowing from the finding of a violation. They do not indicate which measures should be taken to remedy the breach or the time-scale within which they should be taken. However, the execution of the judgments is monitored by the Committee of Ministers of the Council of Europe. If a State were to refuse to apply a judgment given against it—a possibility which unfortunately cannot be ruled out—the Committee Would doubtless adopt a recommendation, but the conflict would probably result in the withdrawal or exclusion of the offending State from the Council of Europe.

1 See Vol. I, 106–108

840. How can the practical effectiveness of the judgments be assessed? Although they are binding only on the States directly involved in the proceedings, it is desirable and natural that they should influence authorities in other countries which are faced with similar problems. Their consequences may take the form of both 'redress' and 'preventive' action.

The first consequences are the most obvious ones. Usually they are individual in scope: the grant of 'just satisfaction' to an injured party will consist in the award of a sum of money, or the withdrawal of a measure or the mere declaration that a right has been violated. Sometimes the consequences are general in scope: in such a case, the judgment will give rise to or accelerate legal reform.

Consequences of the second type are more difficult to gauge, but they are no less beneficial. In such a case, during the proceedings before the Court domestic law undergoes changes or the Government gives certain undertakings. More generally and above all in those countries which have accepted the right of individual petition to the Commission, the national authorities, in particular the courts, will take care to ensure that the Convention is complied with in the day-to-day exercise of their functions. Indeed, precisely because of the often vague nature of the Convention, they may find inspiration in the solutions adopted by the Court.

841. Following awkward and somewhat lethargic beginnings—so much so, that some doubted its ability to survive—the Court has developed a rich and influential body of case-law. In parallel to the number of judgments delivered, which has been tending to accelerate for some years, the variety of the problems dealt with and their interest for the 'ordinary' citizen—in other words, for people who are neither in detention or convicts—are increasing. Does that expansion reflect a heightened disregard for human rights in Europe, a disturbing erosion of freedoms? Probably not. In point of fact, the Commission and to a smaller extent the States are showing less reluctance—or more enthusiasm, if it is preferred—to address themselves to the Court now that they are more aware of its utility. No one can tell if this trend will prove to be long-lived, but in all probability it will be pursued at least by the applicants after the entry into force of Protocol No. 9. It any event, one thing is certain—the cases already decided or pending have not exhausted the field of intervention of the Court of Human Rights. Many provisions of the Convention will sooner or later need interpreting and those which have already been considered will inevitably be faced with new situations, if only as a result of changes in our societies and in our attitudes.

APPENDIX A

Convention for the Protection of Human Rights and Fundamental Freedoms[1]

(at 31 December 1993)

The Governments signatory hereto, being Members of the Council of Europe,

Considering the Universal Declaration of Human Rights proclaimed by the General Assembly of the United Nations on 10th December 1948;

Considering that this Declaration aims at securing the universal and effective recognition and observance of the Rights therein declared;

Considering that the aim of the Council of Europe is the achievement of greater unity between its Members and that one of the methods by which that aim is to be pursued is the maintenance and further realisation of Human Rights and Fundamental Freedoms;

Reaffirming their profound belief in those Fundamental Freedoms which are the foundation of justice and peace in the world and are best maintained on the one hand by an effective political democracy and on the other by a common understanding and observance of the Human Rights upon which they depend;

Being resolved, as the Governments of European countries which are likeminded and have a common heritage of political traditions, ideals, freedom and the rule of law to take the first steps for the collective enforcement of certain of the Rights stated in the Universal Declaration,

Have agreed as follows:

Article 1

The High Contracting Parties shall secure to everyone within their jurisdiction the rights and freedoms defined in Section 1 of this Convention.

SECTION 1

Article 2

1. Everyone's right to life shall be protected by law. No one shall be deprived of his life intentionally save in the execution of a sentence of a court following his conviction of a crime for which this penalty is provided by law.

---

1. As amended by Protocols Nos. 3, 5 and 8, which entered into force on 21 September 1970, 20 December 1971 and 1 January 1990 respectively.

2. Deprivation of life shall not be regarded as inflicted in contravention of this Article when it results from the use of force which is no more than absolutely necessary:

(a) in defence of any person from unlawful violence;

(b) in order to effect a lawful arrest or prevent the escape of a person lawfully detained;

(c) in action lawfully taken for the purpose of quelling a riot or insurrection.

Article 3

No one shall be subjected to torture or inhuman or degrading treatment or punishment.

Article 4

1. No one shall be held in slavery or servitude.

2. No one shall be required to perform forced or compulsory labour.

3. For the purpose of this Article the term 'forced or compulsory labour' shall not include:

(a) any work required to be done in the ordinary course of detention imposed according to the provisions of Article 5 of this Convention or during conditional release from such detention;

(b) any service of a military character or, in case of conscientious objectors in countries where they are recognised, service exacted instead of compulsory military service;

(c) any service exacted in case of an emergency or calamity threatening the life or well-being of the community;

(d) any work or service which forms part of normal civic obligations.

Article 5

1. Everyone has the right to liberty and security of person. No one shall be deprived of his liberty save in the following cases and in accordance with a procedure prescribed by law:

(a) the lawful detention of a person after conviction by a competent court;

(b) the lawful arrest or detention of a person for non-compliance with the lawful order of a court or in order to secure the fulfilment of any obligation prescribed by law;

(c) the lawful arrest or detention of a person effected for the purpose of bringing him before the competent legal authority on a reasonable suspicion of having committed an offence or when it is reasonably considered necessary to prevent his committing an offence or fleeing after having done so;

(d) the detention of a minor by lawful order for the purpose of educational supervision or his lawful detention for the purpose of bringing him before the competent legal authority;

(e) the lawful detention of persons for the prevention of the spreading of infectious diseases, of persons of unsound mind, alcoholics or drug addicts or vagrants;

(f) the lawful arrest or detention of a person to prevent his effecting an unauthorised entry into the country or of a person against whom action is being taken with a view to deportation or extradition.

2. Everyone who is arrested shall be informed promptly, in a language which he understands, of the reasons for his arrest and of any charge against him.

3. Everyone arrested or detained in accordance with the provisions of paragraph 1 (c) of this Article shall be brought promptly before a judge or other officer authorized by law to exercise judicial power and shall be entitled to trial within a reasonable time or to release pending trial. Release may be conditioned by guarantee to appear for trial.

4. Everyone who is deprived of his liberty by arrest or detention shall be entitled to take proceedings by which the lawfulness of his detention shall be decided speedily by a court and his release ordered if the detention is not lawful.

5. Everyone who has been the victim of arrest or detention in contravention of the provisions of this Article shall have an enforceable right to compensation.

Article 6

1. In the determination of his civil rights and obligations or of any criminal charge against him, everyone is entitled to a fair and public hearing within a reasonable time by an independent and impartial tribunal established by law. Judgment shall be pronounced publicly but the press and public may be excluded from all or part of the trial in the interests of morals, public order or national security in a democratic society, where the interests of juveniles or the protection of the private life of the parties so require, or to the extent strictly necessary in the opinion of the court in special circumstances where publicity would prejudice the interests of justice.

2. Everyone charged with a criminal offence shall be presumed innocent until proved guilty according to the law.

3. Everyone charged with a criminal offence has the following minimum rights:

(a) to be informed promptly, in a language which he understands and in detail, of the nature and cause of the accusation against him;

(b) to have adequate time and facilities for the preparation of his defence;

(c) to defend himself in person or through legal assistance of his own choosing or, if he has not sufficient means to pay for legal assistance, to be given it free when the interests of justice so require;

(d) to examine or have examined witnesses against him and to obtain the attendance and examination of witnesses on his behalf under the same conditions as witnesses against him;

(e) to have the free assistance of an interpreter if he cannot understand or speak the language used in court.

Article 7

1. No one shall be held guilty of any criminal offence on account of any act or omission which did not constitute a criminal offence under national or international law at the time when it was committed. Nor shall a heavier penalty be imposed than the one that was applicable at the time the criminal offence was committed.

2. This Article shall not prejudice the trial and punishment of any person for any act or omission which, at the time when it was committed, was criminal according to the general principles of law recognised by civilised nations.

Article 8

1. Everyone has the right to respect for his private and family life, his home and his correspondence.

2. There shall be no interference by a public authority with the exercise of this right except such as is in accordance with the law and is necessary in a democratic society in the interests of national security, public safety or the economic well-being of the country, for the prevention of disorder or crime, for the protection of health or morals, or for the protection of the rights and freedoms of others.

Article 9

1. Everyone has the right to freedom of thought, conscience and religion; this right includes freedom to change his religion or belief and freedom, either alone or in community with others and in public or private, to manifest his religion or belief, in worship, teaching, practice and observance.

2. Freedom to manifest one's religion or belief shall be subject only to such limitations as are prescribed by law and are necessary in a democratic society in the interests of public safety, for the protection of public order, health or morals, or for the protection of the rights and freedoms of others.

Article 10

1. Everyone has the right to freedom of expression. This right shall include freedom to hold opinions and to receive and impart information and ideas without interference by public authority and regardless of frontiers. This article shall not prevent States from requiring the licensing of broadcasting, television or cinema enterprises.

2. The exercise of these freedoms, since it carries with it duties and responsibilities, may be subject to such formalities, conditions, restrictions or penalties as are prescribed by law and are necessary in a democratic society, in the interests of national security, territorial integrity or public safety, for the prevention of disorder or crime, for the protection of health or morals, for the protection of the reputation or rights of others, for preventing the disclosure of information received in confidence, or for maintaining the authority and impartiality of the judiciary.

Article 11

1. Everyone has the right to freedom of peaceful assembly and freedom of association with others, including the right to form and join trade unions for the protection of his interests.

2. No restrictions shall be placed on the exercise of these rights other than such as are prescribed by law and are necessary in a democratic society in the interests of national security or public safety, for the prevention of disorder or crime, for the protection of health or morals or for the protection of the rights and freedoms of others. This article shall not prevent the imposition of lawful restrictions on the exercise of these rights by members of the armed forces, of the police or of the administration of the State.

Article 12

Men and women of marriageable age have the right to marry and found a family, according to the national laws governing the exercise of this right.

Article 13

Everyone whose rights and freedoms as set forth in this Convention are violated shall have an effective remedy before a national authority notwithstanding that the violation has been committed by persons acting in an official capacity.

Article 14

The enjoyment of the rights and freedoms set forth in this Convention shall be secured without discrimination on any ground such as sex, race, colour, language, religion, political or other opinion, national or social origin, association with a national minority, property, birth or other status.

Article 15

1. In time of war or other public emergency threatening the life of the nation, any High Contracting Party may take measures derogating from its obligations under this Convention to the extent strictly required by the exigencies of the situation, provided that such measures are not inconsistent with its other obligations under international law.

2. No derogation from Article 2, except in respect of deaths resulting from lawful acts of war, or from Articles 3, 4 (paragraph 1) and 7 shall be made under this provision.

3. Any High Contracting Party availing itself of this right of derogation shall keep the Secretary General of the Council of Europe fully informed of the measures which it has taken and the reasons therefor. It shall also inform the Secretary General of the Council of Europe when such measures have ceased to operate and provisions of the Convention are again being fully executed.

Article 16

Nothing in Articles 10, 11 and 14 shall be regarded as preventing the High Contracting Parties from imposing restrictions on the political activity of aliens.

Article 17

Nothing in this Convention may be interpreted as implying for any State, group or person any right to engage in any activity or perform any act aimed at the destruction of any of the rights and freedoms set forth herein or at their limitation to a greater extent than is provided for in the Convention.

Article 18

The restrictions permitted under this Convention to the said rights and freedoms shall not be applied for any purpose other than those for which they have been prescribed.

SECTION II

Article 19

To ensure the observance of the engagements undertaken by the High Contracting Parties in the present Convention, there shall be set up:

(a) A European Commission of Human Rights, hereinafter referred to as 'the Commission';

(b) A European Court of Human Rights, hereinafter referred to as 'the Court'.

SECTION III

Article 20

1. The Commission shall consist of a number of members equal to that of the High Contracting Parties. No two members of the Commission may be nationals of the same State.

2. The Commission shall sit in plenary sessions. It may, however, set up Chambers, each composed of at least seven members. The Chambers may examine petitions submitted under Article 25 of this Convention which can be dealt with on the basis of established case law or which raise no serious question affecting the interpretation or application of the Convention. Subject to this restriction and to the provisions of paragraph 5 of this Article, the Chambers shall exercise all the powers conferred on the Commission by the Convention.

The member of the Commission elected in respect of a High Contracting party against which a petition has been lodged shall have the right to sit on a Chamber to which that petition has been referred.

3. The Commission may set up committees, each composed of a least three members, with the power, exercisable by a unanimous vote, to declare inadmissible or strike from its list of cases a petition submitted under Article 25, when such a decision can be taken without further examination.

4. A Chamber or committee may at any time relinquish jurisdiction in favour of the plenary Commission, which may also order the transfer to it of any petition referred to a Chamber or committee.

5. Only the plenary Commission can exercise the following powers:

(a) The examination of applications submitted under Article 24;

(b) the bringing of a case before the Court in accordance with Article 48(a).

(c) the drawing up of rules of procedure in accordance with Article 36.

Article 21

1. The members of the Commission shall be elected by the Committee of Ministers by an absolute majority of votes, from a list of names drawn up by the Bureau of the Consultative Assembly; each group of the Representatives of the High Contracting Parties in the Consultative Assembly shall put forward three candidates, of whom two at least shall be its nationals.

2. As far as applicable, the same procedure shall be followed to complete the Commission in the event of other States subsequently becoming Parties to this Convention, and in filling casual vacancies.

3. The candidates shall be of high moral character and must either possess the qualifications required for appointment to high judicial office or be persons of recognised competence in national or international law.

Article 22

1. The members of the Commission shall be elected for a period of six years. They may be re-elected. However, of the members elected at the first election, the terms of seven members shall expire at the end of three years.

2. The members whose terms are to expire at the end of the initial period of three years shall be chosen by lot by the Secretary General of the Council of Europe immediately after the first election has been completed.

3. In order to ensure that, as far as possible, one half of the membership of the Commission shall be renewed every three years, the Committee of Ministers may decide, before proceeding to any subsequent election, that the term or terms of office of one or more members to be elected shall be for a period other than six years but not more than nine and not less than three years.

4. In cases where more than one term of office is involved and the Committee of Ministers applies the proceeding paragraph, the allocation of the terms of office shall be effected by the drawing of lots by the Secretary General, immediately after the election.

5. A member of the Commission elected to replace a member whose term of office has not expired shall hold office for the remainder of his predecessor's term.

6. The members of the Commission shall hold office until replaced. After having been replaced, they shall continue to deal with such cases as they already have under consideration.

Article 23

The members of the Commission shall sit on the Commission in their individual capacity. During their term of office they shall not hold any position which is incompatible with their independence and impartiality as members of the Commission or the demands of this office.

Article 24

Any High Contracting Party may refer to the Commission, through the Secretary General of the Council of Europe, any alleged breach of the provisions of the Convention by another High Contracting Party.

Article 25

1. The Commission may receive petitions addressed to the Secretary General of the Council of Europe from any person, non-governmental organisation or group of individuals claiming to be the victim of a violation by one of the High Contracting Parties of the rights set forth in this Convention, provided that the High Contracting Party against which the complaint has been lodged has declared that it recognises the competence of the Commission to receive such petitions. Those of the High Contracting

Parties who have made such a declaration undertake not to hinder in any way the effective exercise of this right.

2. Such declarations may be made for a specific period.

3. The declarations shall be deposited with the Secretary General of the Council of Europe who shall transmit copies thereof to the High Contracting Parties and publish them.

4. The Commission shall only exercise the powers provided for in this Article when at least six High Contracting Parties are bound by declarations made in accordance with the preceding paragraphs.

Article 26

The Commission may only deal with the matter after all domestic remedies have been exhausted, according to the generally recognised rules of international law, and within a period of six months from the date on which the final decision was taken.

Article 27

1. The Commission shall not deal with any petition submitted under Article 25 which:

(a) is anonymous, or

(b) is substantially the same as a matter which has already been examined by the Commission or has already been submitted to another procedure of international investigation or settlement and if it contains no relevant new information.

2. The Commission shall consider inadmissible any petition submitted under Article 25 which it considers incompatible with the provisions of the present Convention, manifestly ill-founded, or an abuse of the right of petition.

3. The Commission shall reject any petition referred to it which it considers inadmissible under Article 26.

Article 28

1. In the event of the Commission accepting a petition referred to it:

(a) it shall, with a view of ascertaining the facts, undertake together with the representatives of the parties an examination of the petition and, if need be, an investigation, for the effective conduct of which the States concerned shall furnish all necessary facilities, after an exchange of view with the Commission;

(b) it shall at the same time place itself at the disposal of the parties concerned with a view to securing a friendly settlement of the matter on the basis of respect for human rights as defined in this Convention.

Article 29

After it has accepted a petition submitted under Article 25, the Commission may nevertheless decide by a majority of two-thirds of its members to reject the petition if, in the course of its examination, it finds that the existence of one of the grounds for non-acceptance provided for in Article 27 has been established.

In such a case, the decision shall be communicated to the parties.

Article 30

1. The Commission may at any stage of the proceedings decide to strike a petition out of its list of cases where the circumstances lead to the conclusion that:

(a) the applicant does not intend to pursue his petition, or

(b) the matter has been resolved, or

(c) for any other reason established by the Commission, it is no longer justified to continue the examination of the petition.

However, the Commission shall continue the examination of a petition if respect for human rights as defined in this Convention so requires.

2. If the Commission decides to strike a petition out of its list after having accepted it, it shall draw up a Report which shall contain a statement of the facts and the decision striking out the petition together with the reasons therefor. The Report shall be transmitted to the parties as well as to the Committee of Ministers for information. The Commission may publish it.

3. The Commission may decide to restore a petition to its list of cases if it considers that the circumstances justify such a course.

Article 31

1. If a solution is not reached, the Commission shall draw up a report on the facts and state its opinion as to whether the facts found disclose a breach by the State concerned of its obligations under the Convention. The opinions of all the members of the Commission on this point may be stated in the report.

2. The report shall be transmitted to the Committee of Ministers. It shall also be transmitted to the States concerned, who shall be at a liberty to publish it.

3. In transmitting the report to the Committee of Ministers the Commission may make such proposals as it thinks fit.

Article 32

1. If the question is not referred to the Court in accordance with Article 48 of this Convention within a period of three months from the date of the

transmission of the report to the Committee of Ministers, the Committee of Ministers shall decide by a majority of two-thirds of the members entitled to sit on the Committee whether there has been a violation of the Convention.

2. In the affirmative case the Committee of Ministers shall prescribe a period during which the High Contracting Party concerned must take the measures required by the decision of the Committee of Ministers.

3. If the High Contracting Party concerned has not taken satisfactory measures within the prescribed period, the Committee of Ministers shall decide by the majority provided for in paragraph 1 above what effect shall be given to its original decision and shall publish the report.

4. The High Contracting Parties undertake to regard as binding on them any decision which the Committee of Ministers may take in application of the preceding paragraphs.

Article 33

The Commission shall meet in camera.

Article 34

Subject to the provisions of Articles 20 (paragraph 3) and 29, the Commission shall take its decisions by a majority of the members present and voting.

Article 35

The Commission shall meet as the circumstances require. The meetings shall be convened by the Secretary General of the Council of Europe.

Article 36

The Commission shall draw up its own rules of procedure.

Article 37

The secretariat of the Commission shall be provided by the Secretary General of the Council of Europe.

SECTION IV

Article 38

The European Court of Human Rights shall consist of a number of judges equal to that of the Members of the Council of Europe. No two judges may be nationals of the same State.

Article 39

1. The members of the Court shall be elected by the Consultative Assembly by a majority of the votes cast from a list of persons nominated by the Members of the Council of Europe; each Member shall nominate three candidates, of whom two at least shall be its nationals.

2. As far as applicable, the same procedure shall be followed to complete the Court in the event of the admission of new Members of the Council of Europe, and in filling casual vacancies.

3. The candidates shall be of high moral character and must either possess the qualifications required for appointment to high judicial office or be jurisconsults of recognised competence.

Article 40

1. The members of the Court shall be elected for a period of nine years. They may be re-elected. However, of the members elected at the first election the terms of four members shall expire at the end of three years, and the terms of four more members shall expire at the end of six years.

2. The members whose terms are to expire at the end of the initial periods of three and six years shall be chosen by lot by the Secretary General immediately after the first election has been completed.

3. In order to ensure that, as far as possible, one third of the membership of the Court shall be renewed every three years, the Consultative Assembly may decide, before proceeding to any subsequent election, that the term or terms of office of one or more members to be elected shall be for a period other than nine years but not more than twelve and not less than six years.

4. In cases where more than one term of office is involved and the Consultative Assembly applies the preceding paragraph, the allocation of the terms of office shall be effected by the drawing of lots by the Secretary General immediately after the election.

5. A member of the Court elected to replace a member whose term of office has not expired shall hold office for the remainder of his predecessor's term.

6. The members of the Court shall hold office until replaced. After having been replaced, they shall continue to deal with such cases as they already have under consideration.

7. The members of the Court shall sit on the Court in their individual capacity. During their term of office, they shall not hold any position which is incompatible with their independence and impartiality as members of the Court or the demands of this office.

Article 41

The Court shall elect its President and one or two Vice-Presidents for a period of three years. They may be re-elected.

Article 42

The members of the Court shall receive for each day of duty a compensation to be determined by the Committee of Ministers.

Article 43

For the consideration of each case brought before it the Court shall consist of a Chamber composed of nine judges. There shall sit as an ex officio member of the Chamber the judge who is a national of any State Party concerned, or, if there is none, a person of its choice who shall sit in the capacity of judge; the names of the other judges shall be chosen by lot by the President before the opening of the case.

Article 44

Only the High Contracting Parties and the Commission shall have the right to bring a case before the Court.

Article 45

The jurisdiction of the Court shall extend to all cases concerning the interpretation and application of the present Convention which the High Contracting Parties or the Commission shall refer to in accordance with Article 48.

Article 46

1. Any of the High Contracting Parties may at any time declare that it recognises as compulsory ipso facto and without special agreement the jurisdiction of the Court in all matters concerning the interpretation and application of the present Convention.

2. The declarations referred to above may be made unconditionally or on condition of reciprocity on the part of several or certain other High Contracting Parties or for a specified period.

3. These declarations shall be deposited with the Secretary General of the Council of Europe who shall transmit copies thereof to the High Contracting Parties.

Article 47

The Court may only deal with a case after the Commission has acknowledged the failure of efforts for a friendly settlement and within the period of three months provided for in Article 32.

Article 48

The following may bring a case before the Court, provided that the High Contracting Party concerned, if there is only one, or the High Contracting

Parties concerned, if there is more than one, are subject to the compulsory jurisdiction of the Court or, failing that, with the consent of the High Contracting Party concerned, if there is only one, or of the High Contracting Parties concerned if there is more than one:

(a) the Commission;

(b) a High Contracting Party whose national is alleged to be a victim;

(c) a High Contracting Party which referred the case to the Commission;

(d) a High Contracting Party against which the complaint has been lodged.

Article 49

In the event of dispute as to whether the Court has jurisdiction, the matter shall be settled by decision of the Court.

Article 50

If the Court finds that a decision or a measure taken by a legal authority or any other authority of a High Contracting Party is completely or partially in conflict with the obligations arising from the present Convention, and if the internal law of the said Party allows only partial reparation to be made for the consequences of this decision or measure, the decision of the Court shall, if necessary, afford just satisfaction to the injured party.

Article 51

1. Reasons shall be given for the judgment of the Court.

2. If the judgment does not represent in whole or in part the unanimous opinion of the judges, any judge shall be entitled to deliver a separate opinion.

Article 52

The judgment of the Court shall be final.

Article 53

The High Contracting Parties undertake to abide by the decision of the Court in any case to which they are parties.

Article 54

The judgment of the Court shall be transmitted to the Committee of Ministers which shall supervise its execution.

Article 55

The Court shall draw up its owns rules and shall determine its own procedure.

Article 56

1. The first election of the members of the Court shall take place after the declarations by the High Contracting Parties mentioned in Article 46 have reached a total of eight.

2. No case can be brought before the Court before this election.

SECTION V

Article 57

On receipt of a request from the Secretary General of the Council of Europe any High Contracting Party shall furnish an explanation of the manner in which its internal law ensures the effective implementation of any of the provision of this Convention.

Article 58

The expenses of the Commission and the Court shall be borne by the Council of Europe.

Article 59

The members of the Commission and the Court shall be entitled, during the discharge of their functions, to the privileges and immunities provided for in Article 40 of the Statute of the Council of Europe and in the agreements made thereunder.

Article 60

Nothing in this Convention shall be construed as limiting or derogating from any of the human rights and fundamental freedoms which may be ensured under the laws of any High Contracting Party or under any other agreement to which it is a Party.

Article 61

Nothing in this Convention shall prejudice the powers conferred on the Committee of Ministers by the Statute of the Council of Europe.

Article 62

The High Contracting Parties agree that, except by special agreement, they will not avail themselves of treaties, conventions or declarations in force between them for the purpose of submitting, by way of petition, a dispute arising out of the interpretation or application of this Convention to a means of settlement other than those provided for in this Convention.

Article 63

1. Any State may at the time of its ratification or at any time thereafter declare by notification addressed to the Secretary General of the Council of Europe that the present Convention shall extend to all or any of the territories for whose international relations it is responsible.

2. The Convention shall extend to the territory or territories named in the notification as from the thirtieth day after the receipt of this notification by the Secretary General of the Council of Europe.

3. The provisions of this Convention shall be applied in such territories with due regard, however, to local requirements.

4. Any State which has made a declaration in accordance with paragraph 1 of this Article may at any time thereafter declare on behalf of one or more of the territories to which the declaration relates that it accepts the competence of the Commission to receive petitions from individuals, non-governmental organisations or groups of individuals in accordance with Article 25 of the present Convention.

Article 64

1. Any State may, when signing this Convention or when depositing its instrument of ratification, make a reservation in respect of any particular provision of the Convention to the extent that any law then in force in its territory is not in conformity with the provision. Reservations of a general character shall not be permitted under this Article.

2. Any reservation made under this Article shall contain a brief statement of the law concerned.

Article 65

1. A High Contracting Party may denounce the present Convention only after the expiry of five years from the date on which it became a Party to it and after six months' notice contained in a notification addressed to the Secretary General of the Council of Europe, who shall inform the other High Contracting Parties.

2. Such a denunciation shall not have the effect of releasing the High Contracting Party concerned from its obligations under this Convention in respect of any act which, being capable of constituting a violation of such

obligations, may have been performed by it before the date at which the denunciation became effective.

3. Any High Contracting Party which shall cease to be a member of the Council of Europe shall cease to be a Party to this Convention under the same conditions.

4. The Convention may be denounced in accordance with the provisions of the preceding paragraghs in respect of any territory to which it has been declared to extend under the terms of Article 63.

Article 66

1. This Convention shall be open to the signature of the Members of the Council of Europe. It shall be ratified. Ratifications shall be deposited with the Secretary General of the Council of Europe.

2. The present Convention shall come into force after the deposit of ten instruments of ratification.

3. As regards any signatory ratifying subsequently, the Convention shall come into force at the date of the deposit of its instrument of ratification.

4. The Secretary General of the Council of Europe shall notify all Members of the Council of Europe of the entry into force of the Convention, the names of the High Contracting Parties who have ratified it, and the deposit of all instruments of ratification which may be effected subsequently.

Done at Rome this 4th day of November 1950 in English and French, both texts being equally authentic, in a single copy which shall remain deposited in the archives of the Council of Europe. The Secretary General shall transmit certified copies to each of the signatories.

PROTOCOL No. 1

The Governments signatory hereto, being Members of the Council of Europe,
Being resolved to take steps to ensure the collective enforcement of certain rights and freedoms other than those already included in Section I of the Convention for the Protection of Human Rights and Fundamental Freedoms signed at Rome on 4th November, 1950 (hereinafter referred to as 'the Convention'),
Have agreed as follows:

Article 1

Every natural or legal person is entitled to the peaceful enjoyment of his possessions. No one shall be deprived of his possessions except in the public interest and subject to the conditions provided for by law and by the general principles of international law.

The preceding provisions shall not, however, in any way impair the right of a State to enforce such laws as it deems necessary to control the use of property in accordance with the general interest or to secure the payment of taxes or other contributions or penalties.

Article 2

No person shall be denied the right to education. In exercise of any functions which it assumes in relation to education and teaching, the State shall respect the right of parents to ensure such education and teaching in conformity with their own religious and philosophical convictions.

Article 3

The High Contracting Parties undertake to hold free elections at reasonable intervals by secret ballot, under conditions which will ensure the free expression of opinion of the people in the choice of the legislature.

Article 4

Any High Contracting Party may at the time of signature or ratification or at any time thereafter communicate to the Secretary General of the Council of Europe a declaration stating the extent to which it undertakes that the provisions of the present Protocol shall apply to such of the territories for the international relations of which it is responsible as are named therein.

Any High Contracting Party which has communicated a declaration in virtue of the preceding paragraph may from time to time communicate a further declaration modifying the terms of any former declaration or terminating the application of the provisions of this Protocol in respect of any territory.

A declaration made in accordance with this Article shall be deemed to have been made in accordance with paragraph 1 of Article 63 of the Convention.

Article 5

As between the High Contracting Parties the provisions of Articles 1, 2, 3 and 4 of this Protocol shall be regarded as additional articles to the Convention and all the provisions of the Convention shall apply accordingly.

Article 6

This Protocol shall be open for signature by the Members of the Council of Europe, who are the signatories of the Convention; it shall be ratified at the same time as or after the ratification of the Convention. It shall enter into force after the deposit of ten instruments of ratification. As regards any signatory ratifying subsequently, the Protocol shall enter into force at the date of the deposit of its instrument of ratification.

The instruments of ratification shall be deposited with the Secretary General of the Council of Europe, who will notify all Members of the names of those who have ratified.

Done at Paris on the 20th day of March 1952, in English and French, both texts being equally authentic, in a single copy which shall remain deposited in the archives of the Council of Europe. The Secretary General shall transmit certified copies to each of the signatory Governments.

PROTOCOL No. 2
conferring upon the European Court of Human Rights competence to give advisory opinions

The member States of the Council of Europe signatory hereto:

Having regard to the provisions of the Convention for the Protection of Human Rights and Fundamental Freedoms signed at Rome on 4th November 1950 (hereinafter-referred to as 'the Convention') and, in particular, Article 19 instituting, among other bodies, a European Court of Human Rights (hereinafter referred to as 'the Court');

Considering that it is expedient to confer upon the Court competence to give advisory opinions subject to certain conditions,

Have agreed as follows:

Article 1

1. The Court may, at the request of the Committee of Ministers, give advisory opinions on legal questions concerning the interpretation of the Convention and the Protocols thereto.

2. Such opinions shall not deal with any question relating to the content or scope of the rights or freedoms defined in Section 1 of the Convention and in the Protocols thereto, or with any other question which the Commission, the Court or the Committee of Ministers might have to consider in consequence of any such proceedings as could be instituted in accordance with the Convention.

3. Decisions of the Committee of Ministers to request an advisory opinion of the Court shall require a two-thirds majority vote of the representatives entitled to sit on the Committee.

Article 2

The Court shall decide whether a request for an advisory opinion submitted by the Committee of Ministers is within its consultative competence as defined in Article 1 of this Protocol.

Article 3

1. For the consideration of request for an advisory opinion, the Court shall sit in plenary session.

2. Reasons shall be given for advisory opinions of the Court.

3. If the advisory opinion does not represent in whole or in part the unanimous opinion of the judges, any judge shall be entitled to deliver a separate opinion.

4. Advisory opinions of the Court shall be communicated to the Committee of Ministers.

Article 4

The power of the Court under Article 55 of the Convention shall extend to the drawing up of such rules and the determination of such procedure as the Court may think necessary for the purpose of this Protocol.

Article 5

1. This Protocol shall be open to signature by member States of the Council of Europe, signatories to the Convention, who may become Parties to it by:

(a) signature without reservation in respect of ratification or acceptance;

(b) signature with reservation in respect of ratification or acceptance, followed by ratification or acceptance.

Instruments of ratification or acceptance shall be deposited with the Secretary General of the Council of Europe.

2. This Protocol shall enter into force as soon as all States Parties to the Convention shall have become Parties to the Protocol, in accordance with the provisions of paragraph 1 of this Article.

3. From the date of the entry into force of this Protocol, Articles 1 and 4 shall be considered an integral part of the Convention.

4. The Secretary General of the Council of Europe shall notify the members States of the Council of:

(a) any signature without reservation in respect of ratification or acceptance;

(b) any signature with reservation in respect of ratification or acceptance;

(c) the deposit of any instrument of ratification or acceptance;

(d) the date of entry into force of this Protocol in accordance with paragraph 2 of this Article.

In witness whereof, the undersigned, being duly authorised thereto, have signed this Protocol.

Done at Strasbourg, this 6th day of May 1963, in English and French, both texts being equally authoritative, in a single copy which shall remain deposited in the archives of the Council of Europe. The Secretary General of the Council of Europe shall transmit certified copies to each of the signatory States.

PROTOCOL No. 4
securing certain rights and freedoms other than those already
included in the Convention and in the first Protocol thereto

The Governments signatory hereto, being Members of the Council of Europe,

Being resolved to take steps to ensure the collective enforcement of certain rights and freedoms other than those already included in Section I of the Convention for the Protection of Human Rights and Fundamental Freedoms signed at Rome on 4th November 1950 (hereinafter referred to as 'the Convention') and in Articles 1 and 3 of the First Protocol to the Convention, signed at Paris on 20th March 1952,

Have agreed as follows:

Article 1

No one shall be deprived of his liberty merely on the ground of inability to fulfil a contractual obligation.

Article 2

1. Everyone lawfully within the territory of a State shall, within that territory, have the right to liberty of movement and freedom to choose his residence.

2. Everyone shall be free to leave any country, including his own.

3. No restrictions shall be placed on the exercise of these rights other than such as are in accordance with law and are necessary in a democratic society in the interest of national security or public safety, for the maintenance of order public, for the prevention of crime, for the protection of health or morals, or for the protection of the rights and freedoms of others.

4. The rights set forth in paragraph 1 may also be subject, in particular areas, to restrictions imposed in accordance with law and justified by the public interest in a democratic society.

Article 3

1. No one shall be expelled, by means either of an individual or of a collective measure, from the territory of the State of which he is a national.

2. No one shall be deprived of the right to enter the territory of the State of which he is a national.

Article 4

Collective expulsion of aliens is prohibited.

Article 5

1. Any High Contracting Party may, at the time of signature or ratification of this Protocol, or at any time thereafter, communicate to the Secretary General of the Council of Europe a declaration stating the extent to which it undertakes that the provisions of this Protocol shall apply to such of the territories for the international relations of which it is responsible as are named therein.

2. Any High Contracting Party which has communicated a declaration in virtue of the preceding paragraph may, from time to time, communicate a further declaration modifying the terms of any former declaration or terminating the application of the provisions of this Protocol in respect of any territory.

3. A declaration made in accordance with this Article shall be deemed to have been made in accordance with paragraph 1 of Article 63 of the Convention.

4. The territory of any State to which this Protocol applies by virtue of ratification or acceptance by that State under this Article, shall be treated as separate territories for the purpose of the references in Articles 2 and 3 to the territory of a State.

Article 6

1. As between the High Contracting Parties the provisions of Articles 1 to 5 of this Protocol shall be regarded as additional Articles to the Convention, and all the provisions of the Convention shall apply accordingly.

2. Nevertheless, the right of individual recourse recognised by a declaration made under Article 25 of the Convention, or the acceptance of the compulsory jurisdiction of the Court by a declaration made under Article 46 of the Convention, shall not be effective in relation to this Protocol unless the High Contracting Party concerned has made a statement recognising such right, or accepting such jurisdiction, in respect of all or any of Articles 1 to 4 of the Protocol.

Article 7

1. This Protocol shall be open for signature by the Members of the Council of Europe who are the signatories of the Convention; it shall be ratified at the same time as or after the ratification of the Convention. It shall enter into force after the deposit of five instruments of ratification. As regards any signatory ratifying subsequently, the Protocol shall enter into force at the date of the deposit of its instrument of ratification.

2. The instruments of ratification shall be deposited with the Secretary General of the Council of Europe, who will notify all Members of the names of those who have ratified.

In witness whereof, the undersigned, being duly authorised thereto, have signed this Protocol.

402

Done at Strasbourg, this 16th day of September 1963, in English and French, both texts being equally authoritative, in a single copy which shall remain deposited in the archives of the Council of Europe. The Secretary General of the Council of Europe shall transmit certified copies to each of the signatory States.

PROTOCOL No. 6
concerning the abolition of the death penalty

The member States of the Council of Europe, signatory to this Protocol to the Convention for the Protection of Human Rights and Fundamental Freedoms, signed at Rome on 4 November 1950 (hereinafter referred to as 'the Convention'),

Considering that the evolution that has occurred in several member States of the Council of Europe expresses a general tendency in favour of abolition of the death penalty,

Have agreed as follows:

Article 1

The death penalty shall be abolished. No one shall be condemned to such penalty or executed.

Article 2

A State may make provision in its law for the death penalty in respect of acts committed in time of war or of imminent threat of war; such penalty shall be applied only in the instances laid down in the law and in accordance with its provisions. The State shall communicate to the Secretary General of the Council of Europe the relevant provisions of that law.

Article 3

No derogation from the provisions of this Protocol shall be made under Article 15 of the Convention.

Article 4

No reservation may be made under Article 64 of the Convention in respect of the provisions of this Protocol.

Article 5

1. Any State may at the time of signature or when depositing its instrument of ratification, acceptance or approval, specify the territory or territories to which this Protocol shall apply.

403

2. Any State may at any later date, by a declaration addressed to the Secretary General of the Council of Europe, extend the application of this Protocol to any other territory specified in the declaration. In respect of such territory the Protocol shall enter into force on the first day of the month following the date of receipt of such a declaration by the Secretary General.

3. Any declaration made under the two preceding paragraphs may, in respect of any territory specified in such declaration, be withdrawn by a notification addressed to the Secretary General. The withdrawal shall become effective on the first day of the month following the date of receipt of such notification by the Secretary General.

Article 6

As between the States Parties the provisions of Articles 1 to 5 of this Protocol shall be regarded as additional articles to the Convention and all the provisions of the Convention shall apply accordingly.

Article 7

This Protocol shall be open for signature by the member States of the Council of Europe, signatories to the Convention. It shall be subject to ratification, acceptance or approval. A member State of the Council of Europe may not ratify, accept or approve this Protocol unless it has, simultaneously or previously, ratified the Convention. Instruments of ratification, acceptance or approval shall be deposited with the Secretary General of the Council of Europe.

Article 8

1. This Protocol shall enter into force on the first day of the month following the date on which five member States of the Council of Europe have expressed their consent to be bound by the Protocol in accordance with the provisions of Article 7.

2. In respect of any member State which subsequently expresses its consent to be bound by it, the Protocol shall enter into force on the first day of the month following the date of the deposit of the instrument of ratification, acceptance or approval.

Article 9

The Secretary General of the Council of Europe shall notify the member States of the Council of:

(a) any signature;

(b) the deposit of any instrument of ratification, acceptance or approval;

(c) any date of entry into force of this Protocol in accordance with Articles 5 and 8;

(d) any other act, notification or communication relating to this Protocol.

In witness whereof the undersigned, being duly authorised thereto, have signed this Protocol.

Done at Strasbourg, the 28th day of April 1983, in English and French, both texts being equally authentic, in a single copy which shall be deposited in the archives of the Council of Europe. The Secretary General of the Council of Europe shall transmit certified copies to each member State of the Council of Europe.

PROTOCOL No. 7

The member States of the Council of Europe signatory hereto,

Being resolved to take further steps to ensure the collective enforcement of certain rights and freedoms by means of the Convention for the protection of Human Rights and Fundamental Freedoms signed at Rome on 4 November 1950 (hereinafter referred to as 'the Convention'),

Have agreed as follows:

Article 1

1. An alien lawfully resident in the territory of the State shall not be expelled therefrom except in pursuance of a decision reached in accordance with law and shall be allowed:

(a) to submit reasons against his expulsion;

(b) to have his case reviewed, and

(c) to be represented for these purposes before the competent authority or a person or persons designated by that authority.

2. An alien may be expelled before the exercise of his rights under paragraph 1(a), (b) and (c) of this Article, when such expulsion is necessary in the interests of public order, or is grounded on reasons of national security.

Article 2

1. Everyone convicted of a criminal offence by a tribunal shall have the right to have conviction or sentence reviewed by a higher tribunal. The exercise of this right, including the grounds on which it may be exercised, shall be governed by law.

2. This right may be subject to exceptions in regard to offences of a minor character, as prescribed by law, or in cases in which the person concerned was tried in the first instance by the highest tribunal or was convicted following an appeal against acquittal.

Article 3

When a person has by a final decision been convicted of a criminal offence and when subsequently his conviction has been reversed, or he has been pardoned, on the ground that a new or newly discovered fact shows conclusively that there has been a miscarriage of justice, a person who has suffered punishment as a result of such conviction shall be compensated according to the law or the practice of the State concerned, unless it is proved that the non-disclosure of the unknown fact in time is wholly or partly attributable to him.

Article 4

1. No one shall be liable to be tried or punished again in criminal proceedings under the jurisdiction of the same State for an offence for which he has already been finally acquitted or convicted in accordance with the law and penal procedure of that State.

2. The provisions of the preceding paragraph shall not prevent the re-opening of the case in accordance with the law and penal procedure of the State concerned, if there is evidence of new or newly discovered facts, or if there has been a fundamental defect in the previous proceedings, which could affect the outcome of the case.

3. No derogation from this Article shall be made under Article 15 of the Convention.

Article 5

1. Spouses shall enjoy equality of rights and responsibilities of a private law character between them, and in their relations with their children, as to marriage, during marriage and in the event of its dissolution. This Article shall not prevent States from taking such measures as are necessary in the interest of the children.

Article 6

1. Any State may at the time of signature or when depositing its instrument of ratification, acceptance or approval, specify the territory or territories to which this Protocol shall apply and state the extent to which it undertakes that the provisions of this Protocol shall apply to this or these territories.

2. Any state may at any later date, by a declaration addressed to the Secretary General of the Council of Europe, extend the application of this Protocol to any other territory specified in the declaration. In respect of such territory the Protocol shall enter into force on the first day of the month following the expiration of a period of two months after the date of receipt by the Secretary General of such declaration.

3. Any declaration made under the two preceding paragraphs may, in respect of any territory specified in such declaration, be withdrawn or modi-

fied by a notification addressed to the Secretary General. The withdrawal or modification shall become effective on the first day of the month following the expiration of a period of two months after the date of receipt of such notification by the Secretary General.

4. A declaration made in accordance with this Article shall be deemed to have been made in accordance with paragraph 1 of Article 63 of the Convention.

5. The territory of any State to which this Protocol applies by virtue of ratification, acceptance or approval by that State, and each territory to which this Protocol is applied by virtue of a declaration by that State under this Article, may be treated as separate territories for the purpose of the reference in Article 1 to the territory of a State.

Article 7

1. As between the State Parties, the provisions of Articles 1 to 6 of this Protocol shall be regarded as additional Articles to the Convention, and all the provisions of the Convention shall apply accordingly.

2. Nevertheless, the right of individual recourse recognised by a declaration made under Article 25 of the Convention, or the acceptance of the compulsory jurisdiction of the Court by a declaration made under Article 46 of the Convention, shall not be effective in relation to this Protocol unless the State concerned has made a statement recognising such right, or accepting such jurisdiction in respect of Articles 1 to 5 of this Protocol.

Article 8

This Protocol shall be open for signature by member States of the Council of Europe which have signed the Convention. It is subject to ratification, acceptance or approval. A member state of the Council of Europe may not ratify, accept or approve this Protocol without previously or simultaneously ratifying the Convention. Instruments of ratification, acceptance or approval shall be deposited with the Secretary General of the Council of Europe.

Article 9

1. This Protocol shall enter into force on the first day of the month following the expiration of a period of two months after the date on which seven member States of the Council of Europe have expressed their consent to be bound by the Protocol in accordance with the provisions of Article 8.

2. In respect of any member State which subsequently expresses its consent to be bound by it, the Protocol shall enter into force on the first day of the month following the expiration of a period of two months after the date of the deposit of the instrument of ratification, acceptance or approval.

Article 10

The Secretary General of the Council of Europe shall notify all the member States of the Council of:

(a) any signature;

(b) the deposit of any instrument of ratification, acceptance or approval;

(c) any date of entry into force of this Protocol in accordance with Articles 6 and 9;

(d) any other act, notification or declaration relating to this Protocol.

In witness whereof the undersigned, being duly authorised thereto, have signed this Protocol.

Done at Strasbourg, the 22nd day of November 1984, in English and French, both texts being equally authentic, in a single copy which shall be deposited in the archives of the Council of Europe. The Secretary General of the Council of Europe shall transmit certified copies to each member State of the Council.

PROTOCOL No. 9[1]

The member States of the Council of Europe, signatories to this Protocol to the Convention for the Protection of Human Rights and Fundamental Freedoms, signed at Rome on 4 November 1950 (hereinafter referred to as 'the Convention'),

Being resolved to make further improvements to the procedure under the Convention,

Have agreed as follows:

Article 1

For Parties to the Convention which are bound by this Protocol, the Convention shall be amended as provided in Articles 2 to 5.

Article 2

Article 31, paragraph 2, of the Convention, shall read as follows:

'2. The Report shall be transmitted to the Committee of Ministers. The Report shall also be transmitted to the States concerned and, if it deals with a petition submitted under Article 25, the applicant. The States concerned and the applicant shall not be at liberty to publish it.'

1. Not yet in force.

Article 3

Article 44 of the Convention shall read as follows:

'Only the High Contracting Parties, the Commission, and persons, non-governmental organisations or groups of individuals having submitted a petition under Article 25 shall have the right to bring a case before the Court.'

Article 4

Article 45 of the Convention shall read as follows:

'The jurisdiction of the Court shall extend to all cases concerning the interpretation and application of the present Convention which are referred to it in accordance with Article 48.'

Article 5

Article 48 of the Convention shall read as follows:

'1. The following may refer a case to the Court, provided that the High Contracting Party concerned, if there is only one, or the High Contracting Parties concerned, if there is more than one, are subject to the compulsory jurisdiction of the Court, or, failing that, with the consent of the High Contracting Party concerned, if there is only one, or of the High Contracting Parties concerned if there is more than one:

(a) the Commission;

(b) a High Contracting Party whose national is alleged to be a victim;

(c) a High Contracting Party which referred the case to the Commission;

(e) a High Contracting Party against which the complaint has been lodged;

(e) the person, non-governmental organisation or group of individuals having lodged the complaint with the Commission.

2. If a case is referred to the Court only in accordance with paragraph 1e., it shall first be submitted to a panel composed of three members of the Court. There shall sit as an ex officio member of the panel the judge elected in respect of the High Contracting Party against which the complaint has been lodged, or, if there is none, a person of its choice who shall sit in the capacity of judge. If the complaint has been lodged against more than one High Contracting Party, the size of the panel shall be increased accordingly.

If the case does not raise serious question affecting the interpretation or application of the Convention and does not for any other reason warrant consideration by the Court, the panel may, by a unanimous vote, decide that it shall not be considered by the Court. In that event, the Committee of Ministers shall decide, in accordance with the provisions of Article 32, whether there has been a violation of the Convention.'

409

Article 6

1. This Protocol shall be open for signature by member States of the Council of Europe signatories to the Convention, which may express their consent to be bound by:

(a) signature without reservation as to ratification, acceptance or approval, or

(b) signature subject to ratification, acceptance or approval, followed by ratification, acceptance or approval.

2. The instruments of ratification, acceptance or approval shall be deposited with the Secretary General of the Council of Europe.

Article 7

1. This Protocol shall enter into force on the first day of the month following the expiration of a period of three months after the date on which ten member States of the Council of Europe have expressed their consent to be bound by the Protocol in accordance with the provisions of Article 6.

2. In respect of any member State which subsequently expresses its consent to be bound by it, the Protocol shall enter into force on the first day of the month following the expiration of a period of three months after the date of signature or of the deposit of the instrument of ratification, acceptance or approval.

Article 8

The Secretary General of the Council of Europe shall notify all the member States of the Council of Europe of:

(a) any signature;

(b) the deposit of any instrument of ratification, acceptance or approval;

(c) any date of entry into force of this Protocol in accordance with Article 7;

(d) any other act, notification or declaration relating to this Protocol.

In witness thereof, the undersigned, being duly authorised thereto, have signed this Protocol.

Done at Rome, this 6 November 1990, in English and French, both texts being equally authentic, in a single copy which shall be deposited in the archives of the Council of Europe. The Secretary General of the Council of Europe shall transmit certified copies to each member State of the Council of Europe.

PROTOCOL No. 10[1]

The member States of the Council of Europe, signatories to this Protocol to the Convention for the Protection of Human Rights and Fundamental Freedoms, signed at Rome on 4 November 1950 (hereinafter referred to as 'the Convention'),

Considering that it is advisable to amend Article 32 of the Convention with a view to the reduction of the two-thirds majority provided therein,

Have agreed as follows:

Article 1

The words 'of two-thirds' shall be deleted from paragraph 1 of Article 32 of the Convention.

Article 2

1. This Protocol shall be open for signature by member States of the Council of Europe signatories to the Convention, which may express their consent to be bound by:

(a) signature without reservation as to ratification, acceptance or approval; or

(b) signature subject to ratification, acceptance or approval, followed by ratification, acceptance or approval.

2. Instruments of ratification, acceptance or approval shall be deposited with the Secretary General of the Council of Europe.

Article 3

This Protocol shall enter into force on the first day of the month following the expiration of a period of three months after the date on which all Parties to the Convention have expressed their consent to be bound by the Protocol in accordance with the provisions of Article 2.

Article 4

The Secretary General of the Council of Europe shall notify the member States of the Council of:

(a) any signature;

(b) the deposit of any instrument of ratification, acceptance or approval;

(c) the date of entry into force of this Protocol in accordance with Article 3;

(d) any other act, notification or communication relating to this Protocol.

1   Not yet in force.

In witness whereof the undersigned, being duly authorised thereto, have signed this Protocol.

Done at Strasbourg, this 25th day of March 1992, in English and French, both texts being equally authentic, in a single copy which shall be deposited in the archives of the Council of Europe. The Secretary General of the Council of Europe shall transmit certified copies to each member State of the Council of Europe.

APPENDIX B

Table of ratifications of the Convention and declarations of acceptance of optional articles

(at 31 December 1993)

Member States of the Council of Europe (entry into force)	Convention (3.9.1953)	Declarations		Protocol No. 1 (18.5.1954)	Protocol No. 2 (21.9.1970)	Protocol No. 4 (2.4.1968)	Protocol No. 6 (1.3.1985)	Protocol No. 7 (1.11.1988)	Protocol No. 9[3]	Protocol No. 10[3]
		Art. 25[1]	Art. 46[2]							
Austria	3.9.1958	3.9.1958	3.9.1958	3.9.1958	21.9.1970	18.6.1989	1.3.1985	1.11.1988	27.4.1992	1.6.1993
Belgium	14.6.1955.	5.7.1955	5.7.1955	14.6.1955	21.9.1970	21.9.1970	–	–	–	21.12.1992
Bulgaria	7.9.1992	7.9.1992	7.9.1992	7.9.1992	7.9.1992	–	–	–	–	–
Cyprus	6.10.1962	1.1.1989	24.1.1980	6.10.1962	21.9.1970	3.10.1989	–	–	–	–
Czech Rep.	1.1.1993	18.3.1992	18.3.1992	1.1.1993	1.6.1993	1.1.1993	1.1.1993	1.1.1993	7.5.1992	26.6.1992
Denmark	3.9.1953	13.4.1953	13.4.1953	18.5.1954	21.9.1970	2.5.1968	1.3.1985	1.11.1988	–	–
Estonia	–	–	–	–	–	–	–	–	–	–
Finland	10.5.1990	10.5.1990	10.5.1990	10.5.1990	10.5.1990	10.5.1990	1.6.1990	1.8.1990	11.12.1992	21.7.1992
France	3.5.1974	2.10.1981	3.5.1974	3.5.1974	2.10.1981	3.5.1974	1.3.1986	1.11.1988	–	–
Germany (FRG)	3.9.1953	5.7.1955	5.7.1955	13.2.1957	21.9.1970.	1.6.1968	1.8.1989	–	–	–
Greece	28.11.1974	2.11.1985	30.1.1979	28.11.1974	28.11.1974	–	–	1.11.1988	–	–
Hungary	5.11.1992	5.11.1992	5.11.1992	5.11.1992	5.11.1992	5.11.1992	1.12.1992	1.2.1993	5.11.1992	–
Iceland	3.9.1953	29.3.1955	3.9.1958	18.5.1954	21.9.1970	2.5.1968	1.6.1987	1.11.1988	–	–
Ireland	3.9.1953	25.2.1953	25.2.1953	18.5.1954	21.9.1970	29.10.1968	–	–	–	–
Italy	26.10.1955	1.8.1973	1.8.1973	26.10.1955	21.9.1970	27.5.1982	1.1.1989	1.2.1992	13.12.1992	–
Liechtenstein	8.9.1982	8.9.1982	8.9.1982	–	8.9.1982	–	1.12.1990	–	–	–
Lithuania	–	–	–	–	–	–	–	–	–	–
Luxembourg	3.9.1953	28.4.1958	28.4.1958	18.5.1954	21.9.1970	2.5.1968	1.3.1985	1.7.1989	9.7.1992	–
Malta	23.1.1967	1.5.1987	1.5.1987	23.1.1967	21.9.1970	–	1.4.1991	–	–	7.5.1992
Netherlands	31.8.1954	28.6.1960	31.8.1954	31.8.1954	21.9.1970	23.6.1982	1.5.1986	–	23.11.1992	23.11.1992
Norway	3.9.1953	10.12.1955	30.6.1964	18.5.1954	21.9.1970	2.5.1968	1.11.1988	1.1.1989	15.1.1992	25.3.1993
Poland	19.1.1993	1.5.1993	1.5.1993	–	19.1.1993	–	–	–	–	–
Portugal	9.11.1978	9.11.1978	9.11.1978	9.11.1978	9.11.1978	9.11.1978	1.11.1986	–	–	–
Romania	–	–	–	–	–	–	–	–	–	–
San Marino	22.3.1989	22.3.1989	22.3.1989	22.3.1989	22.3.1989	22.3.1989	1.4.1989	1.6.1989	–	–
Slovakia	1.1.1993	18.3.1992	18.3.1992	1.1.1993	1.6.1993	1.1.1993	1.1.1993	1.1.1993	7.5.1992	26.6.1992
Slovenia	–	–	–	–	–	–	–	–	–	–
Spain	4.10.1979	1.7.1981	15.10.1979	27.11.1990	6.4.1982	–	1.3.1985	1.11.1988	–	–
Sweden	3.9.1953	4.2.1952	13.5.1966	18.5.1954	21.9.1970	2.5.1968	1.3.1985	1.11.1988	–	19.10.1992
Switzerland	28.11.1974	28.11.1974	28.11.1974	–	28.11.1974	–	1.11.1987	1.11.1988	–	–
Turkey	18.5.1954	28.1.1987	22.1.1990	18.5.1954	21.9.1970	–	–	–	–	–
United Kingdom	3.9.1953	14.1.1966	14.1.1966	18.5.1954	21.9.1970	–	–	–	–	9.3.1993

1 Declarations recognising the right of individual petition to the Commission.
2 Declarations recognising the compulsory jurisdiction of the Court.
3 Not yet in force. Dates are those of ratifications.

APPENDIX C

Scheme of the procedure introduced by the Convention

(at 31 December 1993)

1) Initial phase

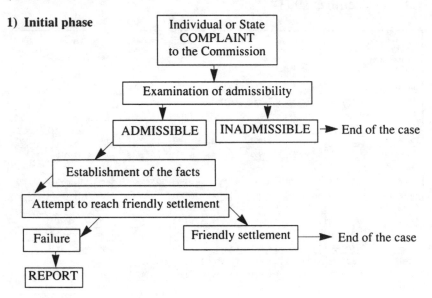

Sent to the Committee of Ministers
Beginning of the period of three months

2) Final phase

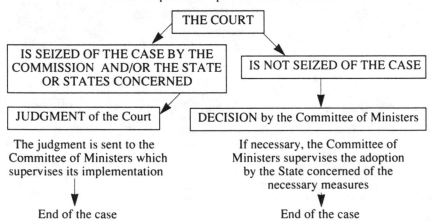

Table of referrals to and judgments of the Court

(at 31 December 1993)

State concerned	Cases brought	Cases resulting in a finding of		Cases struck out of the list	Cases not examined as to merits	Cases pending		
		one breach	no breach			On the merits	Article 50	Total
Austria	43	26	10	3	–	4	–	4
Belgium	32	19	6	4	1	2	1	3
Cyprus	1	1	–	–	–	–	–	–
Denmark	6	1	4	–	–	1	–	1
Finland	2	–	–	–	–	2	–	2
France	44	23[1]	8	6	2	5	–	5
Germany	27	10	15	–	–	2	–	2
Greece	7	4	–	–	1	2	1	3
Iceland	3	2	–	1	–	–	–	–
Ireland	7	5	1	–	–	1	–	1
Italy	114	79[2]	9	18[3]	3	5	–	5
Malta	1	1	–	–	–	1	–	1
Netherlands	29	17	4	–	–	8	–	8
Norway	1	1	–	–	–	–	–	–
Portugal	8	5	–	1	–	2	–	2
Spain	10	4	–	–	1	5	1	6
Sweden	31	20	7	2	–	2	–	2
Switzerland	24	13	8	–	–	3	1	4
Turkey	1	–	–	–	–	1	–	1
United Kingdom	57	31[4]	15	3	–	8	–	8
Total[5]	447	262	87	38[2]	8	53	4	57

1 Including the two *Kemmache* cases, which were joined by the Court but are here counted as two.
2 The *Colozza and Rubinat* case, after being severed, gave rise to two judgments, one finding a violation (*Colozza*) and the other striking the case out of the list (*Rubinat*). Only *Colozza* has been taken into account.
3 Not including *Rubinat*.
4 Including the *Soering* case: finding of a potential violation (which finally did not occur).
5 Certain totals do not tally as the *Drozd and Janousek* case is entered under each of the two respondent states (France and Spain).

Cases pending before the Court

(at 31 December 1993)

1. *Barberà, Messegué and Jabardo v. Spain* (application of Article 50).
2. *Clooth v. Belgium* (application of Article 50).
3. *Schuler-Zgraggen v. Switzerland* (application of Article 50).
4. *Papamichalopoulos and Others v. Greece* (application of Article 50).
5. *Burghartz v. Switzerland* (husband not permitted to put own surname in front of wife's which had been taken as family name).
6. *Stanford v. the United Kingdom* (alleged inability of accused to hear some of evidence given in court).
7. *Raimondo v. Italy* (preventive measures imposed on mafia suspect and length of civil proceedings).
8. *Bendenoun v. France* (access to file of customs authority during administrative court proceedings concerning tax surcharges and supplementary tax assessments).
9. *Tripodi v. Italy* (absence of defence lawyer from hearing before Court of Cassation).
10. *Ravnsborg v. Sweden* (refusal of civil courts to hold hearing before imposing fine on party for written statements judged to be improper).
11. *Silva Pontes v. Portugal* (length of civil proceedings).
12. *Jacubowski v. Germany* (prohibition imposed on journalist restraining him from disseminating letter containing adverse comments on news agency).
13. *Casado Coca v. Spain* (imposition of disciplinary sanction on lawyer for having infringed rule forbidding advertisement of professional services).
14. *Van de Hurk v. the Netherlands* (independence of Industrial Appeals Tribunal, in view of Crown's power to limit effects of that Tribunal's decisions).
15. *The Holy Monasteries v. Greece* (legislation transferring to State a substantial proportion of property of monasteries belonging to the Greek Church).
16. *Otto-Preminger-Institut v. Austria* (seizure and forfeiture of film found to be blasphemous).
17. *Karlheinz Schmidt v. Germany* (duty imposed in Baden–Württemberg on men but not on women, to serve in fire brigade or, failing that, to pay levy).
18. *Murray v. the United Kingdom* (suspect arrested and held in police custody in accordance with State of Emergency legislation in Northern Ireland).
19. *Saraiva de Carvalho v. Portugal* (composition of criminal court).

20. *Boyle v. the United Kingdom* (refusal of local authority to allow uncle contact with nephew).

21. *Keegan v. Ireland* (placement of child for adoption without natural father's consent or knowledge and lack of possibility for him to be named guardian).

22. *Debled v. Belgium* (composition of Medical Association appeals board when considering challenges involving several members of board).

23. *De Moor v. Belgium* (proceedings to consider requests for admission to Bar and length of proceedings before Conseil d'Etat).

24. *Scherer v. Switzerland* (conviction for showing pornographic film in sex shop and length of criminal proceedings).

25. *Fredin v. Sweden (no. 2)* (refusal of Supreme Administrative Court to hold oral hearing).

26. *Katte Klitsche de la Grange v. Italy* (prohibition of development without compensation and length of civil proceedings).

27. *Stran Greek Refineries and Andreadis v. Greece* (annulment by Act of Parliament of arbitral award recognising existence of debt owed by State).

28. *Hentrich v. France* (pre-emption by tax authorities of real property purchased by private individuals and fairness and length of civil proceedings).

29. *Venditelli v. Italy* (length of criminal proceedings and sealing of flat).

30. *Lala v. the Netherlands* (appeal proceedings conducted in absence of accused and refusal to allow counsel to defend him).

31. *Wynne v. the United Kingdom* (review of legality of continued detention of accused sentenced to life imprisonment).

32. *Pelladoah v. the Netherlands* (appeal proceedings conducted in absence of accused and refusal to allow counsel to defend him).

33. *Fayed v. the United Kingdom* (publication by Government of independent report on takeover of company and access to court to challenge conclusions of report).

34. *Kroon and Others v. the Netherlands* (lack of possibility for father to obtain legal recognition of paternity in respect of child by adulterous relationship).

35. *Boner v. the United Kingdom* (lack of legal aid for criminal appeal hearing).

36. *Maxwell v. the United Kingdom* (lack of legal aid for criminal appeal hearing).

37. *Muti v. Italy* (length of proceedings in Audit Court).

38. *Ortenberg v. Austria* (scope of review of the Administrative Court and the Constitutional Court and fairness of proceedings before latter).

39. *Vereinigung Demokratischer Soldaten and Gubi v. Austria* (prohibition of distribution in barracks of magazine published by association of soldiers).

40. *Beaumartin v. France* (fairness of proceedings before Conseil d'Etat, which considered itself bound by interpretation of international agreement given by Minister of Foreign Affairs who was defendant; length of proceedings before administrative courts).

41. *Jersild v. Denmark* (conviction of journalist for aiding and abetting dissemination of racist remarks through television programme).

42. *Hurtado v. Switzerland* (treatment during arrest and in police custody).

43. *Stjerna v. Finland* (refusal of authorisation to change surname).

44. *Ruiz Torija v. Spain* (failure of Court of Appeal, ruling in civil proceedings, to address argument already raised at first instance).

45. *Loizidou v. Turkey* (treatment during arrest and detention by Turkish armed forces stationed in northern Cyprus and lack of access of property owner to land in region; temporal and territorial scope of Turkey's declarations under Article 46 of the Convention).

46. *Lopez Ostra v. Spain* (nuisance caused by waste-treatment plant in vicinity of residential accommodation).

47. *Diaz Ruano v. Spain* (death of suspect in police custody).

48. *Gasus v. the Netherlands* (seizure and sale by tax authorities of machine which belonged to third party without compensation).

49. *Vereniging 'Bluf!' v. the Netherlands* (seizure and confiscation of issue of magazine containing survey of activities of Internal Security Service).

50. *Kemmache v. France (no. 3)* (continued detention of accused pending trial).

51. *Hiro Balani v. Spain* (failure of Supreme Court, ruling on merits in civil proceedings, to address argument adduced at first instance).

52. *Quinn v. France* (legality and length of detention pending extradition).

53. *Schouten v. the Netherlands* (length and fairness of social security proceedings).

54. *Meldrum v. the Netherlands* (length and fairness of social security proceedings).

55. *Hokkanen v. Finland* (enforcement of father's custody and visiting rights in respect of daughter residing with maternal grandparents and transfer of custody to them).

56. *McMichael v. the United Kingdom* (parents' access to confidential documents submitted to body deciding on compulsory care measures in respect of child).

57. *Fischer v. Austria* (scope of review of the Administrative Court and the Constitutional Court and lack of public hearing before them).

General Bibliography[1]

The publications of the Court comprise two series: Series A—completely bilingual (English and French)—includes the judgments and decisions (279 volumes have appeared so far); Series B—partly bilingual—reproduces the main documents of the case (Commission's report, memorials, complete record of the hearings, etc.) (98 volumes have appeared so far). They are published in Cologne by Carl Heymanns Verlag.

The sections relating to each case are followed by a specific bilibiography. Therefore, only the most significant general studies are listed here.

I. BOOKS

BERGER (V.).—*Case Law of the European Court of Human Rights. Volume II: 1988–1990*, Dublin, The Round Hall Press, 1992, XIV–291 p.

CLAPHAM (A.).—*Human rights in the private sphere*, Oxford, Clarendon Press, 1993, 385 p.

CONSEIL DE L'EUROPE.—*Répertoire de la jurisprudence relative à la Convention européenne des droits de l'homme, Vol. 1* (articles 1–5), Cologne, Carl Heymanns, 1992.

CONSEJO GENERAL DEL PODER JUDICIAL.—*La jurisprudencia del Tribunal europeo de Derechos Humanos*, Madrid, Consejo General del Poder Judicial, 1993, 488 p.

DIPLA (H.).—*La responsabilité de l'Etat pour violation des droits de l'homme —Problèmes d'imputation*, Paris, Pedone, 1994, 116 p.

FACULTÉ DE DROIT ET DES SCIENCES SOCIALES DE POITIERS.—*Les incidences des jurisprudences internationales sur les droits néerlandais et français, notamment sur les droits de l'homme*, Paris, P.U.F., 1992, 287 p.

FETERIS (M.W.C.).—*Fiscale administratieve sancties en het recht op een behoorlijk proces*, Deventer, Kluwer, 1993, 816 p.

GREGORI (G.).—*La tutela europea dei diritti dell' uomo*, Milano, Sugar, 1979, 323 p.

JACOT-GILLARMOD (O.).—*Le juge national face au droit européen : perspective suisse et communautaire*, Bâle, Helding & Hahn, and Brussels, Bruylant, 1993, 379 p.

KINLEY (D.).—*The European Convention on Human Rights: compliance without incorporation*, Aldershot, Dartmouth, 1993, 202 p.

MERRILLS (J.G.).—*The development of international law by the European Court of Human Rights*, Manchester, Manchester University Press, 1933, 265 p.

MORENILLA RODRIGUEZ (J.M.).—*El convenio Europeo de Derechos Humanos: Ambito, organos y procedimientos*, Madrid, Ministerio de Justicia, Secretaría General Técnica, Centro de Publicaciones, 1985, 77 p.

---

1 See also Vol. I, pp. 447–459, and Vol. II, pp. 269–276

Bibliography

ORAÁ (J.).—*Human rights in states of emergency in international law*, Oxford, Clarendon Press, 1992, 288 p.

PARISI (N.).—*Estradizione e diritti dell' uomo fra diritto internazionale convenzionale e generale*, Milano, Giuffrè, 1993, 119 p.

POLAKIEWICKZ (J.).—*Die Verpflichtungen der Staaten aus den Urteilen des Europäischen Gerichtshofs für Menschenrechte*, Berlin, Springer, 1993, 392 p.

RIGAUX (F.).—*La protection de la vie privée et des autres biens de la personnalité*, Brussels, Bruylant, and Paris, L.G.D.J., 1990, 849 p.

RIGAUX (F.).—*La vie privée. Une liberté parmi d' autres?*, Brussels, Larcier, 1992, 318 p.

ROBERTSON (A.H.) et MERRILLS (J.G.).—*Human rights in Europe. A study of the European Convention on Human Rights*, Manchester and New-York, Manchester University Press, 1993, 422 p.

SALVIA (M. de).—*Lineamenti di diritto europeo dei diritti dell' uomo*, Padova, CEDAM, 1991, 476 p.

SOYER (J.-C.) and SALVIA (M. de).—*Convention européenne des droits de l' homme. Le recours individuel supranational. Mode d' emploi*, Paris, L.G.D.J., 1992, 287 p.

STARACE (V.).—*La Convenzione europea dei diritti dell' uomo e l' ordinamento italiano*, Bari, Levante, 1992, 299 p.

STAVROS (S.).—*The guarantees for accused persons under Article 6 of the European Convention on Human Rights*, Dordrecht, Nijhoff, 1992, 400 p.

VILLIGER (M.E.).—*Handbuch der europaïschen Menschenrechtskonvention*, Zürich, Schulthess, 1993, 469 p.

II. ARTICLES

ABRAHAM (R.).—'The effects of the ECHR on constitutional and administrative law in Contracting Parties', *A.E.H.R.Y.B.* 1992, p. 127–146.

ALLEWELDT (R.).—'Protection against expulsion under Article 3 of the European Convention on Human Rights', *E.J.I.L./J.E.D.I.* 1993, p. 360–376.

BARRETO (I.).—'Notas para un processo equitativo. Análise do artigo 6.° da Convençao Europeia dos Direitos do Homen', *Documentaçâo e direito comparado* 1992, p. 69–133.

BARTSCH (H.J.).—'The effects of decisions of the European Court of Human Rights', in *Les effets des décisions de la Cour de justice des Communautés européennes dans les Etats membres*, Brussels, U.G.A.,1983, p. 217–245.

BATTAGLINI (G.).—'Convenzione europea, misure di emergenza e controllo del giudice', *Giurisprudenza costitutionale* 1982, p. 404 *et seq.*

BECHLIVANOU (G.).—'Symbole et verbe au sein du droit. À propos des lieux fermés et de la notion de privation de liberté dans la jurisprudence européenne', in *Présence du droit public et des droits de l' homme. Mélanges offerts à Jacques Velu*, Brussels, Bruylant, 1992, Vol. III, p. 1607–1625.

BENGOENTXAE (J.) and JUNG (H.).—'Towards a European jurisprudence? The justification of criminal law by the Strasbourg Court', *Legal Studies* 1991, p. 239 *et seq.*

BERGER (V.), GIAKOUMOPOULOS (G.), LABAYLE (H.) and SUDRE (F.).—'Droit administratif et Convention européenne des droits de l'homme', *R.F.D.A.* 1992, p. 510–532, and 1993, p. 963–1001.

BERNHARDT (R.).—'Einwirkungen der Entscheidungen internationaler Meschenrechtsinstitutionen auf das nationale Recht', in *Staat und Völkerrechtsordnung. Festschrift für K. Doehring*, Berlin, 1989, p. 23–35.

BERTENS (G.), HUUSSEN (I.) and LABUSCHAGNE (B.).—'De Nederlandse wetgever en de implementatie van arresten van het Europese Hof voor de Rechten van de Mens', *NJCM–Bulletin* 1994, p. 519–538.

BOULAN (F.).—'La Convention européenne des droits de l'homme et le droit pénal procédural', *Vorträge, Reden und Berichte aus dem Europa-Institut der Universität des Saarlandes*, no. 252, Sarrebrücken, 1991, 20 p.

CALLEWAERT (J.).—'La Cour européenne des droits de l'homme et l'urgence', *R.T.D.H.* 1994, p. 391–403.

CALLEWAERT (J.).—'The judgments of the Court : background and content', in *The European system for the protection of human rights*, Dordrecht, Nijhoff, 1993, p. 713–731.

CASSESE (A.).—'Prohibition of torture and inhuman or degrading treatment', in *The European system for the protection of human rights*, Dordrecht, Nijhoff, 1993, p. 225–261.

CHIAVARIO (M.).—'Cour européenne des droits de l'homme et Cour constitutionnelle italienne : quelques notes pour une comparaison', in Carpi (F.) and Orlandi (C.G.) (ed.), *Judicial protection of human rights at the national and international level*, Vol. II, Milano, Giuffrè, 1991, p. 555–563.

CHOLEWINSKI (R.).—'Strasbourg's "hidden agenda"? The protection of second-generation migrants from expulsion under Article 8 of the European Convention on Human Rights', *N.Q.H.R.* 1994, p. 287–306.

CHURCHILL (R.R.).—'Aspects of compliance with findings of the Committee of Ministers and judgments of the Court with reference to the United Kingdom', in *Aspects of incorporation of the European Convention on Human Rights into domestic law*, London, The British Institute of International and Comparative Law and The British Institute of Human Rights, 1993, p. 103–119.

CHURCHILL (R.R.) and YOUNG (J.).—'Compliance with judgements of the European Court of Human Rights and decisions of the Committee of Ministers: the experience of the United Kingdom 1975–1987', *B.Y.B.L.* 1991, p. 283–346.

CLAPHAM (A.).—'The "Drittwirkung" of the Convention', in *The European system for the protection of human rights*, Dordrecht, Nijhoff, 1993, p. 163–206.

COHEN–JONATHAN (G.).—'La Convention européenne des droits de l'homme. Caractères généraux', *J.C.P.* 1990, Europe, Section 6500, 23 p.

COHEN–JONATHAN (G.).—'Responsabilité pour atteinte aux droits de l'homme', in *La responsabilité dans le système international*, Paris, Pedone, 1991, p. 101–135.

COHEN–JONATHAN (G.).—'Convention européenne des droits de l'homme. Système international de contrôle', *J.C.P.* 1991, Europe, Section 6510, 27 p.

COHEN–JONATHAN (G.).—'Convention européenne des droits de l'homme. Droits garantis', *J.C.P.* 1992, Europe, Sections 6520, 6521 and 6522, 25, 32 et 32 p.

COHEN–JONATHAN (G.).—'Liberté d'expression et message publicitaire', *R.T.D.H.* 1993, p. 69–93.

COHEN–JONATHAN (G.).—'Convention européenne des droits de l'homme et procédure civile', *J.C.P.* April 1993, procédure civile, 18 p.

COHEN–JONATHAN (G.).—'Respect for private and family life', in *The European system for the protection of human rights*, Dordrecht, Nijhoff, 1993, p. 405–444.

COHEN–JONATHAN (G.).—'La liberté d'expression dans la Convention européenne des droits de l'homme—1ère partie', *L.P.* , January–February 1994, no. 108, p. 1–10.

COHEN–JONATHAN(G.).—'Fiscalité et Convention européenne des droits de l'homme : quelques observations', *L.P. A.*, 6 July 1994, no. 80,p. 15–24.

CONNELLY (A.).—'Ireland and the European Convention on Human Rights: an overview', in Hefferman (L.) (ed.), *Human rights. A European perspective*, Dublin, The Round Hall Press, 1994, p. 33–47.

COUSSIRAT–COUSTÈRE (V.).—'Convention européenne des droits de l'homme et droit interne : primauté et effet direct', in *La Convention européenne des droits de l' homme*, Brussels, Némésis, 1992, p. 11–23.

DANELIUS (H.).—'L'indipendenza e l'imparzialità della giustizia alla luce della giurisprudenza della Corte europea dei diritti dell'uomo', *Riv.I.D.U.* 1993, p. 443–452.

DAVIDSON (J.S.).—'The European Convention on Human Rights and the "illegitimate" child', in Freestone (D.) (éd.), *Children and the law*, Hull, Hull University Press, 1990, p. 75 *et seq.*

DELGADO BARRIO (J.).—'Proyección de las decisiones del Tribunal Europeo de Derechos Humanos en la jurisprudencia española', *Revista de Administración Pública* 1989, p. 233–252.

DELMAS–MARTY (M.).—'La Convention européenne des droits de l'homme et le droit pénal des affaires. Aspects de droit processuel', *D.P. C.I.* 1991, p. 366-379.

DELMAS–MARTY (M.).—'La Convention européenne de sauvegarde des droits de l'homme et le droit pénal de fond', in *Mélanges offerts à Georges Levasseur*, Paris, Gazette du Palais and Litec, 1992, p. 195–203, and *I diritti dell' uomo. Cronache e battaglie* 1992, no. 3, p. 13–18.

DELMAS–MARTY (M.).—'La jurisprudence de la Cour européenne des droits de l'homme et la "logique du flou"', *R.D.P. C.* 1992, p. 1031–1046.

DE MEYER (J.).—'La Cour européenne des droits de l'homme et la liberté d'expression', in *Jornadas : Jurisprudencia europea en materia de Derechos Humanos*, Vitoria, Servicio Central de Publicaciones del Gobierno Vasco, 1991, p. 235–256.

DE SCHUTTER (O.).—'L'interprétation de la Convention européenne des droits de l'homme : un essai en démolition', *Revue de droit international, de sciences diplomatiques et politiques* 1992, p. 83–127.

DE SCHUTTER (O.) and FIERENS (J.).—'Examen de jurisprudence : Convention européenne des droits de l'homme (1992–1993)', *J.T. Droit européen* 1993, p. 68–73, and 1994, p. 48–52.

DICKSON (B.).—'The European Convention on Human Rights and Northern Ireland', in *Présence du droit public et des droits de l'homme. Mélanges offerts à Jacques Velu*, Brussels, Bruylant, 1932, Vol. III, p. 1407–1429.

DIJK (P. van).—'Access to court', in *The European system for the protection of human rights*, Dordrecht, Nijhoff, 1993, p. 345–379.

DIJK (P. van).—'Toelating en verblijf van vreemdelingen in Nederland: de eerbieding van het familie— en gezinsleven op grond van artikel 8 EVRM', *Nederlands tijdschrift voor de mensenrechten* 1994, p. 6–33.

DI MARTINO (V.).—'Il Consiglio d'Europa e la tutela della libertà sindacale. La Convenzione europea dei diritti dell'uomo', *Diritto del lavoro* 1977, p. 248 *et seq.*

DOURAKI (T.).—'Les associations devant la Commission et la Cour européennes des droits de l'homme', *Annuaire de l'Association des auditeurs et anciens auditeurs de l'Académie de droit international de La Haye* 1989, p. 139–146.

DUBBER (M.R.).—'Homosexual privacy rights before the United States Supreme Court and the European Court of Human Rights', *Stanford Journal of International Law* 1990, p. 189–214.

DUFFAR (J.).—'La protection du droit au respect de la vie familiale des étrangers. Jurisprudence récente des organes de la Convention européenne des droits de l'homme', *L.P. A.*, 24 May 1991, no. 62, p. 32–34.

DUFFAR (J.).—'Religion et travail dans la jurisprudence de la Cour de justice des Communautés européennes et des organes de la Convention européenne des droits de l'homme', *R.D.P.* 1993, p. 695–718.

DURAND (D.).—'Les garanties apportées par la Convention européenne des droits de l'homme dans le procès pénal', in *La Convention européenne des droits de l'homme*, Brussels, Némésis, 1992, p. 53–76.

ECOCHARD (B.) and PEYROT (B.).—'Activités de la Cour européenne des droits de l'homme—1992', *Cahiers de l'I.D.E.D.H.* no. 2, 1993, p. 159–174.

ECOCHARD (B.) and PEYROT (B.).—'Activités de la Cour européenne des droits de l'homme—1993', *Cahiers de l'I.D.E.D.H.*, no. 3, 1994, p. 125–141.

EISSEN (M.-A.).—'La Cour européenne des droits de l'homme', *Les cahiers de droit* 1984, p. 873–933.

EISSEN (M.-A.).—'La Cour européenne des droits de l'homme. Bilan d'un quart de siècle', in *Fondation Marangopoulos pour les droits de l'homme, Annales*, Athens, Sakkoulas, 1991, p. 33–46.

EISSEN (M.-A.).—'Discipline de vote à la Cour européenne des droits de l'homme ?', in *Human rights and constitutionnal law. Essays in honour of Brian Walsh*, Dublin, The Round Hall Press, 1992, p. 71–83.

EISSEN (M.-A.).—'Disciplina del voto alla Corte europea dei diritti dell'uomo?', *Riv.I.D.U.* 1992, p. 14–28.

EISSEN (M.-A.).—'Le principe de proportionnalité dans la jurisprudence de la Cour européenne des droits de l'homme', *Documentaçâo e direito comparado* 1993, p. 279–309.

EISSEN (M.-A.).—'The principle of proportionality in the case-law of the European Court of Human Rights', in *The European system for the protection of human rights*, Dordrecht, Nijhoff, 1993, p. 125–146.

ENGEL (C.).—'Der Ordnungsvorbehalt in den Schranken der EMRK', *A.S.D.I.* 1989, p. 41–91.

ENRICH MAS (M.).—'Les droits sociaux dans la jurisprudence de la Cour et de la Commision européennes des droits de l'homme', *Affari sociali internazionali* 1992, p. 163–187, and *R.T.D.H.* 1992, p. 147–180.

ENRICH MAS (M.).—'Right to compensation under Article 50', in *The European system for the protection of human rights*, Dordrecht, Nijhoff, 1993, p. 775–790.

ERGEC (R.).—'Les libertés fondamentales et le maintien de l'ordre dans une société démocratique : un équilibre délicat', in *Maintien de l'ordre et droits de l'homme*, Brussels, Bruylant, 1987, p. 3–33.

ERGEC (R.).—'Le droit disciplinaire et les droits de l'homme', *Revue de droit de l'ULB* 1991, no. 4, p. 35–55.

ERGEC (R.).—'L'incidence du droit du Conseil de l'Europe sur le développement du droit administratif', *Administration publique* 1992, p. 1–11.

ERGEC (R.).—'La liberté d'expression, l'autorité et l'impartialité du pouvoir judiciaire', *R.T.D.H.* 1993, p. 171–181.

EVRIGENIS (D.).—'L'interaction entre la dimension internationale et la dimension nationale de la CEDH. Notions autonomes et effet direct', in *Völkerrecht als Rechtsordnung. Internationale Gerichtsbarkeit. Menschenrechte. Festschrift für Hermann Mosler*, Berlin, Springer, 1983, p. 193–202.

FAVREAU (B.).—'L'urgence et le raisonnable ou "de la diligence exceptionnelle des juridictions"', *U.A.E. Journal* octobre 1994, supplément n° 1, p. 12–16.

FERNANDEZ SANCHEZ (p. A.).—'L'autorité de la chose jugée dans les arrêts de la Cour européenne des droits de l'homme', in Carpi (F.) and Orlandi (C.G.) (ed.), *Judicial protection of human rights at the national and international level*, Vol. II, Milano, Giuffré, 1991, p. 589–601.

FITZMAURICE (G.).—'Strasbourg and The Hague', in *Studi in onore di Giorgio Balladore Pallieri*, Milano, Vita e Pensiero, 1978, Vol. 2, p. 280–305.

FLAUSS (J.-F.).—'Fiscalité et droits substantiels garantis par la Convention européenne des droits de l'homme', *L.P. A.*, 6 July 1994, no. 80, p. 15–24.

FLAUSS (J.-F.).—'Le règlement amiable devant la Cour européenne des droits de l'homme', *L.P. A.*, 24 November 1989, no. 141, p. 4–9.

FLAUSS (J.-F.).—'Les droits de l'homme comme élément d'une constitution et de l'ordre européen', *Vorträge, Reden und Berichte aus dem Europa–Institut der Universität des Saarlandes* no. 264, Sarrebrücken, 1992, 21 p.

FLAUSS (J.-F.).—'La "satisfaction équitable" devant les organes de la Convention européenne des droits de l'homme. Développements récents', *Europe*, June 1992, chronique, p. 1–4.

FLAUSS (J.-F.).—'Actualité de la Convention européenne des droits de l'homme. Droit administratif et Convention européenne des droits de l'homme : l'année 1991', *A.J.D.A.* 1992, p. 15–34.

FLAUSS (J.-F.).—'Actualité de la Convention européenne des droits de l'homme. Droit administratif et Convention européenne des droits de l'homme : janvier–avril 1992', *A.J.D.A.* 1992, p. 416–426.

FONTBRESSIN (P. de).—'La liberté d'expression et la protection de la santé ou de la morale', *R.T.D.H.* 1993, p. 129–146.

FORDER (C.J.).—'Positieve verplichtingen in bet kader van bet Europees Verdrag tot Bescherning van de Rechten van de Mens em de Fundamentele Vrijheden', *Nederlands tijdschrift voor de mensenrechten* 1992, p. 611–637.

FROWEIN (J.A.).—'The protection of property', in *The European system for the protection of human rights*, Dordrecht, Nijhoff, 1993, p. 515–530.

GAJA (G.).—'Il divieto di discriminazioni in ragione del sesso nella giurisprudenza della Corte europea dei diritti dell'uomo', *Riv.I.D.U.* 1991, p. 441–451.

GARCIA DE ENTERRIA (E.).—'Valeur de la jurisprudence de la Cour européenne des droits de l'homme en droit espagnol', in *Protecting human rights: the European dimension. Protection des droits de l'homme : la dimension européenne*, Cologne, Carl Heymanns, 1988, p. 221–230.

GARIBALDI (O.M.).—'On the ideological content of human rights instruments: the clause "in a democratic society"', in *Contemporary issues in international law. Essays in honor of Louis B. Sohn*, Kehl, Engel, 1984, p. 23–68.

GEARTY (C.A.).—'The European Court of Human Rights and the protection of civil liberties: an overview', *C.L.J.* 1993, p. 89–127.

GÖLCÜKLÜ (F.).—'Legal aspects of privatisation', *Revue des droits de l'homme/Human Rights Review* [Ankara] 1992, p. 13–19.

GÖLCÜKLÜ (F.).—'Le procès équitable et l'administration des preuves dans la jurisprudence de la Cour européenne des droits de l'homme', in *Présence du droit public et des droits de l'homme. Mélanges offerts à Jacques Velu*, Brussels, Bruylant, 1992, Vol. III, p. 1361–1377.

GOLSONG (H.).—'L'effet direct ainsi que le rang en droit interne des normes de la Convention européenne des droits de l'homme et des décisions prises par les organes institués par celle-ci', in *Les recours des individus devant les instances nationales en cas de violation du droit européen*, Brussels, Larcier, 1978, p. 59–83.

GOLSONG (H.).—'Interpreting the European Convention on Human Rights beyond the confines of the Vienna Convention on the Law of Treaties?', in *The European system for the protection of human rights*, Dordrecht, Nijhoff, 1993, p. 147–162.

GOUTTES (R. de).—'La Convention européenne des droits de l'homme et la justice française en 1992', *G.P.*, 6–7 March 1992, doctrine, p. 3–11.

GOUTTES (R. de).—'Vers un droit pénal européen ?', *R.S.C.D.P.C.* 1993, p. 643–661.

HAMPSON (F.).—'The United Kingdom before the European Court of Human Rights', *Y.E.L.* 1989, p. 121 *et seq.*

HAMPSON (F.).—'The concept of an "arguable claim" under Article 13 of the European Convention on Human Rights', *I.C.L.Q.* 1990, p. 891–899.

HAMPSON (F.).—'Children in care and the European Convention on Human Rights', in *Aspects of incorporation of the European Convention on Human Rigths into domestic law*, London, The British Institute of International and Comparative Law and The British Institute of Human Rights, 1993, p. 77–86.

HERINGA (A.W.).—'Artikel 6 EVRM: civil rights and obligations revisited', *NJCM–Bulletin* 1994, p. 575–579.

HUNT (p.) and DICKSON (B.).—'Northern Ireland's emergency laws and international human rights', *Netherlands Quarterly of Human Rights* 1993, p. 173–184.

ISRAEL (J.-J.).—'La Convention européenne des droits de l'homme et le droit français de l'utilisation des sols', *D.P. C.I.* 1991, p. 381–392.

JACOT-GILLARMOD (O.).—'Les liens familiaux dans la jurisprudence de Strasbourg', *Recueil de jurisprudence neuchâteloise* 1980–1981, p. 79–92.

JACOT-GILLARMOD (O.).—'Rights related to good administration of justice (Article 6)', in *The European system for the protection of human rights*, Dordrecht, Nijhoff, 1993, p. 381–404.

JACQ (C.).—'Les pratiques policières et pénitentiaires à l'épreuve ·de la Convention européenne de sauvegarde des droits de l'homme', *Documentaçâo e direito comparado* 1991, p. 57–115.

JANIS (M.W.).—'The European Court of Human Rights', in Janis (M.W.) (ed.), *International courts for the twenty–first century*, Nijhoff, Dordrecht, 1992, p. 105–116.

KAYSER (p.).—'Le regroupement familial dans le droit communautaire, la Convention européenne des droits de l'homme et le droit interne français', *La semaine juridique*, édition générale, n° 21–22, 2 June 1993, I (doctrine), p. 235–244.

KERCHOVE (M. van de).—'La preuve en matière pénale dans la jurisprudence de la Cour et de la Commission européennes des droits de l'homme', *R.S.C.D.P. C.* 1992, p. 1–14

KIDD (C.J.F.).—'Disciplinary proceedings and the right to a fair criminal trial under the European Convention on Human Rights', *I.C.L.Q.* 1987, p. 856–872.

KINGSTON (J.).—'Sex and sexuality under the European Convention on Human Rights', in Hefferman (L.) (ed.), *Human rights. A European perspective*, Dublin, The Round Hall Press, 1994 p. 179–194.

KINGSTON (J.).—'Rich people have rights too? The status of property as a fundamental human right', in Hefferman (L.) (ed.), *Human Rights. A European perspective*, Dublin, The Round Hall Press, 1994, p. 284–297.

KISS (A.).—'La protection du droit de propriété', in *Jornadas: Jurisprudencia en materia de Derechos Humanos*, Vitoria, Servicio Central de Publicaciones del Gobierno Vasco, 1991, p. 185–198.

KISS (A.).—'Conciliation', in *The European system for the protection of human rights*, Dordrecht, Nijhoff, 1993, p. 703–711.

KOERING–JOULIN (R.).—'La notion européenne de tribunal indépendant et impartial au sens de l'article 6 § 1 de la Convention européenne des droits de l'homme', *R.S.C.D.P. C.* 1990, p. 765–774.

KOERING–JOULIN (R.).—'La phase préparatoire du procès pénal : grandes lignes de la jurisprudence européenne', in Delmas–Marty (M.) (ed.), *Procès pénal et droits de l'homme. Vers une conscience européenne*, Paris, P.U.F., 1992, p. 47–55.

LABAYLE (H.).—'L'effectivité de la protection juridictionnelle des particuliers. Le droit administratif français et les exigences de la jurisprudence européenne', *R.F.D.A.* 1992, p. 619–642.

LABAYLE (H.).—'Le droit de l'étranger à mener une vie familiale normale, lecture internationale et exigences européennes', *R.F.D.A.* 1993, p. 511–540.

LABAYLE (H.).—'Le droit de l'étranger à mener une vie familiale normale', in *Le droit français et la Convention européenne des droits de l'homme. 1974–1992*, Kehl, Engel, 1994, p. 111–142.

LAMBERT (P.).—'Le droit à un procès équitable au sens de l'article 6, 1° de la Convention européenne des droits de l'homme', in *La Convention européenne des droits de l'homme*, Brussels, Némésis, 1992, p. 25–51.

LAMBERT (P.).—'Les procédures d'arbitrage et la Convention européenne des droits de l'homme', in *Présence du droit public et des droits de l'homme. Mélanges offerts à Jacques Velu*, Brussels, Bruylant, 1992, Vol. II, p. 1281–1291.

LAMBERT (P.).—'La liberté d'expression et la sécurité nationale, l'intégrité territoriale ou la sûreté publique, la défense de l'ordre et la prévention du crime', *R.T.D.H.* 1993, p. 119–128.

LASSALLE (J.–Y.).—'Les délais de la Convention européenne des droits de l'homme et le droit pénal français', *R.T.D.H.* 1993, p. 263–294.

LAURIN (Y.).—'L'opinion séparée des juges de la Cour européenne des droits de l'homme', *G.P.* , 1–5 January 1993, p. 13.

LECLERC (H.).—'Liberté de la presse et Convention européenne des droits de l'homme', *L.P.*, décembre 1991, no. 87, chroniques et opinions, p. 97–108.

LEIGH (L.H.).—'The influence of the European Convention on Human Rights on English criminal law and procedure', *E.J.C.* 1993, p. 3–19.

LEMMENS (P.).—'Effects of the ECHR on certain areas of civil law', *A.E.H.R.Y.B.* 1992, p. 213–233.

LESTER (A.).—'Freedom of expression', in *The European system for the protection of human rights*, Dordrecht, Nijhoff, 1993, p. 465–491.

LEUPRECHT (P.).—'The execution of judgments and decisions', in *The European system for the protection of human rights*, Dordrecht, Nijhoff, 1993, p. 791–800.

LEVINET (M.).—'Le transsexualisme et la Convention européénne des droits de l'homme. Vers un statut des minorités sexuelles en droit européen des droits de l'homme', in *Perspectives du droit international et européen. Recueil d'études à la mémoire de Gilbert Appolis*, Paris, Pedone, 1992, p. 125–138.

LIÑAN NOGUERAS (D.).—'Efectos de las sentencias del Tribunal Europeo de Derechos Humanos y derecho espagñol', *R.E.D.I.* 1985, p. 356–376.

MACDONALD (R. St. J.).—'The margin of appreciation in the jurisprudence of the European Court of Human Rights', in *Collected Courses of the Academy of European Law*, Dordrecht, Nijhoff, Vol. I–1, p. 95–161.

MACDONALD (R. St. J.).—'The margin of appreciation', in *The European system for the protection of human rights*, Dordrecht, Nijhoff, 1993, p. 83–124.

MAHONEY (P.) and SUNDBERG (F.).—'The European Convention on Human Rights : a case study of the international law response to violence', in Mahoney (K.E. and P.) (ed), *Human rights in the twenty–first century: a global challenge*, Dordrecht, Nijhoff, 1993, p. 361–376.

MALINVERNI (G.).—'Il diritto ad un ricorso effettivo ad un'instanza nazionale: osservazionni sull'art. 13 della Convenzione europea dei diritti dell'uomo', *Riv.I.D.U.* 1989, p. 396–405.

MALINVERNI (G.).—'Les fonctions des droits fondamentaux dans la jurisprudence de la Commission et de la Cour européennes des droits de l'homme', in *Im Dienst an der Gemeinschaft. Festschrift für Dietrich Schindler am 65. Geburtstag*, Basel, Helbing & Lichtenhahn, 1989, p. 539–560.

MALINVERNI (G.).—'L'indemnité pour cause d'expropriation selon la jurisprudence de la Cour européenne des droits de l'homme', in *Problemi giuridici dell'orientamento economico attuale*, Bellinzona, Quaderni della Banca del Gottardo, 1989, p. 113–123.

MARTENS (S.K.).—'Individual complaints under Article 53 of the European Convention on Human Rights', in *Essays in honour of Henry G. Schermers, vol. III, The dynamics of the protection of human rights in Europe*, Dordrecht, Nijhoff, 1994, p. 253–292.

MARTÍNEZ RUIZ (L.F.).—'La exigencia de equidad en el proceso civil. Jurisprudencia europea', in *Jornadas: Jurisprudencia en materia de Derechos Humanos*, Vitoria, Servicio Central de Publicaciones del Gobierno Vasco, 1991, p. 151–183.

MARTÍNEZ RUIZ (L.F.).—'L'esigenza di equità nel processo civile. Giurisprudenza europea', *Riv.I.D.U.* 1991, p. 325–352.

MARZADURI (E.).—'Processo penale e procedimento disciplinare : giurisprudenza europea e prospettive per la legislazione interna italiana', in *L'influenza del diritto europea sul diritto italiano*, Milano, Giuffrè, 1982, p. 589 *et seq.*

MASSIAS (F.).—'L'influence de la Convention européenne des droits de l'homme sur le droit de propriété', *European Review of Private Law* 1994, p. 47–78.

MATSCHER (F.).—'Art. 6 EMRK und verfassungsgerichtliche Verfahren', *EuGRZ* 1993, p. 449–453.

MATSCHER (F.).—'Methods of interpretation of the Convention', in *The European system for the protection of human rights*, Dordrecht, Nijhoff, 1993, p. 63–81.

MAURO (J.).—'Chronique des droits de l'homme : le "délai raisonnable" de la procédure devant la Cour européenne des droits de l'homme. Un droit fondamental sanctionné par la Cour', *G.P.* 1988, doctrine, p. 54.

MELCHIOR (M.).—'Rapport sur la jurisprudence relative à l'article 8 de la Convention', in *Jornadas: Jurisprudencia en materia de Derechos Humanos*, Vitoria, Servicio Central de Publicaciones del Gobierno Vasco, 1991, p. 199–233.

MELCHIOR (M.).—'Le principe de non–discrimination dans la Convention européenne des droits de l'homme', in Alen (A.) and Lemmens (P.) (ed.), *Egalité et non-discrimination*, Antwerp, Kluwer, 1991, 228 p.

MELCHIOR (M.).—'La notion de compétence de pleine juridiction en matière civile dans la jurisprudence de la Cour européenne des droits de l'homme', in *Présence du droit public et des droits de l'homme. Mélanges offerts à Jacques Velu*, Brussels, Bruylant, 1992, Vol. III, p. 1327–1346.

MOITRY (J.–H.).—'Right to a fair trial and the European Convention on Human Rights', *Journal of International Arbitration* 1989, p. 115-122.

MORENILLA RODRIGUEZ (J.M.).—'Las garantias del proceso penal segun el Convenio Europeo de Derechos Humanos', *Poder Judicial* 1988, special issue, p. 191–216.

MORENILLA RODRIGUEZ (J.M.).—'La ejecución de las sentencias del Tribunal Europeo de Derechos Humanos', *Poder Judicial* 1989, n° 15, p. 53–90.

MORENILLA RODRIGUEZ (J.M.).—'La ejecución de las sentencias del Tribunal Europeo de Derechos Humanos', in *Jornadas: Jurisprudencia en materia de Derechos Humanos*, Vitoria, Servicio Central de Publicaciones del Gobierno Vasco, 1991, p. 71–97.

MORENILLA RODRIGUEZ (J.M.).—'El derecho al respeto de la esfera privada en la jurisprudencia del Tribunal Europeo de Derechos Humanos', in *La jurisprudencia del Tribunal Europeo de Derechos Humanos*, Madrid, Consejo General del Poder Judicial, 1993, p. 291–333.

MURDOCH (J.).—'Safeguarding the liberty of the person : recent Strasbourg jurisprudence', *I.C.L.Q.* 1993, p. 494–522.

MYJER (E.).—'The European dimension : more than a non–committal ornament. Notes on the consequences of the ECHR for the administration of Dutch criminal justice', *A.E.H.R.Y.B.* 1992, p. 195–212.

NGÔ DINH LÊ QUYÊN.—'I refugiati *de facto* e l'art. 3 della Convenzione europea per la salvaguardia dei diritti dell'uomo e delle libertà fondamentali', *Affari sociali internazionali* 1993, p. 189–196.

NUNIN (R.).—'Osservazioni sulla tutela dei diritto di proprietà nel sistema della Convenzione europea dei diritti dell'uomo', *Riv.I.D.U.* 1991, p. 669–713.

O'BOYLE (M.).—'The reconstruction of the Strasbourg human rights system', *Dublin University Law Journal* 1992, p. 41 *et seq.*

O'BOYLE (M.).—'Right to speak and associate under Strasbourg case-law with reference to Eastern and Central Europe', *Connecticut Journal of International Law* 1993, p. 263–287.

OST (F.) and KERCHOVE (M. van de).—'Les directives d'interprétation adoptées par la Cour européenne des droits de l'homme', in *Entre la lettre et l'esprit. Les directives d'interprétation en droit*, Brussels, Bruylant, 1989, p. 235–323.

PANZERA (A.F.).—'Il potere della Corte europea dei diritti dell'uomo di accordare un'equa riparazione alla parte lesa', *Riv.D.E.* 1974, p. 317–325.

PARTSCH (K.J.).—'Discrimination', in *The European system for the protection of human rights*, Dordrecht, Nijhoff, 1993, p. 571–592.

PEKKANEN (R.).—'Freedom of expression according to the European Convention on Human Rights', *The Finnish Yearbook of International Law* 1993, p. 453–470.

PETTITI (L.-E.).—'La giurisprudenza della Commissione e della Corte europea dei diritti dell'uomo e la sua influenza sulla legislazione degli Stati membri in materia di ascolti e intercettazioni telefoniche', *Riv.I.D.U.* 1991, p. 603–616.

PETTITI (L.-E.).—'Les droits de l'inculpé et de la défense selon la jurisprudence de la Cour européenne des droits de l'homme', in *Mélanges offerts à Georges Levasseur*, Paris, Gazette du Palais and Litec, 1992, p. 249–262.

PETTITI (L.-E.).—'Le rôle de l'équité dans le système juridique de la Convention européenne des droits de l'homme', in *Justice, médiation et équité*, Paris, La Documentation française, 1992, p. 35–45.

PETTITI (L.-E.).—'Una limitazione nell'applicazione dell'art. 6 per rafforzare il nocciolo duro della Convenzione europea', *Riv.I.D.U.* 1993, p. 839–854.

PETTITI (L.-E.).—'La France et la Cour européenne des droits de l'homme. La jurisprudence de 1992. Présentation générale', *Cahiers du CREDHO*, no. 1, 1994, p. 17–34.

PETZOLD (H.).—'The Convention and the principle of subsidiarity', in *The European system for the protection of human rights*, Dordrecht, Nijhoff, 1993, p. 41–62.

PHILLIPS (B.).—'The long road to the European Court of Human Rights', *New Law Journal* 1994, p. 1126–1129.

PICARD (E.).—'La juridiction administrative et les exigences du procès équitable', in *Le droit français et la Convention européenne des droits de l'homme. 1974–1992*, Kehl, Engel, 1994, p. 217–283.

PISANI (M.).—'Le sanzioni per le violazioni dei diritti dell'imputato', *L'indice penale* 1990, p. 37–54.

PIRET (J.–M.).—'Impartialité du juge et suspicion légitime', in *Présence du droit public et des droits de l'homme. Mélanges offerts à Jacques Velu*, Brussels, Bruylant, 1992, Vol. II, p. 857–870.

POLAKIEWICZ (J.G.).—'The implementation of the ECHR and of the decisions of the Strasbourg Court in Western Europe', *A.E.H.R.Y.B.* 1992, p. 147–171.

PRADEL (J.).—'L'arrestation et la détention provisoire sous l'angle notamment de la Convention européenne des droits de l'homme', in *Droits fondamentaux et détention pénale. Human rights an penal detention*, Neuchâtel, Ides et Calendes, 1993, p. 101–116.

PRADEL (J.).—'Le déroulement du procès pénal', in *Le droit français et la Convention européenne des droits de l'homme. 1974–1992*, Kehl, Engel, 1994, p. 197–209.

RESS (G.).—'The effects of judgments and decisions in domestic law', in *The European system for the protection of human rights*, Dordrecht, Nijhoff, 1993, p. 801–851.

RIMANQUE (K.).—'Overwegingen bij de jurisprudentie van de organen van bet Europese Verdrag tot bescherning van de rechten van de mens', in *Opstellen aangeboden aan Prof. Ridder René Victor*, Deurne, Kluwer, Vol. 2, 1973, p. 785–798.

RIMANQUE (K.).—'De nakoming van Straatsburgse beslissingen : een taak voor regelgevers en rechters', in *Présence du droit public et des droits de l'homme. Mélanges offerts à Jacques Velu*, Brussels, Bruylant, 1992, Vol. III, p. 1347–1360.

ROGGE (K.).—'Fact-finding', in *The European system for the protection of human rights*, Dordrecht, Nijhoff, 1993, p. 677–701.

RYSSDAL (R.).—'The expanding role of the European Court of Human Rights', in *The future of human rights protection in a changing world. Fifty years since the four freedoms address. Essays in honour of Torkel Opsahl*, Oslo, Norwegian University Press, 1991, p. 115–124.

SALVIA (M. de).—'Maintien de l'ordre et respect des droits de l'homme : la jurisprudence des organes de la Convention au regard des articles 3 et 5 de la Convention', in *Jornadas : Jurisprudencia europea en materia de Derechos Humanos*, Vitoria, Servicio Central de Publicaciones del Gobierno Vasco, 1991, p. 109–121.

SALVIA (M. de).—'La Convenzione europea dei diritti dell'uomo e la parità fra i sessi : minimo comune denominatore o evoluzione annunciata?', *Riv.I.D.U.* 1991, p. 452–461.

SALVIA (M. de).—'Minoranze storiche e "nuove" minoranze : diritti, doveri e spirito di tolleranza nella giurisprudenza della Commissione e della Corte europea dei diritti dell'uomo', *Riv.I.D.U.* 1992, p. 148–158.

SALVIA (M. de).—'Riflessioni in tema di esecuzione civile ed equo processo nel quadro dell'art. 6 della Convenzione europea dei diritti dell'uomo', *Riv.I.D.U.* 1993, p. 15–23.

SANSONETIS (N.).—'Costs and expenses', in *The European system for the protection of human rights*, Dordrecht, Nijhoff, 1993, p. 755–773.

SAPIENZA (R.).—'Sul margine d'apprezzamento statale nel sistema della Convenzione europea dei diritti dell'uomo', *Riv.D.I.* 1991, p. 571–614.

SCHERMERS (H.).—'The right to a fair trial under the European Convention on Human Rights', in Blackburn (R.) and Taylor (J.) (ed.), *Human rights for the 1990s*, London, Mansell, 1991, p. 59–66.

SCHERMERS (H.G.).—'Human rights and free movement of persons : the role of the European Commission and Court of Human Rights', in *Free movement of persons in Europe. Legal problems and experiences*, Dordrecht, Nijhoff, 1993, p. 235–247.

SCHWARZE (J.).—'Der Beitrag des Europarates zur Entwicklung von Rechtsschutz und Verfahrensgarantien im Verwaltungsrecht', *EuGRZ* 1993, p. 377–384.

SCOFFONI (G.).—'Jurisprudence fiscale et Convention européenne des droits de l'homme : vers une protection "européenne" du contribuable national ?', *Cahiers de l'I.D.E.D.H.* no. 3, 1993, p. 110–125.

SPERDUTI (G.).—'Il principio della preminenza del diritto e sua garanzia nella Convenzione europea dei diritti dell'uomo', in Carpi (F.) and Orlandi

(C.G.) (ed.), *Judicial protection of human rights at the national and international level*, Vol. II, Milano, Giuffrè, 1991, p. 521–538.

SPIELMANN (A.).—'Chroniques de jurisprudence—Cour européenne des droits de l'homme—La liberté d'expression et ses limites', *Annales du droit luxembourgeois* 1991, p. 263–299.

SPIELMANN (D.).—'Les mesures provisoires et les organes de protection prévus par la Convention européenne des droits de l'homme', in *Présence du droit public et des droits de l'homme. Mélanges offerts à Jacques Velu*, Brussels, Bruylant, 1992, Vol. II, p. 1293–1317.

STERN (B.).—'Le droit de propriété, l'expropriation et la nationalisation dans la Convention européenne des droits de l'homme', *D.P. C.I.* 1991, p. 394–423.

STOLZLECHNER (H.).—'Der Schutz des Privat- und Familielebens (Art. 8 EMRK) im Licht der Rechtsprechung des VfGH und der Strassburger Instanzen', *Ö.J.Z.* 1980, p. 85–93 and 123–129.

STROZZI (G.).—'Liberté de l'information et droit international', *R.G.D.I.P.* 1990, p. 947–995.

SUDRE (F.).—'L'Europe des droits de l'homme', *Droits* 1991, p. 105–114.

SUDRE (F.).—'Y a–t–il un pilote à la Cour européenne des droits de l'homme ?', *La lettre d'Avocats et juristes sans frontières*, n° 2, March 1993, p. 3.

SUDRE (F.).—'Droit de la Convention européenne des droits de l'homme', *La semaine juridique* 1993, édition générale, I, n° 3654, p. 93–98.

SUDRE (F.).—'Droit de la Convention européenne des droits de l'homme', *La semaine juridique*, édition générale, 23 February 1994, doctrine, p. 108–114.

SUDRE (F.).—'Misère et Convention européenne des droits de l'homme', *Cahiers de l'I.D.E.D.H.*, no. 3, 1994, p. 113–124.

SUDRE (F.), LEVINET (M.), PEYROT (B.) and ECOCHARD (B.).—'Chronique de la jurisprudence de la Cour européenne des droits de l'homme—1992', *R.U.D.H.* 1992, p. 1–15.

TABORY (M.).—'Language rights as human rights', *Israel Yearbook on Human Rights* 1980, p. 167–223.

TAVERNIER (P.), GREWE (C.) and RUIZ–FABRI (H.).—'Conseil de l'Europe. Convention européenne des droits de l'homme. Droits protégés', *J.C.P.* 1992, Section 155–D, 25 p.

TAVERNIER (P.), GREWE (C.) and RUIZ–FABRI (H.).—'Conseil de l'Europe. Convention européenne des droits de l'homme. Interprétation et application par les organes de Strasbourg et par les organes nationaux', *J.C.P.* 1993, droit international, Section 115–E, 28 p.

THUNE (G.H.).—'The right to an effective remedy in domestic law : Article 13 of the European Convention on Human Rights', in Gomien (D.) (ed.), *Broadening the frontiers of human rigths. Essays in honour of Asbjørn Eide*, Oslo, Scandinavian University Press, 1993, p. 79–95.

TOMUSCHAT (C.).—'Quo vadis Argentoratum ? The success story of the European Convention on Human Rights—and a few dark stains', *H.R.L.J.* 1992, p. 401–406.

TOMUSCHAT (C.).—'Freedom of association', in *The European system for the protection of human rights*, Dordrecht, Nijhoff, 1993, p. 493–513.

TRECHSEL (S.).—'Aus der Rechtsprechung des Europäischen Gerichtshofs für Menschenrechte', *Strafverteidiger* 1992, p. 187–194.

TRECHSEL (S.).—'La exigencia de equidad en el proceso penal. Jurisprudencia europea', in *Jornadas : Jurisprudencia en materia de Derechos Humanos*, Vitoria, Servicio Central de Publicaciones del Gobierno Vasco 1991, p. 123–150.

TRECHSEL (S.).—'Liberty and security of person', in *The European system for the protection of human rights*, Dordrecht, Nijhoff, 1993, p. 277–344.

TRICHILO (P.).—'Trent'anni di giurisprudenza della Corte europea dei diritti dell'uomo in materia di libertá personale (1960–1990)', *Riv.I.D.U.* 1993, p. 103–115.

TULKENS (F.).—'Chronique annuelle des droits de l'homme', *R.I.D.P.* 1992, p. 1415–1445.

VALTICOS (N.).—'La jurisprudence de la Cour européenne des droits de l'homme sur l'art. 3 de la Convention européenne des droits de l'homme', in Cassese (A.) (ed.), *The international fight against torture. La lutte internationale contre la torture*, Baden–Baden, Nomos, 1991, p. 121–134.

VALTICOS (N.).—'Les diverses formes de la protection des droits de l'homme en Europe', in *Hacia un nuevo orden internacional y europeo. Estudios en homenaje al Professor Don Manuel Diez de Velasco*, Madrid, Editorial Tecnos, 1993, p. 793–805.

VELU (J.).—'A propos de l'autorité jurisprudentielle des arrêts de la Cour européenne des droits de l'homme : vues de droit comparé sur des évolutions en cours', in *Nouveaux itinéraires en droit. Hommage à François Rigaux*, Brussels, Bruylant, 1993, p. 527–562.

VIENNE (R.).—'Les écoutes téléphoniques au regard de la Cour européenne des droits de l'homme', in *Mélanges offerts à Georges Levasseur*, Paris, Gazette du Palais and Litec, 1992, p. 263–285.

WACHENFIELD (M.G.).—'The human rights of the mentally ill in Europe under the European Convention on Human Rights', *Nordic Journal of International Law* 1991, p. 109–292.

WACHSMANN (P.).—'La Cour européenne des droits de l'homme et la liberté d'expression : renforcement ou affaiblissement du contrôle ?', in *Perspectives du droit international et européen. Recueil d'études à la mémoire de Gilbert Appolis*, Paris, Pedone, 1992, p. 151–164.

WARBRICK (C.).—'Rights, the European Convention on Human Rights and English law', *E.L.R.* 1994, p. 34–46.

WILDHABER (L.).—'Die Koalitionsfreiheit gemäß Art. 11 EMRK', *G.Y.I.L.* 1976, p. 238–253.

WILDHABER (L.).—"Civil rights' nacht Art. 6 Ziff. 1 EMRK', in Juristische Fakultät der Universität Basel (ed.), *Privatrecht. Öffentliches Recht. Strafrecht. Grenzen und Grenzüberschreitungen, Festgabe zum schweizerischen Juristentag 1985*, Basel, 1985, p. 469 *et seq.*

WILDHABER (L.).—'Nouvelle jurisprudence concernant l'art. 8 CEDH', in *Mélanges en l'honneur de Jacques-Michel Grossen*, Basel, Helbing & Lichtenhahn, 1992, p. 97–106.

Bibliography

WILDHABER (L.).—'Right to education and parental rights', in *The European system for the protection of human rights*, Dordrecht, Nijhoff, 1993, p. 531–551.

WILDHABER (L.) and BREITENMOSER (S.).—'Kommentierung des Artikels 8', in *Internationaler Kommentar zur europäischen Menschenrechtskonvention*, Cologne, Carl Heymanns, 1992, 264 p.

WYLER (E.).—'Victime "actuelle" et victime "virtuelle" d'une violation des droits de l'homme dans la jurisprudence relative à l'art. 25 de la Convention européenne des droits de l'homme', *Revue suisse de droit international et de droit européen* 1993, p. 3–38.

Index of Articles of the Convention for the Protection of Human Rights and Fundamental Freedoms

(Numbers refer to paragraphs.)

Table of Cases

(Numbers refer to paragraphs.)

Index

(The numbers refer to paragraphs.)